TAKING↻SIDES

Clashing Views on

Moral Issues

THIRTEENTH EDITION, EXPANDED

Selected, Edited, and with Introductions by

Stephen Satris
Clemson University

Connect
Learn
Succeed™

The McGraw-Hill Companies

Mc Graw Hill

Connect
Learn
Succeed™

TAKING SIDES: CLASHING VIEWS ON MORAL ISSUES, THIRTEENTH EDITION, EXPANDED

Published by McGraw-Hill, a business unit of The McGraw-Hill Companies, Inc., 1221 Avenue of the Americas, New York, NY 10020. Copyright © 2013 by The McGraw-Hill Companies, Inc. All rights reserved. Printed in the United States of America. Previous edition(s) © 2012, 2010, and 2008. No part of this publication may be reproduced or distributed in any form or by any means, or stored in a database or retrieval system, without the prior written consent of The McGraw-Hill Companies, Inc., including, but not limited to, in any network or other electronic storage or transmission, or broadcast for distance learning.

Some ancillaries, including electronic and print components, may not be available to customers outside the United States.

Taking Sides® is a registered trademark of the McGraw-Hill Companies, Inc.
Taking Sides is published by the **Contemporary Learning Series** group within the McGraw-Hill Higher Education division.

1 2 3 4 5 6 7 8 9 0 DOC/DOC 1 0 9 8 7 6 5 4 3 2

MHID: 0-07-805013-8
ISBN: 978-0-07-805013-8
ISSN: 1094-7604

Managing Editor: *Larry Loeppke*
Senior Developmental Editor: *Dave Welsh*
Content License Specialist: *Rita Hingten*
Marketing Specialist: *Alice Link*
Lead Project Manager: *Jane Mohr*
Design Coordinator: *Brenda A. Rolwes*
Cover Graphics: *Rick D. Noel*
Buyer: *Nicole Baumgartner*
Media Project Manager: *Sridevi Palani*

Compositor: MPS Limited
Cover Image: © Ingram Publishing

www.mhhe.com

Editors/Academic Advisory Board

Members of the Academic Advisory Board are instrumental in the final selection of articles for each edition of TAKING SIDES. Their review of articles for content, level, and appropriateness provides critical direction to the editors and staff. We think that you will find their careful consideration well reflected in this volume.

TAKING SIDES: Clashing Views on MORAL ISSUES

Thirteenth Edition, Expanded

EDITOR

Stephen Satris
Clemson University

ACADEMIC ADVISORY BOARD MEMBERS

Preface

This text contains 34 essays, arranged in pro and con pairs, that address 17 controversial issues in morality and moral philosophy. Each of the issues is expressed in terms of a single question in order to draw the lines of debate more clearly.

Some of the questions that are included here have been in the mainstream of moral philosophy for hundreds (or even thousands) of years and are central to the discipline. I have not shied away from abstract questions about relativism and the relationship between morality and religion. Other questions relate to specific topics of contemporary concern, such as human cloning, abortion, affirmative action, and drug legalization.

The authors of the selections included here take a strong stand on a given issue and provide their own best defenses of a pro or con position. The selections were chosen for their usefulness in defending a position and for their accessibility to students. The authors are philosophers, scientists, and social critics from a wide variety of backgrounds. Each presents us with a determinant answer on an issue—even if we ultimately cannot accept the answer as our own.

Each issue is accompanied by an *introduction,* which sets the stage for the debate, and each issue concludes with a *postscript* that summarizes the debate, considers other views on the issue, and suggests additional readings. The introductions and postscripts do not preempt what is the reader's own task: to achieve a critical and informed view of the issue at stake. I have also provided relevant Internet site addresses (URLs) on the *Internet References* page that accompanies each unit opener. And at the back of the book is a list of all the *contributors to this volume,* which provides information on the philosophers and social commentators whose views are debated here.

Taking Sides: Clashing Views on Moral Issues is a tool to encourage critical thought on important moral issues. Readers should not feel confined to the views expressed in the selections. Some readers may see important points on both sides of an issue and may construct for themselves a new and creative approach, which may incorporate the best of both sides or provide an entirely new vantage point for understanding.

Changes to this edition Several new articles have been added to this edition which have aided in the currency and refinement of the issue questions. These would include "Is Abortion Immoral?" (Issue 4); "Should Drugs Be Legalized?" (Issue 9); and "Is Torture Ever Justified?" (Issue 13). One issue is new to this edition: "Is Price Gouging Wrong?" (Issue 10). In addition, this expanded edition includes two entirely new issues: "Should College Athletes Be Paid?" (Issue 16) and "Is It Right to Produce Genetically Modified Food?" (Issue 17).

A word to the instructor An *Instructor's Resource Guide with Test Questions* (multiple-choice and essay) is available through the publisher for the instructor using *Taking Sides* in the classroom. A general guidebook, *Using Taking Sides in the Classroom,* which discusses methods and techniques for using the pro–con approach in any classroom setting, is also available. An online version of *Using Taking Sides in the Classroom* and a correspondence service for *Taking Sides* adopters can be found at www.mhhe.com/cls/UsingTS2.pdf.

Taking Sides: Clashing Views on Moral Issues is only one title in the *Taking Sides* series. If you are interested in seeing the table of contents for any of the other titles, please visit the Taking Sides website at www.mhhe.com/cls.

Acknowledgments   Finally, a unique debt of thanks is owed to those who tolerated my strange hours and the time spent away from them as this book was being prepared and revised: Kim, Angela, and Michelle.

Stephen Satris
Clemson University

To the memory of my mother and father

Contents In Brief

Contents

Philosopher Gilbert Harman argues that relativism is true for morality—much as Einstein proved it was true for motion. Just as motion always presupposes some framework in which it occurs (and something can be in motion relative to one person but not to another), morality too always presupposes some framework. Louis Pojman carefully distinguishes what he calls the diversity thesis—that moral rules differ from society to society—from ethical relativism. The diversity thesis is a straightforward description of what are acknowledged differences in the moral beliefs and practices of various human groups. But he argues that moral relativism does not follow from this diversity.

Philosopher C. Stephen Layman argues that morality makes the most sense from a theistic perspective and that a purely secular perspective is insufficient. The secular perspective, Layman asserts, does not adequately deal with secret violations, and it does not allow for the possibility of fulfillment of people's deepest needs in an afterlife. Philosopher John Arthur counters that morality is logically independent of religion, although there are historical connections. Religion, he believes, is not necessary for moral guidance or moral answers; morality is social.

and the supposed unnaturalness of asexual reproduction) that are inadequate and fail to express what is really wrong with cloning. We need, instead, to address fundamental questions about our stance toward nature. Law professor John A. Robertson maintains that there should not be a complete ban on human cloning but that regulatory policy should be focused on ensuring that it is performed in a responsible manner.

UNIT 3   LAW AND SOCIETY   129

Issue 7.   Is Cloning Pets Ethically Justified?   130

YES: Autumn Fiester, from "Creating Fido's Twin: Can Pet Cloning Be Ethically Justified?" *Hastings Center Report* (July/ August 2005)   *132*

NO: Hilary Bok, from "Cloning Companion Animals Is Wrong," *Journal of Applied Animal Welfare Science* (vol. 5, no. 3, 2002)   *142*

Autumn Fiester argues in support of cloning animals (in particular, people's pets). She emphasizes the point that pet owners really care about their pets. One result of this is that they spend large amounts of money on veterinary care for their pets. Cloning their pets could serve as a useful extension of this idea—and also serve as a positive demonstration of society in general that individual pets have intrinsic value and cannot simply be replaced by new pets. Hilary Bok argues that cloning pets is immoral first of all because it causes great harm to animals. The animal that results from cloning, for example, is much more likely to have physical defects than the animal from which it was cloned. Moreover, the process of cloning itself necessarily involves harm to other animals (e.g., the animal that will carry the new pet to term). Finally, the end result simply does not provide pet owners with what they were looking for.

Issue 8.   Should Congress Allow the Buying and Selling of Human Organs?   148

YES: Lewis Burrows, from "Selling Organs for Transplantation," *The Mount Sinai Journal of Medicine* (September 2004)   *150*

NO: James F. Childress, from "Should Congress Allow the Buying and Selling of Human Organs? No," *Insight on the News* (May 7, 2001)   *155*

Lewis Burrows, M.D., begins with the observation that the need for organs far outstrips the supply: each year, hundreds of patients die while waiting for transplants. Burrows argues that payment to the donor (or payment to the donor's family, in cases in which the donor is deceased) would increase the supply of organs, regulations could restrain possible abuses, and a payment-for-organs system could meet relevant medical ethical principles. James F. Childress, professor of ethics and professor of medical education, argues that a free market would cause the loss of important altruistic motivations and would turn organs into commodities; moreover, such an untried market might make fewer—not more—organs available.

Issue 9.   Should Drugs Be Legalized?   161

YES: Meaghan Cussen and Walter Block, from "Legalize Drugs Now! An Analysis of the Benefits of Legalized Drugs," *American Journal of Economics and Sociology* (July 2000)   *163*

Meaghan Cussen (a student in economics) and Walter Block (her economics professor) argue that the legalization of drugs would provide many sorts of benefits (e.g., crime would fall, the quality of life in inner cities would rise, and taxpayers would no longer have to pay for an unwinnable "war on drugs"). Moreover, the legalization of drugs would promote the American value of liberty. Theodore Dalrymple stresses the harm that drugs can do and the danger of "giving up" in the "war on drugs." He takes issue with most of the claims of the supporters of legalization, and more generally with Mill's "harm principle": the idea that in a free society, adults should be permitted to do whatever they please (provided that they are willing to accept the consequences of their own actions, and those actions don't cause harm to others).

Issue 10.   Is Price Gouging Wrong?   182

Health science professor Jeremy Snyder argues that although there are arguments from a business perspective which emphasize the economic benefits of raising prices in the wake of disasters, price gouging in fact fails to respect persons as persons and is morally wrong insofar as it undermines fair access to essential goods. Political philosopher Matt Zwolinski's article is a direct response to Snyder. He argues that although price gougers may not be morally virtuous agents, they—unlike most of use—are nevertheless doing something that the victims of the disaster can benefit from. In addition, he argues that the allocation of goods via the market is a more just system than other alternatives, including those suggested by Snyder.

Issue 11.   Is Affirmative Action Fair?   209

Professor of philosophy Albert G. Mosley argues that affirmative action is a continuation of the history of black progress since the *Brown v. Board of Education* desegregation decision of 1954 and the Civil Rights Act of 1964. He defends affirmative action as a "benign use of race." Professor of philosophy Louis P. Pojman contends that affirmative action violates the moral principle that maintains that each person is to be treated as an individual, not as representative of a group. He stresses that individual merit needs to be appreciated and that respect should be given to each person on an individual basis.

Issue 12.   Should the Death Penalty Be Abolished?   235

Criminologist Michael Welch argues that the death penalty encourages murder and is applied in a biased and mistake-laden way to growing groups of people. Much of the recent popular support of capital punishment is due to ignorance of the facts. Professor of law Ernest van den Haag argues that the death penalty is entirely in line with the U.S. Constitution and that although studies of its deterrent effect are inconclusive, the death penalty is morally justified and should not be abolished.

Bagaric and Clarke remind us, first of all, that torture, although prohibited by international law, is nevertheless widely practiced. A rational examination of torture and a consideration of hypothetical (but realistic) cases show that torture is justifiable in order to prevent great harm. Torture should be regulated and carefully practiced as an information-gathering technique in extreme cases. Philosopher Philip E. Devine argues for an absolute (or virtually absolute) position against torture. Devine suggests that the wrongness of torture and the repugnance that we feel toward it ultimately go beyond any moral theory. In addition, the examination of extreme cases should not inform our general thought about these and other matters.

Admitting that religiously based grounds for the wrongness of killing an innocent person are not convincing to many people, Doerflinger argues on mainly secular grounds having to do with inconsistencies in the arguments of supporters of physician-assisted suicide. He examines the idea of autonomy, and the tendency for something like physician-assisted suicide to spread once it becomes initially accepted in a limited way. Watts and Howell first claim that it is very important to distinguish between *assisted suicide* and *voluntary active euthanasia*. Basically, the first of these is suicide or killing oneself; the second involves being killed by someone else (e.g., a physician). Watts and Howell argue that most of the opposition to physician-assisted suicide turns out to be really opposition to voluntary active euthanasia; furthermore, they argue that physician-assisted suicide would not have the dire consequence that its opponents predict.

Michael Allen Fox believes that the common practice of eating meat is something that we need to apply critical thinking to. He argues that if we care about pain, suffering, and death, and if we are to live up to the demands of justice, then we should take responsibility for our diets and become vegetarians. Environmental thinker Holmes Rolston III maintains that meat eating by humans is a natural part of the ecosystem. He states that it is important that animals do not suffer needlessly, but it would be a mistake to think that animals, like humans, are members of a culture. Rolston concludes that people too readily project human nature on animal nature.

UNIT 5   OTHER MORAL ISSUES   329

Issue 16.   Should College Athletes Be Paid?   330

Taylor Branch argues that college athletics is big business, and everyone involved is allowed a share of the wealth—except for the students who make it all possible. So-called "student athletes" are exploited. The phrase "student athletes" is itself a cop-out. Seth Davis addresses Branch's article directly, but he denies much of Branch's case. College sports, he says, are not big business; most teams lose money for their colleges. To think that college athletes, such as football players, come away empty-handed is simply false. For one thing, they receive an education (which itself could be valued at about $200,000 in tuition). They also receive training, coaching, and special tutoring.

Issue 17.   Is It Right to Produce Genetically Modified Food?   351

Ronald Bailey is a strong supporter of genetically modified food (GMF). He argues that it is feared by many activists, but there is no strong proof that there are any problems with it. In fact, he suggests that there are great benefits that can be provided by GMFs, especially to the world's poor and to those suffering from natural calamities. Michael Fox is cautious about the spread of *scientism* and the morally blind push for technological development. This scientism, when combined with an aggressive spirit of enterprise, threatens to upset the balance of nature. We may try to rearrange natural things (including plants and animals) to serve our own purposes, but Fox believes that in this way we end up alienating ourselves from the natural world.

Correlation Guide

The *Taking Sides* series presents current issues in a debate-style format designed to stimulate student interest and develop critical thinking skills. Each issue is thoughtfully framed with an issue summary, an issue introduction, and a postscript. The pro and con essays—selected for their liveliness and substance—represent the arguments of leading scholars and commentators in their fields.

Taking Sides: Clashing Views on Moral Issues, 13/e, Expanded is an easy-to-use reader that presents issues on important topics in moral philosophy. For more information on *Taking Sides* and other *McGraw-Hill Contemporary Learning Series* titles, visit www.mhhe.com/cls.

This convenient guide matches the issues in **Taking Sides: Moral Issues, 13/e, Expanded** with the corresponding chapters in three of our best-selling McGraw-Hill Philosophy textbooks by Bonevac, Rosenstand, and Rachels/Rachels.

Taking Sides: Moral Issues, 13/e, Expanded	Today's Moral Issues: Classic and Contemporary Perspectives, 7/e by Bonevac	The Moral of the Story: An Introduction to Ethics, 7/e by Rosenstand	The Elements of Moral Philosophy, 7/e by Rachels/Rachels
Issue 1: Is Moral Relativism Correct?		Chapter 3: Ethical Relativism	Chapter 2: The Challenge of Cultural Relativism
Issue 2: Does Morality Need Religion?	**Part I: First Principles:** Theoretical Approaches	Chapter 1: Thinking About Values Chapter 3: Ethical Relativism	Chapter 4: Does Morality Depend on Religion?
Issue 3: Must Sex Involve Commitment?	**Part I: First Principles:** Sexual Behavior **Part I: First Principles:** Sexual Orientation and Gay Marriage	Chapter 5: Using Your Reason, Part 1: Utilitarianism	Chapter 8: The Debate Over Utilitarianism
Issue 4: Is Abortion Immoral?	**Part III: Rights and Responsibilities:** Abortion	Chapter 13: Applied Ethics: A Sampler	Chapter 4: Does Morality Depend on Religion?
Issue 5: Is It Right to Prohibit Same-Sex Marriage?	**Part I: First Principles:** Sexual Orientation and Gay Marriage		Chapter 6: The Social Contract Theory
Issue 6: Should Human Cloning Be Banned?		Chapter 7: Personhood, Rights, and Justice	Chapter 10: Kant and Respect for Persons
Issue 7: Is Cloning Pets Ethically Justified?	**Part I: First Principles:** Animals	Chapter 5: Using Your Reason, Part 1: Utilitarianism Chapter 13: Applied Ethics: A Sampler	Chapter 7: The Utilitarian Approach Chapter 8: The Debate Over Utilitarianism

(continued)

Taking Sides: Moral Issues, 13/e, Expanded	Today's Moral Issues: Classic and Contemporary Perspectives, 7/e by Bonevac	The Moral of the Story: An Introduction to Ethics, 7/e by Rosenstand	The Elements of Moral Philosophy, 7/e by Rachels/ Rachels
Issue 8: Should Congress Allow the Buying and Selling of Human Organs?			**Chapter 7:** The Utilitarian Approach **Chapter 8:** The Debate Over Utilitarianism
Issue 9: Should Drugs Be Legalized?	**Part II: Liberty:** Drug Legalization		**Chapter 5:** Ethical Egoism
Issue 10: Is Price Gouging Wrong?	**Part IV: Justice and Equality:** Economic Equality		**Chapter 5:** Ethical Egoism **Chapter 6:** The Social Contract Theory
Issue 11: Is Affirmative Action Fair?	**Part IV: Justice and Equality:** Affirmative Action	**Chapter 7:** Personhood, Rights, and Justice	**Chapter 8:** The Debate Over Utilitarianism
Issue 12: Should the Death Penalty Be Abolished?	**Part III: Rights and Responsibilities:** Capital Punishment	**Chapter 13:** Applied Ethics: A Sampler	**Chapter 9:** Are There Absolute Moral Rules? **Chapter 10:** Kant and Respect for Persons
Issue 13: Is Torture Ever Justified?		**Chapter 5:** Using Your Reason, Part 1: Utilitarianism	**Chapter 9:** Are There Absolute Moral Rules? **Chapter 10:** Kant and Respect for Persons
Issue 14: Is Physician-Assisted Suicide Wrong?	**Part III: Rights and Responsibilities:** Euthanasia and Physician-Assisted Suicide	**Chapter 13:** Applied Ethics: A Sampler	**Chapter 7:** The Utilitarian Approach **Chapter 8:** The Debate Over Utilitarianism **Chapter 9:** Are There Absolute Moral Rules? **Chapter 10:** Kant and Respect for Persons
Issue 15: Does Morality Require Vegetarianism?	**Part I: First Principles:** Animals	**Chapter 13:** Applied Ethics: A Sampler	**Chapter 12:** Virtue Ethics
Issue 16: Should College Athletes Be Paid?			**Chapter 7:** The Utilitarian Approach **Chapter 8:** The Debate Over Utilitarianism **Chapter 9:** Are There Absolute Moral Rules? **Chapter 10:** Kant and Respect for Persons
Issue 17: Is It Right to Produce Genetically Modified Food?			**Chapter 12:** Virtue Ethics

Introduction

Thinking About Moral Issues

Stephen Satris

Getting Started

If you were asked in your biology class to give the number of bones in the average human foot, you could consult your textbook, you could go to the library and have the librarian track down the answer, you could search the Internet, or you could ask your friend who always gets A's in biology. Most likely you have not previously had any reason to consider this question, but you do know for certain that it has one right answer, which you will be expected to provide for the final exam.

What do you do, however, when faced with a moral question like one of the ones raised in this text? Whereas it is a relatively straightforward matter to find out how many bones there are in the human foot, in addressing moral issues, understanding cannot be acquired as easily. Someone cannot report back to you on the right answer. You will have to discuss the ideas raised by these moral questions and determine the answers for yourself. And you will have to arrive at an answer through reason and careful thought; you cannot just rely on your *feelings* to answer these questions. Keep in mind, too, that these are questions you will be facing your entire life—understanding will not end with the final exam.

In approaching the issues in this book, you should maintain an open mind toward both sides of the question. Otherwise, it will be more difficult for you to see, appreciate, and, most importantly, *learn* from the opposing position. Therefore, you should first ask yourself what your own assumptions are about an issue and become aware of any preconceived notions you may have. And then, after such reflection, you should assume the posture of an impartial judge. If you have a strong prior attachment to one side, do not let it prevent you from giving a sympathetic ear to the opposing side.

Once the arguments have been laid out and you have given them careful consideration, do not remain suspended in the middle. Now is the time for informed judgment.

A natural dramatic sequence is played out for each of the 17 issues discussed in *Taking Sides: Clashing Views on Moral Issues*. A question is posed, and you must open yourself to hear each author's arguments, reasons, and examples, which are meant to persuade you to take the author's viewpoint. But then comes the second part of the drama. Having heard and considered both sides of an issue, what will *you* say? What understanding of the issue can *you* achieve?

You can choose aspects of the "yes" answer and aspects of the "no" answer and weave them together to construct a coherent whole. You can accept one answer and build some qualifications or limitations into it. Or you might be stimulated to think of a completely new angle on the issue.

Be aware of three dangers. The first is a premature judgment or fixed opinion that rules out a fair hearing of the opposing side. The second danger is in many ways like the first, but is somewhat more insidious. It is an unconscious assumption (or set of assumptions) that makes it impossible to hear the other side correctly. (The best antidote for this is to be able to give a fair and accurate account of the issue as it appears to someone on the opposing side.) Finally, the third danger is to lack a judgment after having considered the issue. In this case, two contrary positions simply cannot both be right, and it is up to the reader to make an effort to distinguish what is acceptable from what is unacceptable in the arguments and positions that have been defended.

Fundamental Issues in Morality

The 17 issues in this book are divided into five units. The first unit deals with fundamental questions about morality as a whole. In this context, it might be said that "morality is a religious matter" or, perhaps, that "it's all relative." The issues in the first unit do not directly confront specific moral problems; they question the nature of morality itself.

Already in Unit 1, we see something that is a recurring feature of moral thought and of this book: Moral issues are interrelated. Suppose, for example, that you answer the question "Is Moral Relativism Correct?" (Issue 1) in the affirmative and also answer the question "Does Morality Need Religion?" (Issue 2) in the affirmative. How can these two answers fit together? A positive answer to the second question is generally thought to involve a source for morality that is supernatural, beyond the customs and traditions of any one particular social group. But an affirmative answer to the first question suggests that morality is grounded in what is cultural and *not* supernatural. (It may be possible to maintain affirmative answers to both of these questions, but a person who does so owes us an explanation as to how these two ideas fit together.) Many other issues that at first sight might seem distinct have connections among one another.

Another point, and one that applies not only to the issues in Unit 1 but to controversial issues in general, is this: In evaluating any position, you should do so on the merits (or lack of merit) of the specific case that is made. Do not accept or reject a position on the basis of what the position (supposedly) tells you about the author, and do not criticize or defend a position by reducing it to simplistic slogans. The loss of articulation and sophistication that occurs when a complex position is reduced to a simple slogan is significant and real. For example, a "no" answer to the question "Does Morality Need Religion?" might be superficially labeled as "antireligion" and a "yes" answer might seem as "proreligion." Yet Saint Thomas Aquinas, who has always been regarded as the foremost theologian of the Christian tradition, would respond with a "no" to that question. Moral questions are complex, and the reduction of answers to simple reactions or superficial slogans will not be helpful. The questions and issues that are raised here require careful analysis, examination, and argumentation.

Gender, Sex, and Reproduction

Unit 2 includes several questions that have to do with ways of looking at society, especially sex roles, sexual relationships, and reproduction. In many ways, the issues in this section are basic to an understanding of our own place in society, our relation to others, and what we expect of men and women.

Specific issues considered in Unit 2 are "Must Sex Involve Commitment?," "Is Abortion Immoral?," "Is It Right To Prohibit Same-Sex Marriage?," and "Should Human Cloning Be Banned?"

The question "Must Sex Involve Commitment?" (Issue 3) has traditionally been answered in the positive—the conservative answer certainly tends to be positive. But after the social changes that have liberalized society's sexual attitudes, does the traditional answer still stand? What, exactly, has changed in people's attitudes? Have people come to see premarital sex as morally permissible (where it was once thought to be immoral)? Or do people still see it as immoral, but they are no longer shocked by its widespread occurrence in real life, films, etc.? The word *must* in "Must Sex Involve Commitment?" is moral. The view that sex must involve commitment is not intended to be one that reflects how things actually are. In fact, those who answer this question positively would probably think that how things actually are is not at all how they should be.

The question "Is Abortion Immoral?" (Issue 4) is not at all new, and threatens immediately to polarize people into pro-life and pro-choice camps. But it is best to leave such labels and superficial slogans behind. Whenever an issue seems to demand answers very quickly, as this one might, it is better to go slowly and to first consider the arguments, examples, and rationale of each position before making up your mind. Both of the writers on this topic, for example, stay away from religious arguments—which could very quickly polarize people.

The question "Is It Right to Prohibit Same-Sex Marriage?" (Issue 5) arises in a social context of changing practices and values. Certainly, same-sex relationships are more widely tolerated now than in the past. Some people may think that this shows a moral decline and would naturally be against same-sex marriage. But even some people who think of this increased tolerance as a good thing are hesitant to accept same-sex marriage. Marriage is something for a man and a woman, they might say. Traditionally, this may have indeed been so. But the question now arises whether any changes should be made to this idea. Is marriage for heterosexual unions only? And if same-sex marriage is allowed, what would be the social repercussions?

The question "Should Human Cloning Be Banned?" (Issue 6) has arisen because technology may some day (soon) exist that could clone human beings. Some people think that science would be going too far here and that cloning people would be akin to "playing God." They also feel that not everything that technology makes possible should actually be done. Others see no problem with proceeding with experimentation toward human cloning. Is cloning just a case of using science to manipulate natural facts and achieve some desired results, or are the results here not to be desired?

Law and Society

Unit 3 focuses on questions that involve our social nature. We ask what particular arrangements will (or will not) be tolerated in society. We also ask what laws we should have (or not have).

This section considers the questions "Is Cloning Pets Ethically Justified?," "Should Congress Allow the Buying and Selling of Human Organs?," "Should Drugs Be Legalized?," "Is Price Gouging Wrong?," "Is Affirmative Action Fair?," "Should the Death Penalty Be Abolished?," "Is Torture Ever Justified?" and "Is Physician-Assisted Suicide Wrong?"

The first question, "Is Cloning Pets Ethically Justified?" (Issue 7), raises many of the same questions that arise in the case of cloning human beings. People may have unrealistic expectations of cloning in both cases. And in both cases the cloned individual may be held to those expectations. However, it may be felt that human beings are in a class by themselves and should not be cloned—while we can do virtually anything in the case of animals. Yet, here again, objectors to cloning stress the failures of the technique and the problems that it always seems to bring with it. If our pets really are at our mercy (unlike human beings), perhaps it is not right to treat them in ways that seem to be problematic.

The second question, "Should Congress Allow the Buying and Selling of Human Organs?" (Issue 8), is one that might initially sound quite gruesome. But the fact is that there are many more people needing organs than there are organs available for transplant. Part of the problem with the shortage of organs is that there is no financial incentive for donors to provide kidneys. Doctors and hospitals are compensated for their roles in the organ transplant process, but the donor—by law—cannot be compensated. There cannot be payment for organs. Yet there is a demand for organs on the part of those in need. Would a market in which there was buying and selling help? Is this even something we should think about? Why not, if it can help?

Asking "Should Drugs Be Legalized" (Issue 9) raises a number of points that require consideration. Here we ask about the future and what kind of society is worth aiming for. Should we strive for a society in which certain substances are available on the open market to consumers who choose them, or should we aim to eliminate certain substances and legally punish drug dealers and users? This is one of several issues in which we are drawn to two incompatible values; in this case, the values are complete liberty and social order. It seems impossible to have both.

The question "Is Affirmative Action Fair?" (Issue 11) confronts a policy that is intended to address problems arising from the history and the current state of race relations in the United States. Most arguments in favor of affirmative action can be seen as either backward-looking or forward-looking. Arguments that regard affirmative action as a form of compensation or as a response to previous injustices are backward-looking because they focus on prior events. Arguments that regard affirmative action as a means of achieving integration or diversity or as a means of providing minority role models are forward-looking because they point to the future. Critics of programs of affirmative action, however, have charged that such programs lead to (or themselves amount to) "reverse discrimination" and unfairly focus on "group rights," whereas the only actual rights are rights of individuals.

Many subsidiary questions enter into the issue of "Should the Death Penalty Be Abolished?" (Issue 12). Does the death penalty deter crime? Does it, in fact, encourage crime? Is it the only way to give some criminals what they deserve? Does it fall unfairly on minorities and the poor? How much should we be concerned about errors? And, finally, even if we had the answers to all these questions, could we use those answers to address the overarching question of whether or not the death penalty should be abolished?

The question "Is Torture Ever Justified?" (Issue 13) was, until 9/11, mainly a hypothetical question. Now, it is asked by government interrogators—who have suspects and want answers, and by concerned citizens as well, who might feel that torture makes us no better than the terrorists. The problem is that arguments on both sides seem fairly strong. To use torture against terrorists who have killed some innocent Americans and may want to kill us too does not seem very far from self-defense. However, if we engage in torture, then we seem to be the very devils we are said by the terrorists to be. But aren't Americans supposed to be the "good guys"? With torture, we seem to be stooping to the same level as the terrorists.

The question "Is Physician-Assisted Suicide Wrong?" (Issue 14) is another question about life or death, but this time the person who would die would not be regarded as a criminal. Such a person, who may have a terminal illness and perhaps be in great pain, requests the physician's assistance in killing himself or herself. (Why would such assistance even be needed? Some people may be so bad off as not to be able to do it themselves; still others may be better off—but might end up botching things and making the situation worse. Hence, the physician is asked to lend expertise and assistance.) The question is whether this request may be fulfilled. If so, the end comes quickly. If not, the end will come, but not so quickly. But is helping to bring the situation to a quick end something that physicians may do?

Human Beings and Other Species

Unit 4 has only one question: "Does Morality Require Vegetarianism?" (Issue 15). This is a question that probably would not have been taken seriously in earlier times. However, today there are people and organizations that promote vegetarianism on moral grounds. The simplest idea here is that animals are beings that can be harmed, and they generally do suffer when they are raised and killed for meat. Most people can live without eating meat, so meat-eating seems to be a practice that we have in our power to change. Of course, many people *like* meat-eating and are very reluctant to change. From their point of view, animals are part of nature, human beings are part of nature, and meat-eating—where one species eats another—is also part of nature. But the meat-eating question remains and forces itself upon people, who pride themselves on their ability to be self-aware and have knowledge—knowledge that in this case includes awareness of the fact that they share the planet with other species.

Unit 5 contains the final two questions, "Should College Athletes Be Paid?" (Issue 16) and "Is It Right to Produce Genetically Modified Food?" (Issue 17). These questions are currently being debated but are not easily placed into the other categories in this book. The question "Should College Athletes Be Paid?" (Issue 16) has to do with fairness. After all, the athletes are the ones who play the sports that attract so much money and attention to the schools. Everyone associated with college sports seems to profit—except the athletes themselves. So it's partly a question of fairness. But this issue also has to do with both college and sports, and their essential natures. There is something not quite right about regarding college athletes as professional athletes—who must be paid. We are drawn to the amateur ideal as part of the nature of the college athlete. Student athletes really are playing for their alma mater, their college or university home. They shouldn't have to be paid, we feel. In some ways, too much money detracts from the idea of a college or a university as a place of academic value, a place set apart, a place of teaching and learning.

The question "Is It Right to Produce Genetically Modified Food?" (Issue 17) is another question that wouldn't have been asked years ago since we didn't have the technical means to modify living things in this way. But now that we do have the technical ability, we have to ask ourselves how we are to act. Supporters of genetically modified food will sing its praises.

But its critics would have us pause rather than rush to embrace a technology that is both new and powerful. We have to ask ourselves whether we can envision the long-term effects of this new technology. Not everything that we *can* do is something that we *should* do.

Internet References . . .

The Internet Encyclopedia of Philosophy

This is a very useful reference tool for the serious philosophy student. It contains an excellent collection of readings from classic philosophy texts and original contributions by professional philosophers around the Internet.

www.iep.utm.edu/

Ethics Updates

Ethics Updates is an online resource edited by Lawrence M. Hinman, a well-respected ethicist at the University of San Diego. The site includes definitions of basic ideas, online articles, audio files, video files, discussion boards, and sophisticated search engines. There is a wide variety of subject matter, running from ethical theory to applied ethics, and the site offers frequent opportunities for user input.

http://ethics.sandiego.edu

Internet Philosophical Resources on Moral Relativism

This *Ethics Updates* site contains discussion questions and Internet resources devoted to moral, cultural, and ethical relativism.

http://ethics.sandiego.edu/theories/

Fundamental Issues in Morality

*E*ven *before confronting particular moral issues, we find that there are several conflicting assertions that have been made about morality considered as a whole. Some people state that there is no such thing as objective moral knowledge and that morality can provide no answers. Among them, relativists contend that all moral talk is simply the expression of subjective feelings or cultural norms, and these vary from case to case. Others maintain that morality does not have a source in purely human experience and interaction. Religion, they say, is the ground of morality. These and other ideas are discussed in this section.*

- Is Moral Relativism Correct?
- Does Morality Need Religion?

ISSUE 1

Is Moral Relativism Correct?

YES: Gilbert Harman, from "Moral Relativism," in Gilbert Harman and Judith Jarvis Thomson, eds., *Moral Relativism and Moral Objectivity* (Blackwell, 1996)

NO: Louis P. Pojman, from "The Case Against Moral Relativism," in Louis P. Pojman and Lewis Vaughn, eds., *The Moral Life: An Introductory Reader in Ethics and Literature* (Oxford University Press, 2007)

ISSUE SUMMARY

YES: Philosopher Gilbert Harman argues that relativism is true for morality—much as Einstein proved it was true for motion. Just as motion always presupposes some framework in which it occurs (and something can be in motion relative to one person but not to another), morality too always presupposes some framework.

NO: Louis Pojman carefully distinguishes what he calls the diversity thesis—that moral rules differ from society to society—from ethical relativism. The diversity thesis is a straightforward description of what are acknowledged differences in the moral beliefs and practices of various human groups. But he argues that moral relativism does not follow from this diversity.

Many people are drawn to the idea that moral relativism is correct, but most people who have thought and written about this issue think that it is not. As a result, the supporters of moral relativism are in the minority. Among those, however, who think moral relativism is correct, Gilbert Harman's work—excerpted here—stands out.

Harman draws attention to what is probably one of the most common sources of the idea of moral relativism, namely, the fact that there is vast diversity among the moral views of different people at different times and places; furthermore, he emphasizes there is even a diversity of moral views among people in the very same society.

Diversity of views by itself proves nothing, and Harman acknowledges this. Consider the fact that among people of different times and places, there is also a diversity of views about many other things (e.g., about the origin of the earth, whether thunder is caused by Zeus, and so on). But no one would say that there is no truth of the matter, or that such matters are relative.

Of course, one might argue that *beliefs* are relative, at least in the following sense. If you time-traveled back to ancient Greece and asked people whether it was Zeus who caused thunder, you'd receive a large number of affirmative answers, whereas asking the same question of almost anyone today would most probably yield negative answers. So the *beliefs* might be in some sense relative. Both Harman and Pojman would agree that their own disagreement is not over what the beliefs of people would be but what the situation actually is.

As for the belief that Zeus causes thunder, we can probably chalk that one up to the lack of scientific sophistication of the ancient Greeks. But it is also worthwhile considering a more modern question—such as the origin and nature of black holes. There may be competing theories about black holes, and (unlike the case of thunder) the matter might not be settled at all. But no one would say that the nature of thunder or black holes is *relative*. There's a definite truth there to find out. In the case of thunder, we may know the truth; in the case of black holes, we may not. So here is a case in which we ourselves may lack the knowledge. But that doesn't mean that the matter is relative.

From Pojman's point of view, he could easily grant that the views of the people of different times and places are different. Nevertheless, he might say, what different people (e.g., the ancient Greeks and modern-day scientists) say or believe about something may have little or nothing to do with the truth of the matter. Perhaps one of these groups is correct. Perhaps neither is correct. But in any case, the truth of the matter does not depend on what they might say or believe.

Likewise, an opponent of relativism, such as Pojman himself, will insist that the same holds true for moral belief and for physical belief. In any case, the moral objectivist (or non-relativist) will certainly hold that moral judgments are not dependent on cultural acceptance for their validity. So, it's possible for some people to promote a certain moral position, and for that moral position to be correct, while the majority of the population rejects the position. Pojman would admit that in some cases it's *hard* to see the validity, or lack of validity, behind a moral point of view. (Perhaps many controversial ideas—like those in this book—are *hard* in this sense.) Of course, in some cases it's quite easy to see whether or not we have moral validity. (For example, consider an obvious wrong like rape. No one defends rape, it's not controversial, and there is no issue about it in this book.)

In the following essays, Gilbert Harman first defends relativism, invoking, in fact, Einstein's relativistic theory about physical phenomena. Louis Pojman, a supporter of moral objectivism, then argues that moral relativism is not correct.

YES

Gilbert Harman

Moral Relativism

Introduction

Motion is a relative matter. Motion is always relative to a choice of spatio-temporal framework. Something that is moving in relation to one spatio-temporal framework can be at rest in relation to another. And no spatio-temporal framework can be singled out as the one and only framework that captures the truth about whether something is in motion.

According to Einstein's Theory of Relativity even an object's mass is relative to a choice of spatio-temporal framework. An object can have one mass in relation to one such framework and a different mass in relation to another. Again, there is no privileged spatio-temporal framework that determines the real mass of an object.

I am going to argue for a similar claim about moral right and wrong. That is, . . . I am going to defend *moral relativism*. I am going to argue that moral right and wrong (good and bad, justice and injustice, virtue and vice, etc.) are always relative to a choice of moral framework. What is morally right in relation to one moral framework can be morally wrong in relation to a different moral framework. And no moral framework is objectively privileged as the one true morality.

Einstein's relativistic conception of mass involves the following claim about the truth conditions of judgments of mass.

> (1) For the purposes of assigning truth conditions, a judgment of the form, *the mass of X is M* has to be understood as elliptical for a judgment of the form, *in relation to spatio-temporal framework F the mass of X is M.*

The word *elliptical* might be misleading here. Einstein's Theory of Relativity does not involve a claim about meaning or about what people intend to be claiming when they make judgments about an object's mass. The point is, rather, that the only truth there is in this area is relative truth.

Before Einstein, judgments about mass were not intended as relative judgments. But it would be mean-spirited to invoke an "error theory" and conclude that these pre-Einsteinian judgments were all false![1] Better to suppose that such a judgment was true to the extent that an object had the relevant mass in relation to a spatio-temporal framework that was conspicuous to the

From *Moral Relativism and Moral Objectivity* (Blackwell 1996), pp. 3–6, 8–15, 17–19 (excerpts). Copyright © 1996 by Gilbert Harman and Judith Jarvis Thompson, eds. Reprinted by permission of Blackwell Publishing, Ltd.

person making the judgment, for example, a framework in which that person was at rest.

Similarly, the moral relativism I will argue for is not a claim what people *mean* by their moral judgments. Moral relativism does not claim that people intend their moral judgments to be "elliptical" in the suggested way; just as relativism about mass does not claim that people intend their judgments about mass to make implicit reference to a spatio-temporal framework.

To a first approximation, moral relativism makes the following claim about moral judgments.

(2) For the purposes of assigning truth conditions, a judgment of the form, *it would be morally wrong of P to D,* has to be understood as elliptical for a judgment of the form, *in relation to moral framework M, it would be morally wrong of P to D.* Similarly for other moral judgments.[2]

As before, it is important not to put too much stress on the word *elliptical.* The moral relativism I will argue for is no more a claim about what people mean by their moral judgments than relativism about mass is a claim about what people mean when they make judgments about mass. Moral relativism does not claim that people intend their moral judgments to be "elliptical" in the suggested way; just as relativism about mass does not claim that people intend their judgments about mass to make implicit reference to a spatio-temporal framework. . . .

<◦>

(2) is only part of a definition of moral relativism because it is important to distinguish moral relativism both from moral absolutism on the one side and from moral nihilism on the other side. Moral absolutism holds that there is a single true morality. Moral relativism claims instead:

(3) There is no single true morality. There are many different moral frameworks, none of which is more correct than the others.

Moral nihilism agrees with (3) and takes that conclusion to be a reason to reject morality altogether including any sort of relative morality.

Moral nihilism can be compared to religious nihilism. Religious nihilism would be a natural response to the conclusion that there is no single true religion but only many different religious outlooks, none of which is more correct than the others. Such a conclusion would seem to provide a reason to reject religion and religious judgments altogether, rather than a reason to accept "religious relativism." It might then be possible to assign objective truth conditions to religious judgments in relation to one or another religious framework, but it is hard to see how such relative religious judgments could play a serious role in religious practices. Moral nihilism argues that the same is true of morality: given (3), there is no point to engaging in morality and moral judgment.

Moral relativism rejects moral nihilism and asserts instead

(4) Morality should not be abanboned.

Furthermore, moral relativism insists. . . .

(5) Relative moral judgments can continue to play a serious role in moral thinking. . . .

Explaining Moral Diversity

In this and the following section I argue that the following claim is a reasonable inference from the most plausible explanation of moral diversity.

> There is no single true morality. There are many different moral frameworks, none of which is more correct than the others.

I begin by mentioning data to be explained: the nature and extent of moral diversity.

Members of different cultures often have very different beliefs about right and wrong and often act quite differently on their beliefs. To take a seemingly trivial example, different cultures have different rules of politeness and etiquette: burping after eating is polite in one culture, impolite in another. Less trivially, some people are cannibals, others find cannibalism abhorrent.

The institution of marriage takes different forms in different societies. In some, a man is permitted to have several wives, in others bigamy is forbidden. More generally, the moral status of women varies greatly from one society to another in many different ways.

Some societies allow slavery, some have caste systems, which they take to be morally satisfactory, others reject both slavery and caste systems as grossly unjust.

It is unlikely that any nontrivial moral principles are universally accepted in all societies. The anthropologist George Silberbauer (1993, p. 15) is able to say only that "there are values which can be seen as common to nearly all societies," a remark limited by the phrases "can be seen as" and "nearly all." He further limits this claim by adding, "there are sometimes strong contrasts in the ways in which [these values] are expressed in precepts, principles and evaluations of behaviour."

Some say that there is a universally recognized central core of morality consisting of prohibitions against killing and harming others, against stealing, and against lying to others. Walzer (1987, p. 24) offers a more limited list of universal prohibitions: "murder, deception, betrayal and gross cruelty." It makes sense for Walzer to leave theft off the list, since some societies do not recognize private property, so they would have no rules against stealing. (Without property, there can be no such thing as stealing. It is trivial to say that all societies that recognize private property have rules against stealing, because having such rules is a necessary condition of recognizing private property!)

It may be that *murder* is always considered wrong, if murder is defined as "wrongful killing." But few societies accept *general* moral prohibitions on killing or harming other people. There are societies in which a "master" is thought to have an absolute right to treat his slaves in any way he chooses, including arbitrarily beating and killing them. Similarly, there may be no limitations on what a husband can do to his wife, or a father to his young children. Infanticide is considered acceptable in some societies. When moral prohibitions on harming and killing and lying exist, they are sometimes supposed to apply only with respect to the local group and not with respect to outsiders. A person who is able successfully to cheat outsiders may be treated as an admirable person. Similarly for someone who is able to harm and kill outsiders.

Any universally accepted principle in this area must verge on triviality, saying, for example, that one must not kill or harm members of a certain group, namely the group of people one must not kill or harm![3]

Thomson (1990) appears to disagree. She states certain principles and says of them, "it is not at all clear how their negations could be accommodated into what would be recognizable as a moral code" (Thomson, 1990, p. 20). The principles she mentions are, "Other things being equal, one ought not act rudely," "Other things being equal, one ought to do what one promised," "Other things being equal, one ought not cause others pain," and "One ought not torture babies to death for fun."

On the contrary, it is clear that many moral codes have accommodated the negations of all these general principles by accepting instead principles restricted to insiders. And, if the phrase "other things being equal" is supposed to include a restriction to insiders, then triviality looms in the manner I have already mentioned.

Now, mere moral diversity is not a disproof of moral absolutism. Where there are differences in custom, there are often differences in circumstance. Indeed, differences in custom are themselves differences in circumstance that can affect what is right or wrong without entailing moral relativism. You do not need to be a moral relativist to recognize that in England it is wrong to drive on the right, whereas in France it is not wrong to drive on the right.

Even where circumstances are relevantly the same, mere differences in moral opinion no more refute moral absolutism than scientific differences in opinion about the cause of canal-like features on the surface of Mars establish that there is no truth to that matter.

But, even though the rejection of moral absolutism is not an immediate logical consequence of the existence of moral diversity, it is a reasonable inference from the most *plausible explanation* of the range of moral diversity that actually exists (Wong, 1984).

One of the most important things to explain about moral diversity is that it occurs not just between societies but also within societies and in a way that leads to seemingly intractable moral disagreements. In the contemporary

United States, deep moral differences often seem to rest on differences in basic values rather than on differences in circumstance or information. Moral vegetarians, who believe that it is wrong to raise animals for food, exist in the same community as nonvegetarians, even in the same family. A disagreement between moral vegetarians and nonvegetarians can survive full discussion and full information and certainly appears to rest on a difference in the significance assigned to animals as compared with humans. Is there a nonrelative truth concerning the moral importance of animals? How might that "truth" be discovered?

In a similar way, disagreements about the moral acceptability of abortion or euthanasia survive extensive discussion and awareness of all relevant information about abortion. Such disagreements appear to depend on basic disagreements concerning the intrinsic value or "sanctity" of human life as compared with the value of the things that life makes possible, such as pleasurable experience and fulfilling activity (Dworkin, 1993).

There are similarly intractable disagreements about the relative value of artifacts of culture as compared with human life. Some people think that it is worse when terrorists bomb famous old museums than when they bomb crowded city streets; others feel that the loss of human life is worse than the loss of architecture and art. Again, there are disagreements about how much help one person should be prepared to give to others. Is it morally wrong to purchase a new record player instead of trying to help people who cannot afford food? Singer (1972) says yes; others say no. There are intractable disputes about whether it is morally worse to kill someone than it is to let that person die (Rachels, 1975) and about the relative importance of liberty versus equality in assessing the justice of social arrangements (Rawls, 1971; Nozick, 1972). . . .

It is hard to see how to account for all moral disagreements in terms of differences in situation or beliefs about nonmoral facts. Many moral disagreements seem to rest instead on basic differences in moral outlook.

Explaining Basic Differences

Suppose that many moral disagreements do indeed rest on basic differences in moral outlook rather than on differences in situation or beliefs about nonmoral facts. What explanation might there be for that?

An "absolutist" explanation might be that some people are simply not well placed to discover the right answers to moral questions.[4] The point to this response is not just that different people have different evidence but that what one makes of evidence depends on one's antecedent beliefs, so that starting out with some beliefs can help one reach the truth, whereas starting out with other beliefs can prevent one from reaching the truth. Rational change in belief tends to be conservative. It is rational to make the least change in one's view that is necessary in order to obtain greater coherence in what one believes (Goodman, 1965; Rawls, 1971; Harman, 1986). Different people with different starting points will rationally respond in different ways to the same evidence. There is no guarantee that people who start sufficiently far apart in belief will tend to converge in view as the evidence comes in. Someone whose initial view is relatively close to the truth may be led by the evidence to come closer to the truth. Someone who starts further away from the truth may be led even further away by the same evidence. Such a person is simply not well placed to discover the truth.

Here then is one absolutist's explanation of why moral disagreements that rest on basic differences in moral outlook cannot be rationally resolved, supposing that is in fact the case.

Moral relativists instead see an analogy with other kinds of relativity.

Consider the ancient question whether the earth moves or the sun moves. Here the relativistic answer is correct. Motion is a relative matter. Something can be in motion relative to one system of spatio-temporal coordinates and not in motion relative to another system. The particular motion an object exhibits will differ from one system to another. There is no such thing as absolute motion, apart from one or another system of coordinates.

A relativistic answer is also plausible in the moral case. Moral right and wrong are relative matters. A given act can be right with respect to one system of moral coordinates and wrong with respect to another system of moral coordinates. And nothing is absolutely right or wrong, apart from any system of moral coordinates.

By "a moral system of coordinates" I mean a set of values (standards, principles, etc.), perhaps on the model of the laws of one or another state. Whether something is wrong in relation to a given system of coordinates is to [be] determined by the system together with the facts of the case in something like the way in which whether something is illegal in a given jurisdiction is determined by the laws of that jurisdiction together with the facts of the case.

Why does it seem (to some people) that there are objective nonrelative facts about moral right and wrong? Well, why does it seem to some people that there [are] objective nonrelative facts about motion or mass? In the case of motion or mass, one particular system of coordinates is so salient that it seems to have a special status. Facts about motion or mass in relation to the salient system of coordinates are treated as nonrelational facts.

In a similar way, the system of moral coordinates that is determined by a person's own values can be so salient that it can seem to that person to have a special status. Facts about what is right or wrong in relation to that system of coordinates can be misidentified as objective nonrelational facts.

To be sure, the system of moral coordinates that is determined by a given person's values cannot in general be *identified* with all and only exactly those very values. Otherwise a person could never be mistaken about moral issues (in relation to the relevant system of coordinates) except by being mistaken about his or her own values!

For the same reason, a legal system cannot be simply identified with existing legislation, the record of prior court decisions, and the principles currently accepted by judges. Otherwise legislation could not be unconstitutional and judges could not be mistaken in the legal principles they accept or the decisions they reach. . . .

Evaluative Relativity: "Good For"

We might compare the relativity of moral wrongness with the way in which something that is good for one person may not be good for another person. If Tom has bet on a horse that runs well in the rain and Sue has bet on a horse that does not run well in the rain, then rain is good for Tom and bad for Sue. This is an uncontroversial example of evaluative relativity. The rain is good in relation to Tom's goals and bad in relation to Sue's.

Similarly, abortion can be immoral with respect to (the moral coordinates determined by) Tom's values and not immoral with respect to Sue's. Moral relativists sometimes express this by saying that abortion is immoral "for Tom" and not immoral "for Sue." Of course, what is meant here is not that abortion is bad for Tom but not bad for Sue in the sense of harmful to one but not the other, not is it just to say that Tom may think abortion immoral and Sue may think it moral. The rain might be good for Tom even if he doesn't realize it and abortion might be immoral for Tom whether or not he realizes that it is.

Notice, by the way, that a speaker does not always have to make explicit for whom a given situation is good. In particular, if Max has bet on the same horse as Alice and he is speaking to Alice, out of the hearing of Sue, he can say simply. "This rain is bad," meaning that it is bad for him and Alice.

Similarly, a moral relativist talking to another moral relativist can suppress reference to a particular set of values if the judgment is supposed to hold in relation both to the (moral coordinates determined by the) values accepted by the speaker and to the (moral coordinates determined by the) values accepted by the hearer. If Sue and Arthur both have values with the same implications for abortion, and Tom isn't listening, Sue might say simply, "Abortion is not morally wrong," meaning that it is not wrong in relation to her and Arthur's values. It is not wrong for either of them. . . .

Relativity Theory

Something that is good for some people is bad for others, indifferent to yet others. Moral relativism says that the same is true of moral values and moral norms. According to moral relativism whether something is morally good, right, or just is always relative to a set of moral coordinates, a set of values or moral standards, a certain moral point of view. . . .

[Moral] relativism makes the following claim about moral judgments:

> For the purpose of assigning truth conditions, a judgment of the form, it would be morally wrong of P to D, has to be understood as elliptical for a judgment of the form, in relation to moral framework M, it would be morally wrong of P to D. Similarly for other moral judgments.

Recall that moral relativism is not by itself a claim about meaning. It does not say that speakers always *intend* their moral judgments to be relational in this respect. It is clear that many speakers do not. Moral relativism is a thesis about how things are and a thesis about how things aren't! Moral relativism claims that there is no such thing as objectively absolute good, absolute right, or absolute justice; there is only what is good, right, or just in relation to this or that moral framework. What someone takes to be absolute rightness is only rightness in relation to (a system of moral coordinates determined by) that person's values.

Earlier, I compared moral relativism with Einstein's theory of relativity in physics, which says that physical magnitudes, like mass, length, or temporal duration, are relative to a frame of reference, so that two events that are simultaneous with respect to one frame of reference can fail to be simultaneous with respect to another. In saying this, Einstein's theory does not make a claim about speakers' intentions. It does not claim that speakers intend to be making relational judgments when they speak of mass or simultaneity. The claim is, rather, that there is no such thing as absolute simultaneity or absolute mass. There is only simultaneity or mass with respect to one or another frame of reference. What someone might take to be absolute magnitudes are really relative magnitudes: magnitudes that are relative to that person's frame of reference.

Imagine a difference of opinion about whether event E precedes event F. According to Einstein's theory of relativity, there may be no uniform answer to this question: perhaps, in relation to one framework E precedes F, while in relation to a different framework E does not precede F.

Similarly, consider a moral disagreement about whether we are right to raise animals for food. Moral relativism holds that there is no uniform answer to this question: in relation to (the system of moral coordinates determined by) one person's values it is permissible to raise animals for food and in relation to (the system of moral coordinates determined by) a different person's values it is not permissible to raise animals for food. To repeat: what someone takes to be absolute rightness is only rightness in relation to (a system of moral coordinates determined by) that person's values.

Moral relativism does not claim that moral differences by themselves entail moral relativism, any more than Einstein claimed that differences in opinion about simultaneity by themselves entailed relativistic physics. We have to consider what differences there are or could be and why this might be so. How are we to explain the sorts of moral differences that actually occur? Can we seriously suppose that there is an answer to the question about the justice of our treatment of animals that is independent of one or another moral framework? What is the best explanation of differences in this and other areas of seeming intractability?

I emphasize again that moral relativism does not identify what is right in relation to a given moral framework with whatever is taken to be right by those who accept that framework. That would be like saying Einstein's theory of relativity treats two events as simultaneous with respect to a given coordinate system if people at rest with respect to the coordinate system believe the events are simultaneous.

Notes

1. Mackie, 1977, chapter one, advocates an error theory of this sort about ordinary moral judgments.
2. So, for example, a judgment of the form, *P ought morally to D,* has to be understood as elliptical for a judgment of the form, *in relation to moral framework M, P ought morally to D.*

3. There will be universal truths about moralities just as there are universal truths about spatio-temporal frameworks. Perhaps all spatio-temporal frameworks must admit of motion and rest. And perhaps all moralities have some rules against killing, harm, and deception. The existence of universal features of spatio-temporal frameworks is compatible with and is even required by Einstein's Theory of Relativity and the existence of universal features of morality is compatible with moral relativism.

4. I am indebted to Nicholas Sturgeon for this suggestion.

Bibliography

Dworkin, R. (1993). *Life's Dominion,* New York: Knopf.

Goodman, N. (1965). *Fact, Fiction, and Forecast.* Cambridge, Mass.: Harvard University Press.

Harman, G. (1986). *Change in View: Principles of Reasoning,* Cambridge, Massachusetts: Bradford Books/MIT Press.

Mackie, J. (1977). *Ethics: Inventing Right and Wrong,* London: Penguin Books.

Nozick, R. (1972). *Anarchy, State, and Utopia,* New York: Basic Books.

Rachels, J. (1975). "Active and passive euthanasia," *New England Journal of Medicine* 292.

Rawls, J. (1971). *A Theory of Justice,* Cambridge, Mass.: Harvard University Press.

Silberbauer, G. (1993). "Ethics in small-scale societies," *A Companion to Ethics,* ed. Peter Singer, Oxford: Blackwell.

Singer, P. (1972). "Famine, affluence, and morality," *Philosophy and Public Affairs* 1.

Thomson, J. (1990). *The Realm of Rights,* Cambridge, Mass.: Harvard University Press.

Walzer, M. (1987). *Interpretation and Social Criticism.* Cambridge, Massachusetts: Harvard University Press.

Wong, D. B. (1984). *Moral Relativity,* Berkeley, California: University of California Press.

The Case Against Moral Relativism

"Who's to Judge What's Right or Wrong?"

Like many people, I have always been instinctively a moral relativist. As far back as I can remember . . . it has always seemed to be obvious that the dictates of morality arise from some sort of convention or understanding among people, that different people arrive at different understandings, and that there are no basic moral demands that apply to everyone. This seemed so obvious to me I assumed it was everyone's instinctive view, or at least everyone who gave the matter any thought in this day and age.

—Gilbert Harman[1]

Ethical relativism is the doctrine that the moral rightness and wrongness of actions vary from society to society and that there are not absolute universal moral standards on all men at all times. Accordingly, it holds that whether or not it is right for an individual to act in a certain way depends on or is relative to the society to which he belongs.

—John Ladd[2]

Gilbert Harman's intuitions about the self-evidence of ethical relativism contrast strikingly with Plato's or Kant's equal certainty about the truth of objectivism, the doctrine that universally valid or true ethical principles exist. . . . "Two things fill the soul with ever new and increasing wonder and reverence the oftener and more fervently reflection ponders on it: the starry heavens above and the moral law within," wrote Kant. On the basis of polls taken in my ethics and introduction to philosophy classes in recent years, Harman's views may signal a shift in contemporary society's moral understanding. The polls show a two-to-one ratio in favor of moral relativism over moral absolutism, with fewer than five percent of the respondents recognizing that a third position between these two polar opposites might exist. Of course, I'm not suggesting that all of these students had a clear understanding of what relativism entails, for many who said they were relativists also contended in the same polls that abortion except to save the mother's life is always wrong, that capital punishment is always wrong, or that suicide is never morally permissible. . . .

1. An Analysis of Relativism

Let us examine the theses contained in John Ladd's succinct statement on ethical (conventional) relativism that appears at the beginning of this essay. If we analyze it, we derive the following argument:

1. Moral rightness and wrongness of actions vary from society to society, so there are no universal moral standards held by all societies.
2. Whether or not it is right for individuals to act in a certain way depends on (or is relative to) the society to which they belong.
3. Therefore, there are no absolute or objective moral standards that apply to all people everywhere.

1. The first thesis, which may be called the *diversity thesis,* is simply a description that acknowledges the fact that moral rules differ from society to society. The Spartans of ancient Greece and the Dobu of New Guinea believe that stealing is morally right, but we believe it is wrong. The Roman father had the power of life and death . . . over his children, whereas we condemn parents for abusing their children. A tribe in East Africa once threw deformed infants to the hippopotamuses, and in ancient Greece and Rome infants were regularly exposed, while we abhor infanticide. Ruth Benedict describes a tribe in Melanesia that views cooperation and kindness as vices, whereas we see them as virtues. While in ancient Greece, Rome, China and Korea parricide was condemned as "the most execrable of crimes," among Northern Indians aged persons, persons who were no longer capable of walking, were left alone to starve. Among the California Gallinomero, when fathers became feeble, a burden to their sons, "the poor old wretch is not infrequently thrown down on his back and securely held while a stick is placed across his throat, and two of them seat themselves on the ends of it until he ceases to breathe."[3] Sexual practices vary over time and place. Some cultures permit homosexual behavior, while others condemn it. Some cultures practice polygamy, while others view it as immoral. Some cultures condone while others condemn premarital sex. Some cultures accept cannibalism, while the very idea revolts us. Some West African tribes perform clitoridectomies on girls, whereas we deplore such practices. Cultural relativism is well documented, and "custom is the king o'er all." There may or may not be moral principles that are held in common by every society, but if there are any, they seem to be few at best. Certainly it would be very difficult to derive any single "true" morality by observing various societies' moral standards.

2. The second thesis, the *dependency thesis,* asserts that individual acts are right or wrong depending on the nature of the society from which they emanate. Morality does not occur in a vacuum, and what is considered morally right or wrong must be seen in a context that depends on the goals, wants, beliefs, history, and environment of the society in question. As William G. Sumner says,

> We learn the morals as unconsciously as we learn to walk and hear and breathe, and [we] never know any reason why the [morals] are what they are. The justification of them is that when we wake to consciousness of life we find them facts which already hold us in the bonds of tradition, custom, and habit.[4]

Trying to see things from an independent, noncultural point of view would be like taking out our eyes in order to examine their contours and qualities. There is no "innocent eye." We are simply culturally determined beings.

We could, of course, distinguish between a weak and a strong thesis of dependency, for the nonrelativist can accept a certain degree of relativity in the way moral principles are *applied* in various cultures, depending on beliefs, history, and environment. For example, Jewish men express reverence for God by covering their heads when entering places of worship, whereas Christian men uncover their heads when entering places of worship. Westerners shake hands upon greeting each other, whereas Hindus place their hands together and point them toward the person to be greeted. Both sides adhere to principles of reverence and respect but apply them differently. But the ethical relativist must maintain a stronger thesis, one that insists that the moral principles themselves are products of the cultures and may vary from society to society." The ethical relativist contends that even beyond environmental factors and differences in beliefs, a fundamental disagreement exists among societies. . . .

In a sense we all live in radically different worlds. But the relativist wants to go further and maintain that there is something conventional about *any* morality, so that every morality really depends on a level of social acceptance. Not only do various societies adhere to different moral systems, but the very same society could (and often does) change its moral views over place and time. For example, the majority of people in the southern United States now view slavery as immoral, whereas one hundred and forty years ago they did not. Our society's views on divorce, sexuality, abortion, and assisted suicide have changed somewhat as well—and they are still changing.

3. The conclusion that there are no absolute or objective moral standards binding on all people follows from the first two propositions. Combining cultural relativism (*the diversity thesis*) with *the dependency thesis* yields ethical relativism in its classic form. If there are different moral principles from culture to culture and if all morality is rooted in culture, then it follows that there are no universal moral principles that are valid (or true) for all cultures and peoples at all times.

2. Subjectivism

Some people think that this conclusion is still too tame, and they maintain that morality is dependent not on the society but rather on the individual. As my students sometimes maintain, "Morality is in the eye of the beholder." They treat morality like taste or aesthetic judgments—person relative. This form of moral subjectivism has the sorry consequence that it makes morality a very useless concept, for, on its premises, little or no interpersonal criticism or judgment is logically possible. Suppose that you are repulsed by observing John torturing a child. You cannot condemn him if one of his principles is "torture little children for the fun of it." The only basis for judging him wrong might be that he was a hypocrite who condemned others for torturing. But suppose that another of his principles is that hypocrisy is morally permissible (for him); thus we cannot condemn him for condemning others for doing what he does.

On the basis of subjectivism Adolf Hitler and the serial murderer Ted Bundy could be considered as moral as Gandhi, so long as each lived by his own standards, whatever those might be. . . .

Notions of good and bad, or right and wrong, cease to have interpersonal evaluative meaning. We might be revulsed by the views of Ted Bundy, but that is just a matter of taste. A student might not like it when her teacher gives her an F on a test paper, while he gives another student an A for a similar paper, but there is no way to criticize him for injustice, because justice is not one of his chosen principles.

Absurd consequences follow from subjectivism. If it is correct, then morality reduces to aesthetic tastes about which there can be neither argument nor interpersonal judgment. Although many students say they espouse subjectivism, there is evidence that it conflicts with other of their moral views. They typically condemn Hitler as an evil man for his genocidal policies. A contradiction seems to exist between subjectivism and the very concept of morality, which it is supposed to characterize, for morality has to do with *proper* resolution of interpersonal conflict and the amelioration of the human predicament. . . . Whatever else it does, morality has a minimal aim of preventing a Hobbesian state of nature . . . , wherein life is "solitary, poor, nasty, brutish, and short. But if so, subjectivism is no help at all, for it rests neither on social agreement of principle (as the conventionalist maintains) nor on an objectively independent set of norms that bind all people for the common good. If there were only one person on earth, there would be no occasion for morality, because there wouldn't be any interpersonal conflicts to resolve or others whose suffering he or she would have a duty to ameliorate. Subjectivism implicitly assumes something of this solipsism, an atomism in which isolated individuals make up separate universes.

Subjectivism treats individuals like billiard balls on a societal pool table where they meet only in radical collisions, each aimed at his or her own goal and striving to do in the others before they themselves are done in. This atomistic view of personality is belied by the facts that we develop in families and mutually dependent communities in which we share a common language, common institutions, and similar rituals and habits, and that we often feel one another's joys and sorrows. As the poet John Donne wrote, "No man is an island, entire of itself; every man is a piece of the continent."

Radical individualistic ethical relativism is incoherent. If so, it follows that the only plausible view of ethical relativism must be one that grounds morality in the group or culture. This form is called *conventionalism*.

3. Conventionalism

Conventional ethical relativism, the view that there are no objective moral principles but that all valid moral principles are justified (or are made true) by virtue of their cultural acceptance, recognizes the social nature of morality. That is precisely its power and virtue. It does not seem subject to the same absurd consequences which plague subjectivism. Recognizing the importance of our social environment in generating customs and beliefs, many people suppose that ethical relativism is the correct metaethical theory. Furthermore, they are drawn to it for its liberal philosophical stance. It seems to be an enlightened response to the sin of ethnocentricity, and it seems to entail or strongly imply an attitude of tolerance toward other cultures. Anthropologist Ruth Benedict says, that in recognizing ethical relativity, "We shall arrive at a more realistic social faith, accepting as grounds of hope and as new bases for tolerance the coexisting and equally valid patterns of life which mankind has created for itself from the raw materials of existence."[5] The most famous of those holding this position is the anthropologist Melville Herskovits, who argues even more explicitly than Benedict that ethical relativism entails intercultural tolerance.

1. If morality is relative to its culture, then there is no independent basis for criticizing the morality of any other culture but one's own.
2. If there is no independent way of criticizing any other culture, we ought to be tolerant of the moralities of other cultures.
3. Morality is relative to its culture. Therefore,
4. We ought to be tolerant of the moralities of other cultures.[6]

Tolerance is certainly a virtue, but is this a good argument for it? I think not. If morality simply is relative to each culture, then if the culture in question does not have a principle of tolerance, its members have no obligation to be tolerant. Herskovits seems to be treating the *principle of tolerance* as the one exception to his relativism. He seems to be treating it as an absolute moral principle. But from a relativistic point of view there is no more reason to be tolerant than to be intolerant and neither stance is objectively morally better than the other.

Not only do relativists fail to offer a basis for criticizing those who are intolerant, but they cannot rationally criticize anyone who espouses what they might regard as a heinous principle. If, as seems to be the case, valid criticism supposes an objective or impartial standard, relativists cannot morally criticize anyone outside their own culture. Adolf Hitler's genocidal actions, so long as they are culturally accepted, are as morally legitimate as Mother Teresa's works of mercy. If Conventional Relativism is accepted, racism, genocide of unpopular minorities, oppression of the poor, slavery, and even the advocacy of war for its own sake are as equally moral as their opposites. And if a subculture decided that starting a nuclear war was somehow morally acceptable, we could not morally criticize these people. Any actual morality, whatever its content, is as valid as every other, and more valid than ideal moralities—since the latter aren't adhered to by any culture.

There are other disturbing consequences of ethical relativism. It seems to entail that reformers are always (morally) wrong since they go against the tide of cultural standards. William Wilberforce was wrong in the eighteenth century to oppose slavery; the British were immoral in opposing suttee in India (the burning of widows, which is now illegal in India). The early Christians were wrong in refusing to serve in the Roman army or to bow down to Caesar, since the majority in the Roman Empire believed that these two acts were moral duties. In fact, Jesus himself was immoral in breaking the law of His day by healing on the Sabbath day and by advocating the principles of the Sermon on the Mount, since it is clear that few in His time (or in ours) accepted them.

Yet we normally feel just the opposite, that the reformer is a courageous innovator who is right, who has the truth, against the mindless majority. Sometimes the individual must stand alone with the truth, risking social censure and persecution. . . . Yet if relativism is correct, the opposite is necessarily the case. Truth is with the crowd and error with the individual. . . .

There is an even more basic problem with the notion that morality is dependent on cultural acceptance for its validity. The problem is that the notion of a *culture* or *society* is notoriously difficult to define. This is especially so in a pluralistic society like our own where the notion seems to be vague with unclear boundary lines. One person may belong to several societies (subcultures) with different value emphases and arrangements of principles. A person may belong to the nation as a single society with certain values of patriotism, honor, courage, laws (including some which are controversial but have majority acceptance, such as the current law on abortion). But he or she may also belong to a church which opposes some of the laws of the State. He may also be an integral member of a socially mixed community where different principles hold sway, and he may belong to clubs and a family where still other rules are adhered to. Relativism would seem to tell us that where he is a member of societies with conflicting moralities he must be judged both wrong and not-wrong whatever he does. For example, if Mary is a U.S. citizen and a member of the Roman Catholic Church, she is wrong (qua Catholic) if she chooses to have an abortion and not-wrong (qua citizen of the U.S.A.) if she acts against the teaching of the Church on abortion. As a member of a racist university fraternity, KKK, John has no obligation to treat his fellow Black student as an equal, but as a member of the university community itself (where the principle of equal rights is accepted) he does have the obligation; but as a member of the surrounding community (which may reject the principle of equal rights) he again has no such obligation; but then again as a member of the nation at large (which accepts the principle) he is obligated to treat his fellow with respect. What is the morally right thing for John to do? The question no longer makes much sense in this moral Babel. It has lost its action-guiding function.

Perhaps the relativist would adhere to a principle which says that in such cases the individual may choose which group to belong to as primary. If Mary chooses to have an abortion, she is choosing to belong to the general society relative to that principle. And John must likewise choose among groups. The trouble with this option is that it seems to lead back to counter-intuitive results. If Murder Mike of Murder, Incorporated, feels like killing Bank President Ortcutt and wants to feel good about it, he identifies with the Murder, Incorporated society rather than the general public morality. Does this justify the killing? In fact, couldn't one justify anything simply by forming a small subculture that approved of it? Ted Bundy would be morally pure in raping and killing innocents simply by virtue of forming a little coterie. How large must the group be in order to be a legitimate subculture or society? Does it need ten or fifteen people? How about just three? Come to think about it, why can't my burglary partner and I found our own society with a morality of its own? Of course, if my partner dies, I could still claim that I was acting from an originally social set of norms. But why can't I dispense with the interpersonal agreements altogether and invent my own morality—since morality, on this view, is only an invention anyway? Conventionalist relativism seems to reduce to subjectivism. And subjectivism leads, as we have seen, to moral solipsism, to the demise of morality altogether. . . .

. . . I don't think you can stop the move from conventionalism to subjectivism. The essential force of the validity of the chosen moral principle is that it is dependent on choice. The conventionalist holds that it is the choice of the group, but why should I accept the group's silly choice, when my own is better (for me)? Why should anyone give such august authority to a culture of society? If this is all morality comes to, why not reject it altogether—even though one might want to adhere to its directives when others are looking in order to escape sanctions?

4. A Critique of Ethical Relativism

However, while we may fear the demise of morality, as we have known it, this in itself may not be a good reason for rejecting relativism. That is, for judging it false. Alas, truth may not always be edifying. But the consequences of this position are sufficiently alarming to prompt us to look carefully for some weakness in the relativist's argument. So let us examine the premises and conclusion listed at the beginning of this essay as the three theses of relativism.

1. *The Diversity Thesis.* What is considered morally right and wrong varies from society to society, so that there are no moral principles accepted by all societies.
2. *The Dependency Thesis.* All moral principles derive their validity from cultural acceptance.
3. *Ethical Relativism.* Therefore, there are no universally valid moral principles, objective standards which apply to all people everywhere and at all times.

Does any one of these seem problematic? Let us consider the first thesis, the diversity thesis, which we have also called cultural relativism. Perhaps there is not as much diversity as anthropologists like Sumner and Benedict suppose. One can also see great similarities between the moral codes of various cultures. E. O. Wilson has identified over a score of common features,[7] and before him Clyde Kluckhohn has noted much significant common ground between cultures.

> Every culture has a concept of murder, distinguishing this from execution, killing in war, and other "justifiable homicides." The notions of incest and other regulations upon sexual behavior, the prohibitions upon untruth under defined circumstances, of restitution and reciprocity, of mutual obligations between parents and children—these and many other moral concepts are altogether universal.[8]

Colin Turnbull's description of the sadistic, semidisplaced, disintegrating Ik in Northern Uganda supports the view that a people without principles of kindness, loyalty, and cooperation will degenerate into a Hobbesian state of nature.[9] But he has also produced evidence that underneath the surface of this dying society, there is a deeper moral code from a time when the tribe flourished, which occasionally surfaces and shows its nobler face.

On the other hand, there is enormous cultural diversity and many societies have radically different moral codes. Cultural relativism seems to be a fact, but, even if it is, it does not by itself establish the truth of ethical relativism. Cultural diversity in itself is neutral between theories. For the objectivist could concede complete cultural relativism, but still defend a form of universalism; for he or she could argue that some cultures simply lack correct moral principles.

On the other hand, a denial of complete cultural relativism (i.e., an admission of some universal principles) does not disprove ethical relativism. For even if we did find one or more universal principles, this would not prove that they had any objective status. We could still *imagine* a culture that was an exception to the rule and be unable to criticize it. So the first premise doesn't by itself imply ethical relativism and its denial doesn't disprove ethical relativism.

We turn to the crucial second thesis, the dependency thesis. Morality does not occur in a vacuum, but rather what is considered morally right or wrong must be seen in a context, depending on the goals, wants, beliefs, history, and environment of the society in question. We distinguished a weak and a strong thesis of dependency. The weak thesis says that the application of principles depends on the particular cultural predicament, whereas the strong thesis affirms that the principles themselves depend on that predicament. The nonrelativist can accept a certain relativity in the way moral principles are *applied* in various cultures, depending on beliefs, history, and environment. For example, a raw environment with scarce natural resources may justify the Eskimos' brand of euthanasia to the objectivist, who in another environment would consistently reject that practice. The members of a tribe in the Sudan throw their deformed children into the river because of their belief that such infants *belong* to the hippopotamus, the god of the river. We believe that they have a false belief about this, but the point is that the same principles of respect for property and respect for human life are operative in these contrary practices. They differ with us only in belief, not in substantive moral principle. This is an illustration of how nonmoral beliefs (e.g., deformed children belong to the hippopotamus) when applied to common moral principles (e.g., give to each his due) generate different actions in different cultures. In our own culture the difference in the nonmoral belief about the status of a fetus generates opposite moral prescriptions. The major difference between pro-choicers and pro-lifers is not whether we should kill persons but whether fetuses are really persons. It is a debate about the facts of the matter, not the principle of killing innocent persons.

So the fact that moral principles are weakly dependent doesn't show that ethical relativism is valid. In spite of this weak dependency on nonmoral factors, there could still be a set of general moral norms applicable to all cultures and even recognized in most, which are disregarded at a culture's own expense.

What the relativist needs is a strong thesis of dependency, that somehow all principles are essentially cultural inventions. But why should we choose to view morality this way? Is there anything to recommend the strong thesis over the weak thesis of dependency? The relativist may argue that in fact we don't have an obvious impartial standard from which to judge. "Who's to say which culture is right and which is wrong?" But this seems to be dubious. We can reason and perform thought experiments in order to make a case for one system over another. We may not be able to know with certainty that our moral beliefs are closer to the truth than those of another culture or those of others within our own culture, but we may be *justified* in believing that they are. If we can be closer to the truth regarding factual or scientific matters, why can't we be closer to the truth on moral matters? Why can't a culture be simply confused or wrong about its moral perceptions? Why can't we say that the society like the Ik which sees nothing wrong with enjoying watching its own children fall into fires is less moral in that regard than the culture that cherishes children and grants them protection and equal rights? To take such a stand is not to commit the fallacy of ethnocentricism, for we are seeking to derive principles through critical reason, not simply uncritical acceptance of one's own mores.

Many relativists embrace relativism as a default position. Objectivism makes no sense to them. I think this is Ladd and Harman's position, as the latter's quotation at the beginning of this article seems to indicate. Objectivism has insuperable problems, so the answer must be relativism. . . .

In conclusion I have argued (1) that cultural relativism (the fact that there are cultural differences regarding moral principles) does not entail ethical relativism (the thesis that there are no objectively valid universal moral principles) [and] (2) that the dependency thesis (that morality derives its legitimacy from individual cultural acceptance) is mistaken. . . .

So "Who's to judge what's right or wrong?" We are. We are to do so on the basis of the best reasoning we can bring forth, and with sympathy and understanding.[10]

Notes

1. Gilbert Harman, "Is There a Single True Morality?" in *Morality, Reason and Truth,* eds. David Copp and David Zimmerman (Rowman & Allenheld, 1984).

2. John Ladd, *Ethical Relativism* (Wadsworth, 1973).

3. Reported by the anthropologist Powers, *Tribes of California,* p. 178. Quoted in E. Westermarck, *Origin and Development of Moral Ideals* (London, 1906), p. 386. This work is a mine of examples of cultural diversity.

4. W. G. Sumner, *Folkways* (Ginn & Co., 1906), p. 76.

5. Ruth Benedict, *Patterns of Culture* (New American Library, 1934), p, 257.

6. Melville Herskovits, *Cultural Relativism* (Random House, 1972).

7. E. O. Wilson, *On Human Nature* (Bantam Books, 1979), pp. 22–23.

8. Clyde Kluckhohn, "Ethical Relativity: Sic et Non," *Journal of Philosophy,* LII (1955).

9. Colin Turnbull, *The Mountain People* (New York: Simon & Schuster, 1972).

10. Bruce Russell, Morton Winston, Edward Sherline, and an anonymous reviewer made important criticisms on earlier versions of this article, issuing in this revision.

POSTSCRIPT

Is Moral Relativism Correct?

One important feature about this issue is that there is a difference between the well-known and widely recognized facts about moral diversity and the claim of moral relativism. Harman's claim goes beyond the observed facts about moral diversity. He claims that moral diversity can be *explained* by moral relativism; it's not identical with it. In fact, he admits that the existence of moral diversity doesn't by itself disprove moral absolutism.

Harman draws an analogy between physical (or Einsteinian) relativism and moral relativism. Just as Einstein has showed that there is no absolute motion, and something may be in motion according to one framework but not according to another, Harman suggests that there is no such thing as absolute good, but that something can be good according to one framework but not another.

If Harman is correct about good and bad (and right and wrong, etc.), then it is very important to be able to identify the *frameworks* that he says are involved. Note that these are not simply people's moral beliefs—as if believing that something is good would make it good! (Compare, for example, the idea of believing that something is in motion—the belief doesn't mean that it's really in motion.) Harman specifically rejects the idea of identifying the framework with a person's own values. If we did make such an identification, then— unless a person could be mistaken about his or her own values—we would all be right whenever we made moral claims. We'd be infallible when it comes to moral belief—but this is absurd. *Some* moral claims are mistaken. (One way to see this is to imagine that you held some moral belief in the past that you now regard as wrong; this is quite different from merely liking or disliking something, where your tastes could change without "right" and "wrong" coming into it at all.) Harman draws an analogy to law. The law is not infallible either. The view of "separate but equal" may have been the law in the past, but we see now that this is wrong, and we have changed our ways.

An objectivist like Pojman would want to focus on the part that says "we see that this is wrong." In order to see that something is wrong, it would have to be objectively wrong. Sometimes—and civil rights may provide a good example—we do see that something in the law needs to be changed. The Constitution, which is the highest law in the land, has been amended numerous times. There are several different possibilities as to what is going on when we amend the Constitution. One possibility is that things just come into fashion and go out of fashion. At one time, the Constitution allowed for slavery, for instance, and now it doesn't. Is slavery something that just came into fashion at one time and then passed out of fashion at another? A second possibility is that slavery was thought to be objectively wrong—and so egregiously wrong that it needed to be ruled out by the Constitution.

In some sense, Harman would be prepared for these considerations, since the Constitution could function similarly to his idea of a *framework*. He runs into a problem when we are changing frameworks (for example, when the Constitution is amended, or even when the Congress is just talking about the value of amending it). When we are "in between frameworks," as it were, relativism seems to make little sense.

Another difficulty comes about when we have a great number of frameworks, for example, as we do in a multicultural and pluralistic society. Here, any single individual may look at things in terms of religious, political, regional, generational, etc. frameworks. Someone may simultaneously belong to groups that use a number of frameworks. And not all of these frameworks will agree. Relativism seems to provide no way to get a handle on the kind of uncertainty that a person may have in choosing between the ways of his church, his family, his friends, his country, etc.

Strangely, it is just this kind of uncertainly in the face of diverse views that has cast doubt on the idea of moral objectivity, but moral relativism seems to fare no better.

Issues associated with moral relativism and absolutism, and the relation of all this to cultural variation and diversity, are quite complex. See Peter Kreeft, *A Refutation of Moral Relativism: Interviews with an Absolutist* (Ignatius Press, 1999); John Cook, *Morality and Cultural Differences* (Oxford University Press, 1999); Paul K. Moser and Thomas L. Carson, eds., *Moral Relativism: A Reader* (Oxford University Press, 2000); Neil Levy, *Moral Relativism: A Short Introduction* (OneWorld Publications, 2002); and Maria Baghramian, *Relativism* (Routledge, 2004); and Michael C. Brannigan, *Ethics across Cultures* (McGraw-Hill, 2005).

ISSUE 2

Does Morality Need Religion?

YES: C. Stephen Layman, from *The Shape of the Good: Christian Reflections on the Foundations of Ethics* (University of Notre Dame Press, 1991)

NO: John Arthur, from "Religion, Morality, and Conscience," in John Arthur, ed., *Morality and Moral Controversies*, 4th ed. (Prentice Hall, 1996)

ISSUE SUMMARY

YES: Philosopher C. Stephen Layman argues that morality makes the most sense from a theistic perspective and that a purely secular perspective is insufficient. The secular perspective, Layman asserts, does not adequately deal with secret violations, and it does not allow for the possibility of fulfillment of people's deepest needs in an afterlife.

NO: Philosopher John Arthur counters that morality is logically independent of religion, although there are historical connections. Religion, he believes, is not necessary for moral guidance or moral answers; morality is social.

Thereis a widespread feeling that morality and religion are connected. One view is that religion provides a ground for morality, so without religion there is no morality. Thus, a falling away from religion implies a falling away from morality.

Such thoughts have troubled many people. The Russian novelist Dostoyevsky (1821–1881) wrote, "If there is no God, then everything is permitted." Many Americans today also believe that religious faith is important. They often maintain that even if doctrines and dogmas cannot be known for certain, religion nevertheless leads to morality and good behavior. President Dwight D. Eisenhower is reputed to have said that everyone should have a religious faith but that it did not matter what that faith was. And many daily newspapers throughout the country advise their readers to attend the church or synagogue of their choice. Apparently, the main reason why people think it is important to subscribe to a religion is that only in this way will one be able to attain morality. If there is no God, then everything is permitted and there is moral chaos. Moral chaos can be played out in societies and, on a smaller scale, within the minds of individuals. Thus, if you do not believe in God, then you will confront moral chaos; you will be liable to permit (and permit yourself to do) anything, and you will have no moral bearings at all.

Such a view seems to face several problems, however. For example, what are we to say of the morally good atheist or of the morally good but completely nonreligious person? A true follower of the view that morality derives from religion might reply that we are simply begging the question if we believe that such people *could* be morally good. Such people might do things that are morally right and thus might *seem* good, the reply would go, but they would not be acting for the right reason (obedience to God). Such people would not have the same anchor or root for their seemingly moral attitudes that religious persons do.

Another problem for the view that links morality with religion comes from the following considerations: If you hold this view, what do you say of devoutly religious people who belong to religious traditions and who support moralities that are different from your own? If morality is indeed derived from religion, if different people are thus led to follow different moralities, and if the original religions are not themselves subject to judgment, then it is understandable how different people arrive at different moral views. But the views will still be different and perhaps even incompatible. If so, the statement that morality derives from religion must mean that one can derive *a* morality from *a* religion (and not that one derives morality itself from religion). The problem is that by allowing this variation among religions and moralities back into the picture, we seem to allow moral chaos back in, too.

The view that what God commands is good, what God prohibits is evil, and without divine commands and prohibitions nothing is either good or bad in itself is called the *divine command theory,* or the *divine imperative view.* This view resists the recognition of any source of good or evil that is not tied to criteria or standards of God's own creation. Such a recognition is thought to go against the idea of God's omnipotence. A moral law that applied to God but was not of God's own creation would seem to limit God in a way in which he cannot be limited. But, on the other hand, this line of thought (that no moral law outside of God's own making should apply to him) seems contrary to the orthodox Christian view that God is good. For if good means something in accordance with God's will, then when we say that God is good, we are only saying that he acts in accordance with his own will—and this just does not seem to be enough.

In the following selections, C. Stephen Layman argues that a religious perspective makes better sense of moral commitment than a secular perspective. Indeed, in his view, it is not even clear that a secular individual who followed the dictates of morality would be rational. John Arthur asserts that morality does not need a religious foundation at all and that morality is social.

YES

C. Stephen Layman

Ethics and the Kingdom of God

Why build a theory of ethics on the assumption that there is a God? Why not simply endorse a view of ethics along . . . secular lines . . . ? I shall respond to these questions in [two] stages. First, I contrast the secular and religious perspectives on morality. Second, I explain why I think the moral life makes more sense from the point of view of theism [belief in God] than from that of atheism. . . .

⌘

As I conceive it, the modern secular perspective on morality involves at least two elements. First, there is no afterlife; each individual human life ends at death. It follows that the only goods available to an individual are those he or she can obtain this side of death.[1]

Second, on the secular view, moral value is an *emergent* phenomenon. That is, moral value is "a feature of certain effects though it is not a feature of their causes" (as wetness is a feature of H_2O, but not of hydrogen or oxygen).[2] Thus, the typical contemporary secular view has it that moral value emerges only with the arrival of very complex nervous systems (viz., human brains), late in the evolutionary process. There is no Mind "behind the scenes" on the secular view, no intelligent Creator concerned with the affairs of human existence. As one advocate of the secular view puts it, "Ethics, though not consciously created [either by humans or by God], is a product of social life which has the function of promoting values common to the members of society."[3]

By way of contrast, the religious point of view (in my use of the phrase) includes a belief in God and in life after death. God is defined as an eternal being who is almighty and perfectly morally good. Thus, from the religious point of view, morality is not an emergent phenomenon, for God's goodness has always been in existence, and is not the product of nonmoral causes. Moreover, from the religious point of view, there are goods available after death. Specifically, there awaits the satisfaction of improved relations with God and with redeemed creatures.

It is important to note that, from the religious perspective, *the existence of God and life after death* are not independent hypotheses. If God exists, then at least two lines of reasoning lend support to the idea that death is not final.

From *The Shape of the Good: Christian Reflections on the Foundations of Ethics*, by Stephen Layman. Copyright © 1991 by the University of Notre Dame Press, Notre Dame, IN 46556.

While I cannot here scrutinize these lines of reasoning, I believe it will be useful to sketch them.[4] (1) It has often been noted that we humans seem unable to find complete fulfillment in the present life. Even those having abundant material possessions and living in the happiest of circumstances find themselves, upon reflection, profoundly unsatisfied. . . . [I]f this earthly life is the whole story, it appears that our deepest longings will remain unfulfilled. But if God is good, He surely will not leave our deepest longings unfulfilled provided He is able to fulfill them—at least to the extent that we are willing to accept His gracious aid. So, since our innermost yearnings are not satisfied in this life, it is likely that they will be satisfied after death.

(2) Human history has been one long story of injustice, of the oppression of the poor and weak by the rich and powerful. The lives of relatively good people are often miserable, while the wicked prosper. Now, if God exists, He is able to correct such injustices, though He does not correct all of them in the present life. But if God is also good, He will not leave such injustices forever unrectified. It thus appears that He will rectify matters at some point after death. This will involve benefits for some in the afterlife—it may involve penalties for others. (However, the . . . possibility of post-mortem punishment does not necessarily imply the possibility of hell as *standardly conceived*.)

We might sum up the main difference between the secular and religious views by saying that the only goods available from a secular perspective are *earthly* goods. Earthly goods include such things as physical health, friendship, pleasure, self-esteem, knowledge, enjoyable activities, an adequate standard of living, etc. The religious or theistic perspective recognizes these earthly goods *as good,* but it insists that there are non-earthly or *transcendent* goods. These are goods available only if God exists and there is life after death for humans. Transcendent goods include harmonious relations with God prior to death as well as the joys of the afterlife—right relations with both God and redeemed creatures.

⚜

[One secular] defense of the virtues amounts to showing that society cannot function well unless individuals have moral virtue. If we ask, "Why should we as individuals care about society?", the answer will presumably be along the following lines: "Individuals cannot flourish apart from a well-functioning society, *so morality pays for the individual*."

This defense of morality raises two questions we must now consider. First, is it misguided to defend morality by an appeal to self-interest? Many people feel that morality and self-interest are fundamentally at odds: "If you perform an act because you see that it is in your interest to do so, then you aren't doing the right thing *just because it's right*. A successful defense of morality must be a defense of duty for duty's sake. Thus, the appeal to self-interest is completely misguided." Second, *does* morality really pay for the individual? More particularly, does morality always pay in terms of earthly goods? Let us take these questions up in turn.

(1) Do we desert the moral point of view if we defend morality on the grounds that it pays? Consider an analogy with etiquette. Why should one bother with etiquette? Should one do the well-mannered thing simply for its own sake? Do we keep our elbows off the table or refrain from belching just because these things are "proper"?

To answer this question we must distinguish between the *justification of an institution* and *the justification of a particular act within that institution*. (By 'institution' I refer to any system of activities specified by rules.) This distinction can be illustrated in the case of the game (institution) of baseball. If we ask a player why he performs a particular act during a game, he will probably give an answer such as, "To put my opponent out" or "To get a home run." These answers obviously would not be relevant if the question were, "Why play baseball at all?" Relevant answers to this second question would name some advantage for the individual player, e.g., "Baseball is fun" or "It's good exercise." Thus, a justification of the institution of baseball (e.g., "It's good exercise") is quite different from a justification of a particular act within the institution (e.g., "To get a home run").

Now let's apply this distinction to our question about etiquette. If our question concerns the justification of a particular act within the institution of etiquette, then the answer may reasonably be, in effect, "This is what's proper. This is what the rules of etiquette prescribe." . . .

But plainly there are deeper questions we can ask about etiquette. Who hasn't wondered, at times, what the point of the institution of etiquette is? Why do we have these quirky rules, some of which seem to make little sense? When these more fundamental questions concerning the entire institution of etiquette are being asked, it makes no sense to urge etiquette for etiquette's sake. What is needed is a description of the human *ends* the institution fulfills— ends which play a justificatory role similar to fun or good exercise in the case of baseball. And it is not difficult to identify some of these ends. For example, the rules of etiquette seem designed, in part, to facilitate social interaction; things just go more smoothly if there are agreed upon ways of greeting, eating, conversing, etc.

If anyone asks, "Why should I as an individual bother about etiquette?", an initial reply might be: "Because if you frequently violate the rules of etiquette, people will shun you." If anyone wonders why he should care about being shunned, we will presumably reply that good social relations are essential to human flourishing, and hence that a person is jeopardizing his own best interests if he places no value at all on etiquette. Thus, in the end, a defense of the institution of etiquette seems to involve the claim that the institution of etiquette *pays* for those who participate in it; it would not be illuminating to answer the question, "Why bother about etiquette?" by saying that etiquette is to be valued for its own sake.

Now, just as we distinguish between justifying the institution of etiquette (or baseball) and justifying a particular act within the institution, so we must distinguish between justifying the institution of morality and justifying a particular act within the institution. When choosing a particular course of action we may simply want to know what's right. But a more ultimate question also cries out for an answer: "What is the point of the institution of morality, anyway? Why should one bother with it?" It is natural to respond by saying that society cannot function well without morality, and individuals cannot flourish apart from a well-functioning society. In short, defending the institution of morality involves claiming that morality pays for the individual in the long run. It seems obscurantist to preach duty for duty's sake, once the more fundamental question about the point of the institution of morality has been raised.

But if morality is defended on the grounds that it pays, doesn't this distort moral motivation? Won't it mean that we no longer do things because they are right, but rather because they are in our self-interest? No. We must bear in mind our distinction between the reasons that justify a particular act within an institution and the reasons that justify the institution itself. A baseball player performs a given act in order to get on base or put an opponent out; he does not calculate whether this particular swing of the bat (or throw of the ball) is fun or good exercise. A well-mannered person is not constantly calculating whether a given act will improve her relations with others, she simply does "the proper thing." Similarly, even if we defend morality on the grounds that it pays, it does not follow that the motive for each moral act becomes, "It will pay" for we are not constantly thinking of the philosophical issues concerning the justification of the entire system of morality; for the most part we simply do things because they are right, honest, fair, loving, etc. Nevertheless, our willingness to plunge wholeheartedly into "the moral game" is apt to be vitiated should it become clear to us that the game does not pay.

At this point it appears that the institution of morality is justified only if it pays for the individuals who participate in it. For if being moral does not pay for individuals, it is difficult to see why they should bother with it. The appeal to duty for duty's sake is irrelevant when we are asking for a justification of the institution of morality itself.

(2) But we must now ask, "Does morality in fact pay?" There are at least four reasons for supposing that morality does not pay from a *secular* perspective. (a) One problem for the secular view arises from the fact that the moral point of view involves a concern for *all* human beings—or at least for all humans affected by one's actions. Thus, within Christian theology, the parable of the good Samaritan is well known for its expansion of the category of "my neighbor." But human societies seem able to get along well without extending full moral concern to all outsiders; this is the essence of tribal morality. Thus, explorers in the 1700s found that the Sioux Indians followed a strict code in dealing with each other, but regarded themselves as free to steal horses from the Crow. Later on, American whites repeatedly broke treaties with the American Indians in a way that would not have been possible had the Indians been regarded as equals. It is no exaggeration to say that throughout much of human history tribal morality has been the morality humans lived by.

And so, while one must agree . . . that the virtues are necessary for the existence of society, it is not clear that this amounts to anything more than a defense of tribal morality. . . . From a purely secular point of view, it is unclear why the scope of moral concern must extend beyond one's society—or, more precisely, why one's concern must extend to groups of people outside of one's society *who are powerless and stand in the way of things one's society wants.* Why should the members of a modern industrial state extend full moral consideration to a tiny Amazonian tribe? . . .

(b) A second problem for secular views concerns the possibility of secret violations of moral rules. What becomes of conscientiousness when one can break the rules in secret, without anyone knowing? After all, if I can break the rules in secret, I will not cause any social disharmony. Of course, there can be no breaking of the rules in secret if there is a God of the Christian type, who knows every human thought as well as every human act. But there are cases in which it is extraordinarily unlikely that any *humans* will discover one's rule breaking. Hence, from a secular perspective, there are cases in which secret violations of morality are possible.

Consider the following case. Suppose A has borrowed some money from B, but A discovers that B has made a mistake in his records. Because of the mistake, B believes that A has already paid the money back. B even goes out of his way to thank A for prompt payment on the loan. Let us further suppose that B is quite wealthy, and hence not in need of the money. Is it in A's interest to pay the money back? Not paying the money back would be morally wrong; but would it be irrational, from a secular point of view? Not necessarily. Granted, it might be irrational in some cases, e.g., if A would have intense guilt feelings should he fail to repay the loan. But suppose A will not feel guilty because he really needs the money (and knows that B does not need it), and because he understands that secret violations belong to a special and rare category of action. Then, from a secular point of view, it is doubtful that paying the loan would be in A's interest.

The point is not that theists never cheat or lie. Unfortunately they do. The point is rather that secret violations of morality arguably pay off from a secular point of view. And so, once again, it seems that there is a "game" that pays off better (in terms of earthly goods) than the relatively idealistic morality endorsed by the great ethicists, viz., one allowing secret "violations."

(c) Even supposing that morality pays for some people, does it pay for *everyone* on the secular view? Can't there be well-functioning societies in which some of the members are "moral freeloaders"? In fact, don't all actual societies have members who maintain an appearance of decency, but are in fact highly manipulative of others? How would one show, on secular grounds, that it is in the interest of these persons to be moral? Furthermore, according to psychiatrists, some people are highly amoral, virtually without feelings of guilt or shame. Yet in numerous cases these amoral types appear to be happy. These "successful egoists" are often intelligent, charming, and able to evade legal penalties for their unconventional behavior.[5] How could one show, on secular grounds, that it is in the interests of such successful egoists to be moral? They seem to find their amoral lives amply rewarding.

(d) Another problem from the secular perspective stems from the fact that in some cases morality demands that one risk death. Since death cuts one off from all earthly goods, what sense does it make to be moral (in a given case) if the risk of death is high?

This point must be stated with care. In many cases it makes sense, from a secular point of view, to risk one's life. For example, it makes sense if the risk is small and the earthly good to be gained is great; after all, one risks one's life driving to work. Or again, risking one's life makes sense from a secular point of view if failing to do so will probably lead to profound and enduring earthly unhappiness. Thus, a woman might take an enormous risk to save her child from an attacker. She might believe that she would be "unable to live with herself" afterward if she stood by and let the attacker kill or maim her child. Similarly, a man might be willing to die for his country, because he could not bear the dishonor resulting from a failure to act courageously.

But failing to risk one's life does not always lead to profound and enduring earthly unhappiness. Many soldiers play it safe in battle when risk taking is essential for victory; they may judge that victory is not worth the personal risks. And many subjects of ruthless tyrants entirely avoid the risks involved in resistance and reform. Though it may be unpleasant for such persons to find themselves regarded as cowards, this unpleasantness does not necessarily lead to profound and enduring earthly unhappiness. It seems strained to claim that what is commonly regarded as moral courage always pays in terms of earthly goods.

At this point it appears that the institution of morality cannot be justified from a secular point of view. For, as we have seen, the institution of morality is justified only if it pays (in the long run) for the individuals who participate in it. But if by "morality" we mean the relatively idealistic code urged on us by the great moralists, it appears that the institution of morality does not pay, according to the secular point of view. This is not to say that no moral code could pay off in terms of earthly goods; a tribal morality of some sort might pay for most people, especially if it were to include conventions which skirt the problems inherent in my "secret violation" and "risk of death" cases. But such a morality would be a far cry from the morality most of us actually endorse.

Defenders of secular morality may claim that these difficulties evaporate if we look at morality from an evolutionary point of view. The survival of the species depends on the sacrifice of individuals in some cases, and the end of morality is the survival of the species. Hence, it is not surprising that being highly moral will not always pay off for individuals.

This answer is confused for two reasons. First, even if morality does have survival value for the species, we have seen that this does not by itself justify the individual's involvement in the institution of morality. In fact, it does not justify such involvement if what is best for the species is not what is best for the individual member of the species. And I have been arguing that, from a secular point of view, the interests of the species and the individual diverge.

Second, while evolution might explain why humans *feel* obligated to make sacrifices, it is wholly unable to account for genuine moral obligation. If we did not feel obligated to make sacrifices for others, it might be that the species would have died out long ago. So, moral *feelings* may have survival value. However, *feeling obligated* is not the same thing as *being obligated*. . . . Thus, to show that moral feelings have survival value is not to show that there are any actual moral obligations at all. . . . The point is, the evolutionary picture does not require the existence of real obligations; it demands only the existence of moral feelings or beliefs. Moral feelings or beliefs would motivate action even if there were in actuality no moral obligations. For example, the belief that human life is sacred may very well have survival value even if human life is not sacred. Moral obligation, as opposed to moral feeling, is thus an unnecessary postulate from the standpoint of evolution.

At this point defenders of the secular view typically make one of two moves: (i) They claim that even if morality does not pay, there remain moral truths which we must live up to; or (ii) they may claim that morality pays in subtle ways which we have so far overlooked. Let us take these claims up in turn.

(i) It may be claimed that moral obligation is just a fact of life, woven into the structure of reality. Morality may not always pay, but certain moral standards remain true, e.g., "Lying is wrong" or "Human life is sacred." These are not made true by evolution or God, but are necessary truths, independent of concrete existence, like "1 + 1 = 2" or "There are no triangular circles."

There are at least three difficulties with this suggestion. First, assuming that there are such necessary truths about morality, why should we care about them or pay them any attention? We may grant that an act is correct from the moral point of view and yet wonder whether we have good reason to participate in the institution of morality. So, even if we grant that various statements of the form "One ought to do X" are necessarily true, this does not show that the institution of morality pays off. It just says that morality is a "game" whose rules are necessary truths. . . . To defend the institution of morality simply on the grounds that certain moral statements are necessarily true is to urge duty for duty's sake. And . . . this is not an acceptable defense of the institution of morality.

Second, the idea that some moral truths are necessary comports poorly with the usual secular account. As Mavrodes points out, necessary moral truths seem to be what Plato had in mind when he spoke about the Form of the Good. And Plato's view, though not contradicted by modern science, receives no support from it either. Plato's Form of the Good is not an emergent phenomenon, but is rather woven into the very structure of reality, independently of physical processes such as evolution. So, Plato's view is incompatible with the typically modern secular view that moral value is an emergent phenomenon, coming into existence with the arrival of the human nervous system. For this reason, Plato's views have "often been taken to be congenial . . . to a religious understanding of the world."[6]

Third, it is very doubtful that there are any necessary truths of the form "One ought to do X." We have seen that the institution of morality stands unjustified if participation in it does not pay (in the long run) for individuals. And why should we suppose that there are *any* necessary moral truths if the institution of morality is unjustified? . . . [S]tatements of the form "One ought to do X" are not *necessary* truths, though they may be true *if* certain conditions are met. . . . Hence, if there are any necessary moral truths, they appear to be conditional (if-then) in form: If certain conditions exist, one ought to do X. Among the conditions, as we have seen, is the condition that doing X pays for the individual in the long run. So, it is very doubtful that there are any necessary moral truths of the form "One ought to do X."[7] The upshot is that morality is partly grounded in those features of reality which guarantee that morality pays; and the secular view lacks the metaphysical resources for making such a guarantee. . . .

(ii) But some have claimed that, if we look closely at human psychology, we can see that morality does pay *in terms of earthly goods.* For example, Plato suggested that only a highly moral person could have harmony between the various elements of his soul (such as reason and desire). Others have claimed that being highly moral is the only means to inner satisfaction. We humans are just so constituted that violations of morality never leave us with a net gain. Sure, we may gain earthly goods of one sort or another by lying, stealing, etc., but these are always outweighed by inner discord or a sense of dissatisfaction with ourselves.

There are several problems with this. First, some may doubt that moral virtue is the best route to inner peace. After all, one may experience profound inner discord when one has done what is right. It can be especially upsetting to stand up for what is right when doing so is unpopular; indeed, many people avoid "making waves" precisely because it upsets their inner peace. . . .

Second, how good is the evidence that inner peace *always* outweighs the benefits achievable through unethical action? Perhaps guilt feelings and inner discord are a reasonable price to pay for certain earthly goods. If a cowardly act enables me to stay alive, or a dishonest act makes me wealthy, I may judge that my gains are worth the accompanying guilt feelings. A quiet conscience is not everything.

Third, if inner discord or a sense of dissatisfaction stems from a feeling of having done wrong, why not reassess my standards? Therapists are familiar with the phenomenon of false guilt. For example, a married woman may feel guilty for having sex with her spouse. The cure will involve enabling the patient to view sex as a legitimate means of expressing affection. The point is that just because I feel a certain type of act is wrong, it does not follow that the only route to inner peace is to avoid the action. I also have the option of revising my standards, which may enable me to pursue self-interested goals in a less inhibited fashion. Why drag along any unnecessary moral baggage? How could it be shown, on secular grounds, that it is in my interest to maintain the more idealistic standards endorsed by the great moralists? Certainly, some people have much less idealistic standards than others, and yet seem no less happy.

By way of contrast with the secular view, it is not difficult to see how morality might pay if there is a God of the Christian type. First, God loves all humans and wants all included in his kingdom. So, a tribal morality would violate his demands, and to violate his demands is to strain one's most important personal relationship. Second, there are no secret violations of morality if God exists. Since God is omniscient, willful wrongdoing of any sort will estrange the wrongdoer from God. Third, while earthly society may be able to function pretty well even though there exists a small number of "moral freeloaders," the freeloaders themselves are certainly not attaining harmonious relations with God. Accordingly, their ultimate fulfillment is in jeopardy. Fourth, death is the end of earthly life, but it is not the end of conscious existence, according to Christianity. Therefore, death does not end one's opportunity for personal fulfillment; indeed, if God is perfectly good and omnipotent, we can only assume that the afterlife will result in the fulfillment of our deepest needs—unless we willfully reject God's efforts to supply those needs.

So, it seems to me that the moral life makes more sense from a theistic perspective than from a secular perspective. Of course, I do not claim that I have proved the existence of God, and a full discussion of this metaphysical issue would take us too far from matters at hand.[8] But if I have shown that the moral life makes more sense from a theistic perspective than from a secular one, then I have provided an important piece of evidence in favor of the rationality of belief in God. Moreover, I believe that I have turned back one objection to the Christian teleological view, namely, the allegation that theism is unnecessary metaphysical baggage.

Notes

1. It can be argued that, even from a secular perspective, some benefits and harms are available after death. For example, vindicating the reputation of a deceased person may be seen as benefiting that person. See, for example, Thomas Nagel, *Mortal Questions* (London: Cambridge University Press, 1979), pp. 1–10. But even if we grant that these are goods for the deceased, it is obvious that, from the secular point of view, such post-mortem goods cannot be consciously enjoyed by the deceased. They are not available in the sense that he will never take pleasure in them.

2. George Mavrodes, "Religion and the Queerness of Morality," in *Rationality, Religious Belief, and Moral Commitment,* ed. Robert Audi and William J. Wainwright (Ithaca, N.Y.: Cornell University Press, 1986), p. 223.

3. Peter Singer, *Practical Ethics* (London: Cambridge University Press, 1970), p. 209.

4. For an excellent discussion of arguments for immortality, see William J. Wainwright, *Philosophy of Religion* (Belmont, Calif.: Wadsworth, 1988), pp. 99–111.

5. My source for these claims about "happy psychopaths" is Singer, *Practical Ethics,* pp. 214–216. Singer in turn is drawing from Hervey Cleckley, *The Mask of Sanity,* (*An Attempt to Clarify Some Issues About the So-Called Psychopathic Personality*), 5th ed. (St. Louis, Mo.: E. S. Cleckley, 1988).

6. Mavrodes, "Religion and the Queerness of Morality," p. 224. I am borrowing from Mavrodes throughout this paragraph.

7. Those acquainted with modal logic may have a question here. By a principle of modal logic, if p is a necessary truth and p necessarily implies q, then q is a necessary truth. So, if it is necessarily true that "certain conditions are met" and necessarily true that "If they are met, one ought to X," then, "One ought to do X" is a necessary truth. But I assume it is not *necessarily true* that "certain conditions are met." In my judgment it would be most implausible to suppose, e.g., that "Morality pays for humans" is a necessary truth.

8. Two fine discussions of moral arguments for theism are Robert Merrihew Adams, "Moral Arguments for Theistic Belief," in *Rationality and Religious Belief,* ed. C. F. Delaney (Notre Dame, Ind.: University of Notre Dame Press, 1979), pp. 116–140, and J. L. Mackie, *The Miracle of Theism* (Oxford: Oxford University Press, 1982), pp. 102–118.

Religion, Morality, and Conscience

My first and prime concern in this paper is to explore the connections, if any, between morality and religion. I will argue that in fact religion is not necessary for morality. Yet despite the lack of any logical or other necessary connection, I will claim, there remain important respects in which the two are related. In the concluding section I will discuss the notion of moral conscience, and then look briefly at the various respects in which morality is "social" and the implications of that idea for moral education. First, however, I want to say something about the subjects: just what are we referring to when we speak of morality and of religion?

Morality and Religion

A useful way to approach the first question—the nature of morality—is to ask what it would mean for a society to exist without a social moral code. How would such people think and behave? What would that society look like? First, it seems clear that such people would never feel guilt or resentment. For example, the notions that I ought to remember my parent's anniversary, that he **has** a moral responsibility to help care for his children after the divorce, that she has a right to equal pay for equal work, and that discrimination on the basis of race is unfair would be absent in such a society. Notions of duty, rights, and obligations would not be present, except perhaps in the legal sense; concepts of justice and fairness would also be foreign to these people. In short, people would have no tendency to evaluate or criticize the behavior of others, nor to feel remorse about their own behavior. Children would not be taught to be ashamed when they steal or hurt others, nor would they be allowed to complain when others treat them badly. (People might, however, feel regret at a decision that didn't turn out as they had hoped; but that would only be because their expectations were frustrated, not because they feel guilty.)

Such a society lacks a moral code. What, then, of religion? Is it possible that a people lacking a morality would nonetheless have religious beliefs? It seems clear that it is possible. Suppose every day these same people file into their place of worship to pay homage to God (they may believe in many gods or in one all-powerful creator of heaven and earth). Often they can be heard praying to God for help in dealing with their problems and thanking Him for their good fortune. Frequently they give sacrifices to God, sometimes in the form of money spent to build beautiful temples and churches, other times by performing actions they believe God would approve such as helping those in need. These practices might also be institutionalized, in the sense that certain people are assigned important leadership roles. Specific texts might also be taken as authoritative, indicating the ways God has acted in history and His role in their lives or the lives of their ancestors.

To have a moral code, then, is to tend to evaluate (perhaps without even expressing it) the behavior of others and to feel guilt at certain actions when we perform them. Religion, on the other hand, involves beliefs in supernatural power(s) that created and perhaps also control nature, the tendency to worship and pray to those supernatural forces or beings, and the presence of organizational structures and authoritative texts. The practices of morality and religion are thus importantly different. One involves our attitudes toward various forms of behavior (lying and killing, for example), typically expressed using the notions of rules, rights, and obligations. The other, religion, typically involves prayer, worship, beliefs about the supernatural, institutional forms and authoritative texts.

We come, then, to the central question: What is the connection, if any, between a society's moral code and its religious practices and beliefs? Many people have felt that morality is in some way dependent on religion or religious truths. But what sort of "dependence" might there be? In what follows I distinguish various ways in which one might claim that religion is necessary for morality, arguing against those who claim morality depends in some way on religion. I will also suggest, however, some other important ways in which the two are related, concluding with a brief discussion of conscience and moral education.

Religious Motivation and Guidance

One possible role that religion might play in morality relates to motives people have. Religion, it is often said, is necessary so that people will DO right. Typically, the argument begins with the important point that doing what is right often has costs: refusing to shoplift or cheat can mean people go without some good or fail a test; returning a billfold means they don't get the contents. Religion is therefore said to be necessary in that it provides motivation to do the right thing. God rewards those who follow His commands by providing for them a place in heaven or by insuring that they prosper and are happy on earth. He also punishes those who violate the moral law. Others emphasize less self-interested ways in which religious motives may encourage people to act rightly. Since God is the creator of the universe and has ordained that His plan should be followed, they point out, it is important to live one's life in accord with this divinely ordained plan. Only by living a moral life, it is said, can people live in harmony with the larger, divinely created order.

The first claim, then, is that religion is necessary to provide moral motivation. The problem with that argument, however, is that religious motives are far from the only ones people have. For most of us, a decision to do the right thing (if that is our decision) is made for a variety of reasons: "What if

I get caught? What if somebody sees me—what will he or she think? How will I feel afterwards? Will I regret it?" Or maybe the thought of cheating just doesn't arise. We were raised to be a decent person, and that's what we are—period. Behaving fairly and treating others well is more important than whatever we might gain from stealing or cheating, let alone seriously harming another person. So it seems clear that many motives for doing the right thing have nothing whatsoever to do with religion. Most of us, in fact, do worry about getting caught, being blamed, and being looked down on by others. We also may do what is right just because it's right, or because we don't want to hurt others or embarrass family and friends. To say that we need religion to act morally is mistaken; indeed it seems to me that many of us, when it really gets down to it, don't give much of a thought to religion when making moral decisions. All those other reasons are the ones which we tend to consider, or else we just don't consider cheating and stealing at all. So far, then, there seems to be no reason to suppose that people can't be moral yet irreligious at the same time.

A second argument that is available for those who think religion is necessary to morality, however, focuses on moral guidance and knowledge rather than on people's motives. However much people may want to do the right thing, according to this view, we cannot ever know for certain what is right without the guidance of religious teaching. Human understanding is simply inadequate to this difficult and controversial task; morality involves immensely complex problems, and so we must consult religious revelation for help.

Again, however, this argument fails. First, consider how much we would need to know about religion and revelation in order for religion to provide moral guidance. Besides being sure that there is a God, we'd also have to think about which of the many religions is true. How can anybody be sure his or her religion is the right one? But even if we assume the Judeo-Christian God is the real one, we still need to find out just what it is He wants us to do, which means we must think about revelation.

Revelation comes in at least two forms, and not even all Christians agree on which is the best way to understand revelation. Some hold that revelation occurs when God tells us what he wants by providing us with His words: The Ten Commandments are an example. Many even believe, as evangelist Billy Graham once said, that the entire *Bible* was written by God using 39 secretaries. Others, however, doubt that the "word of God" refers literally to the words God has spoken, but believe instead that the *Bible* is an historical document, written by human beings, of the events or occasions in which God revealed Himself. It is an especially important document, of course, but nothing more than that. So on this second view revelation is not understood as *statements* made by God but rather as His *acts* such as leading His people from Egypt, testing Job, and sending His son as an example of the ideal life. The *Bible* is not itself revelation, it's the historical account of revelatory actions.

If we are to use revelation as a moral guide, then, we must first know what is to count as revelation—words given us by God, historical events, or both? But even supposing that we could somehow answer those questions, the problems of relying on revelation are still not over since we still must interpret that revelation. Some feel, for example, that the *Bible* justifies various forms of killing, including war and capital punishment, on the basis of such statements as "An eye for an eye." Others, emphasizing such sayings as "Judge not lest ye be judged" and "Thou shalt not kill," believe the *Bible* demands absolute pacifism. How are we to know which interpretation is correct? It is likely, of course, that the answer people give to such religious questions will be influenced in part at least by their own moral beliefs: if capital punishment is thought to be unjust, for example, then an interpreter will seek to read the *Bible* in a way that is consistent with that moral truth. That is not, however, a happy conclusion for those wishing to rest morality on revelation, for it means that their understanding of what God has revealed is itself dependent on their prior moral views. Rather than revelation serving as a guide for morality, morality is serving as a guide for how we interpret revelation.

So my general conclusion is that far from providing a short-cut to moral understanding, looking to revelation for guidance often creates more questions and problems. It seems wiser under the circumstances to address complex moral problems like abortion, capital punishment, and affirmative action directly, considering the pros and cons of each side, rather than to seek answers through the much more controversial and difficult route of revelation.

The Divine Command Theory

It may seem, however, that we have still not really gotten to the heart of the matter. Even if religion is not necessary for moral motivation or guidance, it is often claimed, religion is necessary in another more fundamental sense. According to this view, religion is necessary for morality because without God there could BE no right or wrong. God, in other words, provides the foundation or bedrock on which morality is grounded. This idea was expressed by Bishop R. C. Mortimer:

> "God made us and all the world. Because of that He has an absolute claim on our obedience. . . . From [this] it follows that a thing is not right simply because we think it is. It is right because God commands it."[1]

What Bishop Mortimer has in mind can be seen by comparing moral rules with legal ones. Legal statutes, we know, are created by legislatures; if the state assembly of New York had not passed a law limiting speed people can travel, then there would be no such legal obligation. Without the statutory enactments, such a law simply would not exist. Mortimer's view, the *divine command theory,* would mean that God has the same sort of relation to moral law as legislature has to statutes it enacts: without God's commands there would be no moral rules, just as without a legislature there would be no statutes.

Defenders of the divine command theory often add to this a further claim, that only by assuming God sits at the foundation of morality can we explain the objective difference between right and wrong. This point was forcefully argued by F. C. Copleston in a 1948 British Broadcasting Corporation radio debate with Bertrand Russell.

Copleston: . . . The validity of such an interpretation of man's conduct depends on the recognition of God's existence, obviously. . . . Let's take a look at the Commandant of the [Nazi] concentration camp at Belsen. That appears to you as undesirable and evil and to me too. To Adolf Hitler we suppose it appeared as something good and desirable. I suppose you'd have to admit that for Hitler it was good and for you it is evil.

Russell: No, I shouldn't go so far as that. I mean, I think people can make mistakes in that as they can in other things. If you have jaundice you see things yellow that are not yellow. You're making a mistake.

Copleston: Yes, one can make mistakes, but can you make a mistake if it's simply a question of reference to a feeling or emotion? Surely Hitler would be the only possible judge of what appealed to his emotions.

Russell: . . . You can say various things about that; among others, that if that sort of thing makes that sort of appeal to Hitler's emotions, then Hitler makes quite a different appeal to my emotions.

Copleston: Granted. But there's no objective criterion outside feeling then for condemning the conduct of the Commandant of Belsen, in your view. . . . The human being's idea of the content of the moral law depends certainly to a large extent on education and environment, and a man has to use his reason in assessing the validity of the actual moral ideas of his social group. But the possibility of criticizing the accepted moral code presupposes that there is an objective standard, that there is an ideal moral order, which imposes itself. . . . It implies the existence of a real foundation of God.[2]

Against those who, like Bertrand Russell, seek to ground morality in feelings and attitudes, Copleston argues that there must be a more solid foundation if we are to be able to claim truly that the Nazis were evil. God, according to Copleston, is able to provide the objective basis for the distinction, which we all know to exist, between right and wrong. Without divine commands at the root of human obligations, we would have no real reason for condemning the behavior of anybody, even Nazis. Morality, Copleston thinks, would then be nothing more than an expression of personal feeling.

To begin assessing the divine command theory, let's first consider this last point. Is it really true that only the commands of God can provide an objective basis for moral judgments? Certainly many philosophers have felt that morality rests on its own perfectly sound footing, be it reason, human nature, or natural sentiments. It seems wrong to conclude, automatically, that morality cannot rest on anything but religion. And it is also possible that morality doesn't have any foundation or basis at all, so that its claims should be ignored in favor of whatever serves our own self-interest.

In addition to these problems with Copleston's argument, the divine command theory faces other problems as well. First, we would need to say much more about the relationship between morality and divine commands. Certainly the expressions "is commanded by God" and "is morally required" do not *mean* the same thing. People and even whole societies can use moral concepts without understanding them to make any reference to God. And while it is true that God (or any other moral being for that matter) would tend to want others to do the right thing, this hardly shows that being right and being commanded by God are the same thing. Parents want their children to do the right thing, too, but that doesn't mean parents, or anybody else, can make a thing right just by commanding it!

I think that, in fact, theists should reject the divine command theory. One reason is what it implies. Suppose we were to grant (just for the sake of argument) that the divine command theory is correct, so that actions are right just because they are commanded by God. The same, of course, can be said about those deeds that we believe are wrong. If God hadn't commanded us not to do them, they would not be wrong.

But now notice this consequence of the divine command theory. Since God is all-powerful, and since right is determined solely by His commands, is it not possible that He might change the rules and make what we now think of as wrong into right? It would seem that according to the divine command theory the answer is "yes": it is theoretically possible that tomorrow God would decree that virtues such as kindness and courage have become vices while actions that show cruelty and cowardice will henceforth be the right actions. (Recall the analogy with a legislature and the power it has to change law.) So now rather than it being right for people to help each other out and prevent innocent people from suffering unnecessarily, it would be right (God having changed His mind) to create as much pain among innocent children as we possibly can! To adopt the divine command theory therefore commits its advocate to the seemingly absurd position that even the greatest atrocities might be not only acceptable but morally required if God were to command them.

Plato made a similar point in the dialogue *Euthyphro*. Socrates is asking Euthyphro what it is that makes the virtue of holiness a virtue, just as we have been asking what makes kindness and courage virtues. Euthyphro has suggested that holiness is just whatever all the gods love.

Socrates: Well, then, Euthyphro, what do we say about holiness? Is it not loved by all the gods, according to your definition?

Euthyphro: Yes.

Socrates: Because it is holy, or for some other reason?

Euthyphro: No, because it is holy.

Socrates: Then it is loved by the gods because it is holy: it is not holy because it is loved by them?

Euthyphro: It seems so.

Socrates: . . . Then holiness is not what is pleasing to the gods, and what is pleasing to the gods is not holy as you say, Euthyphro. They are different things.

Euthyphro: And why, Socrates?

Socrates: Because we are agreed that the gods love holiness because it is holy: and that it is not holy because they love it.[3]

This raises an interesting question: Why, having claimed at first that virtues are merely what is loved (or commanded) by the gods, would Euthyphro so quickly contradict this and agree that the gods love holiness *because* it's holy, rather than the reverse? One likely possibility is that Euthyphro believes that whenever the gods love something they do so with good reason, not without justification and arbitrarily. To deny this, and say that it is merely the gods' love that makes holiness a virtue, would mean that the gods have no basis for their attitudes, that they are arbitrary in what they love. Yet—and this is the crucial point—it's far from clear that a religious person would want to say that God is arbitrary in that way. If we say that it is simply God's loving something that makes it right, then what sense would it make to say God wants us to do right? All that could mean, it seems, is that God wants us to do what He wants us to do; He would have no reason for wanting it. Similarly "God is good" would mean little more than "God does what He pleases." The divine command theory therefore leads us to the results that God is morally arbitrary, and that His wishing us to do good or even God's being just mean nothing more than that God does what He does and wants whatever He wants. Religious people who reject that consequence would also, I am suggesting, have reason to reject the divine command theory itself, seeking a different understanding of morality.

This now raises another problem, however. If God approves kindness because it is a virtue and hates the Nazis because they were evil, then it seems that God discovers morality rather than inventing it. So haven't we then identified a limitation on God's power, since He now, being a good God, must love kindness and command us not to be cruel? Without the divine command theory, in other words, what is left of God's omnipotence?

But why, we may ask, is such a limitation on God unacceptable? It is not at all clear that God really can do anything at all. Can God, for example, destroy Himself? Or make a rock so heavy that He cannot lift it? Or create a universe which was never created by Him? Many have thought that God cannot do these things, but also that His inability to do them does not constitute a serious limitation on His power since these are things that cannot be done at all: to do them would violate the laws of logic. Christianity's most influential theologian, Thomas Aquinas, wrote in this regard that "whatever implies contradiction does not come within the scope of divine omnipotence, because it cannot have the aspect of possibility. Hence it is more appropriate to say that such things cannot be done than that God cannot do them."[4]

How, then, ought we to understand God's relationship to morality if we reject the divine command theory? Can religious people consistently maintain their faith in God the Creator and yet deny that what is right is right because He commands it? I think the answer to this is "yes." Making cruelty good is not like making a universe that wasn't made, of course. It's a moral limit on God rather than a logical one. But why suppose that God's limits are only logical?

One final point about this. Even if we agree that God loves justice or kindness because of their nature, not arbitrarily, there still remains a sense in which God could change morality even having rejected the divine command theory. That's because if we assume, plausibly I think, that morality depends in part on how we reason, what we desire and need, and the circumstances in which we find ourselves, then morality will still be under God's control since God could have constructed us or our environment very differently. Suppose, for instance, that he created us so that we couldn't be hurt by others or didn't care about freedom. Or perhaps our natural environment were created differently, so that all we have to do is ask and anything we want is given to us. If God had created either nature or us that way, then it seems likely our morality might also be different in important ways from the one we now think correct. In that sense, then, morality depends on God whether or not one supports the divine command theory.

"Morality Is Social"

I have argued here that religion is not necessary in providing moral motivation or guidance, and against the divine command theory's claim that God is necessary for there to be morality at all. In this last section, I want first to look briefly at how religion and morality sometimes *do* influence each other. Then I will consider the development of moral conscience and the important ways in which morality might correctly be thought to be "social."

Nothing I have said so far means that morality and religion are independent of each other. But in what ways are they related, assuming I am correct in claiming morality does not *depend* on religion? First, of course, we should note the historical influence religions have had on the development of morality as well as on politics and law. Many of the important leaders of the abolitionist and civil rights movements were religious leaders, as are many current members of the pro-life movement. The relationship is not, however, one-sided: morality has also influenced religion, as the current debate within the Catholic church over the role of women, abortion, and other social issues shows. In reality, then, it seems clear that the practices of morality and religion have historically each exerted an influence on the other.

But just as the two have shaped each other historically, so, too, do they interact at the personal level. I have already suggested how people's understanding of revelation, for instance, is often shaped by morality as they seek the best interpretations of revealed texts. Whether trying to understand a work of art, a legal statute, or a religious text, interpreters regularly seek to understand them in the best light—to make them as good as they can be, which requires that they bring moral judgment to the task of religious interpretation and understanding.

The relationship can go the other direction as well, however, as people's moral views are shaped by their religious training and beliefs. These relationships between morality and religion are often complex, hidden even from ourselves, but it does seem clear that our views on important moral issues, from sexual morality and war to welfare and capital punishment, are often influenced by our religious outlook. So not only are religious and moral practices and understandings historically linked, but for many religious people the relationship extends to the personal level—to their understanding of moral obligations as well as their sense of who they are and their vision of who they wish to be.

Morality, then, is influenced by religion (as is religion by morality), but morality's social character extends deeper even than that, I want to argue. First, of course, we possess a socially acquired language within which we think about our various choices and the alternatives we ought to follow, including whether a possible course of action is the right thing to do. Second, morality is social in that it governs relationships among people, defining our responsibilities to others and theirs to us. Morality provides the standards we rely on in gauging our interactions with family, lovers, friends, fellow citizens, and even strangers. Third, morality is social in the sense that we are, in fact, subject to criticism by others for our actions. We discuss with others what we should do, and often hear from them concerning whether our decisions were acceptable. Blame and praise are a central feature of morality.

While not disputing any of this, John Dewey has stressed another, less obvious aspect of morality's social character. Consider then the following comments regarding the origins of morality and conscience in an article he titled "Morality Is Social":

> In language and imagination we rehearse the responses of others just as we dramatically enact other consequences. We foreknow how others will act, and the foreknowledge is the beginning of judgment passed on action. We know *with* them; there is conscience. An assembly is formed within our breast which discusses and appraises proposed and performed acts. The community without becomes a forum and tribunal within, a judgment-seat of charges, assessments and exculpations. Our thoughts of our own actions are saturated with the ideas that others entertain about them. . . . Explicit recognition of this fact is a prerequisite of improvement in moral education. . . . Reflection is morally indispensable.[5]

To appreciate fully the role of society in shaping morality and influencing people's sense of responsibility, Dewey is arguing, requires appreciating the fact that to think from the moral point of view, as opposed to the selfish one, for instance, means rejecting our private, subjective perspective in favor of the view of others, envisioning how they might respond to various choices we might make. Far from being private and unrelated to others, moral conscience is in that sense "public." To consider a decision from the moral perspective, says Dewey, requires that we envision an "assembly of others" that is "formed within our breast." In that way, our moral conscience cannot be sharply distinguished from our nature as social beings since conscience invariably brings with it, or constitutes, the perspective of the other. "Is this right?" and "What would this look like were I to have to defend it to others?" are not entirely separable questions.[6]

It is important not to confuse Dewey's point here, however. He is *not* saying that what is right is finally to be determined by the reactions of actually existing other people, or even by the reaction of society as a whole. What is right or fair can never be finally decided by a vote, and might not meet the approval of any specific others. But what then might Dewey mean in speaking of such an "assembly of others" as the basis of morality? The answer is that rather than actual people or groups, the assembly Dewey envisions is hypothetical or "ideal." The "community without" is thus transformed into a "forum and tribunal within, a judgment seat of charges, assessments and exculpations." So it is through the powers of our imagination that we can meet our moral responsibilities and exercise moral judgment, using these powers to determine what morality requires by imagining the reaction of Dewey's "assembly of others."

Morality is therefore *inherently* social, in a variety of ways. It depends on socially learned language, is learned from interactions with others, and governs our interactions with others in society. But it also demands, as Dewey put it, that we know "with" others, envisioning for ourselves what their points of view would require along with our own. Conscience demands we occupy the positions of others.

Viewed in this light, God would play a role in a religious person's moral reflection and conscience since it is unlikely a religious person would wish to exclude God from the "forum and tribunal" that constitutes conscience. Rather, for the religious person conscience would almost certainly include the imagined reaction of God along with the reactions of others who might be affected by the action. Other people are also important, however, since it is often an open question just what God's reaction would be; revelation's meaning, as I have argued, is subject to interpretation. So it seems that for a religious person morality and God's will cannot be separated, though the connection between them is not the one envisioned by defenders of the divine command theory.

Which leads to my final point, about moral education. If Dewey is correct, then it seems clear there is an important sense in which morality not only can be taught but must be. Besides early moral training, moral thinking depends on our ability to imagine others' reactions and to imaginatively put ourselves into their shoes. "What would somebody (including, perhaps, God) think if this got out?" expresses more than a concern with being embarrassed or punished; it is also the voice of conscience and indeed of morality itself. But that would mean, thinking of education, that listening to others, reading about what others think and do, and reflecting within ourselves about our actions and whether we could defend them to others are part of the practice of morality itself. Morality cannot exist without the broader, social perspective introduced by others, and this social nature ties it, in that way, with education and with public discussion, both actual and imagined. "Private" moral reflection taking place independent of the social world would be no moral reflection at all; and moral education is not only possible, but essential.

Notes

1. R. C. Mortimer, *Christian Ethics* (London: Hutchinson's University Library, 1950), pp. 7–8.
2. This debate was broadcast on the "Third Program" of the British Broadcasting Corporation in 1948.

3. Plato, *Euthyphro*, tr. H. N. Fowler (Cambridge MA: Harvard University Press, 1947).

4. Thomas Aquinas, *Summa Theologica*, Part I, Q.25, Art. 3.

5. John Dewey, "Morality Is Social" in *The Moral Writings of John Dewey*, revised edition, ed. James Gouinlock (Amherst, NY: Prometheus Books, 1994), pp. 182–184.

6. Obligations to animals raise an interesting problem for this conception of morality. Is it wrong to torture animals only because other *people* could be expected to disapprove? Or is it that the animal itself would disapprove? Or, perhaps, duties to animals rest on sympathy and compassion while human moral relations are more like Dewey describes, resting on morality's inherently social nature and on the dictates of conscience viewed as an assembly of others?

POSTSCRIPT

Does Morality Need Religion?

As Arthur notes, some of the earliest—and indeed some of the best—arguments on this issue can be found in Plato's dialogue *Euthyphro,* which was written in the fourth century B.C. His arguments were in terms of Greek religious practices and Greek gods, but we can reformulate the points and elaborate on the arguments in monotheistic terms.

One key dilemma in the original Greek version asks us to consider whether holy things (i) are holy because they please the gods or (ii) please the gods because they are holy. In monotheistic terms, the dilemma would be whether holy things (i) are holy because they please God or (ii) please God because they are holy. The question can then be broadened and the dilemma posed in terms of good things in general. We then ask whether good things are (i) good because God wills them or (ii) willed by God because they are good.

Plato believed that the gods love what is holy because it is holy (i.e., he believed the second option above), just as Christians have traditionally believed that God wills good things because they are good. Traditionally, a contrast is drawn between God, an infinite and all-good being who always wills the good, and humans, finite beings who are not all-good and do not always will the good.

We might also consider a parallel dilemma concerning truths. Are things true because God knows them, or does God know them because they are true? The traditional view is that God is all-knowing. God knows all truths because they are truths (and no truths lie outside divine knowledge), whereas people do not know all truths (and many truths lie outside human knowledge).

Nevertheless, there has also been in Christianity a tradition that the almighty power of God is not to be constrained by anything—even if we imagine that what constrains God are good things. This view holds that God creates not only good things but the very fact that a good thing (such as honesty) is good while another thing (such as false witness against your neighbor) is not. Thus, in this view, God in his power determines what is good and what is bad.

These topics are further discussed in Glenn Tinder, "Can We Be Good Without God? On the Political Meaning of Christianity," *The Atlantic Monthly* (December 1989); Richard J. Mouw, *The God Who Commands: A Study in Divine Command Ethics* (University of Notre Dame Press, 1990); E. M. Adams, *Religion and Cultural Freedom* (Temple University Press, 1993); D. Z. Phillips, ed., *Religion and Morality* (St. Martin's Press, 1996); and Paul Chamberlain, *Can We Be Good Without God? A Conversation About Truth, Morality, Culture, and a Few Other Things That Matter* (InterVarsity Press, 1996).

Internet References . . .

National Abortion and Reproductive Rights Action League

This is the home page of the National Abortion and Reproductive Rights Action League (NARAL), an organization that works to promote reproductive freedom and dignity for women and their families.

http://www.prochoiceamerica.org/

Pro-Life Action League

This site is pro-life with respect to abortion, but some of the links also concern euthanasia and related topics.

www.prolifeaction.org/

Pro-Life News

This site contains many links to news items and information on abortion, euthanasia, etc.

http://www.lifenews.com/

Literature on Cloning and Reproductive Technologies

This *Ethics Updates* site contains many links to articles, interviews, associations, and other resources that are concerned with cloning and reproductive technologies.

http://ethics.sandiego.edu/

Gender, Sex, and Reproduction

*H*umans are sexual, reproductive, social beings. Given this fact, it is imperative to have some idea of what is socially acceptable and what is not, as well as what is expected of males and females, and what is not.

The issues in this section do not presuppose that there is anything morally questionable about sex itself, but they do raise questions about how, in today's society, we should think about sex roles and matters of sex and reproduction.

- Must Sex Involve Commitment?
- Is Abortion Immoral?
- Is It Right to Prohibit Same-Sex Marriage?
- Should Human Cloning Be Banned?

ISSUE 3

Must Sex Involve Commitment?

YES: Vincent C. Punzo, from *Reflective Naturalism* (Macmillan, 1969)

NO: Alan H. Goldman, from "Plain Sex," *Philosophy and Public Affairs* (Spring 1977)

ISSUE SUMMARY

YES: Philosopher Vincent C. Punzo maintains that the special intimacy of sex requires a serious commitment that is for the most part not required in other human activities.

NO: Philosopher Alan H. Goldman argues for a view of sex that is completely separate from any cultural or moral ideology that might be attached to it.

For many people, sex and morality are interconnected. Some complain that talk about sex, such as in sex education classes, is worse than worthless—it is downright corrupt—if it is divorced from talk about morality. Yet, with the exception of specialized concepts such as sexual harassment, most contemporary moral philosophers have very little to say about sex. In part, this may be due to the modern idea that many traditional beliefs about sex are steeped in superstitious, prejudiced, or misguided views that are in need of scientific correction.

In the traditional thought of ancient and medieval times, the stage of the world contains a large backdrop that is intended to make sense of the place of humans in the world. Ancient Greek philosophers created metaphysical theories and medieval theologians created religious theories to explain the role and purpose of humankind. According to both ancient and medieval views, humans are different from animals and thought to possess traits beyond the physical, which ground this difference. However, the modern and scientific view is that humans have no special metaphysical or supernatural standing above animals. Humans are simply a part of nature. This is not an attempt to provide another backdrop, but instead an attempt to eliminate all backdrops, so that people can be viewed in a more realistic manner. This view supports the idea that sexual urges are simply a part of our nature.

Consider a different example. Eating habits are also considered to be a part of our nature, but traditionalists would remind us that we have to eat the correct foods from a nutritional standpoint. We have to direct our eating habits with reason—we cannot simply eat whatever we feel like whenever we want to. Traditionalists view eating as something beyond the process of digestion. Sexual intercourse has its own physical processes, and, like eating, also involves more than just the physical. Sex involves the use of self-control and reason.

Modernists may argue that in many ways the analogy with eating fails. In the past, eating habits were only minimally affected by superstitious or false ideas, whereas sexual practices were greatly affected.

What we are left with today are elements of ancient, medieval, and modern thought. When it comes to sex, it is clear that modern scientific views have a contribution to make; but it is not clear whether we can simply do away with all previous ideas about sex.

In the following selections, Vincent C. Punzo argues for the view that sex, since it involves the highest level of human intimacy, must involve commitment. Alan H. Goldman counters that a concept of "plain sex" helps us to understand sex for what it is—something that does not need moral ideas attached to it.

YES

Vincent C. Punzo

Morality and Human Sexuality

If one sees man's moral task as being simply that of not harming anyone, that is if one sees this task in purely negative terms, he will certainly not accept the argument to be presented in the following section. However, if one accepts the notion of the morality of aspiration, if one accepts the view that man's moral task involves the positive attempt to live up to what is best in man, to give reality to what he sees to be the perfection of himself as a human subject, the argument may be acceptable.

Sexuality and the Human Subject

[Previous discussion] has left us with the question as to whether sexual intercourse is a type of activity that is similar to choosing a dinner from a menu. The question is of utmost significance in that one's view of the morality of premarital intercourse seems to depend on the significance that one gives to the sexual encounter in human life. Those such as [John] Wilson and [Eustace] Chesser who see nothing immoral about the premarital character of sexual intercourse seem to see sexual intercourse as being no different from myriad of other purely aesthetic matters. This point is seen in Chesser's questioning of the reason for demanding permanence in the relationship of sexual partners when we do not see such permanence as being important to other human relationships.[1] It is also seen in his asking why we raise a moral issue about premarital coition when two people may engage in it, with the resulting social and psychological consequences being no different than if they had gone to a movie.[2]

Wilson most explicitly makes a case for the view that sexual intercourse does not differ significantly from other human activities. He holds that people think that there is a logical difference between the question "Will you engage in sexual intercourse with me?" and the question, "Will you play tennis with me?" only because they are influenced by the acquisitive character of contemporary society.[3] Granted that the two questions may be identical from the purely formal perspective of logic, the ethician must move beyond this perspective to a consideration of their content. Men and women find themselves involved in many different relationships: for example, as buyer-seller, employer-employee, teacher-student, lawyer-client, and partners or competitors in certain games such as tennis or bridge. Is there any morally significant difference between these relationships and sexual intercourse? We cannot examine all the possible relationships into which a man and woman can enter, but we will consider the employer-employee relationship in order to get some perspective on the distinctive character of the sexual relationship.

A man pays a woman to act as his secretary. What rights does he have over her in such a situation? The woman agrees to work a certain number of hours during the day taking dictation, typing letters, filing reports, arranging appointments and flight schedules, and greeting clients and competitors. In short, we can say that the man has rights to certain of the woman's services or skills. The use of the word "services" may lead some to conclude that this relationship is not significantly different from the relationship between a prostitute and her client in that the prostitute also offers her "services."

It is true that we sometimes speak euphemistically of a prostitute offering her services to a man for a sum of money, but if we are serious about our quest for the difference between the sexual encounter and other types of human relationships, it is necessary to drop euphemisms and face the issue directly. The man and woman who engage in sexual intercourse are giving their bodies, the most intimate physical expression of themselves, over to the other. Unlike the man who plays tennis with a woman, the man who has sexual relations with her has literally entered her. A man and woman engaging in sexual intercourse have united themselves as intimately and as totally as is physically possible for two human beings. Their union is not simply a union of organs, but is as intimate and as total a physical union of two selves as is possible of achievement. Granted the character of this union, it seems strange to imply that there is no need for a man and woman to give any more thought to the question of whether they should engage in sexual intercourse than to the question of whether they should play tennis.

In opposition to Wilson, I think that it is the acquisitive character of our society that has blinded us to the distinction between the two activities. Wilson's and Chesser's positions seem to imply that exactly the same moral considerations ought to apply to a situation in which a housewife is bartering with a butcher for a few pounds of pork chops and the situation in which two human beings are deciding whether sexual intercourse ought to be an ingredient of their relationship. So long as the butcher does not put his thumb on the scale in the weighing process, so long as he is truthful in stating that the meat is actually pork, so long as the woman pays the proper amount with the proper currency, the trade is perfectly moral. Reflecting on sexual intercourse from the same sort of economic perspective, one can say that so long as the sexual partners are truthful in reporting their freedom from contagious venereal diseases and so long as they are truthful in reporting that they are interested in the activity for the mere pleasure of it or to try out their sexual techniques, there is nothing immoral about such activity. That in the one case pork chops are being exchanged for money whereas in the other the decision concerns the most complete and intimate merging of one's self with another makes no difference to the moral evaluation of the respective cases.

It is not surprising that such a reductionistic outlook should pervade our thinking on sexual matters, since in our society sexuality is used to sell everything from shave cream to underarm deodorants, to soap, to mouth-wash, to cigarettes, and to automobiles. Sexuality has come to play so large a role in our commercial lives that it is not surprising that our sexuality should itself come to be treated as a commodity governed by the same moral rules that govern any other economic transaction.

Once sexuality is taken out of this commercial framework, once the character of the sexual encounter is faced directly and squarely, we will come to see that Doctor Mary Calderone has brought out the type of questions that ought to be asked by those contemplating the introduction of sexual intercourse into their relationships: "How many times, and how casually, are you willing to invest a portion of your total self, and to be the custodian of a like investment from the other person, without the sureness of knowing that these investments are being made for keeps?"[4] These questions come out of the recognition that the sexual encounter is a definitive experience, one in which the physical intimacy and merging involves also a merging of the nonphysical dimensions of the partners. With these questions, man moves beyond the negative concern with avoiding his or another's physical and psychological harm to the question of what he is making of himself and what he is contributing to the existential formation of his partner as a human subject.

If we are to make a start toward responding to Calderone's questions we must cease talking about human selfhood in abstraction. The human self is an historical as well as a physical being. He is a being who is capable of making at least a portion of his past an object of his consciousness and thus is able to make this past play a conscious role in his present and in his looking toward the future. He is also a being who looks to the future, who faces tomorrow with plans, ideals, hopes, and fears. The very being of a human self involves his past and his movement toward the future. Moreover, the human self is not completely shut off in his own past and future. Men and women are capable of consciously and purposively uniting themselves in a common career and venture. They can commit themselves to sharing the future with another, sharing it in all its aspects—in its fortunes and misfortunes, in its times of happiness and times of tragedy. Within the lives of those who have so committed themselves to each other, sexual intercourse is a way of asserting and confirming the fullness and totality of their mutual commitment.

Unlike those who have made such a commitment and who come together in the sexual act in the fullness of their selfhood, those who engage in premarital sexual unions and who have made no such commitment act as though they can amputate their bodily existence and the most intimate physical expression of their selfhood from their existence as historical beings. Granting that there may be honesty on the verbal level in that two people engaging in premarital intercourse openly state that they are interested only in the pleasure of the activity, the fact remains that such unions are morally deficient because they lack existential integrity in that there is a total merging and union on a physical level, on the one hand, and a conscious decision not to unite any other dimension of themselves, on the other hand. Their sexual union thus involves a "depersonalization" of their bodily existence, an attempt to cut off the most intimate physical expression of their respective selves from their very selfhood. The mutual agreement of premarital sex partners is an agreement to merge with the other not as a self, but as a body which one takes unto oneself, which one possesses in a most intimate and total fashion for one's own pleasure or designs, allowing the other to treat oneself in the same way. It may be true that no physical or psychological harm may result from such unions, but such partners have failed to existentially incorporate human sexuality, which is at the very least the most intimate physical expression of the human self, into the character of this selfhood.

In so far as premarital sexual unions separate the intimate and total physical union that is sexual intercourse from any commitment to the self in his historicity, human sexuality, and consequently the human body, have been fashioned into external things or objects to be handed over totally to someone else, whenever one feels that he can get possession of another's body, which he can use for his own purposes.[5] The human body has thus been treated no differently from the pork chops spoken of previously or from any other object or commodity, which human beings exchange and haggle over in their day-to-day transactions. One hesitates to use the word that might be used to capture the moral value that has been sacrificed in premarital unions because in our day the word has taken on a completely negative meaning at best, and, at worst, it has become a word used by "sophisticates" to mock or deride certain attitudes toward human sexuality. However, because the word "chastity" has been thus abused is no reason to leave it in the hands of those who have misrepresented the human value to which it gives expression.

The chaste person has often been described as one intent on denying his sexuality. The value of chastity as conceived in this section is in direct opposition to this description. It is the unchaste person who is separating himself from his sexuality, who is willing to exchange human bodies as one would exchange money for tickets to a baseball game—honestly and with no commitment of self to self. Against this alienation of one's sexuality from one's self, an alienation that makes one's sexuality an object, which is to be given to another in exchange for his objectified sexuality, chastity affirms the integrity of the self in his bodily and historical existence. The sexuality of man is seen as an integral part of his subjectivity. Hence, the chaste man rejects depersonalized sexual relations as a reduction of man in his most intimate physical being to the status of an object or pure instrument for another. He asserts that man is a subject and end in himself, not in some trans-temporal, nonphysical world, but in the historical-physical world in which he carries on his moral task and where he finds his fellow man. He will not freely make of himself in his bodily existence a thing to be handed over to another's possession, nor will he ask that another treat his own body in this way. The total physical intimacy of sexual intercourse will be an expression of total union with the other self on all levels of their beings. Seen from this perspective, chastity is one aspect of man's attempt to attain existential integrity, to accept his body as a dimension of his total personality.

In concluding this section, it should be noted that I have tried to make a case against the morality of premarital sexual intercourse even in those cases in which the partners are completely honest with each other. There is reason to question whether the complete honesty, to which those who see nothing immoral in such unions refer, is as a matter of fact actually found very often among premarital sex partners. We may well have been dealing with textbook cases which present these unions in their best light. One may be pardoned for wondering whether sexual intercourse often occurs under the following conditions: "Hello, my name is Josiah. I am interested in having a sexual experience with you. I can assure you that I am good at it and that I have no communicable disease. If it sounds good to you and if you have taken the proper contraceptive precautions, we might have a go at it. Of course, I want to make it clear to you that I am interested only in the sexual experience and that I have no intention of making any long-range commitment to you." If those, who defend the morality of premarital sexual unions so long as they are honestly entered into, think that I have misrepresented what they mean by honesty, then they must specify what they mean by an honest premarital union. . . .

Marriage as a Total Human Commitment

The preceding argument against the morality of premarital sexual unions was not based on the view that the moral character of marriage rests on a legal certificate or on a legal or religious ceremony. The argument was not directed against "preceremonial" intercourse, but against premarital intercourse. Morally speaking, a man and woman are married when they make the mutual and total commitment to share the problems and prospects of their historical existence in the world. Although marriages are not to be identified with ceremonies, the words used in marriage ceremonies have captured the character of marriage in the promise which the partners make to each other to join their lives "for better, for worse, for richer, for poorer, in sickness and in health, till death do us part."

. . . The commitment that constitutes marriage is a total commitment of one person to another person of the opposite sex. To understand the character of such commitment, it is necessary to know something about the being of those involved in the commitment; for if it is to be truly total, the commitment must be as rich as the being of those who have made it. It is at this point that the historical character of the human self's existence becomes important. A total commitment to another means a commitment to him in his historical existence. Such a commitment is not simply a matter of words or of feelings, however strong. It involves a full existential sharing on the part of two beings of the burdens, opportunities, and challenges of their historical existence.

Granted the importance that the character of their commitment to each other plays in determining the moral quality of a couple's sexual encounter, it is clear that there may be nothing immoral in the behavior of couples who engage in sexual intercourse before participating in the marriage ceremony. For example, it is foolish to say that two people who are totally committed to each other and who have made all the arrangements to live this commitment are immoral if they engage in sexual intercourse the night before the marriage ceremony. Admittedly this position can be abused by those who have made a purely verbal commitment, a commitment which will be carried out in some vague and ill-defined future. At some time or other, they will unite their two lives totally by setting up house together and by actually undertaking the task of meeting the economic, social, legal, medical responsibilities that are involved in living this commitment. Apart from the reference to a vague and amorphous future time when they will share the full responsibility for each other, their commitment presently realizes itself in going to dances, sharing a box of popcorn at Saturday night movies, and sharing their bodies whenever they can do so without taking too great a risk of having the girl become pregnant.

Having acknowledged that the position advanced in this section can be abused by those who would use the word "commitment" to rationalize what is an interest only in the body of the other person, it must be pointed out that neither the ethician nor any other human being can tell two people whether they actually have made the commitment that is marriage or are mistaking a "warm glow" for such a commitment. There comes a time when this issue falls out of the area of moral philosophy and into the area of practical wisdom. . . .

The characterization of marriage as a total commitment between two human beings may lead some to conclude that the marriage ceremony is a wholly superfluous affair. It must be admitted that people may be morally married without having engaged in a marriage ceremony. However, to conclude from this point that the ceremony is totally meaningless is to lose sight of the social character of human beings. The couple contemplating marriage do not exist in a vacuum, although there may be times when they think they do. Their existences reach out beyond their union to include other human beings. By making their commitment a matter of public record, by solemnly expressing it before the law and in the presence of their respective families and friends and, if they are religious people, in the presence of God and one of his ministers, they sink the roots of their commitment more deeply and extensively in the world in which they live, thus taking steps to provide for the future growth of their commitment to each other. The public expression of this commitment makes it more fully and more explicitly a part of a couple's lives and of the world in which they live.

Notes

1. Eustace Chesser, *Unmarried Love* (New York: Pocket Books, 1965), p. 29.
2. *Op. cit.,* pp. 35–36; see also p. 66.
3. John Wilson, *Logic and Sexual Morality* (Baltimore, Md.: Penguin Books, 1965), p. 67, note 1.
4. Mary Steichen Calderone, "The Case for Chastity," *Sex in America,* ed. by Henry Anatole Grunwald (New York: Bantam Books, 1964), p. 147.
5. The psychoanalyst Rollo May makes an excellent point in calling attention to the tendency in contemporary society to exploit the human body as if it were only a machine. Rollo May, "The New Puritanism," *Sex in America,* pp. 161–164.

Alan H. Goldman  **NO**

Plain Sex

Several recent articles on sex herald its acceptance as a legitimate topic for analytic philosophers (although it has been a topic in philosophy since Plato). One might have thought conceptual analysis unnecessary in this area; despite the notorious struggles of judges and legislators to define pornography suitably, we all might be expected to know what sex is and to be able to identify at least paradigm sexual desires and activities without much difficulty. Philosophy is nevertheless of relevance here if for no other reason than that the concept of sex remains at the center of moral and social consciousness in our, and perhaps any, society. Before we can get a sensible view of the relation of sex to morality, . . . social regulation, and marriage, we require a sensible analysis of the concept itself; one which neither understates its animal pleasure nor overstates its importance within a theory or system of value. I say "before," but the order is not quite so clear, for questions in this area, as elsewhere in moral philosophy, are both conceptual and normative at the same time. Our concept of sex will partially determine our moral view of it, but as philosophers we should formulate a concept that will accord with its proper moral status. What we require here, as elsewhere, is "reflective equilibrium," a goal not achieved by traditional and recent analyses together with their moral implications. Because sexual activity, like other natural functions such as eating or exercising, has become imbedded in layers of cultural, moral, and superstitious superstructure, it is hard to conceive it in its simplest terms. But partially for this reason, it is only by thinking about plain sex that we can begin to achieve this conceptual equilibrium.

I shall suggest here that sex continues to be misrepresented in recent writings, at least in philosophical writings, and I shall criticize the predominant form of analysis which I term "means-end analysis." Such conceptions attribute a necessary external goal or purpose to sexual activity, whether it be reproduction, the expression of love, simple communication, or interpersonal awareness. They analyze sexual activity as a means to one of these ends, implying that sexual desire is a desire to reproduce, to love or be loved, or to communicate with others. All definitions of this type suggest false views of the relation of sex to . . . morality by implying that sex which does not fit one of these models or fulfill one of these functions is in some way deviant or incomplete.

From *Philosophy and Public Affairs,* vol. 6, no. 3, Spring 1977, pp. 267–275, 280–281, 283 (excerpts). Copyright © 1977 by Philosophy and Public Affairs Journal. Reprinted by permission of Wiley-Blackwell.

The alternative, simpler analysis with which I will begin is that sexual desire is desire for contact with another person's body and for the pleasure which such contact produces; sexual activity is activity which tends to fulfill such desire of the agent. Whereas Aristotle and [others] were correct in holding that pleasure is normally a byproduct rather than a goal of purposeful action, in the case of sex this is not so clear. The desire for another's body is, principally among other things, the desire for the pleasure that physical contact brings. On the other hand, it is not a desire for a particular sensation detachable from its causal context, a sensation which can be derived in other ways. This definition in terms of the general goal of sexual desire appears preferable to an attempt to more explicitly list or define specific sexual activities, for many activities such as kissing, embracing, massaging, or holding hands may or may not be sexual, depending upon the context and more specifically upon the purposes, needs, or desires into which such activities fit. The generality of the definition also represents a refusal (common in recent psychological texts) to overemphasize orgasm as the goal of sexual desire or genital sex as the only norm of sexual activity. . . .

Central to the definition is the fact that the goal of sexual desire and activity is the physical contact itself, rather than something else which this contact might express. By contrast, what I term "means-end analyses" posit ends which I take to be extraneous to plain sex, and they view sex as a means to these ends. Their fault lies not in defining sex in terms of its general goal, but in seeing plain sex as merely a means to other separable ends. I term these "means-end analyses" for convenience, although "means-separable-end analyses," while too cumbersome, might be more fully explanatory. The desire for physical contact with another person is a minimal criterion for (normal) sexual desire, but is both necessary and sufficient to qualify normal desire as sexual. Of course, we may want to express other feelings through sexual acts in various contexts; but without the desire for the physical contact in and for itself, or when it is sought for other reasons, activities in which contact is involved are not predominantly sexual. Furthermore, the desire for physical contact in itself, without the wish to express affection or other feelings through it, is sufficient to render sexual the activity of the agent which fulfills it. Various activities with this goal alone, such as kissing and caressing in certain contexts, qualify as sexual even without the presence of genital symptoms of sexual excitement. The latter are not therefore necessary criteria for sexual activity. . . .

Our definition of sex in terms of the desire for physical contact may appear too narrow in that a person's personality, not merely her or his body, may be sexually attractive to another, and in that looking or conversing in a certain way can be sexual in a given context without bodily contact. Nevertheless, it is not the contents of one's thoughts per se that are sexually appealing, but one's personality as embodied in certain manners of behavior. Furthermore, if a person is sexually attracted by another's personality, he or she will desire not just further conversation, but actual sexual contact. While looking at or conversing with someone can be interpreted as sexual in given contexts it is so when intended as preliminary to, and hence parasitic upon, elemental sexual interest. Voyeurism or viewing a pornographic movie qualifies as a sexual activity, but only as an imaginative substitute for the real thing (otherwise a deviation from the norm as expressed in our definition). The same is true of masturbation as a sexual activity without a partner.

That the initial definition indicates at least an ingredient of sexual desire and activity is too obvious to argue. We all know what sex is, at least in obvious cases, and do not need philosophers to tell us. My preliminary analysis is meant to serve as a contrast to what sex is not, at least, not necessarily. I concentrate upon the physically manifested desire for another's body, and I take as central the immersion in the physical aspect of one's own existence and attention to the physical embodiment of the other. One may derive pleasure in a sex act from expressing certain feelings to one's partner or from awareness of the attitude of one's partner, but sexual desire is essentially desire for physical contact itself: it is a bodily desire for the body of another that dominates our mental life for more or less brief periods. Traditional writings were correct to emphasize the purely physical or animal aspect of sex; they were wrong only in condemning it. This characterization of sex as an intensely pleasurable physical activity and acute physical desire may seem to some to capture only its barest level. But it is worth distinguishing and focusing upon this least common denominator in order to avoid the false views of sexual morality . . . which emerge from thinking that sex is essentially something else.

One common position views sex as essentially an expression of love or affection between the partners. It is generally recognized that there are other types of love besides sexual, but sex itself is taken as an expression of one type, sometimes termed "romantic" love.[1] Various factors again ought to weaken this identification. First, there are other types of love besides that which it is appropriate to express sexually, and "romantic" love itself can be expressed in many other ways. I am not denying that sex can take on heightened value and meaning when it becomes a vehicle for the expression of feelings of love or tenderness, but so can many other usually mundane activities such as getting up early to make breakfast on Sunday, cleaning the house, and so on. Second, sex itself can be used to communicate many other emotions besides love, and, as I will argue below, can communicate nothing in particular and still be good sex.

On a deeper level, an internal tension is bound to result from an identification of sex, which I have described as a physical-psychological desire, with love as a long-term, deep emotional relationship between two individuals. As this type of relationship, love is permanent, at least in intent, and more or less exclusive. A normal person cannot deeply love more than a few individuals even in a lifetime. We may be suspicious that those who attempt or claim to love many love them weakly if at all. Yet, fleeting sexual desire can arise in relation to a variety of other individuals one finds sexually attractive. It may even be, as some have claimed, that sexual desire in humans naturally seeks variety, while this is obviously false of love. For this reason, monogamous sex, even if justified, almost always represents a sacrifice or the exercise of self-control on the part of the spouses, while monogamous love generally does not. There is no such thing as casual love in the sense in which I intend the term "love." It may occasionally happen that a spouse falls deeply in love with someone else (especially when sex is conceived in terms of love), but this is relatively rare in comparison to passing sexual desires for others; and while the former often indicates a weakness or fault in the marriage relation, the latter does not.

If love is indeed more exclusive in its objects than is sexual desire, this explains why those who view sex as essentially an expression of love would again tend to hold a repressive or restrictive sexual ethic. . . . [T]here may be good reasons for reserving the total commitment of deep love to the context of marriage and family—the normal personality may not withstand additional divisions of ultimate commitment and allegiance. There is no question that marriage itself is best sustained by a deep relation of love and affection; and even if love is not naturally monogamous, the benefits of family units to children provide additional reason to avoid serious commitments elsewhere which weaken family ties. It can be argued similarly that monogamous sex strengthens families by restricting and at the same time guaranteeing an outlet for sexual desire in marriage. But there is more force to the argument that recognition of a clear distinction between sex and love in society would help avoid disastrous marriages which result from adolescent confusion of the two when sexual desire is mistaken for permanent love, and would weaken damaging jealousies which arise in marriages in relation to passing sexual desires. The love and affection of a sound marriage certainly differs from the adolescent romantic variety, which is often a mere substitute for sex in the context of a repressive sexual ethic.

In fact, the restrictive sexual ethic tied to the means-end analysis in terms of love . . . has failed to be consistent. At least, it has not been applied consistently, but forms part of the double standard which has curtailed the freedom of women. The inconsistency in the sexual ethic typically attached to the sex-love analysis, according to which it has generally been taken with a grain of salt when applied to men, is simply another example of the impossibility of tailoring a plausible moral theory in this area to a conception of sex which builds in conceptually extraneous factors.

I am not suggesting here that sex ought never to be connected with love or that it is not a more significant and valuable activity when it is. Nor am I denying that individuals need love as much as sex and perhaps emotionally need at least one complete relationship which encompasses both. Just as sex can express love and take on heightened significance when it does, so love is often naturally accompanied by an intermittent desire for sex. But again love is accompanied appropriately by desires for other shared activities as well. What makes the desire for sex seem more intimately connected with love is the intimacy which is seen to be a natural feature of mutual sex acts. Like love, sex is held to lay one bare psychologically as well as physically. Sex is unquestionably intimate, but beyond that the psychological toll often attached may be a function of the restrictive sexual ethic itself, rather than a legitimate apology for it. The intimacy involved in love is psychologically consuming in a generally healthy way, while the psychological tolls of sexual relations, often including embarrassment as a correlate of intimacy, are too often the result of artificial sexual ethics and taboos. The intimacy involved in both love and sex is insufficient in any case in light of previous points to render a means-end analysis in these terms appropriate.

. . . To the question of what morality might be implied by my analysis, the answer is that there are no moral implications whatever. Any analysis of sex which imputes a moral character to sex acts in themselves is wrong for that reason. There is no morality intrinsic to sex, although general moral rules apply to the treatment of others in sex acts as they apply to all human relations. We can speak of a sexual ethic as we can speak of a business ethic, without implying that business in itself is either moral or immoral or that special rules are required to judge business practices which are not derived from rules that apply elsewhere as well. Sex is not in itself a moral category, although like business it invariably places us into relations with others in which moral rules apply. It gives us opportunity to do what is otherwise recognized as wrong, to harm others, deceive them or manipulate them against their wills. Just as the fact that an act is sexual in itself never renders it wrong or adds to its wrongness if it is wrong on other grounds (sexual acts towards minors are wrong on other grounds, as will be argued below), so no wrong act is to be excused because done from a sexual motive. If a "crime of passion" is to be excused, it would have to be on grounds of temporary insanity rather than sexual context (whether insanity does constitute a legitimate excuse for certain actions is too big a topic to argue here). Sexual motives are among others which may become deranged, and the fact that they are sexual has no bearing in itself on the moral character, whether negative or exculpatory, of the actions deriving from them. Whatever might be true of war, it is certainly not the case that all's fair in love or sex.

Our first conclusion regarding morality and sex is therefore that no conduct otherwise immoral should be excused because it is sexual conduct, and nothing in sex is immoral unless condemned by rules which apply elsewhere as well. The last clause requires further clarification. Sexual conduct can be governed by particular rules relating only to sex itself. But these precepts must be implied by general moral rules when these are applied to specific sexual relations or types of conduct. The same is true of rules of fair business, ethical medicine, or courtesy in driving a car. In the latter case, particular acts on the road may be reprehensible, such as tailgating or passing on the right, which seem to bear no resemblance as actions to any outside the context of highway safety. Nevertheless their immorality derives from the fact that they place others in danger, a circumstance which, when avoidable, is to be condemned in any context. This structure of general and specifically applicable rules describes a reasonable sexual ethic as well. To take an extreme case, rape is always a sexual act and it is always immoral. A rule against rape can therefore be considered an obvious part of sexual morality which has no bearing on nonsexual conduct. But the immorality of rape derives from its being an extreme violation of a person's body, of the right not to be humiliated, and of the general moral prohibition against using other persons against their wills, not from the fact that it is a sexual act.

The application elsewhere of general moral rules to sexual conduct is further complicated by the fact that it will be relative to the particular desires and preferences of one's partner (these may be influenced by and hence in some sense include misguided beliefs about sexual morality itself). This means that there will be fewer specific rules in the area of sexual ethics than in other areas of conduct, such as driving cars, where the relativity of preference is irrelevant to the prohibition of objectively dangerous conduct. More reliance will have to be placed upon the general moral rule, which in this area holds simply that the preferences, desires, and interests of one's partner or potential partner ought to be taken into account. This rule is certainly not specifically formulated to govern sexual relations; it is a form of the central principle of morality itself. But when applied to sex, it prohibits certain actions, such as molestation of children, which cannot be categorized as violations of the rule without at the same time being classified as sexual. I believe this last case is the closest we can come to an action which is wrong *because* it is sexual, but even here its wrongness is better characterized as deriving from the detrimental effects such behavior can have on the future emotional and sexual life of the naive victims, and from the fact that such behavior therefore involves manipulation of innocent persons without regard for their interests. Hence, this case also involves violation of a general moral rule which applies elsewhere as well. . . .

I suggested earlier that in addition to generating confusion regarding the rightness or wrongness of sex acts, false conceptual analyses of the means-end form cause confusion about the value of sex to the individual. My account recognizes the satisfaction of desire and the pleasure this brings as the central psychological function of the sex act for the individual. Sex affords us a paradigm of pleasure, but not a cornerstone of value. For most of us it is not only a needed outlet for desire but also the most enjoyable form of recreation we know. Its value is nevertheless easily mistaken by being confused with that of love, when it is taken as essentially an expression of that emotion. Although intense, the pleasures of sex are brief and repetitive rather than cumulative. They give value to the specific acts which generate them, but not the lasting kind of value which enhances one's whole life. The briefness of these pleasures contributes to their intensity (or perhaps their intensity makes them necessarily brief), but it also relegates them to the periphery of most rational plans for the good life.

By contrast, love typically develops over a long term relation; while its pleasures may be less intense and physical, they are of more cumulative value. The importance of love to the individual may well be central in a rational system of value. And it has perhaps an even deeper moral significance relating to the identification with the interests of another person, which broadens one's possible relationships with others as well. Marriage is again important in preserving this relation between adults and children, which seems as important to the adults as it is to the children in broadening concerns which have a tendency to become selfish. Sexual desire, by contrast, is desire for another which is nevertheless essentially self-regarding. Sexual pleasure is certainly a good for the individual, and for many it may be necessary in order for them to function in a reasonably cheerful way. But it bears little relation to those other values just discussed, to which some analyses falsely suggest a conceptual connection. . . .

The position I have taken in this paper against those concepts is not totally new. Something similar to it is found in Freud's view of sex, which of course was genuinely revolutionary, and in the body of writings deriving from

Freud to the present time. But in his revolt against romanticized and repressive conceptions, Freud went too far—from a refusal to view sex as merely a means to a view of it as the end of all human behavior, although sometimes an elaborately disguised end. This pansexualism led to the thesis (among others) that repression was indeed an inevitable and necessary part of social regulation of any form, a strange consequence of a position that began by opposing the repressive aspects of the means-end view. Perhaps the time finally has arrived when we can achieve a reasonable middle ground in this area, at least in philosophy if not in society.

Note

1. Even Bertrand Russell, whose writing in this area was a model of rationality, at least for its period, tends to make this identification and to condemn plain sex in the absence of love: "sex intercourse apart from love has little value, and is to be regarded primarily as experimentation with a view to love." *Marriage and Morals* (New York: Bantam, 1959), p. 87.

POSTSCRIPT

Must Sex Involve Commitment?

It is clear that Punzo and Goldman differ fundamentally in their approach to sex and commitment. Goldman maintains that a concept of "plain sex" can be used to view sex without cultural and moral ideology. Punzo's approach counters the idea that an important human concept like sex can be separated from ideology.

A further question is whether men and women regard this issue in different ways. Traditionally, there has been a cultural demand that commitment is required before engaging in sex. However, a "double standard" exists that lets men practice sex in the absence of commitment without cultural disapproval. On the other hand, women are more likely to be viewed as "immoral" if they engage in sex without commitment. If the double standard is to be replaced by a unified standard, should this be one that includes commitment?

Sources relevant to this topic include Russell Vannoy, *Sex Without Love: A Philosophical Exploration* (Prometheus Books, 1981); G. Sidney Buchanan, *Morality, Sex and the Constitution: A Christian Perspective on the Power of Government to Regulate Private Sexual Conduct Between Consenting Adults* (University Press of America, 1985); G. Frankson, *Sex and Morality* (Todd & Honeywell, 1987); Joseph Monti, *Arguing About Sex: The Rhetoric of Christian Sexual Morality* (State University of New York Press, 1995); John Marshall Townsend, *What Women Want—What Men Want: Why the Sexes Still See Love and Commitment so Differently* (Oxford University Press, 1998); and J. Gordon Muir, *Sex, Politics, and the End of Morality* (Pentland Press, 1998).

ISSUE 4

Is Abortion Immoral?

YES: Don Marquis, from "Why Abortion Is Immoral," *The Journal of Philosophy* (April 1989)

NO: Margaret Olivia Little, from "The Moral Permissibility of Abortion," in Andrew I. Cohen and Christopher Heath Wellman, eds., *Contemporary Debates in Applied Ethics* (Blackwell Publishing, 2005)

ISSUE SUMMARY

YES: Professor of philosophy Don Marquis argues that abortion is generally wrong for the same reason that killing an innocent adult human being is generally wrong: it deprives the individual of a future that he or she would otherwise have.

NO: Margaret Little finds several serious problems with the way debates are structured concerning abortion. She stresses three things: first, the continuous development of the earliest stage of the fertilized egg to the birth of a baby; second, the poverty of idea theory that pushes us into all-or-nothing talk of *rights* rather than *values*; and third, the fact that it is a pregnant woman who actively gestates the fetus rather than being merely a passive carrier of it.

$\mathbf{A}$bortion is a divisive topic, and discussions can easily become polarized. Here, we will briefly consider some of the biological facts associated with abortion and review some relevant historical and legal matters. The selections themselves will then look at the moral issues raised by abortion.

Conception occurs when the spermatozoon of a male unites with the ovum of a female. The single cell thus formed is called a zygote. In a normal pregnancy, this zygote will multiply into several cells, travel through the fallopian tube, enter the uterus, and implant itself in the uterine wall. When implantation is complete, 1 to 2 weeks after fertilization (as the original conception is also called), we can say that the pregnancy is established and that the zygote has become an embryo. Once the placenta and umbilical cord are established, the embryo takes nourishment by means of these from the blood of the pregnant woman and quickly grows primitive limbs and organs. At 8 weeks from conception, the first brain waves can be detected and the embryo is now called a fetus. So-called quickening, the first felt spontaneous movement of the fetus, occurs at around 14 or 15 weeks. The threshold of viability (the point at which the fetus can be kept alive outside the uterus) is dependent upon many factors, especially the development of the cardio-pulmonary system. Depending on the level of available medical technology, viability can be reached sometime between 20 and 28 weeks. Birth generally takes place about 38 to 40 weeks after conception, although here too there is significant variation.

There are other possibilities once the spermatozoon and ovum unite. The fertilized ovum, for example, might never be implanted in the wall of the uterus and might be expelled uneventfully, and even without notice, from the body. Or the zygote might implant itself somewhere other than inside the uterus, resulting in an ectopic pregnancy. The embryo will not grow properly outside the uterus, and this kind of pregnancy can be dangerous to the mother. (In the case of an ectopic pregnancy, the Roman Catholic Church will permit an abortion to save the pregnant woman's life.) Another possibility is that the pregnancy will develop normally for a while but then end in miscarriage; this is sometimes called a spontaneous abortion.

The historic *Roe v. Wade* case, decided in 1973 by the U.S. Supreme Court in a split decision of 7–2, ruled that the nineteenth-century Texas statutes against abortion were unconstitutional. The Court divided the normal pregnancy into three trimesters and ruled as follows:

> For the stage prior to approximately the end of the first trimester, the abortion decision and its effectuation must be left to the medical judgment of the pregnant woman's attending physician. For the stage subsequent to approximately the end of the first trimester, the State, in promoting its interest in the health of the mother, may, if it chooses, regulate the abortion procedure in ways that are reasonably related to maternal health. For the stages subsequent to viability, the State, in promoting its interest in the potentiality of human life, may, if it chooses, regulate, and even proscribe, abortion except where it is necessary, in appropriate medical judgment, for the preservation of the life or health of the mother. (410 U.S.113, 93 S. Ct. 705 [1973])

Before *Roe v. Wade,* some states permitted abortion only if a woman's life was in danger; abortion for any other reason or consideration was illegal and punishable by law. *Roe v. Wade* ruled that states do not have the right to regulate abortion procedures in any way during the first trimester of pregnancy. It is important to note that neither the Supreme Court nor the Texas statutes said anything about the relation of the woman to the fetus (or embryo) or about the reasons a woman might have for seeking an abortion.

In the following selections, Don Marquis constructs a secular argument to show that abortion is immoral. He focuses not on the present status of the fetus, but on the *future* status. This avoids the divisive question of whether or not the fetus is a person. Margaret Little also seeks to avoid the standard "pro-life" and "choice" views, but in addition she wants to change the abortion question, or at least our approach to it, by focusing instead on what she calls the *ethics of gestation.*

Don Marquis

Why Abortion Is Immoral

The view that abortion is, with rare exceptions, seriously immoral has received little support in the recent philosophical literature. No doubt most philosophers affiliated with secular institutions of higher education believe that the anti-abortion position is either a symptom of irrational religious dogma or a conclusion generated by seriously confused philosophical argument. The purpose of this essay is to undermine this general belief. This essay sets out an argument that purports to show, as well as any argument in ethics can show, that abortion is, except possibly in rare cases, seriously immoral, that it is in the same moral category as killing an innocent adult human being.

The argument is based on a major assumption. Many of the most insightful and careful writers on the ethics of abortion—such as Joel Feinberg, Michael Tooley, Mary Anne Warren, H. Tristram Engelhardt, Jr., L. W. Sumner, John T. Noonan, Jr., and Philip Devine[1]—believe that whether or not abortion is morally permissible stands or falls on whether or not a fetus is the sort of being whose life it is seriously wrong to end. The argument of this essay will assume, but not argue, that they are correct.

Also, this essay will neglect issues of great importance to a complete ethics of abortion. Some anti-abortionists will allow that certain abortions, such as abortion before implantation or abortion when the life of a woman is threatened by a pregnancy or abortion after rape, may be morally permissible. This essay will not explore the casuistry of these hard cases. The purpose of this essay is to develop a general argument for the claim that the overwhelming majority of deliberate abortions are seriously immoral.

A sketch of standard anti-abortion and pro-choice arguments exhibits how those arguments possess certain symmetries that explain why partisans of those positions are so convinced of the correctness of their own positions, why they are not successful in convincing their opponents, and why, to others, this issue seems to be unresolvable. An analysis of the nature of this standoff suggests a strategy for surmounting it.

Consider the way a typical anti-abortionist argues. She will argue or assert that life is present from the moment of conception or that fetuses look like babies or that fetuses possess a characteristic such as a genetic code that

From *Journal of Philosophy*, vol. 86, no. 4, April 1989, pp. 183–202 (excerpts). Copyright © 1989 by Journal of Philosophy, Inc. Reprinted by permission.

is both necessary and sufficient for being human. Anti-abortionists seem to believe that (1) the truth of all of these claims is quite obvious, and (2) establishing any of these claims is sufficient to show that abortion is morally akin to murder.

A standard pro-choice strategy exhibits similarities. The pro-choicer will argue or assert that fetuses are not persons or that fetuses are not rational agents or that fetuses are not social beings. Pro-choicers seem to believe that (1) the truth of any of these claims is quite obvious, and (2) establishing any of these claims is sufficient to show that an abortion is not a wrongful killing.

In fact, both the pro-choice and the anti-abortion claims do seem to be true, although the "it looks like a baby" claim is more difficult to establish the earlier the pregnancy. We seem to have a standoff. How can it be resolved?

As everyone who has taken a bit of logic knows, if any of these arguments concerning abortion is a good argument, it requires not only some claim characterizing fetuses, but also some general moral principle that ties a characteristic of fetuses to having or not having the right to life or to some other moral characteristic that will generate the obligation or the lack of obligation not to end the life of a fetus. Accordingly, the arguments of the anti-abortionist and the pro-choicer need a bit of filling in to be regarded as adequate.

Note what each partisan will say. The anti-abortionist will claim that her position is supported by such generally accepted moral principles as "It is always prima facie seriously wrong to take a human life" or "It is always prima facie seriously wrong to end the life of a baby." Since these are generally accepted moral principles, her position is certainly not obviously wrong. The pro-choicer will claim that her position is supported by such plausible moral principles as "Being a person is what gives an individual intrinsic moral worth" or "It is only seriously prima facie wrong to take the life of a member of the human community." Since these are generally accepted moral principles, the pro-choice position is certainly not obviously wrong. Unfortunately, we have again arrived at a standoff.

Now, how might one deal with this standoff? The standard approach is to try to show how the moral principles of one's opponent lose their plausibility under analysis. It is easy to see how this is possible. On the one hand, the anti-abortionist will defend a moral principle concerning the wrongness of killing which tends to be broad in scope in order that even fetuses at an early stage of pregnancy will fall under it. The problem with broad principles is that they often embrace too much. In this particular instance, the principle "It is always prima facie wrong to take a human life" seems to entail that it is wrong to end the existence of a living human cancer-cell culture, on the grounds that the culture is both living and human. Therefore, it seems that the anti-abortionist's favored principle is too broad.

On the other hand, the pro-choicer wants to find a moral principle concerning the wrongness of killing which tends to be narrow in scope in order that fetuses will *not* fall under it. The problem with narrow principles is that they often do not embrace enough. Hence, the needed principles such as "It is prima facie seriously wrong to kill only persons" or "It is prima facie wrong to kill only rational agents" do not explain why it is wrong to kill infants or young children or the severely retarded or even perhaps the severely mentally ill. Therefore, we seem again to have a standoff. The anti-abortionist charges, not unreasonably, that pro-choice principles concerning killing are too narrow to be acceptable; the pro-choicer charges, not unreasonably, that anti-abortionist principles concerning killing are too broad to be acceptable.

Attempts by both sides to patch up the difficulties in their positions run into further difficulties. The anti-abortionist will try to remove the problem in her position by reformulating her principle concerning killing in terms of human beings. Now we end up with: "It is always prima facie seriously wrong to end the life of a human being." This principle has the advantage of avoiding the problem of the human cancer-cell culture counterexample. But this advantage is purchased at a high price. For although it is clear that a fetus is both human and alive, it is not at all clear that a fetus is a human *being*. There is at least something to be said for the view that something becomes a human being only after a process of development, and that therefore first trimester fetuses and perhaps all fetuses are not yet human beings. Hence, the anti-abortionist, by this move, has merely exchanged one problem for another.[2]

The pro-choicer fares no better. She may attempt to find reasons why killing infants, young children, and the severely retarded is wrong which are independent of her major principle that is supposed to explain the wrongness of taking human life, but which will not also make abortion immoral. This is no easy task. Appeals to social utility will seem satisfactory only to those who resolve not to think of the enormous difficulties with a utilitarian account of the wrongness of killing and the significant social costs of preserving the lives of the unproductive.[3] A pro-choice strategy that extends the definition of 'person' to infants or even to young children seems just as arbitrary as an anti-abortion strategy that extends the definition of 'human being' to fetuses. Again, we find symmetries in the two positions and we arrive at a standoff.

There are even further problems that reflect symmetries in the two positions. In addition to counterexample problems, or the arbitrary application problems that can be exchanged for them, the standard anti-abortionist principle "It is prima facie seriously wrong to kill a human being," or one of its variants, can be objected to on the grounds of ambiguity. If 'human being' is taken to be a *biological* category, then the anti-abortionist is left with the problem of explaining why a merely biological category should make a moral difference. Why, it is asked, is it any more reasonable to base a moral conclusion on the number of chromosomes in one's cells than on the color of one's skin?[4] If 'human being', on the other hand, is taken to be a *moral* category, then the claim that a fetus is a human being cannot be taken to be a premise in the anti-abortion argument, for it is precisely what needs to be established. Hence, either the anti-abortionist's main category is a morally irrelevant, merely biological category, or it is of no use to the anti-abortionist in establishing (noncircularly, of course) that abortion is wrong.

Although this problem with the anti-abortionist position is often noticed, it is less often noticed that the pro-choice position suffers from an analogous problem. The principle "Only persons have the right to life" also suffers from an ambiguity. The term 'person' is typically defined in terms of psychological characteristics, although there will certainly be disagreement concerning which characteristics are most important. Supposing that this matter can be settled, the pro-choicer is left with the problem of explaining why *psychological* characteristics should make a *moral* difference. If the pro-choicer should attempt to deal with this problem by claiming that an explanation is not necessary, that in fact we do treat such a cluster of psychological properties as having moral significance, the sharp-witted anti-abortionist should have a ready response. We do treat being both living and human as having moral significance. If it is legitimate for the pro-choicer to demand that the anti-abortionist provide an explanation of the connection between the biological character of being a human being and the wrongness of being killed (even though people accept this connection), then it is legitimate for the anti-abortionist to demand that the pro-choicer provide an explanation of the connection between psychological criteria for being a person and the wrongness of being killed (even though that connection is accepted).[5] . . .

[T]he pro-choicer cannot any more escape her problem by making person a purely moral category than the anti-abortionist could escape by the analogous move. For if person is a moral category, then the pro-choicer is left without the resources for establishing (noncircularly, of course) the claim that a fetus is not a person, which is an essential premise in her argument. Again, we have both a symmetry and a standoff between pro-choice and anti-abortion views.

Passions in the abortion debate run high. There are both plausibilities and difficulties with the standard positions. Accordingly, it is hardly surprising that partisans of either side embrace with fervor the moral generalizations that support the conclusions they preanalytically favor, and reject with disdain the moral generalizations of their opponents as being subject to inescapable difficulties. It is easy to believe that the counterexamples to one's own moral principles are merely temporary difficulties that will dissolve in the wake of further philosophical research, and that the counterexamples to the principles of one's opponents are . . . straightforward. . . . This might suggest to an impartial observer (if there are any) that the abortion issue is unresolvable.

There is a way out of this apparent dialectical quandary. The moral generalizations of both sides are not quite correct. The generalizations hold for the most part, for the usual cases. This suggests that they are all *accidental* generalizations, that the moral claims made by those on both sides of the dispute do not touch on the *essence* of the matter.

This use of the distinction between essence and accident is not meant to invoke obscure metaphysical categories. Rather, it is intended to reflect the rather atheoretical nature of the abortion discussion. If the generalization a partisan in the abortion dispute adopts were derived from the reason why ending the life of a human being is wrong, then there could not be exceptions to that generalization unless some special case obtains in which there are even more powerful countervailing reasons. Such generalizations would not be merely accidental generalizations; they would point to, or be based upon, the essence of the wrongness of killing, what it is that makes killing wrong. All this suggests that a necessary condition of resolving the abortion controversy is a more theoretical account of the wrongness of killing. After all, if we merely believe, but do not understand, why killing adult human beings such as ourselves is wrong, how could we conceivably show that abortion is either immoral or permissible?

⋅✦⋅

In order to develop such an account, we can start from the following unproblematic assumption concerning our own case: it is wrong to kill *us*. Why is it wrong? . . .

What primarily makes killing wrong is neither its effect on the murderer nor its effect on the victim's friends and relatives, but its effect on the victim. The loss of one's life is one of the greatest losses one can suffer. The loss of one's life deprives one of all the experiences, activities, projects, and enjoyments that would otherwise have constituted one's future. Therefore, killing someone is wrong, primarily because the killing inflicts (one of) the greatest possible losses on the victim. To describe this as the loss of life can be misleading, however. The change in my biological state does not by itself make killing me wrong. The effect of the loss of my biological life is the loss to me of all those activities, projects, experiences, and enjoyments which would otherwise have constituted my future personal life. These activities, projects, experiences, and enjoyments are either valuable for their own sakes or are means to something else that is valuable for its own sake. Some parts of my future are not valued by me now, but will come to be valued by me as I grow older and as my values and capacities change. When I am killed, I am deprived both of what I now value which would have been part of my future personal life, but also what I would come to value. Therefore, when I die, I am deprived of all of the value of my future. Inflicting this loss on me is ultimately what makes killing me wrong. This being the case, it would seem that what makes killing *any* adult human being prima facie seriously wrong is the loss of his or her future.[6] . . .

The claim that what makes killing wrong is the loss of the victim's future is directly supported by two considerations. In the first place, this theory explains why we regard killing as one of the worst of crimes. Killing is especially wrong, because it deprives the victim of more than perhaps any other crime. In the second place, people with AIDS or cancer who know they are dying believe, of course, that dying is a very bad thing for them. They believe that the loss of a future to them that they would otherwise have experienced is what makes their premature death a very bad thing for them. A better theory of the wrongness of killing would require a different natural property associated with killing which better fits with the attitudes of the dying. What could it be?

The view that what makes killing wrong is the loss to the victim of the value of the victim's future gains additional support when some of its implications are examined. In the first place, it is incompatible with the view that it is wrong to kill only beings who are biologically human. It is possible that there exists a different species from another planet whose members have a future like ours. Since having a future like that is what makes killing someone wrong, this theory entails that it would be wrong to kill members of such a species. Hence, this theory is opposed to the claim that only life that is biologically human has great moral worth, a claim which many anti-abortionists have seemed to adopt. This opposition, which this theory has in common with personhood theories, seems to be a merit of the theory.

In the second place, the claim that the loss of one's future is the wrong-making feature of one's being killed entails the possibility that the futures of some actual nonhuman mammals on our own planet are sufficiently like ours that it is seriously wrong to kill them also. Whether some animals do have the same right to life as human beings depends on adding to the account of the wrongness of killing some additional account of just what it is about my future or the futures of other adult human beings which makes it wrong to kill us. No such additional account will be offered in this essay. Undoubtedly, the provision of such an account would be a very difficult matter. Undoubtedly, any such account would be quite controversial. Hence, it surely should not reflect badly on this sketch of an elementary theory of the wrongness of killing that it is indeterminate with respect to some very difficult issues regarding animal rights.

In the third place, the claim that the loss of one's future is the wrong-making feature of one's being killed does not entail, as sanctity of human life theories do, that active euthanasia is wrong. Persons who are severely and incurably ill, who face a future of pain and despair, and who wish to die will not have suffered a loss if they are killed. It is, strictly speaking, the value of a human's future which makes killing wrong in this theory. This being so, killing does not necessarily wrong some persons who are sick and dying. Of course, there may be other reasons for a prohibition of active euthanasia, but that is another matter. Sanctity-of-human-life theories seem to hold that active euthanasia is seriously wrong even in an individual case where there seems to be good reason for it independently of public policy considerations. This consequence is most implausible, and it is a plus for the claim that the loss of a future of value is what makes killing wrong that it does not share this consequence.

In the fourth place, the account of the wrongness of killing defended in this essay does straightforwardly entail that it is prima facie seriously wrong to kill children and infants, for we do presume that they have futures of value. Since we do believe that it is wrong to kill defenseless little babies, it is important that a theory of the wrongness of killing easily account for this. Personhood theories of the wrongness of killing, on the other hand, cannot straightforwardly account for the wrongness of killing infants and young children.[7] Hence, such theories must add special ad hoc accounts of the wrongness of killing the young. The plausibility of such ad hoc theories seems to be a function of how desperately one wants such theories to work. The claim that the primary wrong-making feature of a killing is the loss to the victim of the value of its future accounts for the wrongness of killing young children and infants directly; it makes the wrongness of such acts as obvious as we actually think it is. This is a further merit of this theory. Accordingly, it seems that this value of a future-like-ours theory of the wrongness of killing shares strengths of both sanctity-of-life and personhood accounts while avoiding weaknesses of both. In addition, it meshes with a central intuition concerning what makes killing wrong.

The claim that the primary wrong-making feature of a killing is the loss to the victim of the value of its future has obvious consequences for the ethics of abortion. The future of a standard fetus includes a set of experiences, projects, activities, and such which are identical with the futures of adult human beings and are identical with the futures of young children. Since the reason that is sufficient to explain why it is wrong to kill human beings after the time of birth is a reason that also applies to fetuses, it follows that abortion is prima facie seriously morally wrong. . . .

How complete an account of the wrongness of killing does the value of a future-like-ours account have to be in order that the wrongness of abortion is a consequence? This account does not have to be an account of the necessary conditions for the wrongness of killing. Some persons in nursing homes may lack valuable human futures, yet it may be wrong to kill them for other reasons. Furthermore, this account does not obviously have to be the sole reason killing is wrong where the victim did have a valuable future. This analysis claims only that, for any killing where the victim did have a valuable future like ours, having that future by itself is sufficient to create the strong presumption that the killing is seriously wrong. . . .

In this essay, it has been argued that the correct ethic of the wrongness of killing can be extended to fetal life and used to show that there is a strong presumption that any abortion is morally impermissible. If the ethic of killing adopted here entails, however, that contraception is also seriously immoral, then there would appear to be a difficulty with the analysis of this essay.

But this analysis does not entail that contraception is wrong. Of course, contraception prevents the actualization of a possible future of value. Hence, it follows from the claim that futures of value should be maximized that contraception is prima facie immoral. This obligation to maximize does not exist, however; furthermore, nothing in the ethics of killing in this paper entails that it does. The ethics of killing in this essay would entail that contraception is wrong only if something were denied a human future of value by contraception. Nothing at all is denied such a future by contraception, however. . . .

At the time of contraception, there are hundreds of millions of sperm, one (released) ovum and millions of possible combinations of all of these. There is no actual combination at all. Is the subject of the loss to be a merely possible combination? Which one? This alternative does not yield an actual subject of harm either. Accordingly, the immorality of contraception is not entailed by the loss of a future-like-ours argument simply because there is no nonarbitrarily identifiable subject of the loss in the case of contraception.

The purpose of this essay has been to set out an argument for the serious presumptive wrongness of abortion subject to the assumption that the moral permissibility of abortion stands or falls on the moral status of the fetus. Since a fetus possesses a property, the possession of which in adult human beings is sufficient to make killing an adult human being wrong, abortion is wrong. This way of dealing with the problem of abortion seems superior to other approaches to the ethics of abortion, because it rests on an ethics of killing which is close to self-evident, because the crucial morally relevant property clearly applies to fetuses, and because the argument avoids the usual equivocations on 'human life', 'human being', or 'person'. The argument rests neither on religious claims nor on Papal dogma. It is not subject to the objection of "speciesism." Its soundness is compatible with the moral permissibility of euthanasia and contraception. It deals with our intuitions concerning young children.

Finally, this analysis can be viewed as resolving a standard problem—indeed, *the* standard problem—concerning the ethics of abortion. Clearly, it is wrong to kill adult human beings. Clearly, it is not wrong to end the life of some arbitrarily chosen single human cell. Fetuses seem to be like arbitrarily chosen human cells in some respects and like adult humans in other respects. The problem of the ethics of abortion is the problem of determining the fetal property that settles this moral controversy. The thesis of this essay is that the problem of the ethics of abortion, so understood, is solvable.

Notes

1. Feinberg, "Abortion," in *Matters of Life and Death: New Introductory Essays in Moral Philosophy,* Tom Regan, ed. (New York: Random House, 1986), pp. 256–293; Tooley, "Abortion and Infanticide," *Philosophy and Public Affairs,* II, 1 (1972): 37–65; Tooley, *Abortion and Infanticide* (New York: Oxford, 1984); Warren, "On the Moral and Legal Status of Abortion," *The Monist,* I.VII, 1 (1973): 43–61; Engelhardt, "The Ontology of Abortion," *Ethics,* I, XXXIV, 3 (1974): 217–234; Sumner, *Abortion and Moral Theory* (Princeton: University Press, 1981); Noonan, "An Almost Absolute Value in History," in *The Morality of Abortion: Legal and Historical Perspectives,* Noonan, ed. (Cambridge: Harvard, 1970); and Devine, *The Ethics of Homicide* (Ithaca: Cornell, 1978).

2. For interesting discussions of this issue, see Warren Quinn, "Abortion: Identity and Loss," *Philosophy and Public Affairs,* XIII, 1 (1984): 24–54; and Lawrence C. Becker, "Human Being: The Boundaries of the Concept," *Philosophy and Public Affairs,* IV, 4 (1975): 334–359.

3. For example, see my "Ethics and the Elderly: Some Problems," in Stuart Spicker, Kathleen Woodward, and David Van Tassel, eds., *Aging and the Elderly: Humanistic Perspectives in Gerontology* (Atlantic Highlands, NJ: Humanities, 1978), pp. 341–355.

4. See Warren, *op. cit.,* and Tooley, "Abortion and Infanticide."

5. This seems to be the fatal flaw in Warren's treatment of this issue.

6. I have been most influenced on this matter by Jonathan Glover, *Causing Death and Saving Lives* (New York: Penguin, 1977), ch. 3; and Robert Young, "What Is So Wrong with Killing People?" *Philosophy,* LIV, 210 (1979): 515–528.

7. Feinberg, Tooley, Warren, and Engelhardt have all dealt with this problem.

 **NO**

The Moral Permissibility
of Abortion

Introduction

When a woman or girl finds herself pregnant, is it morally permissible for her to end that pregnancy? One dominant tradition says "no"; its close cousin says "rarely"—exceptions may be made where the burdens on the individual girl or woman are exceptionally dire, or, for some, when the pregnancy results from rape. On both views, though, there is an enormous presumption against aborting, for abortion involves destruction of something we've no right to destroy. Those who reject this claim, it is said, do so by denying the dignity of early human life—and imperiling their own.[1]

I think these views are deeply flawed. They are, I believe, based on a problematic conception of how we should value early human life; more than that, they are based on a profoundly misleading view of gestation and a deontically crude picture of morality. I believe that early abortion is fully permissible, widely decent, and, indeed, can be honorable. This is not, though, because I regard burgeoning human life as "mere tissue": on the contrary, I think it has a value worthy of special respect. It is, rather, because I believe that the right *way* to value early human life, and the right way to value what is involved in and at stake with its development, lead to a view that regards abortion as both morally sober and morally permissible. Abortion at later stages of pregnancy becomes, for reasons I'll outline, multiply more complicated; but it is early abortions—say, abortions in the first half of pregnancy—that are most at stake for women.

The Moral Status of Embryos and Early Fetuses

According to one tradition, the moral case against abortion is easily stated: abortion is morally impermissible because it is murder. The fetus, it's claimed, is a *person*—not just a life (a frog is a life), or an organism worthy of special regard, but a creature of full moral status imbued with fundamental rights. Abortion, in turn, constitutes a gross violation of one of that person's central-most such rights: namely, its right to life.

Now, for a great many people, the idea of a 2-week blastocyst, or 6-week embryo, or 12-week fetus counting as an equivalent rights-bearer to more usual persons is just an enormous stretch. It makes puzzles of widely shared intuitions, including the greater sense of loss most feel at later rather than earlier miscarriages, or again the greater priority we place on preventing childhood diseases than on preventing miscarriages. However else we may think such life worthy of regard, an embryo or early fetus is so far removed from our paradigmatic notion of a person that regarding it as such seems an extreme view.

The question is why some feel pushed to such an extreme. It's in part a reflection of just how inadequate our usual theories are when they bump up against reproduction. Surely part of the urge to cast a blastocyst as a full-fledged person, for instance, is a by-product of the impoverished resources our inherited theory has for valuing germinating human life: if the only category of moral status one has is a person or rights-holder, then the only way to capture our sense of the kind of respect or honor that embryos might deserve (the only way to capture the loss many feel at early miscarriage, for instance, or the queasiness over certain aspects of human embryo research) is to insist on fetal personhood from the moment of conception. The alternative, of course, is to challenge the assumption: instead of making the fetus match those terms of moral status, we ask what our theory of value should look like to accommodate the value of an entity like the fetus. . . .

If we expand our moral categories beyond *rights* to notions of *value*, and accept *continua* as everyday phenomena rather than special puzzles, the road is paved for a picture of burgeoning human life that accords far better with the intuitions of so many: burgeoning human life has a status and worth that deepen as its development progresses.

But, it will be said, such an account misses something crucial. Unlike other inherently gradualist processes—the building of a house, say—there is here something already extant that should ground full moral status to the embryo: namely, a potential . . . for personhood. The only gradualist element in the picture is its unfolding. This, it will be urged, is what really grounds the moral standing of early human life: it's not because the embryo or early fetus *is* a person, but because the right way to value potential persons is to regard them as deserving the same deference *as* persons.

Now, I think there is a very important sense in which we should regard human embryos and fetuses as potential persons. . . . A human embryo is understood biologically as the kind of organism it is by giving explanatory primacy to the trajectory of its developing into a matured human, i.e. a person—something that cannot be said of a given sperm or egg.[2]

Lest we hang too much on this point, though, we need to remember that biology is not the only rubric that matters here. . . . Indeed, on one view, biological potential is only a candidate for normative upshot for creatures who independently count as having moral standing—a view that grounds moral status in potentiality turns out to have things exactly backwards. More deeply, though, the particular classification at issue here carries an intrinsic tension. For the trajectory in virtue of which we connect this sort of organism with that further state is a trajectory that depends on what *another person*—the pregnant woman—is able and willing to do. That is, *unlike* most biological organisms, the trajectory we privilege as the fetus's "natural" development—against which we classify its "potential" and measure when its existence is "truncated"— depends on the actions and resources of an autonomous *agent*, not the events and conditions of a *habitat*. Knowing what to think of the fetus thus requires assessing moves that have their home in biology . . . applied when the biological "environment" is, at one and the same time, an autonomous agent subsumable under normative, not just biological, categories.

If this is easy to miss, it's in part because of how human gestation itself tends to get depicted. Metaphors abound of passive carriage; the pregnancy is a project of nature's. The woman is, perhaps, an especially close witness to that project, or again its setting, but the project is not her own. Her agency is thus noticed when she cuts off the pregnancy but passes unnoticed when she continues it. If, though, gestation belongs to the *woman*—if its essential resources are hers—her blood, her hormones, her energy, all resources that could be going to other of her bodily projects—then the concept of potential person is a hybrid concept from the start, not something we can read off of the neutral lessons of biology. In an important sense, then, talk of the fetus as potential person is dangerously misleading. For it encourages us to think of the embryo's development as mere *unfolding*—as though all that's needed other than the passage of time is already intrinsically there, or at least there independently of the woman.

In my own view, the biological capacities of early human life provide, once again, a degreed basis for according regard. Such biological potential marks out early human life as specially *respect-worthy*—which is why we should try to avoid conception where children are not what is sought (or again, why we don't think we should tack up human embryos on the wall for art, or provide them for children to dissect at school if fertilized chicken eggs get too pricey). To say that such life is respect-worthy, though, is not the same as claiming we are charged to defer as we would those with moral status.

Abortion and Gestational Assistance

Thus far, I've argued that morally restrictive views of abortion ride atop a problematic view of how we should value early human life. I now want to argue that they also ride atop a problematic misconception of the act of aborting itself. Let me illustrate first by returning to the claim that, if the fetus *were* a person, abortion would be a violation of its right to life.

We noted above that, while certain metaphors depict gestation as passive carriage (as though the fetus were simply occupying a room until it is born), the truth is of course far different. One who is gestating is providing the fetus with sustenance—donating nourishment, creating blood, delivering oxygen, providing hormonal triggers for development—without which it could not live. . . . Whether the assistance is delivered by way of intentional activity (as when the woman eats or takes her prenatal vitamins) or by way of biological mechanism, assistance it plainly is. But this has crucial implications for abortion's alleged status as murder. To put it simply, the right to life, as Judith Thomson famously put it, does not include the right to have all assistance needed to maintain that life (Thomson, 1971). Ending gestation will, at early stages at least, certainly lead to the fetus's demise, but that does not mean that doing so would violate its right to life.

Now Thomson herself illustrated the point with an (in)famous thought experiment in which one person is kidnapped and used as life support for another: staying connected to the Famous Violinist, she points out, may be the kind thing to do, but disconnecting oneself does not violate the Violinist's rights. The details of this rather esoteric example have led to widespread charges that Thomson's point ignores the distinction between killing and letting die, and would apply at any rate only to cases in which the woman was not responsible for procreation occurring. In fact, though, I think the central insight here is broader than the example, or Thomson's own analysis, indicates.[3]

As Frances Kamm's work points out (Kamm, 1992), in the usual case of a killing—if you stab a person on the street, for instance—you interfere with the trajectory the person had independently of you. She faced a happy enough future, we'll say; your action changed that, taking away from her something she would have had but for your action. In ending gestation, though, what you are taking away from this person is something she wouldn't have had to begin with without your aid. She comes to you with a downward trajectory, as it were: but for you she would already be dead. In removing that assistance, you are not violating the person's right to life, judged in the traditional terms of a right against interference. While all killings are tragedies, then, not all are alike: some killings, as Kamm puts it, share the crucial "formal" feature of letting die, which is that they leave the person no worse off than before she encountered you. Of course, if one *could* end the assistance without effecting death, then, absent extraordinary circumstances, one should. . . .

. . . The point . . . is that where I am still in the process of saving—or sustaining or enabling—your life, and that life cannot be thusly saved or sustained by anyone else, ending that assistance, even by active means, does not violate your right to life.

Some, of course, will argue that matters change when the woman is causally responsible for procreation. In such cases, it will be said, she is responsible for introducing the person's need. She isn't like someone happening by an accident on the highway who knows CPR; she's like the person who *caused* the accident. Her actions introduced a set of vulnerabilities or needs, and we have a special duty to lessen vulnerabilities and repair harms we have inflicted on others.

But there is a deep disanalogy between causing the accident and procreating. The fact of causing a crash itself introduces a harm to surrounding drivers: they are in a worse position for having encountered that driver. But the simple act of procreating does not worsen the fetus's position: without procreation, the fetus wouldn't exist at all; and the mere fact of being brought into existence is not a bad thing. To be sure, creating a human is creating someone who comes with needs. But this, crucially, is not the same as inflicting a need *onto* someone (see Silverstein, 1987). It isn't as though the fetus already existed with one level of needs and the woman added a new one. . . .

Even if the fetus were a person, then, abortion would not be murder. More broadly, abortion isn't a species of *wrongful interference*. This isn't to say that abortion is thereby necessarily unproblematic. It is to argue, instead, that the crucial moral issue needs to be relocated to the question of what, if any, positive obligations pregnant women have to continue gestational assistance. The question abortion really asks us to address is a question about the *ethics of gestation*. But this is a question that takes us into far richer, and far more interesting, territory than that occupied by discussions of murder. In particular, it requires us to discuss and assess claimed grounds of obligation, and to assess the very specific kinds of burdens and sacrifice involved in rendering *this* type of assistance.

I've argued elsewhere that if or when the fetus is a person, then the question of when a woman might have some obligation to provide use of her body to save its life turns out to be a fascinatingly deep matter, and one that is ultimately deeply contextual (Little, forthcoming). The issue I want to turn my attention to here is what picture we get when we join the two views I've outlined: a view that regards burgeoning human life as respect-worthy but not endowed with substantial moral status, and a view that recognizes abortion as the ending of gestational support. Abortion, I want to argue, is both permissible and widely decent, for reasons involving what we might call *authorship* and *stewardship*. Let me take them each in turn.

Intimacy, Pregnancy, and Motherhood

When people first ask what's at stake in asking a woman to continue a pregnancy, what usually get emphasized are the physical and medical risks. And indeed, they're important to emphasize. While many pregnancies go smoothly, many do not; and the neutral language of an obstetrics text hardly captures the lived reality. I think of a friend I visited who'd been put in lock-down on the psychiatric ward from pregnancy-related psychosis (and whose physician wouldn't discuss inducing at 39 weeks because there was no "obstetrical indication"). Or my sister, whose two trimester "morning sickness"—actually gut-wrenching dry heaves every 20-minutes and three hospitalizations—was the equal of many an experience of chemotherapy. Or another acquaintance, whose sudden onset of eclampsia during delivery brought her so close to dying that it left us all breathless. Asking women to take on the *ex ante* medical risks of pregnancy is asking a lot.

Then there are the social risks pregnancy can represent for some women—risks it is very hard for those of us in more comfortable lives to fully appreciate. Pregnancy is a marker for increased domestic violence. It leads for many to abandonment by family and community, even as it can lead the woman to feel tied to a relationship she would otherwise leave.

All of these burdens are important to appreciate. But there is something incomplete in such renditions of pregnancy's stakes. For a great many women, it's another set of issues that motivate the desire to end a pregnancy—issues having to do with the extraordinarily *personal* nature of gestation.

To be pregnant is to allow another living creature to live in and off of one's body for nine months. It's to have one's every physical system shaped by its needs, rather than one's own. It is to share one's body in an extraordinarily intimate and extensive—and often radically unpredictable—way. Then there is the aftermath of the nine months: for gestation doesn't just turn cells into a person; it turns the woman into a mother. One of the most common reasons women give for wanting to abort is that they do not want to become a mother—now, ever, again, with this partner, or no reliable partner, with these few resources, or these many that are now, after so many years of mothering, slated finally to another cause. Not because motherhood would bring with it such burdens—though it can—but because motherhood would so thoroughly change what we might call one's fundamental practical identity. The enterprise of mothering restructures the self—changing the shape of one's heart, the primary commitments by which one lives one's life, the terms by which one judges one's life a success or a failure. If the enterprise is eschewed and one decides to give the child over to another, the identity of mother still changes the normative facts that are true of one, as there is now someone by whom one does well or poorly (Ross, 1982). And either way— whether one rears the child or lets it go—to continue a pregnancy means that a piece of one's heart, as the saying goes, will forever walk outside one's body.

Gestation, in short, is not just any activity. It involves sharing one's very body. It brings with it an emotional intertwinement that can reshape one's entire life. It brings another person into one's family. Deciding whether to continue a pregnancy isn't like being asked to write a check for charity, however large; it's an enormous undertaking that has reverberations for an entire lifetime. To argue that women may permissibly decline this need not trade on a view that grants no value to early life; it is, in essence, to argue about the right way to value *pregnancy* and *parenthood*. It is to recognize a level of moral prerogative based not just on the concretely understood burdens of the activity in question, but also on its deep connection to authoring a life. To illustrate, consider the following.

Imagine that the partner of your family's dreams is wildly in love with you and asks for your hand in marriage. As it turns out, substantial utility would accrue by your accepting him: his connections would seal your father's bid for political office, raise the family profile yet higher, and add nicely to its coffers just as your eldest brother faces expensive restoration of the family estate. It would also, and not incidentally, keep the fellow himself from falling into a pit of despair, as it's clear you're the only one for him.

All of this utility notwithstanding, many will believe that you don't thereby have a moral *obligation*—even a prima facie one—to accept the proposal. You might have a responsibility to give the proposal serious thought; but if, on reflection, you realize that marriage to this man—or to any man—is not what you want, then there we are. . . . Nor . . . need we think the resistance must trace to a conviction that it would be morally wrong to accept the proposal—that it would in some way transgress the norms governing marriage. It is, we'll imagine, quite obvious to you that you would come to have an enduring love if you accept; he understands this and relishes the prospective courtship. It isn't that you would *use* him if you accept; it's that you don't *want* to have an enduring love with him, now, or at all.

Or again, imagine that your providing sexual service would help comfort and inspire the soldiers readying for battle. Many will believe this does not ground a requirement, even prima facie, to offer intercourse. This, even if you're the only one around capable of offering such service, and even if doing so wouldn't actually be distressful to you. Such an intuition, again, needn't trade on thinking it would be wrong to give sex for such a purpose. Those with more permissive views of sexuality might well think someone who authentically and with full self-respect wanted to share her body to this purpose would be doing something generous and fine. One just doesn't want to make doing so the subject of obligation.

Now not all agree to these intuitions. If Victorian novels are to be believed, the upper classes of Regency England believed both that marriage and sex were fair candidates for obligation (especially when the family estate was at stake). But for many, there is something about marriage as a relationship, and sexual intercourse as a bodily connection, that makes them deserving of some special kind of deference when assessing moral obligation. . . .

Gestation, like sex, is a bodily intimacy of the first order. Motherhood, like marriage, is a relational intimacy of the first order. If one believes that decisions about whether to continue a pregnancy are deserving of moral prerogative, it need not be because one believes early human life has no value— any more than assigning prerogatives over sex and marriage denies the value of one's family, the boys in fighting blue, or the relationship of marriage. Such views instead stem from the conviction that the proper way to value the relationship of motherhood and the bodily connection of pregnancy is to view them as intimacies deserving of special deference. Even if continuing a pregnancy represents *no* welfare setback to the woman, classically construed, we should recognize a strong moral prerogative over whether to continue that pregnancy.

This isn't a claim that any reason to abort is a good one. Human life, even in nascent forms, should not to be extinguished lightly; one who decides to end a pregnancy because she wants to fit into a party dress, say, is getting wrong the value of burgeoning human life. To abort for such reasons is to act indecently. But this doesn't mean that such a woman now has an obligation to continue the pregnancy. What it means, in the first instance, is that she should not regard such a reason as adequate for the conclusion; not that the conclusion is not available to her. . . .

Norms of Responsible Creation

Now some will urge that those who are (at least jointly) responsible for procreation thereby have a heightened obligation to continue gestating. People, of course, disagree over what it takes to count as "responsible" here. . . . But those who satisfy the relevant criteria, it's often said, must thereby face greater duty to "see the pregnancy through." Unease is expressed at the thought of heterosexual intercourse conducted in callous disregard of procreative potential, of creating only to let wither. If you're going to allow a new life to begin, it's thought, you'd better see it through to fruition.

I think these intuitions point to important issues, but not the ones usually thought. Let's start with that notion of sexual irresponsibility. For many people, there is something troubling about the idea of couples engaging in heterosexual intercourse in complete disregard of contraception—say, when one is highly fertile and birth control is just an arm's reach away. Such a view points to an important set of intuitions about another layer of respect, namely, respect for creation itself. Respect for burgeoning human life carries implications, not just for the accommodation we might owe such life once extant, but for the conditions under which we should undertake activities with procreative potential in the first place. To regard something as a value sometimes enjoins us to make more of it, and sometimes, as with people, to take care about the conditions under which we make any.[4]

There are, as we might put it, norms of responsible creation. Such a view seems exactly right to me. Part of what I imagine teaching my own children about sexuality is that human life as such deserves respect (whatever the metaphysical details), and respect requires that one not treat one's procreative capacities in a cavalier way. But none of this means that one has a special responsibility to gestate if one *does* get pregnant. For one thing, these norms, while very important (and far too little emphasized in our current culture), are norms about the activities that can lead to procreation, not what one owes should procreation take place. They specify, as it were, the good faith conditions one should meet for engaging in certain activities. Even if the norms are [breached]—one has sex in callous disregard to its potential to lead to new human life—that doesn't itself imply that one now (as punishment?) must gestate: it says one shouldn't have had that sort of sex. Indeed, for many of us, the thought that negligence here means one should continue a pregnancy has an internal disconnect: that one had irresponsible sex is no reason at all to bring a new person into the world.

This last point begins to point to a very different approach to the ethics of creation. The salience of responsibility for procreation to the responsibilities of gestation is not just complex: decisions about abortion are often located *within* the norms of responsible creation. Let me explain.

Many people have deeply felt convictions about the circumstances under which they feel it right for them to bring a child into the world—can it be brought into a decent world, an intact family, a society that can minimally respect its agency? These considerations can persist even after conception has taken place; for while the embryo has already been created, a person has not. Some women decide to abort, that is, not because they do not *want* the resulting child—indeed, they may yearn for nothing more, and desperately wish that their circumstances were otherwise—but because they do not think bringing a child into the world the right thing for them to do.

As Barbara Katz Rothman (1989) puts it, decisions to abort often represent not a decision to destroy, but a refusal to create. These are abortions marked by moral language. A woman wants to abort because she knows she couldn't give up a child for adoption but feels she couldn't give the child the sort of life, or be the sort of parent, she thinks a child *deserves*; a woman who would have to give up the child thinks it would be *unfair* to bring a child into existence already burdened by rejection, however well grounded its reasons; a woman living in a country marked by poverty and gender apartheid wants to abort because she decides it would be *wrong* for her to bear a daughter whose life, like hers, would be filled with so much injustice and hardship. . . .

Some will protest the thought of our deciding such matters. We have no dominion, it will be said, to pick and chose the conditions under which human life, once started, proceeds. On what we might call a "stewardship" view of creation, in contrast, this dominion is precisely *part* of the responsibility involved in creation. It's a grave matter to end a developing human life by not nurturing it; but it can be an equally grave decision to continue a process that will result in the creation of a person. The present case, note, is thus importantly different from the other area of controversy over dominion over life, namely, actions intending to hasten death. Whatever one thinks of that matter, it diverges in a key respect from abortion. When we stand by rather than hasten death, we are allowing a trajectory independent of us to proceed without our influence. Not to abort, though, *is* to do something else—namely, to create a person.

Gestation is *itself* a creative endeavor. . . . If personhood emerges through pregnancy, and one has choices about whether to continue pregnancy, then decisions to do so themselves involve norms of respect. And not all norms of respect for creation, it turns out, tell in favor of continuing.

None of this is to say that abortion is morally neutral. Abortion involves loss. Not just loss of the hope various parties have invested in the pregnancy, but loss of something valuable in its own right. Abortion is thus a sober matter, an occasion, often, for moral emotions such as grief and regret. Given the value at stake, it is only fitting to feel grief—a sorrow that life begun is now ended—or to feel moral regret—that the actions needed to help these cells develop into a person would have compromised too significantly the life of someone who already was one. Such regret, that is, can signal appreciation of the fact, not that the action was indecent, but that decent actions sometimes involve loss.

It takes enormous investment to develop early human life into a human being. Understanding the morality of early abortion involves assessing not just welfare, but intimacy, not just destruction, but creation. As profound as the respect we should have for burgeoning human life, we should acknowledge moral prerogatives over associations such as having another inhabit and use one's body in such an extraordinarily enmeshed way, over identity-constituting commitments and enterprises as profound as motherhood, and over the weighty responsibility of bringing a new person into the world.

Notes

1. Portions of this chapter draw on my essay, "Abortion" (Little, 2003).

2. At least, one of a couple of weeks' standing: earlier blastocysts' trajectories turn out to be fascinatingly underdetermined. There is, for instance, no fact of the matter internal to its own cellular information as to whether a one-week blastocyst will be one person or more; and at very early stages there is no fact of the matter as to which cells will become the fetus and which will become the placenta.

3. RU-486, which essentially interrupts the production of progesterone needed to maintain a placenta, provides a good example of an abortion method that is more straightforwardly a "letting die" than an active killing.

4. Of course, just how much "care" one must exert to avoid conception will be heartily contested. Those, like myself, who value spontaneity in sexual relations and have mild views about the value of burgeoning human life will advance something quite modest—urging, say, good faith attempts to use birth control if it is safe, easily obtained, and immediately convenient. Others will advance stringent principles indeed, requiring, say, that one not have sex at all until one is prepared to parent.

References

Herman, Barbara (1993). *The Practice of Moral Judgment*. Cambridge, MA: Harvard University Press.

Kamm, Frances Myrna (1992). *Creation and Abortion: A Study in Moral and Legal Philosophy*. New York: Oxford University Press.

Little, Margaret Olivia (2003). "Abortion." In R. G. Frey and Christopher Heath Wellman (eds.), *A Companion to Applied Ethics* (pp. 313–25). Oxford: Blackwell.

Little, Margaret (forthcoming). *Intimate Duties: Re-thinking Abortion, the Law, and Morality*. Oxford: Oxford University Press.

Ross, Steven (1982). "Abortion and the death of the fetus." *Philosophy and Public Affairs*, 11: 232–45.

Rothman, Barbara Katz (1989). *Recreating Motherhood: Ideology and Technology in a Patriarchal Society*. New York: Norton.

Silverstein, H. S. (1987). "On a woman's 'responsibility' for the fetus." *Social Theory and Practice*, 13: 103–19.

Thomson, Judith Jarvis (1971) "A defense of abortion." *Philosophy and Public Affairs*, 1: 47–66.

POSTSCRIPT

Is Abortion Immoral?

Whether or not a fetus can be considered a person is often at the center of the abortion issue. Marquis, however, does not find that a direct approach to this question breaks the deadlock that is characteristic of many discussions of the morality of abortion. Instead, he argues that the effect of aborting a fetus, which is the loss of that fetus's future experiences, is the reason why abortion is immoral. Marquis considers this loss of future experiences to be the reason why killing adult human beings is wrong, and he carries the logic over to fetuses.

Little regards a newly conceived zygote as quite distant from an ordinary person, but (unlike some supporters of "choice") she recognizes the moral worth of a "potential person" and in fact thinks that most people agree and are careful to use birth control so as to prevent unwanted pregnancy in the first place. But the moral claims of a potential person grow over time as a fetus develops more and more into a person. Thus, the moral worth of a fetus in a quite advanced stage of development is greater than at an early stage—which explains why we feel that the loss of a pregnancy in the advanced stages is greater than the loss at an earlier stage (and why opponents of abortion generally think that so-called partial-birth abortion is the worst of all abortions). We are, she complains, forced by the poverty of our moral language into thinking in all-or-nothing terms. Thus, the fetus (or embryo) either has *all* the rights of an ordinary people or has *none* of them. Little wants instead to use language that admits of degrees. She favors ideas such as *respect*, or *responsibility*. Moreover, she wants to turn the question around so that the discussion is not about what the woman with the unwanted pregnancy can do, or what rights the fetus or woman has, but what she calls the *ethics of gestation*.

Judith Jarvis Thomson, in her ground-breaking article "In Defense of Abortion," *Philosophy and Public Affairs* (Fall 1971), argues that, from the premise that the fetus is a person with a right to life, it does not follow that a woman cannot disconnect herself from it and terminate an unwanted pregnancy. Suppose, she says, that you wake up one day to find yourself medically attached to a famous violinist who would die if you detached yourself. A violinist is a person and has a right to life. Does it then follow, asks Thomson, that you may not detach yourself from this unwanted arrangement? Further readings on this issue are Joel Feinberg, *The Problem of Abortion,* 2d ed. (Wadsworth, 1984); Laurence Tribe, *Abortion: The Clash of Absolutes* (W. W. Norton, 1990); Bonnie Steinbock, *Life Before Birth: The Moral and Legal Status of Embryos and Fetuses* (Oxford University Press, 1992); Frances Myrna Kamm, *Creation and Abortion: An Essay in Moral and Legal Philosophy* (Oxford University Press, 1992); Robert M. Baird and Stuart E. Rosenbaum, eds., *The Ethics of Abortion: Pro-Life vs. Pro-Choice,*

2d ed. (Prometheus Books, 1993); Eva R. Rubin, ed., *The Abortion Controversy: A Documentary History* (Greenwood Press, 1994); Bhavani Sitaraman, *The Middleground: The American Public and the Abortion Debate* (Garland, 1994); Ian Shapiro, ed., *Abortion: The Supreme Court Decisions* (Hackett, 1995); Peter Korn, *Lovejoy: A Year in the Life of an Abortion Clinic* (Atlantic Monthly Press, 1996); Patrick Lee, *Abortion and Unborn Human Life* (Catholic University of America Press, 1996); Eileen McDonagh, *Breaking the Abortion Deadlock: From Choice to Consent* (Oxford University Press, 1996); Kathy Rudy, *Beyond Pro-Life and Pro-Choice: Moral Diversity in the Abortion Debate* (Beacon Press, 1997); Katha Pollitt, "Abortion in American History," *The Atlantic Monthly* (May 1997); and Louis Pojman and Francis Beckwith, eds., *The Abortion Controversy: 25 Years After Roe v. Wade: A Reader,* 2d ed. (Wadsworth Publishing Company, 1998). A CD-ROM on abortion is J. Douglas Butler, ed., *Abortion and Reproductive Rights* (J. Douglas Butler, Inc., 1997).

More recent publications include David Boonin, *A Defense of Abortion* (Cambridge University Press, 2002); Laurie J. Shrage, *Abortion and Social Responsibility: Depolarizing the Debate* (Oxford University Press, 2003); Anne Hendershott, *The Politics of Abortion* (Encounter Books, 2006); and Jennifer Baumgardner, *Abortion & Life* (Akashic Books, 2008).

ISSUE 5

Is It Right to Prohibit Same-Sex Marriage?

YES: Jeff Jordan, from "Is It Wrong to Discriminate on the Basis of Homosexuality?" *Journal of Social Philosophy*, vol. 26, no. 1 (Spring 1995)

NO: David Boonin, from "Same-Sex Marriage and the Argument from Public Disagreement," *Journal of Social Philosophy*, vol. 30, no. 2 (Summer 1999)

ISSUE SUMMARY

YES: Philosopher Jeff Jordan defends the claim that there are situations in which it is morally permissible to discriminate against homosexuals, i.e., to treat homosexuals unfavorably. There is a public dilemma (or a clash of views) concerning the moral status of homosexuality and, unless something of overriding importance—such as human rights—is at stake, the government should refrain from favoring one side by publicly recognizing same-sex marriage.

NO: Philosopher David Boonin argues directly against Jordan that his argument is unsuccessful. He uses Jordan's argument to address some of the questions that seem to lie, unanswered, in the background of this issue: In particular, is it correct that homosexuality is immoral? Do people have a right to marry only certain other people? Is opposition to same-sex marriage comparable to opposition to interracial marriage?

Homosexuality exists in all known human societies, and also among some animals. This, however, has not prevented homosexual behavior from being condemned by virtually all world religions. In some societies, this behavior exists in a hidden, socially unacceptable way; in others, it has been tolerated and even highly esteemed. (The variation here among both existing and historical societies is amazingly wide-ranging.)

Homosexuality is receiving more acceptance in our society. One way this can be seen is in the extension of insurance and other benefits to same-sex "domestic partners." But whereas married heterosexuals can state that they are indeed legally married, homosexual couples generally cannot. The status of homosexual relationships is somewhat unclear as far as the law is concerned. Of course, heterosexuals sometimes have unmarried sexual relationships too—but is that type of relationship the heterosexual counterpart of unmarried homosexual relationships? In a way, it is, but in a way, it isn't. For, at the very least, heterosexual marriage is a recognized possibility, while homosexual marriage is often not. Whereas an unmarried heterosexual relationship is one that could involve marriage, an unmarried homosexual relationship generally cannot. As it is, only a few states recognize same-sex marriage, while several states have specifically ruled it out. There is a great social divide here.

For us, one question that may lie behind issues of same-sex marriage is whether or not homosexuality is immoral. If it is, then it is hard to see why society should support same-sex marriage. Many arguments do aim to show that homosexuality is indeed immoral, but this is much more difficult to demonstrate than many people suppose. Part of the problem is that heterosexuals often know very little about homosexuality and rely upon stereotypical thinking or feelings rather than on facts and logic. But if a successful argument could be made here, then any ground for same-sex marriage would be destroyed.

One argument that is sometimes made does not directly address the morality of homosexuality, but raises practical problems such as the spread of AIDS. Same-sex marriage, however, would probably decrease the spread of AIDS, as homosexuals would presumably indulge in less promiscuous sexual behavior and would tend to become involved in much more stable relationships.

But opponents of same-sex marriage often worry about where (and how) we are to draw the line between two-person same-sex marriage and other forms of marriage such as polygamous marriage. One idea is that we have here a kind of "slippery slope" argument to the effect that if same-sex marriage is allowed, then there is nothing to keep us from sliding farther down this slippery slope and allowing such things as polygamous marriage, incestuous marriage, and so on—at least if this is what the parties to the marriage want. This form of argument depends on just how slippery the slope is. Here, one must face the question: Is it really true that there will be no principled place to stop and draw the line? Won't society be able to articulate some relevant principles? Opponents to same-sex marriage would agree that there are indeed principled lines to be drawn—but would say that on one side of the line we have heterosexual marriages and on the other we have everything else.

In the following selection, Jeff Jordan makes the case that society should prohibit same-sex marriage. The argument is not particularly religiously based, but it does acknowledge that the major monotheistic religions have traditionally prohibited same-sex marriages. David Boonin then takes issue with the argument of Jordan, and examines his conclusion, his premises, and some of the background considerations that do not seem to be explicitly mentioned. One positive feature of both authors is that they deal with the issue in a careful and logical way rather than emotionally.

YES

Jeff Jordan

Is It Wrong to Discriminate on the Basis of Homosexuality?

Much like the issue of abortion in the early 1970s, the issue of homosexuality has exploded to the forefront of social discussion. Is homosexual sex on a moral par with heterosexual sex? Or is homosexuality in some way morally inferior? Is it wrong to discriminate against homosexuals—to treat homosexuals in less favorable ways than one does heterosexuals? Or is some discrimination against homosexuals morally justified? These questions are the focus of this essay.

In what follows, I argue that there are situations in which it is morally permissible to discriminate against homosexuals because of their homosexuality. That is, there are some morally relevant differences between heterosexuality and homosexuality which, in some instances, permit a difference in treatment. The issue of marriage provides a good example. While it is clear that heterosexual unions merit the state recognition known as marriage, along with all the attendant advantages—spousal insurance coverage, inheritance rights, ready eligibility of adoption—it is far from clear that homosexual couples ought to be accorded that state recognition.

The argument of this essay makes no claim about the moral status of homosexuality per se. Briefly put, it is the argument of this essay that the moral impasse generated by conflicting views concerning homosexuality, and the public policy ramifications of those conflicting views justify the claim that it is morally permissible, in certain circumstances, to discriminate against homosexuals.[1]

1. The Issue

The relevant issue is this: does homosexuality have the same moral status as heterosexuality? Put differently, since there are no occasions in which it is morally permissible to treat heterosexuals unfavorably, whether because they are heterosexual or because of heterosexual acts, are there occasions in which it is morally permissible to treat homosexuals unfavorably, whether because they are homosexuals or because of homosexual acts?

A negative answer to the above can be termed the "parity thesis." The parity thesis contends that *homosexuality has the same moral status as*

From *Journal of Social Philosophy,* vol. 26, no. 1, Spring 1995, pp. 39–52 (excerpts). Copyright © 1995 by Journal of Social Philosophy. Reprinted by permission of Wiley-Blackwell.

heterosexuality. If the parity thesis is correct, then it would be immoral to discriminate against homosexuals because of their homosexuality. An affirmative answer can be termed the "difference thesis" and contends that there are morally relevant differences between heterosexuality and homosexuality which justify a difference in moral status and treatment between homosexuals and heterosexuals. The difference thesis entails that *there are situations in which it is morally permissible to discriminate against homosexuals. . . .*

A word should be said about the notion of discrimination. To discriminate against X means treating X in an unfavorable way. The word "discrimination" is not a synonym for "morally unjustifiable treatment." Some discrimination is morally unjustifiable; some is not. For example, we discriminate against convicted felons in that they are disenfranchised. This legal discrimination is morally permissible even though it involves treating one person unfavorably different from how other persons are treated. The difference thesis entails that there are circumstances in which it is morally permissible to discriminate against homosexuals.

2. An Argument for the Parity Thesis

One might suppose that an appeal to a moral right, the right to privacy, perhaps, or the right to liberty, would provide the strongest grounds for the parity thesis. Rights talk, though sometimes helpful, is not very helpful here. If there is reason to think that the right to privacy or the right to liberty encompasses sexuality (which seems plausible enough), it would do so only with regard to private acts and not public acts. Sexual acts performed in public (whether heterosexual or homosexual) are properly suppressible. It does not take too much imagination to see that the right to be free from offense would soon be offered as a counter consideration by those who find homosexuality morally problematic. Furthermore, how one adjudicates between the competing rights claims is far from clear. Hence, the bald appeal to a right will not, in this case anyway, take one very far.

Perhaps the strongest reason to hold that the parity thesis is true is something like the following:

1. Homosexual acts between consenting adults harm no one. And,
2. respecting persons' privacy and choices in harmless sexual matters maximizes individual freedom. And,
3. individual freedom should be maximized. But,
4. discrimination against homosexuals, because of their homosexuality, diminishes individual freedom since it ignores personal choice and privacy. So,
5. the toleration of homosexuality rather than discriminating against homosexuals is the preferable option since it would maximize individual freedom. Therefore,
6. the parity thesis is more plausible than the difference thesis.

Premise (2) is unimpeachable: if an act is harmless and if there are persons who want to do it and who choose to do it, then it seems clear that respecting the choices of those people would tend to maximize their freedom.[2] Step (3) is also beyond reproach: since freedom is arguably a great good and since there does not appear to be any ceiling on the amount of individual freedom—no "too much of a good thing"—(3) appears to be true.

At first glance, premise (1) seems true enough as long as we recognize that if there is any harm involved in the homosexual acts of consenting adults, it would be harm absorbed by the freely consenting participants. This is true, however, only if the acts in question are done in private. Public acts may involve more than just the willing participants. Persons who have no desire to participate, even if only as spectators, may have no choice if the acts are done in public. A real probability of there being unwilling participants is indicative of the public realm and not the private. However, where one draws the line between private acts and public acts is not always easy to discern, it is clear that different moral standards apply to public acts than to private acts.[3]

If premise (1) is understood to apply only to acts done in private, then it would appear to be true. The same goes for (4): discrimination against homosexuals for acts done in private would result in a diminishing of freedom. So (1)–(4) would lend support to (5) only if we understand (1)–(4) to refer to acts done in private. Hence, (5) must be understood as referring to private acts; and, as a consequence, (6) also must be read as referring only to acts done in private.

With regard to acts which involve only willing adult participants, there may be no morally relevant difference between homosexuality and heterosexuality. In other words, acts done in private. However, acts done in public add a new ingredient to the mix; an ingredient which has moral consequence. Consequently, the argument (1)–(6) fails in supporting the parity thesis. The argument (1)–(6) may show that there are some circumstances in which the moral status of homosexuality and heterosexuality are the same, but it gives us no reason for thinking that this result holds for all circumstances.[4]

3. Moral Impasses and Public Dilemmas

Suppose one person believes that X is morally wrong, while another believes that X is morally permissible. The two people, let's stipulate, are not involved in a semantical quibble; they hold genuinely conflicting beliefs regarding the moral status of X. If the first person is correct, then the second person is wrong; and, of course, if the second person is right, then the first must be wrong. This situation of conflicting claims is what we will call an "impasse." Impasses arise out of moral disputes. Since the conflicting parties in an impasse take contrary views, the conflicting views cannot all be true, nor can they all be false.[5] Moral impasses may concern matters only of a personal nature, but moral impasses can involve public policy. An impasse is likely to have public policy ramifications if large numbers of people hold the conflicting views, and the conflict involves matters which are fundamental to a person's moral identity (and, hence, from a practical point of view, are probably irresolvable) and it involves acts done in public. Since not every impasse has public policy ramifications, one can mark off "public dilemma" as a special case of moral impasses: those moral impasses that have public policy consequences. Public dilemmas, then, are impasses located in the public square. Since they have public policy ramifications and since they arise from impasses, one side or another of the dispute will have its views implemented as public policy. Because of the public policy ramifications, and also because social order is sometimes threatened by the volatile parties involved in the impasse, the state has a role to play in resolving a public dilemma.

A public dilemma can be actively resolved in two ways.[6] The first is when the government allies itself with one side of the impasse and, by state coercion and sanction, declares that side of the impasse the correct side. The American Civil War was an example of this: the federal government forcibly ended slavery by aligning itself with the Abolitionist side of the impasse.[7] Prohibition is another example. The 18th Amendment and the Volstead Act allied the state with the Temperance side of the impasse. State mandated affirmative action programs provide a modern example of this. This kind of resolution of a public dilemma we can call a "resolution by declaration." The first of the examples cited above indicates that declarations can be morally proper, the right thing to do. The second example, however, indicates that declarations are not always morally proper. The state does not always take the side of the morally correct; nor is it always clear which side is the correct one.

The second way of actively resolving a public dilemma is that of accommodation. An accommodation in this context means resolving the public dilemma in a way that gives as much as possible to all sides of the impasse. A resolution by accommodation involves staking out some middle ground in a dispute and placing public policy in that location. The middle ground location of a resolution via accommodation is a virtue since it entails that there are no absolute victors and no absolute losers. The middle ground is reached in order to resolve the public dilemma in a way which respects the relevant views of the conflicting parties and which maintains social order. The Federal Fair Housing Act and, perhaps, the current status of abortion (legal but with restrictions) provide examples of actual resolutions via accommodation.[8]

In general, governments should be, at least as far as possible, neutral with regard to the disputing parties in a public dilemma. Unless there is some overriding reason why the state should take sides in a public dilemma—the protection of innocent life, or abolishing slavery, for instance—the state should be neutral, because no matter which side of the public dilemma the state takes, the other side will be the recipient of unequal treatment by the state. A state which is partial and takes sides in moral disputes via declaration, when there is no overriding reason why it should, is tyrannical. Overriding reasons involve, typically, the protection of generally recognized rights.[9] In the case of slavery, the right to liberty; in the case of protecting innocent life, the right involved is the negative right to life. If a public dilemma must be actively resolved, the state should do so (in the absence of an overriding reason) via accommodation and not declaration since the latter entails that a sizable number of people would be forced to live under a government which "legitimizes" and does not just tolerate activities which they find immoral. Resolution via declaration is appropriate only if there is an overriding reason for the state to throw its weight behind one side in a public dilemma.

Is moral rightness an overriding reason for a resolution via declaration? What better reason might there be for a resolution by declaration than that it is the right thing to do? Unless one is prepared to endorse a view that is called "legal moralism"—that immorality alone is a sufficient reason for the state to curtail individual liberty—then one had best hold that moral rightness alone is not an overriding reason. Since some immoral acts neither harm nor offend nor violate another's rights, it seems clear enough that too much liberty would be lost if legal moralism were adopted as public policy.[10] . . .

4. Conflicting Claims on Homosexuality

The theistic tradition, Judaism and Christianity and Islam, has a clear and deeply entrenched position on homosexual acts: they are prohibited. Now it seems clear enough that if one is going to take seriously the authoritative texts of the respective religions, then one will have to adopt the views of those texts, unless one wishes to engage in a demythologizing of them with the result that one ends up being only a nominal adherent of that tradition.[11] As a consequence, many contemporary theistic adherents of the theistic tradition, in no small part because they can read, hold that homosexual behavior is sinful. Though God loves the homosexual, these folk say, God hates the sinful behavior. To say that act X is a sin entails that X is morally wrong, not necessarily because it is harmful or offensive, but because X violates God's will. So, the claim that homosexuality is sinful entails the claim that it is also morally wrong. And, it is clear, many people adopt the difference thesis just because of their religious views: because the Bible or the Koran holds that homosexuality is wrong, they too hold that view.

Well, what should we make of these observations? We do not, for one thing, have to base our moral conclusions on those views, if for no other reason than not everyone is a theist. If one does not adopt the religion-based moral view, one must still respect those who do; they cannot just be dismissed out of hand.[12] And, significantly, this situation yields a reason for thinking that the difference thesis is probably true. Because many religious people sincerely believe homosexual acts to be morally wrong and many others believe that homosexual acts are not morally wrong, there results a public dilemma.[13]

The existence of this public dilemma gives us reason for thinking that the difference thesis is true. It is only via the difference thesis and not the parity thesis, that an accommodation can be reached. Here again, the private/public distinction will come into play.

To see this, take as an example the issue of homosexual marriages. A same-sex marriage would be a public matter. For the government to sanction same-sex marriages—to grant the recognition and reciprocal benefits which attach to marriage—would ally the government with one side of the public dilemma and against the adherents of religion-based moralities. . . .

Of course, some would respond here that by not sanctioning same-sex marriages the state is, and historically has been, taking sides to the detriment of homosexuals. There is some truth in this claim. But one must be careful here. The respective resolutions of this issue—whether the state should recognize and sanction same-sex marriages—do not have symmetrical implications. The asymmetry of this issue is a function of the private/public distinction and the fact that marriage is a public matter. If the state sanctions same-sex marriages, then there is no accommodation available. In that event, the religion-based morality proponents are faced with a public, state sanctioned matter which they find seriously immoral. This would be an example of a resolution via declaration. On the other hand, if the state does not sanction same-sex marriages, there is an accommodation available: in the public realm the state sides with the religion-based moral view, but the state can tolerate private homosexual acts. That is, since homosexual acts are not essentially public acts, they can be, and historically have been, performed in private. The state, by not sanctioning same-sex marriages is acting in the public realm, but it can leave the private realm to personal choice.[14]

5. The Argument From Conflicting Claims

It was suggested in the previous section that the public dilemma concerning homosexuality, and in particular whether states should sanction same-sex marriages, generates an argument in support of the difference thesis. The argument, again using same-sex marriages as the particular case, is as follows:

7. There are conflicting claims regarding whether the state should sanction same-sex marriages. And,
8. this controversy constitutes a public dilemma. And,
9. there is an accommodation possible if the state does not recognize same-sex marriages. And,
10. there is no accommodation possible if the state does sanction same-sex marriages. And,
11. there is no overriding reason for a resolution via declaration. Hence,
12. the state ought not sanction same-sex marriages. And,
13. the state ought to sanction heterosexual marriages. So,
14. there is at least one morally relevant case in which discrimination against homosexuals, because of their homosexuality, is morally permissible. Therefore,
15. the difference thesis is true.

Since proposition (14) is logically equivalent to the difference thesis, then, if (7)–(14) are sound, proposition (15) certainly follows.

Premises (7) and (8) are uncontroversial. Premises (9) and (10) are based on the asymmetry that results from the public nature of marriage. Proposition (11) is based on our earlier analysis of the argument (1)–(6). Since the strongest argument in support of the parity thesis fails, we have reason to think that there is no overriding reason why the state ought to resolve the public dilemma via declaration in favor of same-sex marriages. We have reason, in other words, to think that (11) is true.

Proposition (12) is based on the conjunction of (7)–(11) and the principle that, in the absence of an overriding reason for state intervention via declaration, resolution by accommodation is the preferable route. Proposition (13) is just trivially true. So, given the moral difference mentioned in (12) and (13), proposition (14) logically follows.

6. Two Objections Considered

The first objection to the argument from conflicting claims would contend that it is unsound because a similar sort of argument would permit discrimination against some practice which, though perhaps controversial at some earlier time, is now widely thought to be morally permissible. Take mixed-race marriages, for example. The opponent of the argument from conflicting claims could argue that a similar argument would warrant prohibition against mixed-race marriages. If it does, we would have good reason to reject (7)–(14) as unsound.

There are three responses to this objection. The first response denies that the issue of mixed-race marriages is in fact a public dilemma. It may have been so at one time, but it does not seem to generate much, if any, controversy today. Hence, the objection is based upon a faulty analogy.

The second response grants for the sake of the argument that the issue of mixed-race marriages generates a public dilemma. But the second response points out that there is a relevant difference between mixed-race marriages and same-sex marriages that allows for a resolution by declaration in the one case but not the other. As evident from the earlier analysis of the argument in support of (1)–(6), there is reason to think that there is no overriding reason for a resolution by declaration in support of the parity thesis. On the other hand, it is a settled matter that state protection from racial discrimination is a reason sufficient for a resolution via declaration. Hence, the two cases are only apparently similar, and, in reality, they are crucially different. They are quite different because, clearly enough, if mixed-race marriages do generate a public dilemma, the state should use resolution by declaration in support of such marriages. The same cannot be said for same-sex marriages. . . .

The third response to the first objection is that the grounds of objection differ in the respective cases: one concerns racial identity; the other concerns behavior thought to be morally problematic. A same-sex marriage would involve behavior which many people find morally objectionable; a mixed-race marriage is objectionable to some, not because of the participants' behavior, but because of the racial identity of the participants. It is the race of the marriage partners which some find of primary complaint concerning mixed-race marriages. With same-sex marriages, however, it is the behavior which is primarily objectionable. To see this latter point, one should note that, though promiscuously Puritan in tone, the kind of sexual acts that are likely involved in a same-sex marriage are objectionable to some, regardless of whether done by homosexuals or heterosexuals.[15] So again, there is reason to reject the analogy between same-sex marriages and mixed-race marriages. Racial identity is an immutable trait and a complaint about mixed-race marriages necessarily involves, then, a complaint about an immutable trait. Sexual behavior is not an immutable trait and it is possible to object to same-sex marriages based on the behavior which would be involved in such marriages. Put succinctly, the third response could be formulated as follows: objections to mixed-race marriages necessarily involve objections over status, while objections to same-sex marriages could involve objections over behavior. Therefore, the two cases are not analogues. . . .

The second objection to the argument from conflicting claims can be stated so: if homosexuality is biologically based—if it is inborn[16]—then how can discrimination ever be justified? If it is not a matter of choice, homosexuality is an immutable trait which is, as a consequence, morally permissible. Just as it would be absurd to hold someone morally culpable for being of a certain race, likewise it would be absurd to hold someone morally culpable for being a homosexual. Consequently, according to this objection, the argument from conflicting claims "legitimizes" unjustifiable discrimination.

But this second objection is not cogent, primarily because it ignores an important distinction. No one could plausibly hold that homosexuals act by some sort of biological compulsion. If there is a biological component involved in sexual identity, it would incline but it would not compel. Just because one naturally (without any choice) has certain dispositions, is not in itself a morally cogent reason for acting upon that disposition. Most people are naturally selfish, but it clearly does not follow that selfishness is in any way permissible on that account. Even if it is true that one has a predisposition to do X as a matter of biology and not as a matter of choice, it does not follow that doing X is morally permissible. For example, suppose that pyromania is an inborn predisposition. Just because one has an inborn and, in that sense, natural desire to set fires, one still has to decide whether or not to act on that desire.[17] The reason that the appeal to biology is specious is that it ignores the important distinction between being a homosexual and homosexual acts. One is status; the other is behavior. Even if one has the status naturally, it does not follow that the behavior is morally permissible, nor that others have a duty to tolerate the behavior.

But, while moral permissibility does not necessarily follow if homosexuality should turn out to be biologically based, what does follow is this: in the absence of a good reason to discriminate between homosexuals and heterosexuals, then, assuming that homosexuality is inborn, one ought not discriminate between them. . . . The argument from conflicting claims, however, provides a good reason which overrides this presumption.

7. A Second Argument for the Difference Thesis

A second argument for the difference thesis, similar to the argument from conflicting claims, is what might be called the "no-exit argument." This argument is based on the principle that:

> A. no just government can coerce a citizen into violating a deeply held moral belief or religious belief.

Is (A) plausible? It seems to be since the prospect of a citizen being coerced by the state into a practice which she finds profoundly immoral appears to be a clear example of an injustice. Principle (A), conjoined with there being a public dilemma arising over the issue of same-sex marriages, leads to the observation that if the state were to sanction same-sex marriages, then persons who have profound religious or moral objections to such unions would be legally mandated to violate their beliefs since there does not appear to be any feasible "exit right" possible with regard to state sanctioned marriage. An exit right is an exemption from some legally mandated practice, granted to a person or group, the purpose of which is to protect the religious or moral integrity of that person or group. Prominent examples of exit rights include conscientious objection and military service, home-schooling of the young because of some religious concern, and property used for religious purposes being free from taxation.

It is important to note that marriage is a public matter in the sense that, for instance, if one is an employer who provides health care benefits to the spouses of employees, one must provide those benefits to any employee who is married. Since there is no exit right possible in this case, one would be coerced, by force of law, into subsidizing a practice one finds morally or religiously objectionable.[18]

In the absence of an exit right, and if (A) is plausible, then the state cannot morally force persons to violate deeply held beliefs that are moral or religious in nature. In particular, the state morally could not sanction same-sex marriages since this would result in coercing some into violating a deeply held religious conviction.

8. A Conclusion

It is important to note that neither the argument from conflicting claims nor the no-exit argument licenses wholesale discrimination against homosexuals. What they do show is that some discrimination against homosexuals, in this case refusal to sanction same-sex marriages, is not only legally permissible but also morally permissible. The discrimination is a way of resolving a public policy dilemma that accommodates, to an extent, each side of the impasse and, further, protects the religious and moral integrity of a good number of people. In short, the arguments show us that there are occasions in which it is morally permissible to discriminate on the basis of homosexuality.[19]

Notes

1. The terms "homosexuality" and "heterosexuality" are defined as follows. The former is defined as sexual feelings or behavior directed toward individuals of the same sex. The latter, naturally enough, is defined as sexual feelings or behavior directed toward individuals of the opposite sex.

   Sometimes the term "gay" is offered as an alternative to "homosexual." Ordinary use of "gay" has it as a synonym of a male homosexual (hence, the common expression, "gays and lesbians"). Given this ordinary usage, the substitution would lead to a confusing equivocation. Since there are female homosexuals, it is best to use "homosexual" to refer to both male and female homosexuals, and reserve "gay" to signify male homosexuals, and "lesbian" for female homosexuals in order to avoid the equivocation.

2. This would be true even if the act in question is immoral.

3. The standard answer is, of course, that the line between public and private is based on the notion of harm. Acts which carry a real probability of harming third parties are public acts.

4. For other arguments supporting the moral parity of homosexuality and heterosexuality, see Richard Mohr, *Gays/Justice: A Study of Ethics, Society and Law* (NY: Columbia, 1988); and see Michael Ruse, "The Morality of Homosexuality" in *Philosophy and Sex,* eds. R. Baker & F. Elliston (Buffalo, NY: Prometheus Books, 1984), pp. 370–390.

5. Perhaps it would be better to term the disputing positions "contradictory" views rather than "contrary" views.

6. Resolutions can also be passive in the sense of the state doing nothing. If the state does nothing to resolve the public dilemma, it stands pat with the status quo, and the public dilemma is resolved gradually by sociological changes (changes in mores and in beliefs).

7. Assuming, plausibly enough, that the disputes over the sovereignty of the Union and concerning states' rights were at bottom disputes about slavery.

8. The Federal Fair Housing Act prohibits discrimination in housing on the basis of race, religion, and sex. But it does not apply to the rental of rooms in single-family houses, or to a building of five units or less if the owner lives in one of the units. See 42 U.S.C. Section 3603.

9. Note that overriding reasons involve *generally recognized* rights. If a right is not widely recognized and the state nonetheless uses coercion to enforce it, there is a considerable risk that the state will be seen by many or even most people as tyrannical.

10. This claim is, perhaps, controversial. For a contrary view see Richard George, *Making Men Moral* (Oxford: Clarendon Press, 1993).

11. See, for example, Leviticus 18:22,21:3; and Romans 1:22–32; and Koran IV:13

12. For an argument that religiously-based moral views should not be dismissed out of hand, see Stephen Carter, *The Culture of Disbelief: How American Law and Politics Trivialize Religious Devotion* (NY: Basic Books, 1993).

13. Two assumptions are these: that the prohibitions against homosexuality activity are part of the religious doctrine and not just an extraneous addition; second, that if X is part of one's religious belief or religious doctrine, then it is morally permissible to hold X. Though this latter principle is vague, it is, I think, clear enough for our purposes here (I ignore here any points concerning the rationality of religious belief in general, or in particular cases).

14. This point has implications for the moral legitimacy of sodomy laws. One implication would be this: the private acts of consenting adults should not be criminalized.

15. Think of the sodomy laws found in some states which criminalize certain sexual acts, whether performed by heterosexuals or homosexuals.

16. There is some interesting recent research which, though still tentative, strongly suggests that homosexuality is, at least in part, biologically based.

See Simon LeVay, *The Sexual Brain* (Cambridge, MA: MIT Press, 1993), pp. 120–122; and J.M. Bailey & R.C. Pillard "A Genetic Study of Male Sexual Orientation" *Archives of General Psychiatry* 48 (1991): 1089–1096; and C. Burr, "Homosexuality and Biology" *The Atlantic* 271/3 (March, 1993): 64; and D. Hamer, S. Hu, V. Magnuson, N. Hu, A. Pattatucci, "A Linkage Between DNA Markers on the X Chromosome and Male Sexual Orientation" *Science* 261 (16 July 1993): 321–327; and see the summary of this article by Robert Pool, "Evidence for Homosexuality Gene" *Science* 261 (16 July 1993): 291–292.

17. I do not mean to suggest that homosexuality is morally equivalent or even comparable to pyromania.

18. Is the use of subsidy here inappropriate? It does not seem so since providing health care to spouses, in a society where this is not legally mandatory, seems to be more than part of a salary and is a case of providing supporting funds for a certain end.

19. I thank David Haslett, Kate Rogers, Louis Pojman, and Jim Fieser for helpful and critical comments.

David Boonin  **NO**

Same-Sex Marriage and the Argument from Public Disagreement

Most arguments against same-sex marriage rest at least in part on claims about the moral status of homosexuality: claims to the effect that homosexual behavior is morally objectionable in itself, or that homosexuals as a class are predisposed to commit acts (such as infidelity or child molestation) that are morally objectionable on independent grounds. In "Is It Wrong to Discriminate on the Basis of Homosexuality?" Jeff Jordan claims to produce an argument against same-sex marriage that makes no such assumptions.[1] Rather than relying on claims about the morality of homosexuality per se, Jordan attempts to show that it is morally permissible for the state to refuse to sanction same-sex marriages by appealing to the fact that marriage is a public rather than private institution, and that there is widespread public disagreement about the moral status of homosexuality. I will begin by presenting a brief summary of Jordan's principal argument for this claim and will then argue that it should be rejected for three distinct reasons: the argument itself is unsound, it is subject to a *reductio ad absurdum* that Jordan fails to overcome, and, contrary to Jordan's claim, it does in fact depend on claims about the morality of homosexuality, claims that stand in need of support and that Jordan has not defended.

I

Jordan begins by defining an "impasse" over the moral status of *x* as a situation in which people hold "genuinely conflicting beliefs regarding the moral status of *x*," and a "public dilemma" as an impasse that has "public policy consequences." In cases of genuine public dilemmas, the state will have to act in a way that has some implications with respect to *x*, and as a result will not be able to fully satisfy the interests of everyone on both sides of the impasse. When it does so by putting its power and authority squarely on one side of the impasse, as in the case of the federal government's forcibly ending slavery, it in effect "declares that side of the impasse the correct side," and Jordan refers to this as "resolution by declaration." When it finds a way to stake out some kind of middle ground "in a way that gives as much as possible to all sides of the impasse," it ensures that "there are no absolute victors and no absolute

From *Journal of Social Philosophy*, vol. 30, no. 2, Summer 1999, pp. 251–259. Copyright © 1999 by Journal of Social Philosophy. Reprinted by permission of Wiley-Blackwell.

losers" in the impasse and that the views of all sides are respected. Jordan refers to this as "resolution by accommodation," and cites abortion as a possible example (pornography might be another): the government permits its use, but restricts its availability. Jordan then argues, quite plausibly, that whenever a public dilemma must be actively resolved, the state should institute a resolution by accommodation rather than by declaration, unless there is an "overriding reason" that it should take sides, where such reasons typically involve "the protection of generally recognized rights."

With this general framework in place, Jordan then makes the following claims about same-sex marriage in particular: First, there is a moral impasse over the question of whether or not homosexual acts are morally permissible. Many people think that they are and many think that they are not. Second, whereas engaging in homosexual conduct in itself is essentially a private matter, entering into a relationship of marriage is essentially a public one. Marriage involves a public recognition of a personal relationship between two people and people who are married become eligible for various sorts of public benefits that are unavailable to unmarried couples. As a result, the debate over same-sex marriage represents not merely a moral impasse, but a public dilemma. Third, for the government to sanction same-sex marriage is for it to resolve this public dilemma by declaration in favor of one side of the dispute, in a way that leaves no room for accommodation. If it does this, then members of one segment of the population "are faced with a public, state sanctioned matter which they find seriously immoral." But, fourth, if the state instead refuses to sanction same-sex marriage, this counts as a resolution by accommodation, provided that the state permits private homosexual acts between consenting adults. If it does this, then each side of the impasse gets some but not all of what it wants and thus neither side is an absolute victor or loser. Fifth, and finally, there is no overriding reason for the state to take sides in this dispute. What is at stake is not comparable to what is at stake in those cases, such as the abolition of slavery, where there is plainly reason for the state to resolve the issue by declaration.

If these five claims are correct, and if Jordan's general framework is defensible, the result is that the state should refuse to sanction same-sex marriages. We can represent the argument as follows:

P1 If (a) there is a public dilemma about x, *and* (b) resolution of the dilemma by accommodation is possible, *and* (c) there is no overriding reason to prefer resolution of the dilemma by declaration, *then* (d) the state should resolve the public dilemma about x by accommodation.

P2 There is a public dilemma about same-sex marriage.

P3 It is possible for the state to resolve the dilemma by accommodation if it refuses to sanction same-sex marriage (provided that it permits private homosexual acts between consenting adults).

P4 It is not possible for the state to resolve the dilemma by accommodation if it sanctions same-sex marriage (since that amounts to resolving the dilemma by declaration and leaves no room for accommodation).

P5 There is no overriding reason for the state to resolve the dilemma by declaration.

C The state should refuse to sanction same-sex marriage (provided that it permits private homosexual acts between consenting adults).

At the end of his paper, Jordan characterizes the thesis this argument is meant to defend as one on which it is "morally permissible" for the state to refuse to sanction same-sex marriages, but this puts things far too modestly. If Jordan's argument is successful, it shows not merely that it would be *permissible* for the state to do this, but that this is what the state in fact *ought* to do. Indeed, if the argument is successful, it is difficult to see how one could avoid the conclusion that it would be positively *wrong* for the state to sanction same-sex marriages, because it would be wrong for it, in general, to fully favor one side of a moral dispute over another without a compelling reason for doing so. So a good deal is at stake if Jordan's argument is successful.

But I want now to show that Jordan's argument is not successful. In section II, I will argue that one of the argument's premises is importantly ambiguous, and that either way of resolving the ambiguity renders two of the other premises false. In section III, I will argue that the argument is undermined by a reductio ad absurdum objection that Jordan tries, but fails, to overcome. And in section IV, I will argue that, contrary to Jordan's characterization of the argument, it does, in fact, presuppose a particular and contentious claim about the moral status of homosexuality.

II

Let me begin by raising a question about P2: the claim that there is a public dilemma about same-sex marriage. On the face of it, this might seem to be the clearest and least problematic of all of the premises in Jordan's argument. If anything at all about same-sex marriage is uncontroversial it is the fact that it is controversial. But what, exactly, does the claim made by P2 mean? Jordan, remember, defines a public dilemma as a special case of a moral impasse, and a moral impasse as a situation in which people "hold genuinely conflicting beliefs regarding the moral status of x." The question is: in the case of the public dilemma about same-sex marriage, what does the x stand for?

There are two possibilities: it can stand for acts of homosexual behavior, or it can stand for acts of participating in a same-sex marriage. Jordan at one point speaks of "*the* public dilemma concerning homosexuality, and in particular whether states should sanction same-sex marriages," as if there is a single subject of dispute here, but these are in fact two distinct subjects of disagreement. The former concerns the moral permissibility of certain forms of sexual behavior, regardless of whether the people who engage in them are generally heterosexual or homosexual in their orientation. The latter concerns the moral permissibility of granting certain forms of social recognition and public benefits to same-sex couples, regardless of whether or not they engage in such (or any) sexual behavior.[2]

Suppose that the genuinely conflicting beliefs that generate the dilemma referred to in P2 are beliefs regarding the moral status of acts of participating in a same-sex marriage. This seems to be the most natural interpretation, since the dilemma itself is about same-sex marriage and since a dilemma is simply a special case of an impasse, which is itself a case of conflicting beliefs about something. If this is what is meant by P2, then P3 and P4 are false. P3 says that if the state refuses to sanction same-sex marriages, then it resolves the public dilemma by accommodation (provided that it permits private homosexual acts between consenting adults). If we conflate the two distinct questions about private acts and public benefits into one issue, and think of it as "the" dispute over homosexuality, then this seems plausible enough. Each side gets some of what it wants, and neither side gets all of what it wants. But if the conflict is over the permissibility of same-sex *marriage* in particular, as opposed to about the complex cluster of issues relating to homosexuality taken as a whole, then this is no accommodation at all. It is simply a declaration that one side of the debate is entirely correct (those who oppose same-sex marriages) and the other side entirely incorrect (those who support them). It is as if one were to join together the distinct but related debates about whether or not the government should fund the arts and whether or not it should ban violent pornography, announce that the government will permit violent pornography but will not subsidize it, and declare that "the" debate in question had been settled in a way that accommodates both sides. This would not be a resolution by accommodation of one dilemma, but rather a resolution by declaration of two distinct but related dilemmas.

On this understanding of P2, P4 is also false, for similar but distinct reasons. P4 says that if the state sanctions same-sex marriage, then it resolves the public dilemma by declaration and leaves no room for accommodation. But if the dilemma is over same-sex marriage rather than over same-sex sex, this too is incorrect. If accommodation is reached in controversies such as that over pornography or abortion by permitting but discouraging the controversial practice, then the same would hold here as well. The state could sanction same-sex marriage, but make it more difficult to obtain a same-sex marriage license than to obtain an opposite-sex marriage license. For example, it could require proof that a homosexual couple had been engaged for two years before obtaining a same-sex marriage license, but not require such proof from heterosexual couples, or require extensive premarital counseling, or charge a greater licensing fee. And it could discourage homosexuals from marrying in other ways, such as by taxing married homosexuals at a higher rate (higher than married heterosexuals and/ or higher than unmarried homosexuals), or making it more difficult for them to obtain divorces or to adopt children than it is for heterosexual couples.

None of these suggestions will be fully satisfactory to defenders of same-sex marriage, of course. What they demand is marriage for homosexuals that is on an equal footing with marriage for heterosexuals. Nor will any of these proposals be fully satisfactory to opponents of same-sex marriage. What they demand is that there be no such thing as same-sex marriage. But that is precisely the point. If Jordan is correct that dilemmas of this sort should be resolved by accommodation, and if the dilemma is understood to be one over marriage and not over sex, then following a proposal that is fully satisfactory to neither side is exactly what his argument demands that we do. As in other such cases, the state should find a way to allow those who wish to engage in the disputed behavior to engage in it while at the same time expressing society's disapproval or at least lack of approval of the behavior in question.

Suppose, on the other hand, that the genuinely conflicting beliefs that generate the dilemma referred to in P2 are beliefs regarding the moral status of acts of homosexual behavior. This seems to be what Jordan typically has in mind when he introduces his argument. When he supports the contention that there exists a public dilemma that needs some sort of resolution, for example, he cites the fact that "[t]he theistic tradition, Judaism and Christianity and Islam, has a clear and deeply entrenched position on homosexual *acts:* they are prohibited." And he concludes his argument for the claim by saying that "[b]ecause many religious people sincerely believe homosexual *acts* to be morally wrong and many others believe that homosexual *acts* are not morally wrong, there results a public dilemma."

But if the genuinely conflicting beliefs that generate the dilemma referred to in P2 are beliefs regarding the moral status of acts of homosexual behavior, then P3 and P4 are again false, for different but parallel reasons. If the state sanctions same-sex marriage, it does not resolve the conflicting beliefs about the moral permissibility of acts of homosexual behavior in a way that leaves no room for accommodation. For example, the state could recognize both same-sex and opposite-sex marriage and make it illegal to have homosexual intercourse outside of such a relation while legal to have heterosexual intercourse outside of such a relation. This would have the effect of permitting but restricting the form of behavior whose moral status is the subject of genuinely conflicting beliefs. So if the conflicting beliefs referred to in P2 concern the permissibility of acts of homosexual behavior, then P4 is false. Similarly, if the state refuses to sanction same-sex marriage and permits private homosexual acts between consenting adults, it does not resolve the conflicting beliefs about the moral permissibility of acts of homosexual behavior by accommodation. Rather, it simply declares that one side of the conflict is the correct side, namely, the side that believes that such acts are permissible. Doing so thus renders P3 false as well. So either way that we specify the meaning of the claim made in P2, the argument as a whole proves to be unsound.

III

A second objection to Jordan's argument takes the form of a reductio ad absurdum: if the state should refuse to sanction same-sex marriage because it is the subject of a moral impasse, then it should also refuse to sanction mixed-race marriage on the same ground. But the claim that the state should refuse to sanction mixed-race marriage is surely intolerable. So, therefore, is Jordan's argument. Jordan provides three responses to this objection, but none of them are satisfactory.

His first response is that unlike the issue of same-sex marriage, the issue of mixed-race marriages "does not seem to generate much, if any, controversy today." On this account, there is no such public dilemma in the first place, and so it does not matter that Jordan's position would justify forbidding mixed-race marriage if there were. This response is unsuccessful for two reasons. First, it is not at all clear that there is no such dilemma about mixed-race marriage. In many communities in the South, at least, there remains substantial opposition to interracial *dating,* let alone interracial marriage. And although such opposition is traditionally associated with white racists, there is a more recent and hardly less heated controversy within the black community in all parts of the country about whether or not black men, in particular, have an obligation to marry black women.[3] Second, and more importantly, even if Jordan is right that there is no longer a moral impasse on this issue, this response makes the impermissibility of laws forbidding mixed-race marriage contingent on this fact. And surely such laws were impermissible even when many racists supported them.

Jordan's second response to the mixed-race objection is to say that even if it does represent a public dilemma, it is one in which there is an overriding reason in favor of resolution by declaration. The reason is that "it is a settled matter that state protection from racial discrimination is a reason sufficient for a resolution via declaration" while the same is not true of protection from discrimination according to sexual orientation. This response fails for the simple reason that a law banning mixed-race marriages does not discriminate against people on racial grounds. It says that *every* person, regardless of race, is free to marry anyone else of his or her race, and that *every* person, regardless of race, is prohibited from marrying anyone else of some other race. A white person who falls in love with a black person is adversely affected in just the same way as is [a] black person who falls in love with a white person. And since every black–white couple consists of one black person and one white person, the total number of blacks and whites who are adversely affected in this way is the same. As a result, a law recognizing mixed-race marriage does not protect anyone from racial discrimination that would occur without such a law.

A law forbidding same-sex marriage, it is worth noting, is fundamentally different in this respect. It says that a heterosexual man can marry any member of the sex he is attracted to while a homosexual man can marry any member of the sex he is *not* attracted to, and that a heterosexual man is forbidden to marry any member of the sex that he is not attracted to while a homosexual man is forbidden to marry any member of the sex that he *is* attracted to. This law does discriminate by sexual orientation, since all of the people who are adversely affected by it (at least directly) are homosexuals. And thus a law recognizing same-sex marriage does protect people from discrimination on the basis of sexual orientation that would otherwise occur without such a law. In short, laws banning mixed-race marriage treat people of all races equally while laws banning same-sex marriage do not treat people of all sexual orientations equally. So Jordan has failed to show that there is an overriding reason for the state to resolve the mixed-race marriage issue by declaration that does not also apply to the case of same-sex marriages. Indeed, if anything, he has pointed to an overriding reason to resolve the same-sex marriage issue by declaration that does not apply to the mixed-race marriage issue.

Jordan's final response to the mixed-race marriage objection turns on his attempt to identify a second disanalogy between the two cases: "A same-sex marriage would involve behavior which many people find morally objectionable; a mixed-race marriage is objectionable to some, not because of the participants' behavior, but because of the racial identity of the participants." And since objections based on a person's identity are different from objections based on a person's behavior, it does not follow from the fact that the objection to mixed-race marriage should be overruled by a resolution by declaration that the objection to same-sex marriage should also be overruled in this manner.

This response must be rejected because it rests on a misdescription of the view held by those who object to mixed-race marriage. It is not that they object to the *identity* of the individuals involved. White racists need not have anything against blacks marrying other blacks, and black separatists surely have nothing against white people marrying other whites. It is not the identity of the individuals that they object to, but the act they perform: the act of weakening the purity of the race, or of violating the obligation to put one's own community first. In this sense, they are no different from the antihomosexual people Jordan describes: they say they object not to what homosexuals are, but to what they do.

IV

I have argued that Jordan's argument is unsound, and I have argued that it is subject to an important objection by reductio ad absurdum. In doing this, I have accepted Jordan's claim that if his argument succeeds, it does so without depending on any claims about the moral status of homosexuality. I want to conclude by questioning this claim.

I do so by raising a question about the one premise about same-sex marriage that I have to this point set aside. This is the claim made by P5 that there is no overriding reason for the state to resolve the public dilemma about same-sex marriage by declaration. Jordan does not provide specific criteria for distinguishing overriding reasons from less weighty ones, but his comment that they typically involve "the protection of generally recognized rights" seems to me sufficient for my purposes. The claim that a right is a generally recognized one can be taken in two distinct ways. In the case of the United States prior to the Civil War, for example, there is one sense in which the right not to be enslaved was a generally recognized one. If you tried to enslave a white person during this period, it would have been generally recognized that you were violating his rights. But there is another sense in which the right not to be enslaved was not generally recognized, since it was not generally recognized that it was enjoyed by all people regardless of race.

Now if a right must be generally recognized in this second sense in order for there to be an overriding reason for the state to take sides in a public dilemma, then Jordan will be unable to account for the fact that the morally right thing for the state to do was to abolish slavery. Indeed, if this is what is needed in order for there to be an overriding reason for the state to so act, then P5 will be vacuous: if a right is generally recognized in this sense, there will for that very reason be no public dilemma about it. So the argument can only succeed if the rights that suffice to underwrite an overriding reason in

P5 are ones that are widely agreed to be held by most people, even if many people refrain from attributing them to all people. And this is what creates the final problem with Jordan's argument. For surely it is widely agreed that most people have a right to marry whomever they wish, and to have their marriage publicly recognized. Suppose that the government announced that, starting tomorrow, the state would no longer sanction marriages between heterosexual Jews. For purposes of taxes, child custody, property ownership, next-of-kin visitation rights, and so on, there would no longer be a distinction between married heterosexual Jewish couples and pairs of Jewish people of opposite sexes who happen to live in the same dwelling. Most people would regard this as outrageous. And although I am sympathetic toward those who complain that the language of rights is too often stretched beyond reason, I suspect that most people would object to the edict by saying that it violated a very commonly recognized right, the right of consenting adults to marry whomever they please and to have their marriages publicly recognized. But if it is generally recognized that this is a right that most people have, even if it is not generally recognized that this is a right that all people have, then this is sufficient to establish that there is an overriding reason to resolve the dilemma by declaration in favor of same-sex marriage. It is not sufficient only if there is some morally relevant difference between homosexuals and heterosexuals, just as it would not be sufficient if there were some morally relevant difference between Jews and non-Jews.

Now I do not mean to suggest that this argument provides anything like a conclusive resolution of the debate about same-sex marriage. It is simply the first step that then leaves open any number of responses that might be given to undermine the claim that if heterosexuals have the right to marry whomever they please then so do homosexuals. My point here is simply that it is very difficult to see how any such response could succeed in vindicating P5 without at some point depending at least in part on the claim that there is a morally relevant difference between homosexuals and heterosexuals or between homosexual and heterosexual relationships. This is precisely the sort of argument that Jordan's argument was meant to avoid. And this suggests that even if his argument were not subject to the objections I have presented in the previous two sections, it would still prove incapable of accomplishing the task it set out to accomplish.

Notes

1. *Journal of Social Philosophy,* 25, no. 1 (Spring 1995), reprinted in Robert M. Baird and Stuart E. Rosenbaum, eds., *Same-Sex Marriage: The Moral and Legal Debate* (Amherst, NY: Prometheus Books, 1997), 72–83. . . .

2. It is also worth noting that from the mere claim that a certain kind of behavior is morally impermissible, it does not follow that the state should not sanction marriages between people who engage in such behavior. There are genuinely conflicting moral beliefs about the permissibility of abortion, contraception, pornography, sexual promiscuity, and the use of animals in medical research, to name but a few, but there is no parallel

conflict over whether or not the state should sanction marriages between pornographers, animal researchers, people who use contraception or perform abortion, or who have long and varied sexual histories.

3. That this debate cannot be easily dismissed is shown by Charles W. Mills, "Do Black Men Have a Moral Duty to Marry Black Women?" *Journal of Social Philosophy,* 25th Anniversary Special Issue (1994), 131–53.

POSTSCRIPT

Is It Right to Prohibit Same-Sex Marriage?

Marriage has rather surprisingly changed over time. For example, both now and in the past (as recorded in the Old Testament, for example), there are cases of men with several wives—indeed, King Solomon is said to have had 700 wives and 300 concubines! More recently, interracial marriages have been banned, and then later allowed, in several states. Currently, civil unions for homosexuals are available in Vermont, and several American and Canadian jurisdictions are considering, or have already performed, gay marriages. Meanwhile, there is much heated discussion among both elected lawmakers and the public at large.

Generally, we want to live in a society that is not tied to a specific religion—for we want to recognize diversity and to grant freedom of religion—but we don't want to live in a society that has no specific values; nor do we want to live in a society that allows people to do whatever they want. (We can't allow absolute freedom because we want to maintain some rights against people who are not allowed to transgress those rights.) Hence, we need to draw some lines. The question is whether we should include same-sex marriage inside the line or not.

One general approach that is often recognized by both proponents and opponents of gay marriage is what might be called *liberalism* (in the classical sense): liberalism recognizes that individuals have rights, and that those rights should extend as far as possible until they start to interfere with the rights of other individuals. Classical liberalism is also committed to refraining from endorsing controversial conceptions of the good—it is neutral in this respect. For example, if some people prefer to spend their time reading literary classics (and this is part of *their* conception of "the good"), while other people spend their time playing video games (and this is part of *their* conception of "the good"), the government is not to say that one group of people has the correct conception of the good—it is to remain neutral and let the different parties pursue happiness along the paths that they themselves determine (as long as no rights are violated).

It might seem that classical liberalism must automatically support same-sex marriage. After all, the parties to the marriage are acting according to their own conception of the good, and they are not violating anyone else's rights. But Jeff Jordan has argued that there are several different models of marriage, and that a state endorsement of same-sex marriage *would* endorse one of these as right. So in recognizing same-sex marriage, the state wouldn't be neutral. It would be illiberal. Jonathan Rauch, on the other hand, has argued that the institution of marriage exerts a powerful stabilizing force and contributes to the well-being of society, and is something that *should* be recognized.

This issue is not only about gay rights and the social acceptance of gays, but also about our idea of marriage. It is worthwhile examining Jordan's models and his argumentation to see exactly what is acceptable and what is not.

Relevant literature here includes David Moats, *Civil War: A Battle for Gay Marriage* (Harcourt, 2004); George Chauncey, *Why Marriage? The History Shaping Today's Debate over Gay Equality* (Basic Books, 2004); Evan Wolfson, *Why Marriage Matters: America, Equality, and Gay People's Right to Marry* (Simon & Schuster, 2004); and the TFP Committee on American Issues, *Defending a Higher Law: Why We Must Resist Same-Sex "Marriage" and the Homosexual Movement* (The American Society for the Defense of Tradition, Family and Property, 2004).

ISSUE 6

Should Human Cloning Be Banned?

YES: Michael J. Sandel, from "The Ethical Implications of Human Cloning," *Perspectives in Biology and Medicine* (Spring 2005)

NO: John A. Robertson, from "Human Cloning and the Challenge of Regulation," *The New England Journal of Medicine* (July 9, 1998)

ISSUE SUMMARY

YES: Political philosopher Michael J. Sandel argues that much of the talk about cloning revolves around a few limited concepts (e.g., rights, autonomy, and the supposed unnaturalness of asexual reproduction) that are inadequate and fail to express what is really wrong with cloning. We need, instead, to address fundamental questions about our stance toward nature.

NO: Law professor John A. Robertson maintains that there should not be a complete ban on human cloning but that regulatory policy should be focused on ensuring that it is performed in a responsible manner.

The issue of human cloning requires careful consideration. Each person is believed to be uniquely valuable. Also, many prefer to differentiate humans from animals. If it is accepted that the same technology that allows for the cloning of sheep can also be applied to the cloning of humans, both of these ideas are brought into question. In light of animal cloning, the existence of humans seems to be based on the very same biological processes that exist in sheep and other animals. And if there can be such a thing as human cloning, what happens to the idea that we are all unique? What happens to the idea that we all have our individual lives to lead, and that each person is responsible for his or her own choices?

Moreover, cloning can change ideas about reproduction. In cloning, no male is required. Consider the case of Dolly, the sheep cloned from the cell of an adult ewe. An egg cell, taken from a female sheep, had its nucleus removed; this was replaced with the nucleus of a cell taken from another female sheep. Then the result was implanted and grew in the uterus of a third female sheep, who eventually gave birth to Dolly. Normally, a newborn has genetic input from both the father's side and the mother's side, with the mother supplying the egg cell. But the original egg cell that was used in Dolly's case contributed almost nothing in this regard. The nucleus from the cell of the other sheep contained virtually all of the genetic input for Dolly.

Identical twins are familiar cases of human beings who, like clones, share a common genetic input. When environmental factors connected with identical twins are closely the same, and when they have similar clothes, haircut, etc., they can be difficult to tell apart. But when the environmental factors that impinge on their lives are quite different—as in the case of twins separated at birth—the twins can be quite different in obvious physical ways.

Physical aspects such as height have both genetic and environmental inputs; two people with the same genetic input can have quite different heights if environmental conditions (e.g., their diets) are different.

In some ways, clones are like identical twins, but in many cases there would be far less resemblance between clones than between identical twins, since they would be subject to very different environmental factors. Being conceived and born at different times—perhaps years or even decades apart from each other—they may have radically different environmental input.

Human cloning can be seen as beneficial. Cloning may provide another way for people to utilize technological assistance in reproduction. For example, a couple who could not have children naturally might consider a range of options, including cloning. Some maintain that is a relatively innocent use of human cloning, and can benefit those who are infertile.

Some object to cloning by citing other possible scenarios. Suppose a person wanted numerous clones of himself or herself. Suppose a sports star desired a clone who would then be expected to achieve greatness in sports. Suppose parents wanted a replacement for a child that they had lost, or want a child who could serve as a bone marrow or organ donor. These cases may give some pause, since the motivation for cloning appears to be questionable.

To counter this argument, it is stated that proper regulation would prevent these types of scenarios from occurring. Instead, cloning would be performed only under the correct circumstances, and would promote individual happiness.

In the following selections, Michael Sandel argues that there is something deeply wrong with human cloning. What is wrong goes beyond questions of rights, autonomy, and cloning's supposed "unnaturalness." It involves our fundamental attitudes toward nature and human existence. John A. Robertson counters that human cloning, if properly regulated, need not and would not be sinister. Properly regulated, human cloning should be permitted.

YES

Michael J. Sandel

The Ethical Implications of Human Cloning

In this essay, I will consider the ethics of reproductive and therapeutic cloning. But I want also to advance a more general claim: that the cloning issue, and related debates about genetic engineering, will change the way philosophers think about their subject. Much of the debate about cloning and genetic engineering is conducted in the familiar language of autonomy, consent, and individual rights. Defenders of "liberal eugenics" argue that parents should be free to enhance the genetic traits of their children for the sake of improving their life prospects (Agar 1999; Buchanan et al. 2000; Dworkin 2000). Ronald Dworkin, for example argues that there is nothing wrong with the ambition "to make the lives of future generations of human beings longer and more full of talent and hence achievement." In fact, he maintains, the principle of ethical individualism makes such efforts obligatory (Dworkin 2000, p. 452). Many opponents of cloning and genetic engineering also invoke the language of autonomy and rights. For example, Jurgen Habermas (2003) worries that even favorable genetic enhancements may impair the autonomy and individuality of children by pointing them toward particular life choices, hence violating their right to choose their life plans for themselves.

But talk of autonomy and rights does not address the deepest questions posed by cloning. In order to grapple with the ethical implications of cloning and genetic engineering, we need to confront questions largely lost from view in the modern world—questions about the moral status of nature and about the proper stance of human beings toward the given world. Since questions such as these verge on theology, or at least involve a certain view of the best way for human beings to live their lives, modern philosophers and political theorists tend to shrink from them. But our new powers of biotechnology make these questions unavoidable.

In the United States today, no federal law prohibits human cloning, either for purposes of reproduction or for purposes of biomedical research. This is not because most people favor reproductive cloning. To the contrary, public opinion and almost all elected officials oppose it. But there is strong disagreement about whether to permit cloning for biomedical research. And the opponents of cloning for biomedical research have so far been unwilling to support a separate ban on reproductive cloning, as Britain has enacted. Because of this stalemate, no federal ban on cloning has been enacted.

From *Perspectives in Biology and Medicine,* vol. 48, no. 2, Spring 2005, pp. 241–247. Copyright © 2005 by Johns Hopkins University Press. Reprinted by permission.

The Ethics of Reproductive Cloning

I turn first to the ethics of reproductive cloning, and then to cloning for biomedical research. The case for banning human reproductive cloning is not difficult to make, at least for now. Most scientists agree that it is unsafe and likely to lead to serious abnormalities and birth defects. But suppose that, one day, producing a baby through cloning were no more risky than natural reproduction. Many believe—and I agree—that it would still be ethically objectionable. But it is not easy to say why.

The autonomy argument against cloning is not persuasive, for it wrongly implies that, absent a genetically designing parent, children can choose their physical characteristics for themselves. But none of us has a right to choose our genetic inheritance. The alternative to a cloned or genetically enhanced child is not an autonomous one, but a child at the mercy of the genetic lottery.

Some argue that cloning is wrong because it departs from natural, sexual procreation (Kass and Wilson 1998). But this objection also fails to reach the heart of the matter. What makes reproductive cloning morally troubling is that its primary purpose is to create children of a certain kind. In this respect, it is similar to other forms of genetic engineering by which parents seek to choose the traits of their children—sex, eye color, perhaps one day even their intellectual attributes, athletic prowess, and musical ability. Although a few eccentric narcissists might aspire to create genetic replicas of themselves, the real market for designer children lies elsewhere, in the desire of parents to produce children with genetic traits superior to their own.

The desire to control the genetic characteristics of one's offspring points to the heart of the ethical issue. The moral problem with reproductive cloning lies not in its asexual character, but in its assault on the understanding of children as gifts rather than possessions, or projects of our will, or vehicles for our happiness.

It might be replied that cloning and genetic engineering are in principle no different from other ways in which parents go to great lengths to produce children of a certain kind, or "designer children." But rather than giving us reason to embrace cloning, this observation may give us reason to worry about existing practices of childrearing.

What is most troubling about human cloning and bioengineering is not that they represent a radical departure, but that they carry to full expression troubling tendencies already present in our culture, especially in the way we regard and treat children. We have already traveled some distance down the path of regarding children as vehicles for our own ambitions or fulfillment. Consider the chilling discrepancy in sex ratios in China, South Korea, and parts of India, where boys now outnumber girls by up to 30% (Eberstadt 2002). But think also of the enormous pressure parents put on children in the United States and many other Western societies to qualify for admission to the best schools—not only at the university level, but even, in Manhattan at least, at the preschool level. Sometimes, the drive to produce successful children begins even earlier. The Harvard college newspaper recently carried an advertisement from a couple seeking an egg donor. They did not want just any egg donor.

The ad specified that the donor should be attractive, athletic, at least 5 feet, 10 inches tall, and with a college entrance exam score of 1400 or above. For an egg from a donor meeting these stringent qualifications, the couple was offering a payment of $50,000 (Kolata 1999).

The notion that the project of mastery and choice is subject to certain limits is at odds with the spirit of contemporary liberalism. That is why many who are uneasy with human cloning try to cast their objections in the language of autonomy and rights, arguing that choosing the traits of one's children, by cloning or otherwise, violates their rights. The European Assembly has maintained, for example, that human cloning is wrong because it is a violation of human rights. But the language of rights misses the point. The problem is not that parents usurp the autonomy of the child they design: it is not as if the child could otherwise choose her gender, height, and eye color for herself. The problem lies in the hubris of the designing parents, in their drive to master the mystery of birth. Even if this hubris does not make parents tyrants to their children, it disfigures the relation of parent and child. It deprives the parents of the humility and enlarged human sympathies that an openness to the unbidden "otherness" of our progeny can cultivate.

Like the autonomy objection, the argument that focuses on the asexual character of reproductive cloning misses the point. Understood simply as a departure from sexual procreation, cloning would not represent a serious threat. Sex will survive perfectly well on its own—without the help of federal legislation. By contrast, the sense of life as a gift we cannot summon or control is fragile and vulnerable. In the face of the Promethean drive to mastery that animates modern societies, an appreciation of the giftedness of life is in constant need of support.

The Ethics of Cloning for Biomedical Research

I turn now to the ethics of cloning for biomedical research. It is here that the greatest disagreement prevails. The U.S. Senate is split between those who want to ban all cloning and those who want to ban reproductive cloning but not cloning for stem cell research and regenerative medicine. (For the American debate on cloning, see President's Council 2002.) As in the case of reproductive cloning, the concepts of autonomy and rights cannot by themselves resolve the moral question. In order to assess the moral permissibility of cloning for stem cell research, we need to determine the moral status of the early embryo. If the six-day, pre-implantation embryo (or blastocyst) is morally equivalent to a person, then it is wrong to extract stem cells from it, even for the sake of curing devastating diseases such as Parkinson's, Alzheimer's, or diabetes. If the embryo is a person, then not only should all therapeutic cloning be banned, so also should all embryonic stem cell research.

Before turning to the moral status of the embryo, I would like to consider one influential argument against cloning for biomedical research that stops short of opposing embryonic stem cell research as such. Some opponents of research cloning, troubled by the deliberate creation of embryos for research, support embryonic stem cell research, provided it uses "spare" embryos left over from fertility clinics (Sandel 2002). Since in vitro fertilization (IVF) clinics (at least in the United States) create many more fertilized eggs than are ultimately implanted, some argue that there is nothing wrong with using those spares for research: if excess embryos would be discarded anyway, why not use them (with donor consent) for potentially life-saving research?

This seems to be a sensible distinction. But on closer examination, it does not hold up. The distinction fails because it begs the question whether the "spare" embryos should be created in the first place. If it is immoral to create and sacrifice embryos for the sake of curing or treating devastating diseases, why isn't it also objectionable to create and discard spare IVF embryos in the course of treating infertility? Or, to look at the argument from the opposite end, if the creation and sacrifice of embryos in IVF is morally acceptable, why isn't the creation and sacrifice of embryos for stem cell research also acceptable? After all, both practices serve worthy ends, and curing diseases such as Parkinson's is at least as important as enabling infertile couples to have genetically related children.

Of course, bioethics is not only about ends, but also about means. Those who oppose creating embryos for research argue that doing so is exploitative and fails to accord embryos the respect they are due. But the same argument could be made against fertility treatments that create excess embryos bound for destruction. In fact, a recent study found that some 400,000 frozen embryos are languishing in American fertility clinics, with another 52,000 in the United Kingdom and 71,000 in Australia (Wade 2003).

If my argument is correct, it shows only that stem cell research on IVF spares and on embryos created for research (whether natural or cloned) are morally on a par. This conclusion can be accepted by people who hold very different views about the moral status of the embryo. If cloning for stem cell research violates the respect the embryo is due, then so does stem cell research on IVF spares, and so does any version of IVF that creates and discards excess embryos. If, morally speaking, these practices stand or fall together, it remains to ask whether they stand or fall. And that depends on the moral status of the embryo.

The Moral Status of the Embryo

There are three possible ways of conceiving the moral status of the embryo: as a thing, as a person, or as something in between. To regard an embryo as a mere thing, open to any use we may desire or devise, is, it seems to me, to miss its significance as nascent human life. One need not regard an embryo as a full human person in order to believe that it is due a certain respect. Personhood is not the only warrant for respect: we consider it a failure of respect when a thoughtless hiker carves his initials in an ancient sequoia, not because we regard the sequoia as a person, but because we consider it a natural wonder worthy of appreciation and awe—modes of regard inconsistent with treating it as a billboard or defacing it for the sake of petty vanity. To respect the old growth forest does not mean that no tree may ever be felled or harvested for human purposes. Respecting the forest may be consistent with using it. But the purposes should be weighty and appropriate to the wondrous nature of the thing.

One way to oppose a degrading, objectifying stance toward nascent human life is to attribute full personhood to the embryo. I will call this the "equal moral status" view. One way of assessing this view is to play out its full implications, in order to assess their plausibility. Consider the following hypothetical: a fire breaks out in a fertility clinic, and you have time to save either a five-year-old girl or a tray of 10 embryos. Would it be wrong to save the girl?[1]

A further implication of the equal moral status view is that harvesting stem cells from a six-day-old blastocyst is as morally abhorrent as harvesting organs from a baby. But is it? If so, the penalty provided in the proposed U.S. anti-cloning legislation—a $1 million fine and 10 years in prison—is woefully inadequate. If embryonic stem cell research is morally equivalent to yanking organs from babies, it should be treated as a grisly form of murder, and the scientist who performs it should face life imprisonment or the death penalty.

A further source of difficulty for the equal moral status view lies in the fact that, in natural pregnancies, at least half of all embryos either fail to implant or are otherwise lost. It might be replied that a high rate of infant mortality does not justify infanticide. But the way we respond to the natural loss of embryos or even early miscarriages suggests that we do not regard these events as the moral or religious equivalent of infant mortality. Otherwise, wouldn't we carry out the same burial rituals for the loss of an embryo that we observe for the death of a child?

The conviction that the embryo is a person derives support not only from certain religious doctrines but also from the Kantian assumption that the moral universe is divided in binary terms: everything is either a person, worthy of respect, or a thing, open to use. But this dualism is overdrawn.

The way to combat the instrumentalizing impulse of modern technology and commerce is not to insist on an all-or-nothing ethic of respect for persons that consigns the rest of life to a utilitarian calculus. Such an ethic risks turning every moral question into a battle over the bounds of personhood. We would do better to cultivate a more expansive appreciation of life as a gift that commands our reverence and restricts our use. Human cloning to create designer babies is the ultimate expression of the hubris that marks the loss of reverence for life as a gift. But stem cell research to cure debilitating disease, using six-day-old blastocysts, cloned or uncloned, is a noble exercise of our human ingenuity to promote healing and to play our part in repairing the given world.

Those who warn of slippery slopes, embryo farms, and the commodification of ova and zygotes are right to worry but wrong to assume that cloning for biomedical research necessarily opens us to these dangers. Rather than ban stem cell cloning and other forms of embryo research, we should allow it to proceed subject to regulations that embody the moral restraint appropriate to the mystery of the first stirrings of human life. Such regulations should include licensing requirements for embryo research projects and fertility clinics, restrictions on the commodification of eggs and sperm, and measures to prevent proprietary interests from monopolizing access to stem cell lines. This approach, it seems to me, offers the best hope of avoiding the wanton use of nascent human life and making these biomedical advances a blessing for health rather than an episode in the erosion of our human sensibilities.

Note

1. I am indebted to George Annas for this hypothetical (see Annas 1989).

References

Agar, N. 1999. Liberal eugenics. In *Bioethics,* ed. H. Kuhse and P. Singer. Oxford: Blackwell.

Annas, G. J. 1989. A French homunculus in a Tennessee court. *Hastings Cent Rep* 19(6): 20–22.

Buchanan, A., et al. 2000. *From chance to choice: Genetics and justice.* Cambridge: Cambridge Univ. Press.

Dworkin, R. 2000. Playing God: Genes, clones, and luck. In *Sovereign virtue: The theory and practice of equality,* 427–52. Cambridge: Harvard Univ. Press.

Eberstadt, N. 2002. Testimony to President's Council on Bioethics, Oct. 17. . . .

Habermas, J. 2003. *The future of human nature.* Cambridge, UK: Polity Press.

Kass, L. R., and J. Q. Wilson. 1998. *The ethics of human cloning.* Washington, DC: AEI Press.

Kolata, G. 1999. $50,000 offered to tall, smart egg donor. *NY Times,* March 3.

President's Council on Bioethics. 2002. *Human cloning and human dignity: The report of the President's Council on Bioethics.* Washington, DC: President's Council on Bioethics. Repr. New York: Public Affairs, 2002. . . .

Sandel, M. J. 2002. The anti-cloning conundrum. *NY Times,* May 28.

Wade, N. 2003. Clinics hold more embryos than had been thought. *NY Times,* May 9.

John A. Robertson  **NO**

Human Cloning and the Challenge of Regulation

The birth of Dolly, the sheep cloned from a mammary cell of an adult ewe, has initiated a public debate about human cloning. Although cloning of humans may never be clinically feasible, discussion of the ethical, legal, and social issues raised is important. Cloning is just one of several techniques potentially available to select, control, or alter the genome of offspring.[1-3] The development of such technology poses an important social challenge: how to ensure that the technology is used to enhance, rather than limit, individual freedom and welfare.

A key ethical question is whether a responsible couple, interested in rearing healthy offspring biologically related to them, might ethically choose to use cloning (or other genetic-selection techniques) for that purpose. The answer should take into account the benefits sought through the use of the techniques and any potential harm to offspring or to other interests.

The most likely uses of cloning would be far removed from the bizarre or horrific scenarios that initially dominated media coverage.[4] Theoretically, cloning would enable rich or powerful persons to clone themselves several times over, and commercial entrepreneurs might hire women to bear clones of sports or entertainment celebrities to be sold to others to rear. But current reproductive techniques can also be abused, and existing laws against selling children would apply to those created by cloning.

There is no reason to think that the ability to clone humans will cause many people to turn to cloning when other methods of reproduction would enable them to have healthy children. Cloning a human being by somatic-cell nuclear transfer, for example, would require a consenting person as a source of DNA, eggs to be enucleated and then fused with the DNA, a woman who would carry and deliver the child, and a person or couple to raise the child. Given this reality, cloning is most likely to be sought by couples who, because of infertility, a high risk of severe genetic disease, or other factors, cannot or do not wish to conceive a child.

Several plausible scenarios can be imagined. Rather than use sperm, egg, or embryo from anonymous donors, couples who are infertile as a result of gametic insufficiency might choose to clone one of the partners. If the husband were the source of the DNA and the wife provided the egg that received the nuclear transfer and then gestated the fetus, they would have a child biologically related to each of them and would not need to rely on anonymous gamete or embryo donation. Of course, many infertile couples might still prefer gamete or embryo donation or adoption. But there is nothing inherently wrong in wishing to be biologically related to one's children, even when this goal cannot be achieved through sexual reproduction.

A second plausible application would be for a couple at high risk of having offspring with a genetic disease.[5] Couples in this situation must now choose whether to risk the birth of an affected child, to undergo prenatal or preimplantation diagnosis and abortion or the discarding of embryos, to accept gamete donation, to seek adoption, or to remain childless. If cloning were available, however, some couples, in line with prevailing concepts of kinship, family, and parenting, might strongly prefer to clone one of themselves or another family member. Alternatively, if they already had a healthy child, they might choose to use cloning to create a later-born twin of that child. In the more distant future, it is even possible that the child whose DNA was replicated would not have been born healthy but would have been made healthy by gene therapy after birth.

A third application relates to obtaining tissue or organs for transplantation. A child who needed an organ or tissue transplant might lack a medically suitable donor. Couples in this situation have sometimes conceived a child coitally in the hope that he or she would have the correct tissue type to serve, for example, as a bone marrow donor for an older sibling.[6, 7] If the child's disease was not genetic, a couple might prefer to clone the affected child to be sure that the tissue would match.

It might eventually be possible to procure suitable tissue or organs by cloning the source DNA only to the point at which stem cells or other material might be obtained for transplantation, thus avoiding the need to bring a child into the world for the sake of obtaining tissue.[8] Cloning a person's cells up to the embryo stage might provide a source of stem cells or tissue for the person cloned. Cloning might also be used to enable a couple to clone a dead or dying child so as to have that child live on in some closely related form, to obtain sufficient numbers of embryos for transfer and pregnancy, or to eliminate mitochondrial disease.[5]

Most, if not all, of the potential uses of cloning are controversial, usually because of the explicit copying of the genome. As the National Bioethics Advisory Commission noted, in addition to concern about physical safety and eugenics, somatic-cell cloning raises issues of the individuality, autonomy, objectification, and kinship of the resulting children.[5] In other instances, such as the production of embryos to serve as tissue banks, the ethical issue is the sacrifice of embryos created solely for that purpose.

Given the wide leeway now granted couples to use assisted reproduction and prenatal genetic selection in forming families, cloning should not be rejected in all circumstances as unethical or illegitimate. The manipulation of embryos and the use of gamete donors and surrogates are increasingly common. Most fetuses conceived in the United States and Western Europe are now screened for genetic or chromosomal anomalies. Before conception, screening to identify carriers of genetic diseases is widespread.[9] Such practices also deviate from conventional notions of reproduction, kinship, and medical treatment of infertility, yet they are widely accepted.

Despite the similarity of cloning to current practices, however, the dissimilarities should not be overlooked. The aim of most other forms of assisted reproduction is the birth of a child who is a descendant of at least one member of the couple, not an identical twin. Most genetic selection acts negatively to identify and screen out unwanted traits such as genetic disease, not positively to choose or replicate the genome as in somatic-cell cloning.[3] It is not clear, however, why a child's relation to his or her rearing parents must always be that of sexually reproduced descendant when such a relationship is not possible because of infertility or other factors. Indeed, in gamete donation and adoption, although sexual reproduction is involved, a full descendant relation between the child and both rearing parents is lacking. Nor should the difference between negative and positive means of selecting children determine the ethical or social acceptability of cloning or other techniques. In both situations, a deliberate choice is made so that a child is born with one genome rather than another or is not born at all.

Is cloning sufficiently similar to current assisted-reproduction and genetic-selection practices to be treated similarly as a presumptively protected exercise of family or reproductive liberty?[10] Couples who request cloning in the situations I have described are seeking to rear healthy children with whom they will have a genetic or biologic tie, just as couples who conceive their children sexually do. Whether described as "replication" or as "reproduction," the resort to cloning is similar enough in purpose and effects to other reproduction and genetic-selection practices that it should be treated similarly. Therefore, a couple should be free to choose cloning unless there are compelling reasons for thinking that this would create harm that the other procedures would not cause.[10]

The concern of the National Bioethics Advisory Commission about the welfare of the clone reflects two types of fear. The first is that a child with the same nuclear DNA as another person, who is thus that person's later-born identical twin, will be so severely harmed by the identity of nuclear DNA between them that it is morally preferable, if not obligatory, that the child not be born at all.[5] In this case the fear is that the later-born twin will lack individuality or the freedom to create his or her own identity because of confusion or expectations caused by having the same DNA as another person.[5, 11]

This claim does not withstand the close scrutiny that should precede interference with a couple's freedom to bear and rear biologically related children.[10] Having the same genome as another person is not in itself harmful, as widespread experience with monozygotic twins shows. Being a twin does not deny either twin his or her individuality or freedom, and twins often have a special intimacy or closeness that few non-twin siblings can experience.[12] There is no reason to think that being a later-born identical twin resulting from cloning would change the overall assessment of being a twin.

Differences in mitochondria and the uterine and childhood environment will undercut problems of similarity and minimize the risk of overidentification with the first twin. A clone of Smith may look like Smith, but he or she will not be Smith and will lack many of Smith's phenotypic characteristics. The effects of having similar DNA will also depend on the length of time before the second twin is born, on whether the twins are raised together, on whether they are informed that they are genetic twins, on whether other people are so informed, on the beliefs that the rearing parents have about genetic influence on behavior, and on other factors. Having a previously born twin might in some circumstances also prove to be a source of support or intimacy for the later-born child.

The risk that parents or the child will overly identify the child with the DNA source also seems surmountable. Would the child invariably be expected to match the phenotypic characteristics of the DNA source, thus denying the second twin an "open future" and the freedom to develop his or her own identity?[5, 11, 13] In response to this question, one must ask whether couples who choose to clone offspring are more likely to want a child who is a mere replica of the DNA source or a child who is unique and valued for more than his or her genes. Couples may use cloning in order to ensure that the biologic child they rear is healthy, to maintain a family connection in the face of gametic infertility, or to obtain matched tissue for transplantation and yet still be responsibly committed to the welfare of their child, including his or her separate identity and interests and right to develop as he or she chooses.

The second type of fear is that parents who choose their child's genome through somatic-cell cloning will view the child as a commodity or an object to serve their own ends.[5] We do not view children born through coital or assisted reproduction as "mere means" just because people reproduce in order to have company in old age, to fulfill what they see as God's will, to prove their virility, to have heirs, to save a relationship, or to serve other selfish purposes.[14] What counts is how a child is treated after birth. Self-interested motives for having children do not prevent parents from loving children for themselves once they are born.

The use of cloning to form families in the situations I have described, though closely related to current assisted-reproduction and genetic-selection practices, does offer unique variations. The novelty of the relation—cloning in lieu of sperm donation, for example, produces a later-born identical twin raised by the older twin and his spouse—will create special psychological and social challenges. Can these challenges be successfully met, so that cloning produces net good for families and society? Given the largely positive experience with assisted-reproduction techniques that initially appeared frightening, cautious optimism is justified. We should be able to develop procedures and guidelines for cloning that will allow us to obtain its benefits while minimizing its problems and dangers.

In the light of these considerations, I would argue that a ban on privately funded cloning research is unjustified and likely to hamper important types of research.[8] A permanent ban on the cloning of human beings, as advocated by the Council of Europe and proposed in Congress, is also unjustified.[15, 16] A more limited ban—whether for 5 years, as proposed by the National Bioethics Advisory Commission and enacted in California, or for 10 years, as in the bill of

Senator Dianne Feinstein (D-Calif.) and Senator Edward M. Kennedy (D-Mass.) that is now before Congress—is also open to question.[5, 17, 18] Given the early state of cloning science and the widely shared view that the transfer of cloned embryos to the uterus before the safety and efficacy of the procedure has been established is unethical, few responsible physicians are likely to offer human cloning in the near future.[5] Nor are profit-motivated entrepreneurs, such as Richard Seed, likely to have many customers for their cloning services until the safety of the procedure is demonstrated.[19] A ban on human cloning for a limited period would thus serve largely symbolic purposes. Symbolic legislation, however, often has substantial costs.[20, 21] A government-imposed prohibition on privately funded cloning, even for a limited period, should not be enacted unless there is a compelling need. Such a need has not been demonstrated.

Rather than seek to prohibit all uses of human cloning, we should focus our attention on ensuring that cloning is done well. No physician or couple should embark on cloning without careful thought about the novel relational issues and child-rearing responsibilities that will ensue. We need regulations or guidelines to ensure safety and efficacy, fully informed consent and counseling for the couple, the consent of any person who may provide DNA, guarantees of parental rights and duties, and a limit on the number of clones from any single source.[10] It may also be important to restrict cloning to situations where there is a strong likelihood that the couple or individual initiating the procedure will also rear the resulting child. This principle will encourage a stable parenting situation and minimize the chance that cloning entrepreneurs will create clones to be sold to others.[22] As our experience grows, some restrictions on who may serve as a source of DNA for cloning (for example, a ban on cloning one's parents) may also be defensible.[10]

Cloning is important because it is the first of several positive means of genetic selection that may be sought by families seeking to have and rear healthy, biologically related offspring. In the future, mitochondrial transplantation, germ-line gene therapy, genetic enhancement, and other forms of prenatal genetic alteration may be possible.[3, 23, 24] With each new technique, as with cloning, the key question will be whether it serves important health, reproductive, or family needs and whether its benefits outweigh any likely harm. Cloning illustrates the principle that when legitimate uses of a technique are likely, regulatory policy should avoid prohibition and focus on ensuring that the technique is used responsibly for the good of those directly involved. As genetic knowledge continues to grow, the challenge of regulation will occupy us for some time to come.

References

1. Silver LM. Remaking Eden: cloning and beyond in a brave new world. New York: Avon Books, 1997.
2. Walters L, Palmer JG. The ethics of human gene therapy. New York: Oxford University Press, 1997.
3. Robertson JA. Genetic selection of offspring characteristics. Boston Univ Law Rev 1996;76:421–82.

4. Begley S. Can we clone humans? Newsweek. March 10, 1997:53–60.

5. Cloning human beings: report and recommendations of the National Bioethics Advisory Commission. Rockville, Md.: National Bioethics Advisory Commission, June 1997.

6. Robertson JA. Children of choice: freedom and the new reproductive technologies. Princeton, N.J.: Princeton University Press, 1994.

7. Kearney W, Caplan AL. Parity for the donation of bone marrow: ethical and policy considerations. In: Blank RH, Bonnicksen AL, eds. Emerging issues in biomedical policy: an annual review. Vol. 1. New York: Columbia University Press, 1992:262–85.

8. Kassirer JP, Rosenthal NA. Should human cloning research be off limits? N Engl J Med 1998;338:905–6.

9. Holtzman NA. Proceed with caution: predicting genetic risks in the recombinant DNA era. Baltimore: Johns Hopkins University Press, 1989.

10. Robertson JA. Liberty, identity, and human cloning. Texas Law Rev 1998; 77:1371–456.

11. Davis DS. What's wrong with cloning? Jurimetrics 1997;38:83–9.

12. Segal NL. Behavioral aspects of intergenerational human cloning: what twins tell us. Jurimetrics 1997;38:57–68.

13. Jonas H. Philosophical essays: from ancient creed to technological man. Englewood Cliffs, N.J.: Prentice-Hall, 1974:161.

14. Heyd D. Genethics: moral issues in the creation of people. Berkeley: University of California Press, 1992.

15. Council of Europe. Draft additional protocol to the Convention on Human Rights and Biomedicine on the prohibition of cloning human beings with explanatory report and Parliamentary Assembly opinion (adopted September 22, 1997). XXXVI International Legal Materials 1415 (1997).

16. Human Cloning Prohibition Act, H.R. 923, S. 1601 (March 5, 1997).

17. Act of Oct. 4, 1997, ch. 688, 1997 Cal. Legis. Serv. 3790 (West, WESTLAW through 1997 Sess.).

18. Prohibition on Cloning of Human Beings Act, S. 1602, 105th Cong. (1998).

19. Stolberg SG. A small spark ignites debate on laws on cloning humans. New York Times. January 19, 1998:A1.

20. Gusfield J. Symbolic crusade: status politics and the American temperance movement. Urbana: University of Illinois Press, 1963.

21. Wolf SM. Ban cloning? Why NBAC is wrong. Hastings Cent Rep 1997;27(5):12.

22. Wilson JQ. The paradox of cloning. The Weekly Standard. May 26, 1997:23–7.

23. Zhang J, Grifo J, Blaszczyk A, et al. In vitro maturation of human preovulatory oocytes reconstructed by germinal vesicle transfer. Fertil Steril 1997; 68:Suppl:S1. abstract.

24. Bonnicksen AL. Transplanting nuclei between human eggs: implications for germ-line genetics. Politics and the Life Sciences. March 1998:3–10.

POSTSCRIPT

Should Human Cloning Be Banned?

The social and legal debates about cloning are appropriate because the technology is so fundamentally groundbreaking. Although no human beings have as yet been cloned, note that, as much as Sandel and Robertson disagree in the preceding readings, neither would think it advisable for human cloning to proceed in a totally free and unregulated way.

One problem that might seem small at first but is quite serious is that we do not have a good way of assimilating the new ideas of cloning into our vocabulary and thought. For example, we think of a baby as having both a father and a mother. But a clone would be made from a single person. The clone and the single original person would both have the same set of genes. This set of genes comes from the parents of the original person, who are also the parents, as viewed from one biological standpoint, of the clone. So, this creates a situation in which people can have children when they are very old (or possibly even after their death). Moreover, if the original person and the clone share the same genes, then they seem like identical twins. But they could be of vastly different ages; in fact, one of the "twins" could be an adoptive parent of the other. Thus, for example, if Mr. and Mrs. Jones decide to use Mrs. Jones's egg—but replaced with the nucleus of a cell from Mr. Jones, Mr. Jones could be considered as both father and twin brother of Baby Jones. In addition, we are confused about who the mother is here: it looks like it's Mrs. Jones, since she gave birth, but it also looks like it's the mother of Mr. Jones, since she provided maternal genetic input to Mr. Jones's cells. And what of Baby Jones? Is Baby Jones the child of Mr. and Mrs. Jones—or perhaps a delayed twin of Mr. Jones? Our kinship concepts do not seem to apply, probably because these concepts were developed along other lines, long before cloning was ever imagined.

Some say that the fact that cloning doesn't fit into our normal system for making sense of family relationships is due to the fact that cloning upsets the system in a fundamental way. But others say that the fact that our traditional vocabulary is inadequate to the situation only shows that we are unprepared for this new situation, not that human cloning should be totally banned.

For the original bioethics report discussed by Robertson, see *Cloning Human Beings: Report and Recommendations of the National Bioethics Advisory Commission* (Gem Publications, 1998). A variety of views about cloning can be found in Gregory E. Pence, *Who's Afraid of Human Cloning?* (Rowman & Littlefield, 1998); Glenn McGee, ed., *The Human Cloning Debate* (Berkeley Hills Books, 1998); James C. Hefley and Lane P. Lester, *Human Cloning: Playing God or Scientific Progress?* (Fleming H. Revell, 1998); Gregory E. Pence, ed., *Flesh of My Flesh: The Ethics of Cloning Humans: A Reader* (Rowman & Littlefield, 1998); Martha Nussbaum and Cass R. Sunstein eds., *Clones and Clones: Facts and Fantasies About Human Cloning* (W. W. Norton, 1998); Lori B. Andrews, *The Clone Age: Adventures in the New World of Reproductive Technology* (Henry Holt, 1999); Michael C. Brannigan, ed., *Ethical Issues in Human Cloning: Cross-Disciplinary Perspectives* (Seven Bridges Press, 2000); Leon R. Kass, *Human Cloning and Human Dignity: The Report of the President's Council on Bioethics* (Public Affairs, 2002); Ian Wilmut and Roger Highfield, *After Dolly: The Promise and Perils of Cloning* (2007); and Aaron D. Levine, *Cloning: A Beginner's Guide* (Oneworld Publications, 2007).

Internet References . . .

Drugs

The Drug Reform Coordination Network (DRCN) sponsors this site of links to drug policy organizations and studies.

http://druglibrary.org

The Drug Enforcement Administration's Web site contains numerous useful links.

http://www.justice.gov/dea/index.htm

Affirmative Action

A collection of sites dealing with affirmative action has been posted by Yahoo! at:

http://dir.yahoo.com/society_and_culture/

issues_and_causes/affirmative_action/

Punishment and the Death Penalty

This *Ethics Updates* site contains discussion forums, court decisions, statistical resources, and Internet resources on the death penalty.

http://ethics.sandiego.edu/Applied/DeathPenalty/index.asp

Gun Control and Gun Rights

Numerous links regarding gun control and gun rites are on the following sites:

http://www.guncite.com/

http://jurist.law.pitt.edu/gunlaw.htm

Euthanasia and End-of-Life Decisions

This *Ethics Updates* site contains discussion questions, court decisions, statistical resources, and Internet resources on euthanasia and physician-assisted suicide.

http://ethics.sandiego.edu/Applied/Euthanasia/index.asp

Law and Society

*L*iving in groups is part of the social nature of human beings. And this requires that we have laws or rules that govern our behavior and interpersonal interactions. Morality and shared values can be positive tools for social living. One presupposition in a democratic society is that social differences must be settled by open discussion, argument, and persuasion—not by force. The issues in this section include some that have strongly divided our own society and some that currently challenge existing social institutions and practices.

- Is Cloning Pets Ethically Justified?
- Should Congress Allow the Buying and Selling of Human Organs?
- Should Drugs Be Legalized?
- Is Price Gouging Wrong?
- Is Affirmative Action Fair?
- Should the Death Penalty Be Abolished?
- Is Torture Ever Justified?
- Is Physician-Assisted Suicide Wrong?

ISSUE 7

Is Cloning Pets Ethically Justified?

YES: Autumn Fiester, from "Creating Fido's Twin: Can Pet Cloning Be Ethically Justified?" *Hastings Center Report* (July/August 2005)

NO: Hilary Bok, from "Cloning Companion Animals Is Wrong," *Journal of Applied Animal Welfare Science* (vol. 5, no. 3, 2002)

ISSUE SUMMARY

YES: Autumn Fiester argues in support of cloning animals (in particular, people's pets). She emphasizes the point that pet owners really care about their pets. One result of this is that they spend large amounts of money on veterinary care for their pets. Cloning their pets could serve as a useful extension of this idea—and also serve as a positive demonstration of society in general that individual pets have intrinsic value and cannot simply be replaced by new pets.

NO: Hilary Bok argues that cloning pets is immoral first of all because it causes great harm to animals. The animal that results from cloning, for example, is much more likely to have physical defects than the animal from which it was cloned. Moreover, the process of cloning itself necessarily involves harm to other animals (e.g., the animal that will carry the new pet to term). Finally, the end result simply does not provide pet owners with what they were looking for.

The idea of cloning pets rather than human beings raises some interesting questions for both issues. If there is virtually nothing different between human beings and pets, then the answers to the questions in the issues should be the same. If there is a difference in the answers, then some further explanation should be given in order to show that two different answers are required.

But even if we just consider cloning pets, many questions are raised. For one thing, there are factual (empirical, often scientific) questions about what exactly a clone of a pet is. So, for example, we might wonder about the extent, if any, that it is true to think that having a clone of your beloved pet dog Fido is a way of having Fido live on—or admitting that he died, but bringing him back to life—or having Fido as a puppy all over again—or an exercise in nostalgia perhaps, harkening back to days when Fido was your faithful companion. But further, if it is true (as I think we can all agree) that cloning Fido does not bring him back to life, suppose that a certain percentage of pet owners think that this is indeed the case and want to have the cloning done. In general, even if we can establish the actual truth with respect to factual and scientific matters, does it make a difference that pet owners might not be aware of the truth—or might be in a state of denial? Then there are further questions associated with the fact that some people have more money and resources than others, and might stand to benefit by the use of this cloning, while others, whose relationship with their pets is no different from that in the first group, are nevertheless unable to take advantage of this technology. Moreover, we might wonder whether the newly cloned pets (for example, Fido II) would be done a disservice since their owners might expect them to be just like the original Fido.

Note that the idea of cloning pets seems to be a special case, different from cloning other sorts of animals. We might think that the idea of cloning cows, for example, doesn't give us much pause, because of all the milk (and possibly meat) that they can provide, the benefits are widespread and clear. Anyway, that's the reason most people raise cows in the first place. The situation is similar in the case of animals (such as rats) cloned for scientific or medical research. If cloning animals in this context can provide researchers with important data or even cures for cancer, heart disease, etc., then again the benefit is widespread and clear. Of course, people who support the idea of animal rights might say that the benefits *to us* are clear—but the animals suffer. I think we should put this thought aside, at least for the moment, although it may arise again in the course of the argument about cloning pets. The key point for us right now is that these animals (both the agricultural kind and the laboratory kind) can contribute to human welfare as a whole, whereas the cloning of pets seems to benefit pet owners exclusively. So, whereas we can point to a general benefit (even if it is a benefit *for us*) that we derive from agricultural and laboratory animals, the point here is that these benefits are based on the animals' inpact on human beings in general, while cloning pets seems to benefit only certain private individuals.

Many of these issues arose in the case of the Missyplicity Project, for example. Here, wealthy owners of a dog named Missy spent millions of dollars in an attempt to clone her. Various scientific breakthroughs in the Missyplicity Project allowed the formation of a commercial enterprise, Genetic Savings and Clone, which aimed to clone pets. The following essays discuss these points, both in general and with specific reference to the Missyplicity Project and the commercial enterprise that grew from it. First, Autumn Fiester argues that pet cloning is indeed ethically justified; Hilary Bok argues that it is wrong.

YES

Autumn Fiester

Creating Fido's Twin: Can Pet Cloning Be Ethically Justified?

Commercial pet cloning—currently cats only—is now available from the firm Genetic Savings and Clone for the small price of $30,000. In December 2004, a nine-week-old cat clone was delivered to its owner, the first of six customers waiting for the identical twin of a beloved pet.[1] "Little Nicky," as he's known, has stirred up a great deal of ethical controversy, with more to come as the firm expands to dog cloning. . . .

For many, the cloning of companion animals seems morally suspect in a way that the cloning of animals for agricultural purposes or for biomedical research does not. In judging the ethics of cloning animals that will be healthier to eat or will advance science or medicine, there is a natural argument to be made that the technique will serve the greater human good. But in the case of pet cloning, there is really no analogous argument, however wonderful the original "Missy," the mixed-breed dog whose owner funded the now-famous Missyplicity Project at Texas A&M to make pet cloning possible. Cloned companion animals will not significantly enhance general human well-being. In balancing the cost to animals against the possible benefit to humans, the ethics of pet cloning seems to be a simple equation: a concern for animal welfare equals an anti-cloning stance.

But what if there were benefits to animals, and what if these benefits outweighed the pain and suffering they endure from cloning research and procedures? Then there would be an argument in favor of pet cloning at least as strong as those offered for cloning conducted for agriculture or medical research. The idea of animals suffering for *animal* benefit makes a tidy moral case that just might justify the practice.

Of course, making this case will be a challenge given the serious anti-cloning objections raised by animal advocacy organizations and cloning critics. But the benefit to animals that I will consider is this: the practice of pet cloning—like advanced veterinary care such as transplants, neurosurgery, orthopedics, and psychopharmaceuticals—might improve the public's perception of the moral status of companion animals because it puts animals in the category of being worthy of a very high level of expense and concern. Something that warrants this level of commitment and investment seems valuable

From *Hastings Center Report,* vol. 35, no. 4, July–August 2005, pp. 34–39. Copyright © 2005 by The Hastings Center. Reprinted by permission of the publisher and Autumn Fiester.

intrinsically, not merely instrumentally, and this change in the public's perception could have far-reaching benefits for all animals.

Of course, even if this controversial claim is true—that pet cloning might contribute to an increase in the public's esteem for companion animals—it can justify pet cloning only for those who already find some forms of animal cloning morally acceptable. My case rests on the premise that some types of cloning are morally justified by the benefits that will result from them. People opposed in principle to all forms of animal cloning—for example, because this type of biotechnology is "playing God" or because animals should never be used in research—will not accept this consequentialist starting point. The most straightforward way to make the point is this: we can talk about justifying pet cloning only on the assumption that animal cloning for clearly important ends—like medical or pharmaceutical advances—is morally permissible. If one rejects those types of cloning, the argument about pet cloning cannot get off the ground.

The Anti-Cloning Case

Critics of pet cloning typically offer three objections: (1) the cloning process causes animals to suffer; (2) widely available pet cloning could have bad consequences for the overwhelming numbers of unwanted companion animals; and, (3) companies that offer pet cloning are deceiving and exploiting grieving pet owners.

Animal Suffering   Animal welfare advocates have been quick to point out the cost of animal cloning to the animals involved in the procedures.[2] A large body of literature documents high rates of miscarriage, stillbirth, early death, genetic abnormalities, and chronic diseases among the first cloned animals. These problems occur against a backdrop of what in cloning science is called "efficiency," the percentage of live offspring from the number of transferred embryos. The efficiency of animal cloning has typically been about 1 to 2 percent, meaning that of every one hundred embryos implanted in surrogate animals, ninety-eight or ninety-nine fail to produce live offspring.[3] Given the invasive techniques used to implant the embryos in the surrogate, these numbers represent a certain amount of suffering on the part of the donor animals: for every one or two live animals, one hundred eggs must be harvested and one hundred embryos implanted. In the experiments conducted to clone "CC" the calico cat, one hundred and eighty-eight eggs were harvested, eighty-seven cloned embryos were transferred into eight female cats, two of the females became pregnant, and one live kitten was born.[4]

Further, of the live clones born, many have experienced compromised health status or early death. In one study of cloned pigs, researchers reported a 50% mortality rate for the live offspring, with five out of ten dying between three and one hundred and thirty days of age from ailments including chronic diarrhea, congestive heart failure, and decreased growth rate.[5] A study published last year showed that cloned mice experience early death due to liver failure and lung problems.[6] Another study showed that cloned mice had a high tendency to morbid obesity.[7]

Cloning scientists respond that both efficiency rates and health outcomes are radically improving, and that we can reasonably expect in the very near future to see fewer animals involved in the cloning process and better health status for the clones that are born.[8] Although the process that produced "CC" was inefficient, there were no kittens born with compromised health status. Research on cloned cattle published last year showed that once the animals survived infancy, they had no health problems when compared with non-clones.[9] Genetics Savings and Clone claims that it has pioneered a new cloning technique that not only improves the health status of clones but greatly increases cloning efficiency, achieving pregnancy loss rates on par with those of breeders.[10] Although information is limited, the company claims that six healthy kittens have been born with no deformities. If this proves to be true, then the animal suffering caused by the process is limited to that of the surrogate mothers. There aren't even any donor animals involved, since the company uses eggs harvested from ovaries purchased from spay clinics. And the suffering of the surrogates is surely not greater than that of cats who "donate" kidneys for feline kidney transplants, a practice that has not received widespread criticism on grounds of inordinate feline suffering.[11]

Unwanted Pets   A second objection to pet cloning is that there are millions of unwanted pets in the United States. How can we justify the creation of designer companion animals when so many wonderful animals languish in shelters? This is the main argument behind the Humane Society's anticloning position. Says Senior Vice President Wayne Pacelle, "The Humane Society of the United States opposes pet cloning because it is dangerous for the animals involved, it serves no compelling social purpose, and it threatens to add to the pet overpopulation problem. It doesn't sit well with us to create animals through such extreme and experimental means when there are so many animals desperate for homes."[12] To be sure, the data on the number of companion animals euthanized in American shelters are sobering. The 2001 Humane Society report on the state of animals in the United States found that four to six million dogs and cats were euthanized in shelters in 2001.[13] These figures do not include the millions of stray animals in the country: the ASPCA estimates that 70 million stray dogs and cats live in the United States.[14]

But what is the connection between the sorry state of unwanted companion animals in this country and the anti-pet-cloning stance? Surely one cannot hold that no new animals ought to be intentionally created until all shelter animals are adopted. Anticloners would then have bigger fish to fry than pet cloning—namely, the breeders and puppy farms that produce millions of dogs and cats each year. By comparison, pet cloning, even if it becomes a viable industry, will produce only trivial numbers of animals.

Critics of pet cloning say that pet owners who are so devoted to their animal companions that they would spend thousands of dollars to clone one are precisely the type of adoptive parents who could save an already-existing animal's life through pet adoption, sparing one more dog or cat from euthanasia.[15] But why should a person devoted to a particular animal be more obligated than anyone else to save others of that same species? Being a parent doesn't obligate me more than childless folks to help parentless children. Critics will say this comparison is outrageous. We can't compare animals and children. But for the pet owner willing to clone a deceased pet, there *is* one analogy between a child and a companion animal: you can't substitute or exchange one for another. Pet owners grieving a lost animal see their animal as unique and irreplaceable, so they can't just go to a shelter and get any old animal as a replacement pet. Naturally, this invites the third criticism, which we will discuss below, that this clone *isn't* actually the original pet. But the point is that what these pet owners are after cannot be found in a shelter or purchased from a breeder.

What about the money involved? Isn't there something wrong with spending $30,000 on an animal? Perhaps so, but the problem certainly isn't limited to pet cloning—think of race horses, for example. And if the charge is really that pet cloning is a frivolous use of money that could be better spent on noble causes, then this is just a universal attack on all luxury goods. It doesn't make pet cloning any morally worse than boat-buying.

Exploitation and Deception   But what about the concern that pet owners are being tricked into believing that they are getting Fido back, when in truth, Fido and the clone could be as different as any identical twins? There are two separate charges here: one is about false advertising or exploitation on the part of the cloning firm; the other is about the pet owner's self-deception.

Take the cloning firm first. Opponents argue that grieving pet owners are deceived by companies like Genetic Savings and Clone into believing that cloning is a way of resurrecting a deceased and beloved pet. They argue that the business of pet cloning assumes genetic determinism—that genes alone determine all physical and behavioral characteristics—which is false. For example, criticizing the practice of companion animal cloning, bioethicist David Magnus argues, "The people who want this are spending huge sums of money to get their pet immortalized or to guarantee they're getting a pet exactly like the one they had before—and it's simply not possible."[16] If pet cloning firms are contributing to this false belief, then they are engaging in a type of fraud and are certainly exploiting the grief of the devoted pet owner. Genetic Savings and Clone argues that they have an informed consent process that educates clients about the environmental and in utero factors that influence personality and behavior—maybe even physical characteristics. But whatever policies need to be put in place to make sure the owner has realistic expectations, how cloning firms market pet cloning and educate potential customers does not bear on the moral legitimacy of pet cloning itself. There is a clear need to regulate this emerging industry to ensure truth in advertising, but that could be achieved without eliminating the product.

As for the self-deception of the pet owner, this is a psychological, not an ethical concern. Again, Magnus:

> I can completely sympathize with people who become so attached to their pet that they want to bring it back at any cost, but there is nothing that can bring that animal back. Attempting to do so is unhealthy.

It's trying to pretend that death doesn't exist, which speaks to a larger symptom in our culture of not dealing with death. It's better to just move on.[17]

There are two responses here. First, if the customers don't feel betrayed or deceived (and indeed, they do not) and are satisfied with their investment and comforted by the clone's existence, then it is hard to get this psychological concern going. Second, this argument assumes that there is no good reason to clone a pet unless one *were* deceived[18]—and this is false. The bereft pet owner might know full well that the clone will be nothing more than a genetic twin, and the decision to clone might be merely an attempt to preserve something important from the original animal, rather than *resurrect* it. In the human context, we think of offspring this way. We say things like, "I am so glad my son had children before he died." For animals that were neutered at an early age, who have no offspring, it is perfectly rational to desire the genetic "starting blocks" Fido had, even under complete comprehension that this animal will not be Fido. Wanting to get as close as possible to the original animal is not irrational. In the absence of immortality, genetic identity is the next best thing.

Pet Cloning and "Rising Status"

Now consider an argument in favor of pet cloning: pet cloning may change common views of what in philosophy is called the "moral status" of animals. The fact that companion animals are deemed worthy recipients of this level of effort and expense might encourage people to view animals as having intrinsic value and uniqueness.

The public's perception of the value of animals is not fixed. In fact, the public's estimation of animals' status is arguably rising fast. Getting at perceptions of animal status is difficult, but consider some of the following facts: a 2001 ABC News poll found that 41 percent of Americans believe that animals go to heaven,[19] and a May 2003 Gallup poll found that a full 33 percent of Americans are at least somewhat supportive of an all-out ban on medical research involving laboratory animals.[20] Attitudes among pet owners are even more interesting. For example, a 1999 survey by the American Animal Hospital Association found that 84 percent of pet owners refer to themselves as their pet's "mommy" or "daddy," 63 percent celebrate the pet's birthday, and 72 percent of married respondents greet their pet first when they return home.[21] There are also more pet owners now than ever before; 62 percent of households in the United States own pets in 2005,[22] up from 50 percent in 1975.[23]

The dramatic shift in the status of American pets can also be seen in the resources devoted to them. Americans spent over $30 billion on small animal companions in 2003,[24] a 10 percent increase over 2002 spending,[25] and two and a half times the spending levels of 1978 (in adjusted dollars, Americans spent $11 billion in 1978 vs. $30 billion today).[26] A large part of this figure represents a surge in veterinary service spending: Americans are spending more not only on routine care for companion animals, but on specialty care as well, reflecting a change in priorities and values. For example, pain management expenditures have increased 275 percent in the last six years.[27] Pet owners are now investing in pain control medicines for animals that would have been euthanized a decade ago.

These figures represent what has been called the "pet as family" trend.[28] While it is difficult to empirically document that these figures correspond to an increase in status of companion animals, experts in the field believe they do. Robert Gilbert, associate dean for clinical programs at Cornell Hospital for Animals, describes pet owners' attitudes toward pets as somewhat like parents' attitudes toward children; when he started practicing veterinary medicine in 1977, "a pet was a pet."[29] Thomas Cusick, president of the American Animal Hospital Association, declares, "Pets are clearly becoming an integral part of the American family, enjoying much of the same attention, care, and treatment that is given to a child or spouse."[30]

There is also anecdotal evidence that those who don't own pets are beginning to acknowledge and adopt the changing attitudes of their pet-owning friends and relatives. It is no longer appropriate, for example, to say to a grieving pet owner, "What's the fuss about? Just get another pet." News of an ill pet now engenders concern and sympathy.

The argument I want to advance is that the treatment of companion animals by their caretakers alters what the public in general thinks about them. Attitudes toward companion animals are heavily influenced by the dominant view and mainstream practice (indeed it is the majority of Americans who currently have pets).

More specifically, I want to offer a hypothesis about one mechanism by which this kind of cultural change takes place, namely, that the routinization of certain practices and expenses on the part of pet owners normalizes that behavior, which affects the general view of what care animals deserve; and this in turn enhances the public's estimation of the value of companion animals because it encourages the public to view animals as entities worthy enough to merit this attention and care. One of the most significant influences on the public's perceptions is the effort expended to improve the health and extend the lives of companion animals. Pet cloning is just the extreme form of pet owners' attempts to extend the life (in this case, in the form of the genome) of a beloved animal.

Advanced veterinary care is the paradigm case. Veterinary services are the fastest-growing segment of the companion animal industry, increasing at an annual rate of 4.7 percent, with current expenditures pegged at close to $8 billion.[31] As noted earlier, much of the spending increase is directed at services unheard of a few decades ago. Veterinary medicine has specialized into surgery, dermatology, ophthalmology, orthopedics, neurology, oncology, and even transplant surgery. At a price estimated to be between $5,000 and $15,000 (plus $50–$150 per month in immunosuppressant drugs for life), one's dog or cat can receive a renal transplant at one of the country's new transplant centers.[32] Kidney transplants are still rare, but many other specialty services are not, including x-rays, psychopharmaceuticals, and insulin therapy.

As each new procedure or service is incorporated into veterinary care, pet owners' acceptance of the new standard of care alters the overall public's attitude toward those procedures. No longer seen as a bizarre or exorbitant waste of money and resources, the new procedure starts to seem entirely warranted. Think of the public's attitude toward now commonplace treatments, such as daily shots of insulin, arthritis medicines, corrective surgery for orthopedic problems, or antianxiety medicines. These expenses easily exceed the original price of the animal, but few people would now tell a pet owner to cut her losses and buy a new pet. What is happening to the public's attitude toward companion animals if these advance treatments seem like reasonable measures and expenses to protect animal lives and well-being? At a minimum, the normalization of advanced veterinary care indicates the public's recognition of the "irreplaceability" for the pet owner of one animal with some other. We no longer think of companion animals as disposable or interchangeable, despite the ready supply of homeless animals.

Of course, this argument may suffer from the classic "chicken or the egg" question: is the attention given to animals raising public perceptions of animals' status, or is the perception of animals' status rising independently of the actions of pet owners? In fact, it can go both ways. To the pet owner, the intrinsic value of the companion animal is already recognized, which is why she expends the resources and energy to treat the animal. To someone observing that practice, the effect is to affirm or alter the perception of value that companion animals have—or ought to have. So while only a handful of people may value their pets enough to go through the expense of an organ transplant, the effect of employing "pet organ transplants" is much more widespread. As this type of practice becomes reasonable, it becomes a statement about the intrinsic value and worth of its recipients.

It is plausible that pet cloning will have a parallel effect. Pet cloning makes the statement that one's companion animal is so important that it is worth trying to come as close as possible to preserving it by investing in a genetic twin. The hypothesis is that when pet cloning is seen as a rational, justifiable activity for pet owners as a response to the (impending) death of an animal, the societal effect—as with advanced veterinary care—will be to enhance the companion animal's position on the moral map through the public's recognition that these entities have high value.

One possible rejoinder is that the dignity and uniqueness of the original pet is degraded by an attempt to obtain a clone. Believing that we can replace a companion animal with its clone demonstrates that animals are, in fact, mere objects, not at all like children, and the effect of widespread use of pet cloning will be to downgrade animals' status, not raise it. But whether pet cloning will have this effect will depend on how society interprets it. A pet-cloning-as-mass-production view will undoubtedly reinforce the idea that companion animals are replaceable consumer goods, and this will have a deleterious effect on perceptions of their status. In the cloning-as-solace view as I have described above, however, companion animal cloning will be seen as a tribute to the value of the original animal. There are parents who desperately want to clone their lost children.[33] Pet owners, mirroring their feelings, are making a statement about both the animal's immeasurable value and the level of loss and grief they feel at its death. Whatever one thinks of human cloning, no one argues that the parents who request it don't assign the highest possible worth to the deceased child; the sentiment to clone is a testimony to the parents' belief in the infinite value of that unique person. If this becomes widely understood, the cloning-as-solace interpretation may indeed win out.

If pet cloning bolsters even slightly a perception that companion animals have intrinsic value, then the positive consequences for companion animals will far outweigh the minimal suffering the animals undergo through the cloning process. The rising status of companion animals has already begun to translate into laws that offer more protection for them, including changes in the designation of pet owners to "animal guardians" in some areas.[34] If companion animals' status continues to rise, and if pet cloning contributes at all to that trend, then there is an argument for the moral legitimacy of pet cloning.

References

1. P. Fimrite, "Cat Has 10 Lives, Thanks to $50,000 Cloning," *San Francisco Chronicle,* December 23, 2004.

2. See H. Bok, "Cloning Animals Is Wrong," *Journal of Applied Animal Welfare Science* 5, no. 3 (2002), 233–38.

3. A. Coleman, "Somatic Cell Nuclear Transfer in Mammals: Progress and Application," *Cloning* 1 (1999), 185–200. See also L. Paterson, "Somatic Cell Nuclear Transfer (Cloning) Efficiency." . . .

4. T. Shin et al., "Cell Biology: A Cat Cloned by Nuclear Transplantation," *Nature* 415 (2002): 859.

5. A.B. Carter, "Phenotyping of Transgenic Cloned Pigs," *Cloning and Stem Cells* 4 (2002): 131–45.

6. N. Ogonuki et al., "Early Death of Mice Cloned from Somatic Cells," *Nature Genetics* 30 (2002): 253–54.

7. K. Tamashiro, "Cloned Mice Have an Obese Phenotype Not Transmitted to Their Offspring," *Nature Genetics* 8 (2002): 262–67.

8. *Nature Biotechnology* recently published a metareview of the health status of clones from prior studies, and it reports that 77 percent of cloned animals showed no developmental abnormalities throughout the period of follow-up, although the percentage of healthy clones ranged from 20 percent to 100 percent across the studies. J.B. Cibelli et al. "The Health Profile of Cloned Animals," *Nature Biotechnology* 20 (2002), 13–14.

9. C. Yang, X.C. Tian, and X. Yang, "Serial Bull Cloning by Somatic Cell Nuclear Transfer," *Nature Biotechnology* 22 (2004), 693–94.

10. M. Fox, "Company Says It Cloned Copy Cats," Reuters, August 5, 2004; Fimrite, "Cat Has 10 Lives."

11. Of course, the obvious objection to this comparison is that the kidneys are harvested to save the life of another cat, whereas the animals who suffer through egg harvesting and embryo implantation are not saving an existing cat but creating an entirely new (unneeded) one. But what is in question here is the amount of suffering—not the justification for it.

12. Humane Society of the United States, "Cat Cloning Is Wrong-Headed," February 14, 2002. . . .

13. P.G. Irwin, "Overview: The State of Animals in 2001," in *The State of Animals 2001*, ed. D.J. Salem and A.N. Rowan (Washington, D.C.: Humane Society Press, 2001).

14. American Society for the Prevention of Cruelty to Animals, "Annual Shelter Statistics." . . .

15. The pet owners most likely to request a clone of a deceased pet are those who originally adopted pets from shelters, because these animals are often mixed-breed animals whose personality traits or other features cannot be generated by conventional breeding. It was the owner of a mixed-breed dog, "Missy," that funded the now-famous Missyplicity Project at Texas A&M, which resulted in the cloning of "CC" the cat. But the owner of Missy chose to invest $3.7 million in trying to create Missy's twin; he did not invest the $3.7 million in improving the lives of shelter animals, the original source of Missy herself. . . .

16. M. Shiels, "Carbon Kitty's $50,000 Price Tag," *BBC News,* April 27, 2004.

17. Fimrite, "Cat Has 10 Lives."

18. Magnus reaches this conclusion: "There is no good reason why anybody would do this." Fimrite, "Cat Has 10 Lives."

19. The Roper Center For Public Opinion Research, "Do You Think Animals Go to Heaven When They Die or Only People Go to Heaven?" ABC News/ BeliefNet Poll (June 2001). . . .

20. The Roper Center For Public Opinion Research, "Banning All Medical Research on Laboratory Animals," Gallup Poll (May, 2003). . . .

21. American Animal Hospital Association, Pet Owner Survey, 1999. . . .

22. American Pet Products Manufacturers Association, "APPMA Survey Finds Pet Ownership Continues Growth Trend in U.S." . . .

23. C.W. Schwabe et al., *Veterinary Medicine and Human Health,* third ed. (Baltimore, Md.: Williams & Wilkins Co, 1976).

24. DVM News Magazine, "Pet Spending to Top $37 Billion by '08." . . .

25. S. Aschoff, "Pet RX," *Floridian,* June 10, 2003.

26. Schwabe et al., *Veterinary Medicine and Human Health.*

27. Aschoff, "Pet RX."

28. J.E. Brody. "V.I.P. Medical Treatment Adds Meaning to Dog's (or Cat's) Life," *New York Times,* August 14, 2001: Section F; Page 4; Column 2.

29. J.E. Brody. "V.I.P. Medical Treatment Adds Meaning to Dog's (or Cat's) Life," *New York Times,* August 14, 2001.

30. American Veterinary Medical Association, "Survey Says: Owners Taking Good Care of Their Pets," *Journal of the American Veterinary Medical Association.* . . .

31. *DVM News Magazine,* "Pet Spending to Top $37 Billion by '08." . . .

32. L. Copeland. "Transplant Offers Hope for a Tabby; With Kidney Comes 2nd Chance at 9 Lives," *Washington Post,* March 14, 1999. Also B. Bilger, "The Last Meow," *New Yorker,* September 8, 2003, at 46. Donor cats are taken from local shelters and research labs, and the owners of the transplantee must agree to adopt the donor (p. 49).

33. Offering a pro-pet cloning argument in no way commits me to a pro-human cloning argument, although I can understand the powerful sentiments that would drive a parent to desire the ability to clone a beloved child. The difference is that we can accept a sacrifice in animal lives (we euthanize them, we experiment on them, and we eat them) that we cannot accept in human lives. But if human cloning could be guaranteed never to result in a birth defect, stillbirth, or compromised health status of a child, the debate about human cloning would be quite different.

34. *CBS Evening News,* "Legal Relationship Between Pets and Their Owners," CBS News Transcripts, Aug. 7, 2000; B. Pool, "In West Hollywood, Pets Are Part of the Family," *Los Angeles Times,* February 22, 2001; "Pet Owners in San Francisco Become 'Pet Guardians,'" *The San Diego Union Tribune,* March 1, 2001; and "Students Make History by Helping to Draft & Pass Animal Rights Legislation," *News from General Assembly,* September 26, 2001. . . .

Hilary Bok  **NO**

Cloning Companion Animals Is Wrong

In principle, I have nothing against cloning either nonhuman animals or humans. If cloning were as safe as natural procreation and if those who chose to clone themselves or others completely understood cloning (in particular, how clones are related to their originals), I would not worry about cloning being tantamount to, in Hawthorne's words, "playing God" or "cheating death" (Hawthorne, 2002 . . .). I would view it simply as a complicated and expensive way of producing an identical twin born at a different time and from a different mother than the original. In fact, however, neither of these things is true. Cloning is not safe, and it is not widely understood. Nonetheless, I suppose that some extremely compelling reason might justify our cloning animals. However, there is no such justification for the Missyplicity Project.

Suffering and Complications

Cloning causes animals to suffer. Egg donors must have their ovaries artificially stimulated with hormone treatments and their eggs surgically harvested. Given the unusually high rates of late-term miscarriages and high birth weights among clones, the surrogate mothers are at greater risk of dying or suffering serious complications than animals who become pregnant naturally. The clones, themselves, however, suffer the most serious problems: They are much more likely than other animals to be miscarried, have birth defects, develop serious illnesses, and die prematurely.

Hawthorne (2002 . . .) acknowledges that this is "the ethical issue of greatest concern" (p. 229) raised by animal cloning. However, he greatly understates its seriousness. He claims, for instance, that 20% of cattle clones detectable in utero experience some sort of physical problem resulting in miscarriages, early deaths, or later health problems. In fact, to go by the published reports of cloning surveyed by the National Academy of Sciences (2002) in its recent report on cloning, the numbers are much higher: Of at least 242 pregnancies from cloned adult cattle cells, at least 174 were miscarried. Of the 68 calves born alive, only 42 were still alive at the time of publication, and investigators reported that 5 of those had significant health

From *Journal of Applied Animal Welfare Science,* vol. 5, no. 3, July 2002, pp. 233–238. Copyright © 2002 by ASPCA and Society & Animals Forum. Reprinted by permission of Routledge/Taylor & Francis Group via Rightslink.

problems other than high birth weight. This means that the number of cattle clones detectable in utero who go on to experience serious health problems is not 20% but at least 85%.

In a recent study, Ogonuki et al. (2002) compared the lifespan of 12 cloned mice, 7 genetically matched, naturally conceived mice, and 6 mice produced by a process of spermatid injection performed under the same laboratory conditions as the cloning but resulting in natural conception. Eight hundred days after their birth, 10 of 12 cloned mice had died, compared with 1 of the 7 mice conceived naturally and 2 of the 6 produced by spermatid injection. Autopsies performed on 6 of the cloned mice revealed that all had severe pneumonia, 4 had necrotic livers, and 2 had tumors. In addition, the cloned mice had reduced immune system function, which the researchers believed might account for their pneumonia. Here again, the number of clones with serious health problems is much higher than Hawthorne (2002 . . .) suggests: In Ogonuki et al.'s study, two thirds of the animals who were born alive died prematurely as a result of physical problems associated with their being clones.

Real Problems, Unknown Solutions

Hawthorne (2002 . . .) suggests that these problems may be species specific and that researchers do not know whether dogs and cats will exhibit them. This is disingenuous. It is true that researchers do not yet know what problems cloned dogs and cats might have. No one has yet cloned a dog, and it is too early to tell whether the one cloned cat in existence will develop the kinds of health problems seen in other species. We do know, however, that these problems have turned up in every other species cloned, including goats. Therefore, there is every reason to expect that they will turn up in cats and dogs as well.

Hawthorne also suggests that some test yet to be developed might detect abnormalities prior to implantation. It seems extremely unlikely that in the foreseeable future someone will develop a reliable preimplantation test for problems with gene expression comprehensive enough to ensure that the clones we produce will be healthy. The number of genes whose expression would have to be tested is enormous, and researchers do not now understand the effects of various possible differences in their expression on an animal's subsequent development. In addition, many of these genes are not active before implantation; therefore, it is unclear how one could test their expression at that stage. For these reasons, it is unlikely that such a test will be developed in the near future.

In the meantime, cloned animals will continue to suffer serious health problems at much higher rates than other animals of the same species. Some will be suffocated when their lungs do not inflate, some will be poisoned because of liver or kidney failure, and some will be eaten away by cancer. Some will die from heart failure, and some will have only such "minor" problems as gross obesity or premature arthritis. Almost all clones will suffer and die, and they will do so, not because of some natural illness or misfortune but because researchers have chosen to bring them into existence using a process that is not understood well enough to use safely.

Of course, the only way researchers can learn enough about cloning cats and dogs to do it safely is by trying and learning from their mistakes. This, however, does not justify conducting this process of trial and error on the bodies of dogs and cats, absent some reason to think that learning how to clone dogs and cats is worth the cost in animal suffering. One must ask whether enabling humans to clone their pets is important enough to justify the considerable suffering involved in learning how to do so.

Why Clone Pets?

As the caregiver for two cats, I can easily understand why persons who do not understand what cloning involves might be tempted to clone their pets. Pet owners love their pets. When an animal one loves dies, the most natural thing in the world is to want that animal back. Just as a parent whose child has died is unlikely to be comforted by the thought that there are plenty of other children waiting for adoption, most grieving pet owners are not consoled by the thought that they can always adopt another dog or cat. This is not because pet owners are unduly sentimental or confused about the differences between pets and children. It is because, like parents, they love individuals, and adopting another dog or cat will not replace the individual they have loved and lost.

Cloning is not a way of bringing back the animal one loves. That is the point of loving an individual: Not even an exact replica can be the particular being one loves. Still, to a grieving pet owner an exact replica might seem to be the next best thing, and some pet owners might think that cloning could produce one. This misconception is easy to remove: One need only point out that clones will not have the same memories as their originals and that because their upbringing and environment will differ, their behavior and temperament will differ as well.

However, even after this mistake is corrected, one might still think that cloned animals will be identical to their originals in all respects except those that depend on environment and upbringing. One might, that is, think that although a clone of one's dog will not be a copy of that dog as an adult, the clone, when born, will be identical to the newborn puppy who grew up to be that dog. This is, I think, what many of those who are interested in cloning their pets believe. Unfortunately, they are wrong. Cloning produces animals who are genetically identical to their originals. However, genetic identity is not, and does not ensure, physical identity; the difference between the two is extremely significant.

The genes in an adult animal's somatic cells are programmed not for directing embryonic development but for directing the activities of skin cells, liver cells, and so forth. If researchers tried to clone a cat by inducing one skin cell to divide without reprogramming its DNA, they would end up not with a kitten but with, at best, a kitten-sized mass of skin cells. That mass would be genetically identical to the original cat but, presumably, would not be what the owners had in mind when they asked to clone the cat. To produce not a mass of skin cells but a kitten, the skin cell's DNA needs to be reprogrammed.

To produce a kitten largely, although not entirely, similar to the kitten the cat once was, researchers would have to reprogram the cat's DNA to exactly the state it was in when that cat was a fertilized egg.

In practice, it is extraordinarily unlikely that any animal's DNA can be reprogrammed perfectly. Tens of thousands of genes might need reprogramming, and researchers do not know what they all are, let alone what would count as their correct expression. Nor is it known in most cases, what contribution they make to an animal's subsequent development. Moreover, although the word *reprogramming* might suggest the existence of easily manipulable switches that could be reset one by one, in practice reprogramming is a messy and haphazard process that is neither understood nor controllable.

For these reasons, the likelihood that every gene will be reset correctly is minute. Some problems with reprogramming might be benign. Others might be so serious that any fetus who has them will be miscarried. There is, however, a middle group: problems serious enough to create significant physical differences between clones and their originals but not serious enough to prevent those clones from being born at all. Given the number of such mistakes that it is possible to make and the impossibility in practice of screening for any appreciable number of them, clones probably will differ in unpredictable and potentially significant respects from their originals.

Consider in this light that 85% of cattle clones detected in utero are miscarried, die prematurely, or suffer serious health problems. As far as is known, these cattle were cloned from healthy adults whose lungs, livers, and kidneys did not malfunction; who were born without serious cardiac problems or joint irregularities; and who did not have juvenile diabetes or severe anemia. All these problems appeared among their clones. This indicates three things. First, that clones are genetically identical to their originals does not mean that they will be physically identical to them. Second, the differences between clones and their originals will involve not only relatively unimportant things like coat coloring but also crucial ones like whether their hearts work. Third, these differences are not rare or anomalous: They are the norm.

Cloning, then, is not a way for a pet owner to acquire, say, a puppy just like the puppy who grew up to be his or her dog. It is a way of acquiring a dog who is genetically identical to that dog, but who is much more likely to have major physical defects that cause real suffering and require serious medical care. Moreover, even if that dog is lucky enough not to have serious health problems, he or she is likely to differ from his or her original in subtler ways. In particular, there is no reason to think that the genes that underlie a dog's temperament are less likely than other genes to be reprogrammed incorrectly and, therefore, no reason to think that cloned dogs will necessarily share their originals' temperament and disposition. If pet owners want to get dogs similar to ones who have died, they are much more likely to succeed by adopting puppies of the same breed with similar dispositions than by cloning their pets.

The one goal pet owners might accomplish by cloning their pets is to make it possible for the genes of spayed, neutered, or otherwise infertile pets to be passed on to another generation. Although many clones have serious physical defects because these defects result mostly from problems with gene expression rather than with the genes themselves, clones are unlikely to pass these defects on to their offspring (Tamashiro et al., 2002). Cloning might make sense, then, as a very complicated way of reversing a spaying or neutering operation one had come to regret.

Although a pet owner might achieve this goal through cloning, it is clearly immoral. To clone a dog for this reason is to subject other dogs to hormonal treatments to stimulate their ovaries; surgically harvest their eggs; create hundreds of fetuses; implant them in dogs who will risk unusually dangerous pregnancies; and finally, bring into existence a clone who probably will suffer serious health problems, just to make it possible for this dog to have puppies genetically related to one's original pet. This would display great callousness toward the suffering of animals and a willingness to sacrifice their interests to one's whims.

If the arguments above are sound, then people who want to clone their pets must be either mistaken about what cloning is or immoral. In the first case, it would be wrong of the Missyplicity Project to take advantage of their misconceptions, especially at the expense of other animals. In the second, it would be wrong for the Missyplicity Project to collude in their wrongdoing. In no case is it morally justifiable either to clone one's pet or to enable others to clone theirs.

References

Hawthorne, L. (2002). A project to clone companion animals. *Journal of Applied Animal Welfare Science, 5,* 227–229.

National Academy of Sciences: Committee on Science, Engineering, and Public Policy (2002). *Scientific and medical aspects of human reproductive cloning* (Appendix B). Washington, DC: National Academy Press.

Ogonuki, N., Inove, K., Yamamoto, Y., Noguchi, Y., Tanemura, K., Suzuki, O., et al. (2002, February 11). Early death of mice cloned from somatic cells. *Nature Genetics* [Advance on-line publication]. . . .

Tamashiro, K. L. K., Wakayama, T., Akutsu, H., Yamazaki, Y., Lachey, J. L., Wortman, M. D., et al. (2002). Cloned mice have an obese phenotype not transmitted to their offspring. *Nature Medicine, 8,* 262–267.

POSTSCRIPT

Is Cloning Pets Ethically Justified?

The Missyplicity Project (and the related commercial enterprise called Genetic Savings and Clone) can be a fascinating case study in animal cloning. See the online sources at http://www.the-scientist.com, http://en.wikipedia.org, http://www.mindfully.org, and http://www.pamperedpuppy.com.

As for the idea of cloning pets in general, it is remarkable that some people have immediate reactions that are highly positive, while others have immediate reactions that are highly negative. This suggests that emotions play a great role in the way we think about this. To some extent, we can transcend emotional reactions and try to gain a rational view of the matter. Yet this raises some additional questions because we wonder whether, if emotion is totally removed, this issue can still be appreciated for what it is. Indeed, pet owners can feel such strong emotional bonds with their pets. Nevertheless, even if emotions are allowed a place here, it is undeniable that it is also worthwhile to attend to scientific and factual matters about cloning. Some relevant sources here are http://www.ornl.gov and http://en.wikipedia.org.

A couple of factors still remain, though. First, even though cloning is sometimes discussed in the abstract—as if all the kinks with the procedure had been worked out—there are several severe problems with cloning: It is highly inefficient, often requiring hundreds of implantations in order to generate even one live birth, and even if the clone is successfully born, clones are often subject to serious disease and a shorter-than-normal lifespan. The trouble with discussion that ignores these problems and proceeds as if everything were fine is that these problems may never be solved. There is often a great optimism surrounding discussions of cloning yet problems remain.

Another source of unease is that there is a gap between the two kinds of people who are (or would be) most closely involved with pet cloning: the scientists and the pet owners. Scientists may have accurate ideas about what cloning is, but it is far from clear that pet owners have accurate ideas. For example, pet owners might think that the newly cloned animals will be guaranteed to have the same dispositions and behavioral traits (and perhaps even the same memories) as the original pet. Pet owners may have established emotional bonds here that prevent them from seeing (or acknowledging) the truth. "Idealized" discussion of pet cloning often overlooks this fact, since in the ideal case, everyone knows (and fully acknowledges) the facts.

For further reading, see "Pet Cloning Misses Point," *The Register-Guard*, Eugene, Oregon (February 20, 2002). Pet cloning is also discussed by John Kilner, *Basic Questions in Genetics, Stem Cell Research and Cloning* (Kregel, 2003) and Hwa A. Lim, *Multiplicity Yours* (World Scientific, 2006).

ISSUE 8

Should Congress Allow the Buying and Selling of Human Organs?

YES: Lewis Burrows, from "Selling Organs for Transplantation," *The Mount Sinai Journal of Medicine* (September 2004)

NO: James F. Childress, from "Should Congress Allow the Buying and Selling of Human Organs? No," *Insight on the News* (May 7, 2001)

ISSUE SUMMARY

YES: Lewis Burrows, M.D., begins with the observation that the need for organs far outstrips the supply: each year, hundreds of patients die while waiting for transplants. Burrows argues that payment to the donor (or payment to the donor's family, in cases in which the donor is deceased) would increase the supply of organs, regulations could restrain possible abuses, and a payment-for-organs system could meet relevant medical ethical principles.

NO: James F. Childress, professor of ethics and professor of medical education, argues that a free market would cause the loss of important altruistic motivations and would turn organs into commodities; moreover, such an untried market might make fewer—not more—organs available.

Some facts are important for the proper appreciation of this issue. First, the supply of organs is vastly lower than the demand. This is so not only in the United States, but on a worldwide basis. In America, people who need a new kidney have to be put on a waiting list. In the meantime, they may be able to use a dialysis machine. Receiving dialysis is a noncurative procedure, which must be performed on a regular basis—often three times a week for several hours. Unless people who need new kidneys receive them, the dialysis machine must become a regular part of their lives—forever. Second, when an organ such as a kidney is transplanted into someone selected for transplantation, numerous parties receive compensation for the services they render. Thousands of dollars are paid to physicians and hospitals and others; but donors must be *donors:* they must *give* the organ and must not receive any compensation of any kind, except perhaps a small amount for their time or for their own expenses. (Since 1984 and the passage of the National Organ Transplant Act, it has been a federal offense to buy or sell organs.)

Many people think that there is something wrong, perhaps something distasteful, with buying or selling an organ. By contrast, *donating* an organ is often regarded as an extremely worthy—perhaps heroic—act. But also, to *receive* an organ through transplantation is thought to be extremely beneficial, not distasteful or shameful at all. A donor can give a kidney to a recipient, and both of them will be thought well of. But we tend to look askance at a situation in which money changes hands.

And yet, from one point of view, it seems only fair for the person who gives up a kidney to be compensated for doing so. Everyone else involved in the transplant situation seems to be benefited or compensated. But the donor is supposed to be motivated by pure altruism and not at all by money. This works well when the donor and the recipient are close relations. It is not infrequent for transplantations to occur between family members. (What parent would not give a kidney to a son or daughter who desperately needed one?) But there remains the problem of the general societal lack of organs for transplantation.

In the first of the two selections below, Dr. Lewis Burrows first argues that there should indeed be a (regulated) market for organs. (He speaks, first of all, about kidneys, but suggests that there may also be possibilities for liver, lung, and pancreas transplantation. And if the donor is deceased, the scope for transplantation of organs may be wider still.) This, he claims, would greatly increase the supply. Then, on the other side of the issue, James F. Childress argues against all forms of buying and selling organs; he emphasizes the values that would be lost if there were to be such a market, and he casts doubt on the idea that a market in human organs really would increase the supply. According to Childress, instead of establishing a market in organs—which would likely put a damper on donations—donations and the altruistic motivation that generally lies behind them should be actively encouraged.

YES

Lewis Burrows

Selling Organs for Transplantation

Living donor organ transplantation is the only field of medicine in which two individuals are intimately involved: the donor and the recipient. It is also the only field of medicine in which altruistic giving of oneself is the basis of the medical practice. I have been asked to address a very specific aspect of this process, that is, living organ donation for financial remuneration. No other subject in the transplant experience is as controversial. Many of those involved in the field—surgeons, physicians, social scientists, ethicists, and theologians—have expressed an opinion on this issue.

As a result of impressive gains in this field, organ recipients now have a significant chance for both long-term survival and a reasonable quality of life. These successes have led nearly 80,000 individuals to opt for transplantation as a form of therapy. Unfortunately, the number of organs available has lagged far behind the demand. Every year thousands die while waiting for the gift of life that an organ transplant could provide.

In the case of cadaveric giving, the family of the brain-dead person is asked to donate. There is a serious shortfall in cadaveric organ donations, with only 40–60% of U.S. families consenting to organ recovery. Countries that have adopted the doctrine of "presumed consent" (such as Spain, Austria, and Belgium) have a much higher rate of organ recovery. In these countries, families can "opt out" of donation; if they do not, the organs of deceased family members can be used for transplantation. In most of the rest of the world, families have to "opt in" before organs can be used for transplantation. "Presumed consent" countries that require "opting out" obtain more than 40 donations per million population, as contrasted with half that amount elsewhere. The lower rate is obviously not adequate for meeting current needs.

The number and rate of donations have reached a plateau and leveled off following the enforcement of lower speed limits for automobiles and the introduction of seat belt laws. It is said that donation is a middle class, suburban phenomenon; those groups donate at a somewhat higher rate than others. Why is the rate of donation lower among the poor and in the big cities? We truly do not know. Education, family cohesiveness, trust in medicine, and moral and religious sensibility may all play important roles.

In light of the gap between organ need and organ donation, we are beginning to consider various forms of financial incentives to families as a stimulant for donation (1, 2). I am not referring to the token $399 that the state of

From *Mount Sinai Journal of Medicine*, vol. 71, no. 4, September 2004, pp. 251–254. Copyright © 2004 by Mt. Sinai School of Medicine. Reprinted by permission of Wiley-Blackwell.

Pennsylvania has offered for funeral expenses. That amount would hardly pay for a plain pine coffin. Nor am I referring to the more than $10,000 state income tax credit that the Wisconsin senate approved in January 2004 (3). That incentive would be of little use to the poor. I am referring to a substantial amount, to be included in the financial transactions that occur during the transplant process.

Organ transplantation involves payments of large sums of money. Huge sums go to the hospitals, the transplant surgeons, the physicians, the ancillary staffs and the insurance companies. And most of the money actually goes to the pharmaceutical industry. Many millions of dollars flow into their coffers for the immunosuppressants, antihypertensives, antibiotics, anticholesterols, antacids, and so on, that recipients routinely receive in the course of their treatments. The only people who are not being remunerated are the families of the donors. They alone are being asked to be altruistic.

Just try to do a transplant today on an uninsured patient. I can assure you, the patient will not get through the front door. Medicaid will pay for dialysis treatment of an uninsured alien. But Medicaid will not pay for his or her transplant.

What would be the harm of providing a payment to the donating family of, let's say, $20,000? A liver transplant can cost upward of $300,000, a heart transplant $200,000, and a kidney transplant more than $100,000. In kidney transplantation, even the insurance company would benefit from the payment, since they would no longer have to pay for dialysis therapy.

The most controversial remuneration of all is payment to a living donor who has no relationship to the recipient. Because of the organ shortage, most centers in this country accept the donations of living donors who are related, or emotionally related (for example, a spouse or a friend) as the source of trans-plant organs. In situations where there is an obvious relationship between the donor and recipient, people find no violation of ethical principles. In spite of the inherent risks of donating a kidney or a segment of liver, and the pressures and emotions related to the desire to save a loved one, these organ donations are found acceptable.

But, what of the donor who has no obvious relationship to the recipient? What should we say of someone who only wants to donate an organ to someone with the means to pay for it, perhaps out of financial desperation? About twenty years ago, a foreign-born nephrologist at our institution offered me the opportunity to perform more than two hundred kidney transplants each year. He proposed bringing donor-recipient pairs from his country to our hospital for the surgery. I was to be paid a sizable sum. The apparently wealthy recipients would pay all the involved expenses, and each donor would receive approximately $2,000 for his or her kidney. Apparently, $2,000 was then a sub-stantial sum for a poor person in his country. According to my nephrologist friend, that amount of money would change the donor's life and the standing of his family for generations. Yet even aside from the legal considerations. I rejected the offer outright, because it included no assurance of the donor receiving adequate long-term aftercare. I also felt a sense of revulsion at the idea of a poor, desperate individual peasant being used in this manner by some wealthy businessman or aristocrat.

Nowadays, this form of commercialism is prevalent in the Third World, where either there are no laws prohibiting these transactions or existing laws are not enforced. I shall not address those practices. Instead I want to consider payment for organ donation in an ideal situation. I want to consider the situation where the donor and recipient are carefully selected and carefully matched, and where the operation is well controlled. The donor would be offered long-term care, and the recipient would pay the donor a significant sum. There would be no "middle-men" or brokers involved, and the allocation process would be carefully controlled by the national or regional organ allocation mechanism. Under such circumstances, would it be ethically acceptable for one individual to use another for his own survival and well-being? Would the infliction of pain and suffering on one individual be justified by the benefit to another individual? Should someone with the financial wherewithal be allowed to purchase transplant priority? Does allowing such financial transactions undermine what has been a truly altruistic practice? Would payment to living donors inevitably undermine the public's faith in the process?

Let us examine the proposal in light of the ethical principles involved, to see if they would be violated. But first, I would like to rule out several factors that would be inconsistent with the organ exchange ideal that I imagine:

1. **The donor comes from a country where aftercare is deficient or unavailable.** Such a situation would subject the donor to an unacceptable risk of harm and would therefore exceed a reasonable balance of harms and benefits.

2. **Third-party brokers, profiteers, or entrepreneurs are involved in the transaction.** Removing any portion of the transplant process from the oversight of medical professionals would remove it from the fiduciary relationship that assures that the donor's life and health would be safeguarded. And commercialism introduces possibilities of exploitation and conflict of interest.

3. **The donor does not truly understand the nature of the donation and the potential risks involved.** Evaluation of the donor by an impartial psychiatrist would be a crucial element in assuring that the donor is making an informed choice that reflects personal values and priorities.

4. **There are bidding wars for organs.** The assurance of donor and recipient safety must be a crucial feature of living donor transplantation. Organ auctions could compromise long-term safety or lead to unexpected and untoward outcomes of living donor transplantation. Auctions can only assure price compatibility between buyer and seller. While the selling price should be set high enough to elicit donors, the larger process must take into account the costs of long-term care and emergencies such as primary non-function of the transplanted organ, or organ rejection. Because the transplantation community has the ultimate responsibility for the careful management of these situations, the transplant community must have oversight of any financial exchange.

I would like to summarize the considerations that incline me to accept payment to organ donors in the ideal situation.

1. **Autonomy.** Certainly the donor and the recipient have the right to proceed if those involved in their care are assured that they have freely accepted the transaction with a complete understanding of the risks and benefits involved.
2. **Beneficence.** Both the donor and the recipient stand to gain from their contract, as does everyone else on the waiting list below the recipient. All of the others waiting for a cadaveric organ will benefit by moving up a notch in the process.
3. **The "do no harm" principle (*primum nolle nocere*).** There is obviously some harm done to the donor in the surgery involved in organ donation. There is also the immediate exposure to surgical risks, and the certain disfigurement and loss of an organ. Also there are possible long-term consequences of organ loss. These risks of harm are so well defined in the kidney transplant experience that donors can be assured that the risks, both long- and short-term, are minimal. The risks associated with the liver, lung and pancreas donation process are not as well defined. Perhaps this element of uncertainty justifies a moratorium on these donations until the risks can be carefully assessed in well-controlled clinical studies.
4. **Justice.** I am less confident about whether an ideal organ payment system will conform to the basic principle of fair and equitable distribution of benefits and burdens. The main benefit of payments for organ procurement would go to relatively privileged individuals. They would get transplant organs more readily than others, in addition to all the other privileges that accrue to the wealthy (e.g., better homes, health care, service, etc.). Yet no one else would be harmed by the paid organ donation, unless there is a general loss of faith in the donation process, with a fall in the rate of altruistic giving. This is an empirical question that can only be answered by a trial.

It is clear that I have changed my position somewhat, on this form of donation. I have accepted the libertarian thesis that selling one's organs does not necessarily violate the right of self-determination, and should fall within the protected privacy of free individuals on the basis of the principle of autonomy. I have also been persuaded by pragmatic and utilitarian considerations—the current system is failing, and the benefits for all recipients of an increase in available organs outweigh most objections.

Of course, I would insist on controls. The donor must be healthy, both physically and mentally, as determined by competent physicians and psychiatrists who are not directly involved in the transplant process. We must be assured that the donor fully understands the risks involved and must sign a statement demonstrating true informed consent. Paid donors must be guaranteed long-term medical care and life insurance for themselves and their families in the event that complications occur. The transplant should be controlled by medical professionals and medical agencies that are intimately involved in transplantation and that can administer the process with due care and impartiality.

I offer a final personal note. I am not entirely pleased that I have had to reach this decision. I would certainly prefer that an ample source of cadaveric organs be available to those in need. Available organs would allow us to avoid the dilemmas of living organ donors and paid donations. But for the time being, while my patients are dying for want of an organ, I have accepted this libertarian, utilitarian approach. We do not live in ivory towers. In life, we have to make hard decisions and accept the consequences when all of our options have serious flaws.

References

1. Arnold R, Bartlett S, Bernat J, et al. Financial incentives for cadaver organ donation: an ethical reappraisal. Transplantation 2002; 73(8):1361–1367.
2. Delmonico FL, Arnold R, Scheper-Hughes N, et al. Ethical incentives—not payment—for organ donation. N Engl J Med 2002; 346(25):2002–2005.
3. Napolitano J. Wisconsin senate approves tax deduction for organ donors. N Y Times 2004 Jan 23; A:12.

James F. Childress

Should Congress Allow the Buying and Selling of Human Organs?

A Free Market Would Reduce Donations and Would Commodify the Human Body

The number of patients awaiting an organ transplant exceeded 75,000 in late March [2001]. Yet in 1999, the last year for which there are complete figures, there only were 21,655 transplants with organs from 4,717 living donors and 5,859 from cadavers (many of which provided more than one organ). Organ donation continues to fall further and further behind the demand for organs, and new initiatives have failed to reduce the gap. In this situation, why shouldn't we turn to the free market to increase the supply of transplantable organs, which can save lives and improve the quality of life?

Buying or selling an organ isn't always morally wrong. We don't, and shouldn't, always condemn those who sell or purchase an organ. We can understand why someone might do so. But should we change our laws to permit sales of organs and even enforce contracts to sell organs? Should we turn away from a system of gifts to a market in organs?

Our society has very strong reasons not to allow the transfer of organs from the living or the dead for money. In presenting these reasons, it is useful to separate the acquisition of organs from their distribution. Normally, acquisition and distribution go together. However, if those who need organs had to purchase them directly, then the poor would end up selling organs to the rich—a distribution that would strike many as unfair. Thus, let's assume that the government or a private organization under government regulation will purchase organs and then distribute them in a fair and equitable way. I'll call this an "organ-procurement market."

Such a market could target living donors or cadaveric sources of organs. I use the term "sources" because those who sell their organs are not donors, they are sellers or vendors. Let's begin with cadaveric organs removed after an individual's death.

The main argument for rescinding the federal prohibition on the sale of organs is based on utility—allowing the sale of organs would increase their supply. But would a market actually increase the number of cadaveric organs for transplantation? Despite the claims of market fundamentalists, we simply

From *Insight on the News*, May 7, 2001, pp. 41, 43. Copyright © 2001. Reprinted by permission of The Washington Times.

do not know whether a market would reduce the scarcity of organs, in contrast to many other goods. And we have good reasons to be skeptical.

Indeed, I will argue, we shouldn't legalize a market in organ procurement because it probably would be ineffective, perhaps counterproductive (in reducing donations and possibly even the overall number of organs available for transplantation) and likely change our attitudes and practices by commodifying the human body and its parts. Furthermore, it is unnecessary to take this route, with all its problems, because we can make the system of donation effective without such ethical risks.

It would be unwise to move away from a system of donation unless we have good evidence that a market actually would increase the supply of organs. After all, organ donations provide a substantial (though insufficient) number of organs. Some evidence against a potential market's effectiveness in cadaveric organ procurement comes from the reasons people now give for not signing donor cards. One proponent of the market contends that people now fail to donate "because of inertia, mild doubts about their preferences, a slight distaste for considering the subject or the inconvenience involved in completing or carrying a donor card." If these reasons for nondonation were the only ones, a market in cadaveric organ procurement probably would work. In fact, however, opinion polls indicate that fears of being declared dead prematurely or having one's death hastened in order to provide organs seriously inhibit many from signing donor cards.

The fears and distrust that limit organ donation would render utterly ineffective a system of organ procurement based on sales. A futures market— whereby individuals contract now for delivery of organs upon their deaths—is the most defensible because people sell their own, not others', organs. However, if people at present are reluctant to sign donor cards because they fear they may not receive proper care in the hospital, imagine their fears about accepting money for the delivery of usable organs upon their deaths. Once they have signed the contract, all that remains for its fulfillment is their death. And a regulated market would not eliminate their fears. After all, such fears persist in our regulated system of organ donation.

Critics often contend that allowing sales of organs would turn bodies and parts into commodities. Such commodification could lead us to think about and treat dead bodies in merely instrumental terms, thereby damaging important social values. In addition, many claim, commodification could damage and even reduce altruism. A market in organs would drive out, or very substantially reduce, organ donations, in part because it would redefine acts of donating organs. No longer would donors provide the "gift of life"—they instead would donate the equivalent of the market value of the organs provided.

In short, market defenders have not proposed an effective system to obtain additional cadaveric organs. Not only would a procurement market probably be ineffective, it could be counterproductive and have other social costs. Its financial costs would not be negligible. Furthermore, the system of donation has features, including its connection with altruism, that make it ethically preferable, other things being equal. And we can make our system of express donation more effective.

It works fairly well now. For example, according to some estimates, the acts of cadaveric-organ donation in 1999 represented close to half of the patients who died in circumstances where their organs could be salvaged for transplantation (usually following brain death). It might be possible, and desirable, to expand the categories of potential donors to include many who die according to cardiopulmonary standards. Beyond expanding the criteria of donor eligibility, we need to work to make effective the recently adopted policy of required referral. This policy mandates referral to an organ-procurement organization that can then ask the family about organ donation.

Programs to educate the public about organ donation must attend to attitudes of distrust and mistrust, not merely to the tremendous need for organs. It is difficult to alter those attitudes, but increasing the public's understanding of brain death certainly is one way to proceed.

The public's willingness to donate cadaveric organs generally presupposes trust not only in the society's criteria and procedures for determining death, but in its criteria for fairly and effectively distributing donated organs as well. In addition, the provision of access to basic health care for everyone would create a sense of solidarity that dramatically could increase organ donation, but that vision is a distant one.

I salute the decisions in some states to give the decedent's signed donor card priority over family objections, but it is even more important to educate individuals as members of families. They need to share their decisions with their families and consider their roles as potential donors of a family member's organs. Donor cards may be a useful mechanism to stimulate such conversations, but in and of themselves they are too individualistic, legalistic and formalistic. The process of intrafamilial communication is more important.

Society also provides various incentives for organ donation, such as by recognizing and honoring donors in various ways. Would it be possible to offer some financial incentives without crossing over into a market for organ procurement? Consider the following: As a regular expression of its gratitude for organ donation, society could cover the decedent's funeral expenses up to a certain amount, perhaps $1,000 or more. In this way, the community would recognize with gratitude the decedent's and/or the family's act of donation and also pay respects to the donor or source of the organs by sharing in the disposition of his/her final remains.

Any proposal for such "rewarded gifting" will require careful scrutiny, in part because organ donation is such a highly sensitive area, marked by complex beliefs, symbols, attitudes, sentiments and practices, some of them religious in nature. But a carefully conceived pilot experiment, such as providing death benefits—as Pennsylvania has discussed—may be justifiable. However, it may infringe current laws. In any event, it requires the utmost caution because of its risks. One risk is that it will be perceived as purchasing organs rather than as expressing gratitude and providing incentives for donation.

I have focused on cadaveric organs, but what about a market in organ procurement from living individuals? Such a market probably would be more effective than a futures market in cadaveric organs—more individuals probably would be willing to part with a kidney, especially with reduced risks from kidney removal and with generous compensation. However, the social risk of commodification—of treating living human bodies and their parts as commodities—is very troubling. In addition, the risks of coercion and exploitation, especially of poor people, are substantial. The assertion of a moral right to sell a kidney against the legal prohibition of such a sale is not persuasive; we have good reasons, based on concerns about commodification, coercion and exploitation, to reject such sales as incompatible with our moral vision of the kind of society to which we aspire.

Vigorous efforts along the paths I have indicated should obviate the need to adopt a market in organ procurement, whether from living or cadaveric sources. We have little reason to believe that a futures market will be effective in obtaining cadaveric organs and considerable reason to worry about the risks and social costs of such a market, as well as a market for living organ procurement. We should just say "no" to both markets.

POSTSCRIPT

Should Congress Allow the Buying and Selling of Human Organs?

This is a difficult issue to discuss. One of the difficulties is fairly straight-forward. We need to know the medical facts about kidneys and other organs. In the case of kidneys, we are born with two, but we need only one kidney to survive. (And the form of survival here is not just marginal or borderline. Approximately 98 percent of life insurance companies do not charge a higher premium for people with only one kidney.) If your kidneys don't function properly, and you are unable to receive a transplanted kidney, it may be possible to survive through the use of a kidney dialysis machine—but this requires attachment to such a machine for several hours at a time, several times a week. The use of the machine does not *cure* or solve the problem; it merely "purifies" your blood, removing some of the unwanted products and chemicals, while saving what's useful. However, since the fundamental problem is never cured this way, you must return to the machine in about two days for several hours' more purification—and the process never ends. But if you could have a kidney transplant, and your body didn't reject it, then the kidney could do the blood purifying, and you wouldn't have to use the dialysis machine anymore. Hence, the great need for a functioning kidney.

But at this point, we encounter another problem in dealing with this issue. There is a certain feeling of ghoulishness associated with the buying and selling of human organs. It might be nice, we think, for a good friend or family member to *donate* a kidney—and perhaps it is even somewhat noble—but the buying and selling of human organs threatens to turn them into mere commodities. Childress even suggests that if kidneys can be bought and sold, and have a market value, then there will be fewer donations. This would occur because what used to be *donations* of kidneys would simply be superseded by the market; under a market system, if the good friend or relative wanted to help the person on the dialysis machine, all that would be required is money or a loan. Childress wants to encourage donation, not a market. But as Burrows points out, the supply of donated kidneys falls far short of the demand. And these are the conditions that most favor a market solution.

Recent publications that address this issue are Patrick Waldron, "You Gave Me a New Life: St. Charles Gymnastics Coach Receives Kidney Donation from Her Co-Worker," *Daily Herald* (Arlington Heights, IL, July 2, 2004); James Stacey Taylor, *Stakes and Kidneys: Why Markets in Human Body Parts Are Morally Imperative* (Ashgate, 2005); Mark J. Cherry, *Kidney for Sale by Owner: Human Organs, Transplantation, and the Market* (Georgetown University

Press, 2005); Lesley A. Sharp, *Bodies, Commodities, and Biotechnologies: Death, Mourning, and Scientific Desire in the Realm of Human Organ Transfer* (Columbia University Press, 2006); Rohan J. Hardcastle, *Law and the Human Body: Property Rights, Ownership and Control* (Hart Publishing, 2007); and Donna Dickenson, *Body Shopping: The Economy Fuelled by Flesh and Blood* (Oneworld Publications, 2008).

ISSUE 9

Should Drugs Be Legalized?

YES: Meaghan Cussen and Walter Block, from "Legalize Drugs Now! An Analysis of the Benefits of Legalized Drugs," *American Journal of Economics and Sociology* (July 2000)

NO: Theodore Dalrymple, from "Don't Legalize Drugs," *cjonline.com* (*The City Journal*) (Spring 1997)

ISSUE SUMMARY

YES: Meaghan Cussen (a student in economics) and Walter Block (her economics professor) argue that the legalization of drugs would provide many sorts of benefits (e.g., crime would fall, the quality of life in inner cities would rise, and taxpayers would no longer have to pay for an unwinnable "war on drugs"). Moreover, the legalization of drugs would promote the American value of liberty.

NO: Theodore Dalrymple stresses the harm that drugs can do and the danger of "giving up" in the "war on drugs." He takes issue with most of the claims of the supporters of legalization, and more generally with Mill's "harm principle": the idea that in a free society, adults should be permitted to do whatever they please (provided that they are willing to accept the consequences of their own actions, and those actions don't cause harm to others).

$\mathbf{N}$o one can deny that the use of psychoactive substances has a great impact on society today—from the health effects of cigarettes to the criminal activity of street-corner crack dealers. In some cases, the greatest impact is from the smuggling, trafficking, and consumption of illegal drugs. These practices inevitably lead to bribery, violent crime, babies born addicted to drugs such as crack, and a host of other social ills.

In recent years, there has been a "war on drugs" that is supposed to address (if not solve) these problems. Since the problems still exist, and the war on drugs has been going on now for some time, critics might wonder how effective the war is. Severe critics would say that the so-called war on drugs isn't working at all and that it's time to try another approach.

Some have called for the legalization of drugs. If drugs were legal, proponents say, their sale and use could be regulated and controlled. The government would be able to raise revenue through taxation (instead of having huge drug profits go to organized crime), the quality and quantity of the drugs could be officially monitored, and much street crime could be eliminated. However, even after legalization, there would still be many drug addicts (and perhaps even more of them), "crack babies," and other victims of drug use.

Proponents of drug legalization must offer a realistic plan for the legal market they propose. At least two elements should be addressed. First, what exactly is meant by legalization? Substances that are legal are not necessarily available at all times to everyone. Alcohol, for example, is a legal substance, but when, where, and to whom it may be sold are all regulated by federal and local authorities. And currently some legal drugs are available only by prescription. Second, some further clarification is needed about what is meant by drugs. Talk about drugs can be very vague. Caffeine and nicotine are common drugs, but since they are already legal, we might say that we are considering here only illegal drugs. But why are some drugs legal and others illegal in the first place?

Twentieth-century (alcohol) Prohibition is one of the useful test cases that some people appeal to—while we obviously cannot experiment with changing the legal status of a drug for a limited time to see what would happen, Prohibition is a historical reality. We can check the historical record to see what happened when alcohol was prohibited. Prohibition became effective on January 16, 1920, and was repealed on December 5, 1933. During this time, the Constitution was amended to outlaw "the manufacture, sale, or the transportation of intoxicating liquors within . . . the United States." Also outlawed were all import and export of these items. During Prohibition, many of the problems that we now associate with the modern drug world existed: smuggling, official corruption, murder, large amounts of money being made by violent criminals, and organized criminal networks. Members of the public could—with a little effort, and in some cases with very little effort—buy and consume the very products that were against the law. And what was bought on the black market had no guarantees with respect to health or safety.

In the following selections, Meaghan Cussen and Walter Block and Theodore Dalrymple present radically different cases. Cussen and Block argue that government programs that are meant to control the use of certain substances are misguided; in fact, these efforts are themselves responsible for much drug-related crime; and, for both drug users and the general public, many benefits would follow from the legalization of drugs. However, Theodore Dalrymple argues that it is the drugs themselves that are harmful, and that no matter where we draw the line (allowing drugs for adults, for example, but not for children), drug dealers will strive to cross that line and sell to the group for whom drugs are prohibited. Drug legalization, he claims, would be much more problematic than legalization proponents admit and would certainly lead to an increase in drug abuse and drug addiction. Social ills would follow in the wake of drug legalization.

YES

Meaghan Cussen
and Walter Block

Legalize Drugs Now!
An Analysis of the Benefits
of Legalized Drugs

Abstract: The legalization of drugs would prevent our civil liberties from being threatened any further, it would reduce crime rates, reverse the potency effect, improve the quality of life in the inner cities, prevent the spread of disease, save the taxpayer money, and generally benefit both individuals and the community as a whole. Our arguments are based on a basic appreciation of the benefits provided by voluntary exchange and the role markets play in coordinating human activities. Legalizing drugs would eliminate many inconsistencies, guarantee freedoms, and increase the effectiveness of the government's anti-drug beliefs. The present war on drugs has not and will not produce a decisive victory. We advocate a new approach to this important social problem.

Drug dealers are a thing of the past. Violent crimes and theft are greatly reduced. Drug-related shoot-outs are unheard of. The streets of America begin to "clean up." Communities pull themselves together. Youths and adults once involved in crime rings are forced to seek legitimate work. Deaths due to infected intravenous needles and poisonous street drugs are eliminated. Taxpayers are no longer forced to pay $10,000,000,000 to fund drug-related law enforcement. The $80,000,000,000 claimed by organized crime and drug rings will now go to honest workers (Ostrowski 1993, pp. 203–205). What policy change will bring about such good news? The legalization of drugs! Both practically and philosophically speaking, addictive drugs should be legalized.

I. Basic Constitutional Rights

Many argue that drug prohibition protects addicts from themselves by exerting parental control over their behavior. This government-enforced control, the anti-drug laws, strictly monitors addicts' treatment of their own bodies. For example, the government decides that it wants to protect Fred Brown from destroying his body. The government, therefore, outlaws narcotics and, in effect, takes control of Fred's body. Under the United States Constitution and the anti-slavery laws, this hegemony should not happen. The guiding principles

From *American Journal of Economics & Sociology,* vol. 59, no. 3, July 2000, pp. 525–536. Copyright © 2000 by American Journal of Economics & Sociology, Inc. Reprinted by permission of Wiley-Blackwell via Rightslink.

of the United States, iterated both in the Declaration of Independence and the Constitution, protect Fred's basic civil liberties to "pursue his own happiness" as long as he doesn't infringe on others' rights to life and property. With prohibition, Fred no longer has this constitutional right. He no longer controls his own body. Regulation has stripped him of his civil liberty. Fred's role of "owner of his own body" is taken away from him. This has in effect made him a slave.

Are we being hysterical in categorizing present drug law as a form of servitude? No, our drug laws amount to partial slavery. We must all question the practices of roadblocks, strip-searches, urine tests, locker searches, and money laundering laws. Philosophically speaking, drug prohibition severely threatens our civil liberties and is inconsistent with the anti-slavery philosophy and the founding documents of the United States. The legalization of drugs would give a basic civil liberty back to U.S. citizens, by granting them control over their own bodies.

II. Free Trade

Free trade benefits all parties. It can be assumed that if drugs were legalized, and thus were a part of the market, both the buyer and the seller would gain. Each time a trade occurs, the welfare of both parties is improved. If Joe sold you his shirt for $10, he would benefit because he obviously values the $10 more than the shirt. If he didn't, he would not have traded it. You would also gain from the trade because you obviously value the shirt more than you do the $10. If you didn't, then you would not have agreed to the deal. Free trade in the drug market works the same way. If Joe sells you marijuana for $10, he gains because he values the money more, and you gain because you value the drugs more. Whether or not another person *thinks you should* value the drugs more is not the question. That third party is not involved in the trade. The amount of pleasure the drug brings you is your motivation for buying it. Trade is a positive-sum game. Both parties gain, at least in the ex ante sense.

It cannot be denied that certain third parties will be offended by the drug transaction, on moral or ethical grounds. However, try to find any transaction that does not offend at least one person. Many people object to the sale of alcohol, cigarettes, birth control or animal products, but their feelings or beliefs do not stop these items from being sold. Marxists object to *any* market transactions because they see commercial activity as necessarily exploitative. There is obviously no pleasing everyone when it comes to market transactions. In our free enterprise economy, however, anyone who participates in the market will benefit from it. ". . . For all third parties who say they will be aggrieved by a legalized drug trade, there will be many more benefiting from the reduction in crime" (Block 1993). "A third party can verbally oppose any given trade. But that opposition cannot be revealed through market choices in the same way that trade between the two parties indicates a positive evaluation of the transaction" (Block 1996, p. 434). Free trade of all goods contributes to the number of those who gain. In a free market economy, everybody has opportunity to participate in the market, and therefore, equal opportunity to gain in a positive sum transaction.

Not only would the legalization of drugs protect basic freedoms and lead to individual benefit through free trade, but it would also bring enormous benefits to society as a whole. The first and most important societal benefit is a reduction in crime.

III. Reductions in Crime

When addictive drugs are made legal, crime will decrease substantially, for four main reasons. First, the lowered price of narcotics will eliminate the theft and murder associated with their high prices. When drugs are legalized, law-abiding businesspeople will no longer be deterred by the illegality of drug commerce and will become willing to enter the market. With this increase of supply, assuming a less than proportional increase in demand, the price of narcotics will fall. Addicts who were formerly forced to steal, murder, and engage in illegal employment to earn enough money for their habits will be able to afford the lower prices. Therefore, these types of drug-related crimes will decrease.

Second, substance-related disputes such as gang wars and street violence will be reduced. Dealers will be able to use the courts to settle their disputes instead of taking the law into their own hands. Violations of rights within the drug business will be resolved through the judicial system, thereby decreasing gang violence, and saving the many innocent lives that often get caught in the crossfire.

Third, the drug business creates great profits for cartels. Cartels are often international organizations, many of which support terrorism and add to violent crime in America. If the narcotics market were open, drug revenues would be equally distributed by free-market forces, and would have less of a chance of supporting terrorist organizations, crime rings, and cartel activity and profit.

Finally, and most obviously, with transport, sale, and possession legalized, formerly illegal activities will now become society-approved business transactions. Crime, an act that breaks the law, and in its very insurrectional essence leads to societal instability, will be greatly reduced through the legalization of the inevitable activity of drug transactions.

The prohibition of alcohol in the 1920s provides us with a perfect case in point. The high crime rates during this decade were due to the existence of the black market, spawned from the government-enforced illegalization of alcohol. The black market led to the formation of major crime rings. The underground market for alcohol grew and led many profit-hungry entrepreneurs into a risky lifestyle of crime. Many were jailed due to transport, sale, and possession.

When Prohibition ended, alcohol-related crime ceased. The profit balloon driven by the limited supply of the illegal substance was deflated. The black market disappeared, along with all of the illegal activity associated with it. Crime rings were forced to disband and seek other means of income. How many crime rings exist today for the selling of alcohol? The answer is none. The reason is legalization.

In contrast, drug-related crime is skyrocketing. As Ostrowski (1993, p. 209) notes, "The President's Commission on Organized Crime estimates a total of seventy drug market murders yearly in Miami alone. Based on that figure and FBI data, a reasonable nationwide estimate would be at least 750 murders a year. Recent estimates from New York and Washington are even higher." Anyone who questions whether prohibition is responsible for violence should note the relative peace that prevails in the alcohol and legal drug markets.

IV. The Potency Effect

The end of prohibition also brought the end of the dangerous potency effect. During Prohibition, it was in the best interests of the sellers to carry more potent forms of alcohol. Hence, an alcohol dealer would be more likely to carry vodka and other hard liquor instead of beer and wine because of hard liquor's greater value (per unit of volume). Therefore, people began drinking vodka and other hard liquor, which because of their high potency are more dangerous than beer and wine. Alcohol-related deaths increased. This horrific result is known as the potency effect.

Fifty years after the repeal of Prohibition, the potency effect has been reversed. The average per capita consumption of alcohol has fallen to its lowest level ever (Hamid 1993, p. 184). In fact, people have begun switching to weaker alcohol alternatives, such as wine coolers and nonalcoholic beer. The legalization of alcohol reversed the potency effect. The legalization of drugs will do the same.

For example, the risks involved in transporting marijuana, a low-potency drug, for the purpose of sale are extremely high. It is in the best interests of the dealer to carry more potent, thus more expensive, drugs, which is why he or she will be more likely to carry cocaine because of its greater value (per unit of volume). Because cocaine is more potent, it is also more dangerous. Addicts face increased health risks when using cocaine as opposed to using marijuana. These health risks grow as potency increases. Stronger and more dangerous drugs such as crack, "ice," and PCP are substituted for the weaker, relatively safer drugs. The results are often deadly.

V. Health Benefits

The legalization of drugs would eliminate serious health risks by assuring market-driven high quality substances and the availability of clean needles. Prohibition in the 1920s created a market for cheap versions of alcoholic products, such as bathtub gin. Alcohol was diluted or adulterated in often dangerous ways. Needless deaths occurred because of the poor quality of the product. So is drug prohibition worth the health risks? Fly-by-night goods cannot always be trusted. If narcotics were legalized, purity could be all but guaranteed. Drugstores, held accountable by customers, would deliver safe products. Brand names would bring competition into the market and assure safer, better products. Doctors would now be able to monitor the drug use of seriously addicted patients. Poor quality would be a thing of the past.

In addition, clean needles would be readily available. Drug vendors and health care organizations would be able to provide clean needles for their customers and patients, respectively. Today, needles are shared because they are difficult to obtain. About twenty-five percent of AIDS cases are contracted through the sharing of intravenous needles (Boaz 1990, p. 3). Legalizing drugs would eliminate this problem. "In Hong Kong, where needles are available in drugstores, as of 1987 there were no cases of AIDS among drug users" (ibid).

When was the last time you heard of a diabetic contracting AIDS from contaminated needles? If insulin were prohibited, this situation would surely change for the worse.

VI. Societal Benefits

Illegal drug sale creates a destructive atmosphere. When a criminal culture emerges, a community is torn apart. A booming black market fosters a large criminal presence. Casual recreational users are forced to come in contact with criminals to make their purchases, as prohibition makes it impossible to make a legal transaction. Additionally, basically good citizens often deal with and, unfortunately, become influenced by, the criminals of the area (Boaz 1990, p. 2).

Inner-city youths, surrounded by the booming black market, are influenced by the sheer amount of money dealers make and often fall into a life of crime (Boaz 1990, p. 2). These youths often see themselves as having the choice of remaining in poverty, earning "chump change," or pursuing a life of crime and making thousands of dollars a week. Which do you think all too many young people will choose?

The black market presence often leads to the corruption of police officers and public officials. Police, on average, make $35,000 a year. When they arrest the denizens of the drug world who make ten times that amount, it is often difficult not to be tempted into a life of crime.

> Drug corruption charges have been leveled against FBI agents, police officers, prison guards, U.S. customs inspectors, even prosecutors. In 1986, in New York City's 77th Precinct, twelve police officers were arrested for stealing and selling drugs. Miami's problem is worse. In June 1986, seven officers there were indicted for using their jobs to run a drug operation that used murders, threats, and bribery. Add to that two dozen other cases of corruption in the last three years in Miami alone (Ostrowski 1993, pp. 296–207).

We must question a policy that so frequently turns police officers into the very outlaws they are authorized to bring to justice. We must question a policy that leads to the enormous success of those willing to break the laws of our society. We must question a policy that leaves a criminal profession in a position of great influence over our youth and other honest citizens. Milton Friedman put it best when he wrote, "Drugs are a tragedy for addicts. But criminalizing their use converts the tragedy into a disaster for society, for users and non-users alike" (Friedman 1989a).

VII. Prohibit the Crime, Not the Drug

The laws of the United States prohibit violent acts against other citizens. This is consistent with the founding principles of our nation, which allow each free individual to pursue life, liberty, and happiness. The laws of United States should not prohibit the intake of narcotics that only have an immediate effect on the individual consumer. If I ingest a drug, I am doing possible harm only to myself, and no other. If I subsequently act violently on account of my altered state of mind, only then am I doing harm to others. It is the subsequent action that is harmful, not the drug taking itself. Since I am responsible for my actions, I should be arrested and punished only when I am violent. Alcohol is legal even though people commit rapes, murders, beatings, and other violent crimes when they are drunk. Yet if a person commits these crimes when intoxicated, he or she is held responsible for them. A mere substance should not and does not serve as an excuse for the violent acts. The ingestion of alcohol is not illegal per se. The same standard should be applied to the use of presently illegal drugs.

It should also be noted that every narcotic does not turn the user into a crazed, enraged lunatic capable of all sorts of violent crimes. In fact, it is just the opposite. Most drugs induce lethargy. Remember that opium, now illegal, was used quite often in England, China, and the United States, and tended to induce stupor. The use of traditional opiates did not render users violent. In fact, no drug is "as strongly associated with violent behavior as is alcohol. According to Justice Department statistics, 54 percent of all jail inmates convicted of violent crimes in 1983 reported having just used alcohol just prior to committing their offense" (Nadelmann 1989, p. 22). This statistic renders the prohibition of drugs rather than alcohol a legal inconsistency.

VIII. Save the U.S. Taxpayer Money

According to the U.S. Department of Justice, federal, state, and local governments currently spend over $20 billion per year on drug enforcement. In 1992, there were more than one million arrests for drug law violations. In 1993, sixty percent of the seventy-seven thousand federal prisoners were incarcerated for drug-related crimes (Miron and Zweibel 1995, p. 176). Jails are crowded and large amounts of tax dollars are being spent on enforcement efforts that only aggravate the problem. We can add to this sum the amount of money spent on research and medical care for those infected with AIDS and other diseases caused by needle sharing.

With legalization, the tax dollars spent on enforcement would be saved. The availability of clean needles would reduce the rate of AIDS infections, and would consequently reduce the amount of money spent on medical care, to say nothing of the reduction in human misery.

IX. Don't Help Inflate Criminals' Profit Balloons

If we continue with the same anti-drug policies, we are only helping drug lords get richer. Each time a bust occurs and a shipment is captured and destroyed, the criminals benefit. The seizure reduces supply and takes out one or more black market participants. According to the laws of supply and demand, with a decrease in drug supply, black market prices will rise, creating a larger profit for suppliers. So, every time we think we are winning a battle in the war, we are really strengthening the enemy rather than weakening it. The way to win is not by fighting the alligators, but by draining their swamp (Block 1993, p. 696). It is better to ruin drug lords' businesses by deflating the profit balloon than by acting in a way (i.e., prohibition) that only benefits them. "By taking the profits out of [drugs], we could at one fell swoop do more to reduce their power than decades of fighting them directly" (Holloway, p. 6).

At present, governmental control of the drug lords, while minuscule, is as effective as it will ever be in any sector of society (Thornton 1991). Just think, even in jails, where the lives of residents are completely controlled by the government, drugs still have not been eliminated. If the government cannot even control the drug trade within its own house, how can it expect to control it within the entire nation? Are we to imprison the whole citizenry in an attempt? Legalization will takes the profits out of the narcotics industry.

X. Elasticity of Demand for Drugs

Many believe the elasticity of demand for narcotics is very high. If drugs are legalized and their prices fall, the amount purchased will increase by a large amount. This is not the case. In fact, the elasticity of demand for drugs in general is very low for three main reasons. First, narcotics are seen as necessities for drug users, not luxuries. "While one might severely reduce demand for [luxuries] in the face of an increased price, or even give it up entirely in the extreme, this does not apply to [necessities]" (Block 1993, p. 696). This behavioral pattern indicates that drugs are indeed low elasticity goods. In fact, there is really no good reason to assume that many Americans would suddenly start to ingest or inject narcotics even if given the legal opportunity.

Second, most people recognize the danger of drugs and will avoid them no matter what the price. Third, if drugs are made legal, they will no longer have to be pushed. If they are sold over the counter to adults, criminals will no longer have to pawn these goods off on innocent youths. Competition will be high and dealers will have no reason to resort to this extreme measure. Certainly, market competition will occur which may result in advertisements' targeting particular age groups. However, this would have a negligible effect compared to drug pushers' current youth-targeted tactics.

Finally, we should realize that legalization would cause potency to fall. With normalized supply, people will begin purchasing weaker, safer drugs. This normalized supply, along with the low elasticity of demand for narcotics, will lead to only a small increase in consumption.

XI. Government Regulations

A main driver of anti-drug legislation is the concern that government would be sanctioning an immoral and destructive activity, viewed as sinful in many eyes of the population. However, the legalization of drugs does not mean that government and society would sanction their use. Alcohol and cigarettes are legal but we have pretty successful campaigns against these substances. Gossiping and burping are also legal, but you never see a government sponsored advertisement advocating catty behavior or belching in public. Are we as a society to prohibit automobile racing, extreme skiing, the ingestion of ice cream and fried foods because they may have a detrimental effect on human health? No. Dangers associated with these activities cannot be measured. ". . . Such inherently unquantifiable variables cannot be measured, much less weighed against each other. Interpersonal comparison of utility is incompatible with valid economic analysis" (Block 1996, p. 435). We cannot allow such legal inconsistencies to take place.

Legalizing drugs would eliminate these inconsistencies, guarantee freedoms, and increase the efficiency and effectiveness of the government's anti-drug beliefs. If drugs were legalized, taxes could be cut, with the elimination of government expenditures on enforcement. All of the money saved could be used to promote anti-drug campaigns. Private organizations could take over the tasks of inspecting and regulating. A minimum age of twenty-one would be mandated for the consumption of drugs. Transactions would take place in a drugstore, with upstanding suppliers. Drugs could safely be administered, with clean needles, in hospitals where medical professionals could monitor and rehabilitate the addicted. MADD (Mothers Against Drunk Driving) is a good example of a successful anti-substance abuse campaign. Private, nonprofit groups like this one could help in the fight against drug abuse.

Currently, we are not by any means winning the war on drugs. Our futile attempts at enforcement only exacerbate the problem. We need to de-escalate the war rather than continue fighting the over twenty-three million adult Americans who are obviously determined to enjoy themselves as they see fit (Boaz 1990, p. 5). We must also remember that those that need to be deterred the most, the hard-core drug users, are the least likely to be stopped (Ostrowski 1993, p. 205). Our law enforcement is not working to contain and control the very people the anti-drug laws are designed to control. The war on drugs has done little to reduce narcotics use in the United States and has thus proved counterproductive (Holloway, p. 6). Philosophically and practically speaking, drugs should be legalized. This act would prevent our civil liberties from being threatened, reduce crime rates, reverse the potency effect, improve the quality of life in inner cities, prevent the spread of disease, save the taxpayer money, and generally benefit both individuals and society as a whole.

References

Block, Walter. (1993). "Drug Prohibition: A Legal and Economic Analysis." *Journal of Business Ethics* 12: 689–700.

———. (1996). "Drug Prohibition and Individual Virtue." *Review of Political Economy.* Volume 8, November: 433–436.

Boaz, David. (1990). "The Consequences of Prohibition." In *The Crisis of Drug Prohibition.* Washington, D.C.: Cato Institute.

Friedman, Milton. (1989a). "An Open Letter to Bill Bennett." *Wall Street Journal,* September 7.

Hamid, Ansley. (1993). "To the Editor of the Commentary." In *Drugs in America: The Reference Shelf* (New York: H.W. Wilson) 65 (4): 181–184.

Holloway, Jason and Walter Block. (1998). "Should Drugs Be Legalized?" In *West Coast Libertarian* April: 6–7.

Miron, Jeffrey and Jeffrey Zweibel. (1995). "The Economic Case Against Drug Prohibition." *Journal of Economic Perspectives* 9 (4): 175–192.

Nadelmann, E. (1989). "The Case for Legalization," *Washington Post,* October 8.

Ostrowski, James (1993) [1990]. "Has the Time Come to Legalize Drugs?" *USA Today Magazine* 119 (July 1990): Reprinted in *Drugs in America: The Reference Shelf* (New York: H.W. Wilson) 65 (4): 203–212.

Thornton, M. (1991). *The Economics of Prohibition.* Salt Lake City: The University of Utah Press.

 **NO**

Don't Legalize Drugs

There is a progression in the minds of men: first the unthinkable becomes thinkable, and then it becomes an orthodoxy whose truth seems so obvious that no one remembers that anyone ever thought differently. This is just what is happening with the idea of legalizing drugs: it has reached the stage when millions of thinking men are agreed that allowing people to take whatever they like is the obvious, indeed only, solution to the social problems that arise from the consumption of drugs.

Man's desire to take mind-altering substances is as old as society itself— as are attempts to regulate their consumption. If intoxication in one form or another is inevitable, then so is customary or legal restraint upon that intoxication. But no society until our own has had to contend with the ready availability of so many different mind-altering drugs, combined with a citizenry jealous of its right to pursue its own pleasures in its own way.

The arguments in favor of legalizing the use of all narcotic and stimulant drugs are twofold: philosophical and pragmatic. Neither argument is negligible, but both are mistaken, I believe, and both miss the point.

The philosophic argument is that, in a free society, adults should be permitted to do whatever they please, always provided that they are prepared to take the consequences of their own choices and that they cause no direct harm to others. The locus classicus for this point of view is John Stuart Mill's famous essay On Liberty: "The only purpose for which power can be rightfully exercised over any member of the community, against his will, is to prevent harm to others," Mill wrote. "His own good, either physical or moral, is not a sufficient warrant." This radical individualism allows society no part whatever in shaping, determining, or enforcing a moral code: in short, we have nothing in common but our contractual agreement not to interfere with one another as we go about seeking our private pleasures.

In practice, of course, it is exceedingly difficult to make people take all the consequences of their own actions—as they must, if Mill's great principle is to serve as a philosophical guide to policy. Addiction to, or regular use of, most currently prohibited drugs cannot affect only the person who takes them—and not his spouse, children, neighbors, or employers. No man, except possibly a hermit, is an island; and so it is virtually impossible for Mill's principle to apply to any human action whatever, let alone shooting up heroin or smoking crack. Such a principle is virtually useless in determining what should or should not be permitted.

Perhaps we ought not be too harsh on Mill's principle: it's not clear that anyone has ever thought of a better one. But that is precisely the point. Human affairs cannot be decided by an appeal to an infallible rule, expressible in a few words, whose simple application can decide all cases, including whether drugs should be freely available to the entire adult population. Philosophical fundamentalism is not preferable to the religious variety; and because the desiderata of human life are many, and often in conflict with one another, mere philosophical inconsistency in policy—such as permitting the consumption of alcohol while outlawing cocaine—is not a sufficient argument against that policy. We all value freedom, and we all value order; sometimes we sacrifice freedom for order, and sometimes order for freedom. But once a prohibition has been removed, it is hard to restore, even when the newfound freedom proves to have been ill-conceived and socially disastrous.

Even Mill came to see the limitations of his own principle as a guide for policy and to deny that all pleasures were of equal significance for human existence. It was better, he said, to be Socrates discontented than a fool satisfied. Mill acknowledged that some goals were intrinsically worthier of pursuit than others.

This being the case, not all freedoms are equal, and neither are all limitations of freedom: some are serious and some trivial. The freedom we cherish— or should cherish—is not merely that of satisfying our appetites, whatever they happen to be. We are not Dickensian Harold Skimpoles, exclaiming in protest that "Even the butterflies are free!" We are not children who chafe at restrictions because they are restrictions. And we even recognize the apparent paradox that some limitations to our freedoms have the consequence of making us freer overall. The freest man is not the one who slavishly follows his appetites and desires throughout his life—as all too many of my patients have discovered to their cost.

We are prepared to accept limitations to our freedoms for many reasons, not just that of public order. Take an extreme hypothetical case: public exhibitions of necrophilia are quite rightly not permitted, though on Mill's principle they should be. A corpse has no interests and cannot be harmed, because it is no longer a person; and no member of the public is harmed if he has agreed to attend such an exhibition.

Our resolve to prohibit such exhibitions would not be altered if we discovered that millions of people wished to attend them or even if we discovered that millions already were attending them illicitly. Our objection is not based upon pragmatic considerations or upon a head count: it is based upon the wrongness of the would-be exhibitions themselves. The fact that the prohibition represents a genuine restriction of our freedom is of no account.

It might be argued that the freedom to choose among a variety of intoxicating substances is a much more important freedom and that millions of people have derived innocent fun from taking stimulants and narcotics. But the consumption of drugs has the effect of reducing men's freedom by circumscribing the range of their interests. It impairs their ability to pursue more important human aims, such as raising a family and fulfilling civic obligations. Very often it impairs their ability to pursue gainful employment and promotes parasitism. Moreover, far from being expanders of consciousness, most drugs severely limit it. One of the most striking characteristics of drug takers is their intense and tedious self-absorption; and their journeys into inner space are generally forays into inner vacuums. Drug taking is a lazy man's way of pursuing happiness and wisdom, and the shortcut turns out to be the deadest of dead ends. We lose remarkably little by not being permitted to take drugs.

The idea that freedom is merely the ability to act upon one's whims is surely very thin and hardly begins to capture the complexities of human existence; a man whose appetite is his law strikes us not as liberated but enslaved. And when such a narrowly conceived freedom is made the touchstone of public policy, a dissolution of society is bound to follow. No culture that makes publicly sanctioned self-indulgence its highest good can long survive: a radical egotism is bound to ensue, in which any limitations upon personal behavior are experienced as infringements of basic rights. Distinctions between the important and the trivial, between the freedom to criticize received ideas and the freedom to take LSD, are precisely the standards that keep societies from barbarism.

So the legalization of drugs cannot be supported by philosophical principle. But if the pragmatic argument in favor of legalization were strong enough, it might overwhelm other objections. It is upon this argument that proponents of legalization rest the larger part of their case.

The argument is that the overwhelming majority of the harm done to society by the consumption of currently illicit drugs is caused not by their pharmacological properties but by their prohibition and the resultant criminal activity that prohibition always calls into being. Simple reflection tells us that a supply invariably grows up to meet a demand; and when the demand is widespread, suppression is useless. Indeed, it is harmful, since—by raising the price of the commodity in question—it raises the profits of middlemen, which gives them an even more powerful incentive to stimulate demand further. The vast profits to be made from cocaine and heroin—which, were it not for their illegality, would be cheap and easily affordable even by the poorest in affluent societies—exert a deeply corrupting effect on producers, distributors, consumers, and law enforcers alike. Besides, it is well known that illegality in itself has attractions for youth already inclined to disaffection. Even many of the harmful physical effects of illicit drugs stem from their illegal status: for example, fluctuations in the purity of heroin bought on the street are responsible for many of the deaths by overdose. If the sale and consumption of such drugs were legalized, consumers would know how much they were taking and thus avoid overdoses.

Moreover, since society already permits the use of some mind-altering substances known to be both addictive and harmful, such as alcohol and nicotine, in prohibiting others it appears hypocritical, arbitrary, and dictatorial. Its hypocrisy, as well as its patent failure to enforce its prohibitions successfully, leads inevitably to a decline in respect for the law as a whole. Thus things fall apart, and the center cannot hold.

It stands to reason, therefore, that all these problems would be resolved at a stroke if everyone were permitted to smoke, swallow, or inject anything he chose. The corruption of the police, the luring of children of 11 and 12 into illegal activities, the making of such vast sums of money by drug dealing that legitimate work seems pointless and silly by comparison, and the turf wars that make poor neighborhoods so exceedingly violent and dangerous, would all cease at once were drug taking to be decriminalized and the supply regulated in the same way as alcohol.

But a certain modesty in the face of an inherently unknowable future is surely advisable. That is why prudence is a political virtue: what stands to reason should happen does not necessarily happen in practice. As Goethe said, all theory (even of the monetarist or free-market variety) is gray, but green springs the golden tree of life. If drugs were legalized, I suspect that the golden tree of life might spring some unpleasant surprises.

It is of course true, but only trivially so, that the present illegality of drugs is the cause of the criminality surrounding their distribution. Likewise, it is the illegality of stealing cars that creates car thieves. In fact, the ultimate cause of all criminality is law. As far as I am aware, no one has ever suggested that law should therefore be abandoned. Moreover, the impossibility of winning the "war" against theft, burglary, robbery, and fraud has never been used as an argument that these categories of crime should be abandoned. And so long as the demand for material goods outstrips supply, people will be tempted to commit criminal acts against the owners of property. This is not an argument, in my view, against private property or in favor of the common ownership of all goods. It does suggest, however, that we shall need a police force for a long time to come.

In any case, there are reasons to doubt whether the crime rate would fall quite as dramatically as advocates of legalization have suggested. Amsterdam, where access to drugs is relatively unproblematic, is among the most violent and squalid cities in Europe. The idea behind crime—of getting rich, or at least richer, quickly and without much effort—is unlikely to disappear once drugs are freely available to all who want them. And it may be that officially sanctioned antisocial behavior—the official lifting of taboos—breeds yet more antisocial behavior, as the "broken windows" theory would suggest.

Having met large numbers of drug dealers in prison, I doubt that they would return to respectable life if the principal article of their commerce were to be legalized. Far from evincing a desire to be reincorporated into the world of regular work, they express a deep contempt for it and regard those who accept the bargain of a fair day's work for a fair day's pay as cowards and fools. A life of crime has its attractions for many who would otherwise lead a mundane existence. So long as there is the possibility of a lucrative racket or illegal traffic, such people will find it and extend its scope. Therefore, since even legalizers would hesitate to allow children to take drugs, decriminalization might easily result in dealers turning their attentions to younger and younger children, who—in the permissive atmosphere that even now prevails—have already been inducted into the drug subculture in alarmingly high numbers.

Those who do not deal in drugs but commit crimes to fund their consumption of them are, of course, more numerous than large-scale dealers. And it is true that once opiate addicts, for example, enter a treatment program, which often includes maintenance doses of methadone, the rate at which they commit crimes falls markedly. The drug clinic in my hospital claims an 80 percent reduction in criminal convictions among heroin addicts once they have been stabilized on methadone.

This is impressive, but it is not certain that the results should be generalized. First, the patients are self-selected: they have some motivation to change, otherwise they would not have attended the clinic in the first place. Only a minority of addicts attend, and therefore it is not safe to conclude that, if other addicts were to receive methadone, their criminal activity would similarly diminish.

Second, a decline in convictions is not necessarily the same as a decline in criminal acts. If methadone stabilizes an addict's life, he may become a more efficient, harder-to-catch criminal. Moreover, when the police in our city do catch an addict, they are less likely to prosecute him if he can prove that he is undergoing anything remotely resembling psychiatric treatment. They return him directly to his doctor. Having once had a psychiatric consultation is an all-purpose alibi for a robber or a burglar; the police, who do not want to fill in the 40-plus forms it now takes to charge anyone with anything in England, consider a single contact with a psychiatrist sufficient to deprive anyone of legal responsibility for crime forever.

Third, the rate of criminal activity among those drug addicts who receive methadone from the clinic, though reduced, remains very high. The deputy director of the clinic estimates that the number of criminal acts committed by his average patient (as judged by self-report) was 250 per year before entering treatment and 50 afterward. It may well be that the real difference is considerably less than this, because the patients have an incentive to exaggerate it to secure the continuation of their methadone. But clearly, opiate addicts who receive their drugs legally and free of charge continue to commit large numbers of crimes. In my clinics in prison, I see numerous prisoners who were on methadone when they committed the crime for which they are incarcerated.

Why do addicts given their drug free of charge continue to commit crimes? Some addicts, of course, continue to take drugs other than those prescribed and have to fund their consumption of them. So long as any restriction whatever regulates the consumption of drugs, many addicts will seek them illicitly, regardless of what they receive legally. In addition, the drugs themselves exert a long-term effect on a person's ability to earn a living and severely limit rather than expand his horizons and mental repertoire. They sap the will or the ability of an addict to make long-term plans. While drugs are the focus of an addict's life, they are not all he needs to live, and many addicts thus continue to procure the rest of what they need by criminal means.

For the proposed legalization of drugs to have its much vaunted beneficial effect on the rate of criminality, such drugs would have to be both cheap and readily available. The legalizers assume that there is a natural limit to the demand for these drugs, and that if their consumption were legalized, the demand would not increase substantially. Those psychologically unstable persons currently taking drugs would continue to do so, with the necessity to commit crimes removed, while psychologically stabler people (such as you and I and our children) would not be enticed to take drugs by their new legal status and cheapness. But price and availability, I need hardly say, exert a profound effect on consumption: the cheaper alcohol becomes, for example, the more of it is consumed, at least within quite wide limits.

I have personal experience of this effect. I once worked as a doctor on a British government aid project to Africa. We were building a road through remote African bush. The contract stipulated that the construction company could import, free of all taxes, alcoholic drinks from the United Kingdom. These drinks the company then sold to its British workers at cost, in the local currency at the official exchange rate, which was approximately one-sixth the black-market rate. A liter bottle of gin thus cost less than a dollar and could be sold on the open market for almost ten dollars. So it was theoretically possible to remain dead drunk for several years for an initial outlay of less than a dollar.

Of course, the necessity to go to work somewhat limited the workers' consumption of alcohol. Nevertheless, drunkenness among them far outstripped anything I have ever seen, before or since. I discovered that, when alcohol is effectively free of charge, a fifth of British construction workers will regularly go to bed so drunk that they are incontinent both of urine and feces. I remember one man who very rarely got as far as his bed at night: he fell asleep in the lavatory, where he was usually found the next morning. Half the men shook in the mornings and resorted to the hair of the dog to steady their hands before they drove their bulldozers and other heavy machines (which they frequently wrecked, at enormous expense to the British taxpayer); hangovers were universal. The men were either drunk or hung over for months on end.

Sure, construction workers are notoriously liable to drink heavily, but in these circumstances even formerly moderate drinkers turned alcoholic and eventually suffered from delirium tremens. The heavy drinking occurred not because of the isolation of the African bush: not only did the company provide sports facilities for its workers, but there were many other ways to occupy oneself there. Other groups of workers in the bush whom I visited, who did not have the same rights of importation of alcoholic drink but had to purchase it at normal prices, were not nearly as drunk. And when the company asked its workers what it could do to improve their conditions, they unanimously asked for a further reduction in the price of alcohol, because they could think of nothing else to ask for.

The conclusion was inescapable: that a susceptible population had responded to the low price of alcohol, and the lack of other effective restraints upon its consumption, by drinking destructively large quantities of it. The health of many men suffered as a consequence, as did their capacity for work; and they gained a well-deserved local reputation for reprehensible, violent, antisocial behavior.

It is therefore perfectly possible that the demand for drugs, including opiates, would rise dramatically were their price to fall and their availability to increase. And if it is true that the consumption of these drugs in itself predisposes to criminal behavior (as data from our clinic suggest), it is also possible that the effect on the rate of criminality of this rise in consumption would swamp the decrease that resulted from decriminalization. We would have just as much crime in aggregate as before, but many more addicts.

The intermediate position on drug legalization, such as that espoused by Ethan Nadelmann, director of the Lindesmith Center, a drug policy research institute sponsored by financier George Soros, is emphatically not the answer to drug-related crime. This view holds that it should be easy for addicts to receive opiate drugs from doctors, either free or at cost, and that they should receive them in municipal injecting rooms, such as now exist in Zurich. But just look at Liverpool, where 2,000 people of a population of 600,000 receive official prescriptions for methadone: this once proud and prosperous city is still the world capital of drug-motivated burglary, according to the police and independent researchers.

Of course, many addicts in Liverpool are not yet on methadone, because the clinics are insufficient in number to deal with the demand. If the city expended more money on clinics, perhaps the number of addicts in treatment could be increased five- or tenfold. But would that solve the problem of burglary in Liverpool? No, because the profits to be made from selling illicit opiates would still be large: dealers would therefore make efforts to expand into parts of the population hitherto relatively untouched, in order to protect their profits. The new addicts would still burgle to feed their habits. Yet more clinics dispensing yet more methadone would then be needed. In fact Britain, which has had a relatively liberal approach to the prescribing of opiate drugs to addicts since 1928 (I myself have prescribed heroin to addicts), has seen an explosive increase in addiction to opiates and all the evils associated with it since the 1960s, despite that liberal policy. A few hundred have become more than a hundred thousand.

At the heart of Nadelmann's position, then, is an evasion. The legal and liberal provision of drugs for people who are already addicted to them will not reduce the economic benefits to dealers of pushing these drugs, at least until the entire susceptible population is addicted and in a treatment program. So long as there are addicts who have to resort to the black market for their drugs, there will be drug-associated crime. Nadelmann assumes that the number of potential addicts wouldn't soar under considerably more liberal drug laws. I can't muster such Panglossian optimism.

The problem of reducing the amount of crime committed by individual addicts is emphatically not the same as the problem of reducing the amount of crime committed by addicts as a whole. I can illustrate what I mean by an analogy: it is often claimed that prison does not work because many prisoners are recidivists who, by definition, failed to be deterred from further wrongdoing by their last prison sentence. But does any sensible person believe that the abolition of prisons in their entirety would not reduce the numbers of the law-abiding? The murder rate in New York and the rate of drunken driving in Britain have not been reduced by a sudden upsurge in the love of humanity, but by the effective threat of punishment. An institution such as prison can work for society even if it does not work for an individual.

The situation could be very much worse than I have suggested hitherto, however, if we legalized the consumption of drugs other than opiates. So far, I have considered only opiates, which exert a generally tranquilizing effect. If opiate addicts commit crimes even when they receive their drugs free of charge, it is because they are unable to meet their other needs any other way; but there are, unfortunately, drugs whose consumption directly leads to violence because of their psychopharmacological properties and not merely because of the criminality associated with their distribution. Stimulant drugs such as crack cocaine provoke paranoia, increase aggression, and promote violence. Much of this violence takes place in the home, as the relatives of crack takers will testify. It is something I know from personal acquaintance by working in the emergency room and in the wards of our hospital. Only someone who has not been assaulted by drug takers rendered psychotic by their drug could view with equanimity the prospect of the further spread of the abuse of stimulants.

And no one should underestimate the possibility that the use of stimulant drugs could spread very much wider, and become far more general, than it is now, if restraints on their use were relaxed. The importation of the mildly stimulant khat is legal in Britain, and a large proportion of the community of Somali refugees there devotes its entire life to chewing the leaves that contain the stimulant, miring these refugees in far worse poverty than they would otherwise experience. The reason that the khat habit has not spread to the rest of the population is that it takes an entire day's chewing of disgustingly bitter leaves to gain the comparatively mild pharmacological effect. The point is, however, that once the use of a stimulant becomes culturally acceptable and normal, it can easily become so general as to exert devastating social effects. And the kinds of stimulants on offer in Western cities—cocaine, crack, amphetamines—are vastly more attractive than khat.

In claiming that prohibition, not the drugs themselves, is the problem, Nadelmann and many others—even policemen—have said that "the war on drugs is lost." But to demand a yes or no answer to the question "Is the war against drugs being won?" is like demanding a yes or no answer to the question "Have you stopped beating your wife yet?" Never can an unimaginative and fundamentally stupid metaphor have exerted a more baleful effect upon proper thought.

Let us ask whether medicine is winning the war against death. The answer is obviously no, it isn't winning: the one fundamental rule of human existence remains, unfortunately, one man one death. And this is despite the fact that 14 percent of the gross domestic product of the United States (to say nothing of the efforts of other countries) goes into the fight against death. Was ever a war more expensively lost? Let us then abolish medical schools, hospitals, and departments of public health. If every man has to die, it doesn't matter very much when he does so.

If the war against drugs is lost, then so are the wars against theft, speeding, incest, fraud, rape, murder, arson, and illegal parking. Few, if any, such wars are winnable. So let us all do anything we choose.

Even the legalizers' argument that permitting the purchase and use of drugs as freely as Milton Friedman suggests will necessarily result in less governmental and other official interference in our lives doesn't stand up. To the contrary, if the use of narcotics and stimulants were to become virtually universal, as is by no means impossible, the number of situations in which compulsory checks upon people would have to be carried out, for reasons of public safety, would increase enormously. Pharmacies, banks, schools, hospitals—indeed, all organizations dealing with the public—might feel obliged to check regularly and randomly on the drug consumption of their employees. The general use of such drugs would increase the locus standi of innumerable agencies, public and private, to interfere in our lives; and freedom from interference, far from having increased, would have drastically shrunk.

The present situation is bad, undoubtedly; but few are the situations so bad that they cannot be made worse by a wrong policy decision.

The extreme intellectual elegance of the proposal to legalize the distribution and consumption of drugs, touted as the solution to so many problems at once (AIDS, crime, overcrowding in the prisons, and even the attractiveness of drugs to foolish young people) should give rise to skepticism. Social problems are not usually like that. Analogies with the Prohibition era, often drawn by those who would legalize drugs, are false and inexact: it is one thing to attempt to ban a substance that has been in customary use for centuries by at least nine-tenths of the adult population, and quite another to retain a ban on substances that are still not in customary use, in an attempt to ensure that they never do become customary. Surely we have already slid down enough slippery slopes in the last 30 years without looking for more such slopes to slide down.

POSTSCRIPT

Should Drugs Be Legalized?

Cussen and Block state that governmental efforts to control drug use create serious social problems, and that social conditions would be much improved if drugs were legalized. A strong governmental effort—like the current war on drugs—threatens people's civil liberties and provides criminals with a financial incentive to engage in illegal drug trafficking.

Theodore Dalrymple is skeptical of some of the claims of the proponents of drug legalization. He opposes the claims of Cussen and Block at almost every turn. Moreover, his position is not blind rejection of their views but in many cases is supported by his own experiences with drug users. He notes, for example, that even those who are provided with drugs seek other drugs that they cannot have; and those who have unlimited access tend to overindulge to an extreme extent. Legalization of drugs would lead to many more users, many more social problems. Neither Cussen and Block nor Dalrymple distinguishes "soft" drugs from "hard" drugs. Perhaps, if such a distinction could be well articulated, it might turn out that one side in this dispute (the YES side) is correct for soft drugs, while the other side (the NO side) is correct for hard drugs. Yet, even if only the hard drugs remained illegal, financial incentives for a black market would still be there—along with violence and crime. But how would limited or regulated legalization work in practice? Suppose, for example, that there was an age limit for purchasing drugs, just as there is in the case of tobacco and alcohol. But then again there would still be financial incentives for a black market for underage purchasers. Many of the same social ills that Cussen and Block identify would follow. (But one difference is that the scope of these might be smaller, although drug dealers wouldn't have to worry about their product having to be smuggled into the country, since it would be readily available for adult buyers.) Cussen and Block and Dalrymple sometimes seem to occupy extreme positions. But it is difficult to find and defend a middle position here. Is there a middle position?

For further reading on this issue, see James A. Inciardi, *The War on Drugs III: The Continuing Saga of the Mysteries and Miseries of Intoxication, Addiction, Crime, and Public Policy* (Allyn & Bacon, 2001); Robert J. MacCoun and Peter Reuter, *Drug War Heresies: Learning from Other Vices, Times, and Places* (Cambridge University Press, 2001); Douglas Husak, *Drugs and Rights* (Cambridge University Press, 2002); Jeffrey A. Miron, *Drug War Crimes: The Consequences of Prohibition* (Independent Institute, 2004); DorisMarie Provine, *Unequal Under Law: Race in the War on Drug* (University of Chicago, 2007); Peggy J. Parks, *Drug Legalization* (ReferencePoint Press, 2008). Margaret J. Goldstein, *Legalizing Drugs: Crime Stopper or Social Risk?* (Twenty-First Century, 2010).

ISSUE 10

Is Price Gouging Wrong?

YES: Jeremy Snyder, from "What's the Matter with Price Gouging?" *Business Ethics Quarterly*, vol. 19, no. 2 (April 2009)

NO: Matt Zwolinski, from "Price Gouging, Non-Worseness, and Distributive Justice," *Business Ethics Quarterly*, vol. 19, no. 2 (April 2009)

ISSUE SUMMARY

YES: Health science professor Jeremy Snyder argues that although there are arguments from a business perspective which emphasize the economic benefits of raising prices in the wake of disasters, price gouging in fact fails to respect persons as persons and is morally wrong insofar as it undermines fair access to essential goods.

NO: Political philosopher Matt Zwolinski's article is a direct response to Snyder. He argues that although price gougers may not be morally virtuous agents, they—unlike most of use—are nevertheless doing something that the victims of the disaster can benefit from. In addition, he argues that the allocation of goods via the market is a more just system than other alternatives, including those suggested by Snyder.

The topic of price gouging is one that bothers us. It bothers us in a couple of ways. First, the term itself is not really neutral. It has a negative connotation; it sounds unsavory. But it's hard to think of a neutral term or phrase that would serve to pick out cases of price gouging without a negative judgment being attached or suggested. Here's where the second thing that bothers us comes in. What exactly is wrong with price gouging? If we had a good answer to that question, we'd be able to identify the aspect of price gouging that makes it wrong. Then we could remove that aspect and refer to the idea in more neutral terms.

One problem is that the idea of buying and selling at terms mutually acceptable to the buyer and the seller is part of the very essence of business; and business itself is not inherently wrong. There is, of course, an essential tension in business, a tension between the interests of the buyer and the interests of the seller. The buyer will normally want to charge as much as possible (without pricing himself completely out of the market), and the seller will normally want to pay as little as possible (provided there is no reduction in quality of goods, etc.).

In a settled market, there will often be established prices. Thus, for example, when you go into a supermarket, the goods for sale will generally be for sale at fixed prices. Of course, some supermarkets will be more expensive than others, especially for certain items, but shoppers who have time can normally use this to their advantage by doing a little comparison-shopping and purchasing (say) fresh produce from one store (where it is cheaper, but just as good as elsewhere), meat from another store, and maybe canned goods from yet a third. Prices vary a bit from store to store. Moreover, prices are subject to change, and they can indeed change when market conditions change. Thus, when there was a gas shortage, gas stations charged more for gas. Again, if the American dollar declines in value, while Chinese currency rises, our so-called "cheap" imports from China will no longer be so cheaply priced on our store shelves.

Further, in the wake of a natural disaster such as a hurricane or an earthquake, there may be sudden shortages of power as well shortages of ice, fresh water, etc. Thus, for example, generators may be brought into a hurricane-stricken coastal city after it has been devastated by a hurricane. Perhaps individuals will bring these generators in by truck from locations some distance away from the path of the hurricane. As sellers of generators, their objective is to sell these generators at a high price and to provide themselves with a profit, and to cover the usual costs of the generators as well as the additional shipping costs involved with bringing those generators to the stricken city. Note that, as is common in financial matters, the opportunity for greater than usual profit-making will be accompanied by risks that are also greater than usual. Some particular risks here might include the possibility of damage to the generators while they are being shipped; the possibility of theft; the possibility of the expected profit being not as high as was originally anticipated, due to many other generator sellers being motivated by seemingly greater than usual profits, and so also shipping generators to the city, and consequently raising the supply of generators, and thus lowering their price. Yet another risk might be borne by sellers who position their generators close to where a hurricane is predicted to strike, so as to be the first on the scene and thus reap the greatest profit. But note that the hurricane is only *predicted* to strike in a certain place, while in reality it might come ashore at precisely the place where a risk-taking seller has prepositioned his generators—thus possibly destroying the generators as well as any hope of profiting from their sale.

Yet, even though we acknowledge the risks and added costs that these sellers are taking on, we might still feel that there is something unsavory about what they are doing. It's difficult to specify what exactly the problem is, though. For in the wake of the disaster, people are getting exactly what they need. In the readings that follow, Jeremy Snyder first aims to diagnose the problem, define the problem, and make a moral case for regulation that would address the problem. He is then directly answered by Matt Zwolinski.

YES

Jeremy Snyder

What's the Matter with Price Gouging?

Prices for essential goods are likely to increase when a disaster strikes, should that event decrease available supplies of these goods, increase demand, or both.[1] Sometimes these price increases are condemned as 'price gouging' or 'profiteering.' Such labels are not intended as simply descriptions of price increases; rather, they carry a strong negative moral valence. In many cases, the moral wrong of these price increases is identified as wrongfully gaining from another's misfortune. Consider the common view that "[t]hings like selling generators for four and five times their cost is not free enterprise, that's taking advantage of other people's misery" (Rushing 2004, A-1). In other cases, price gouging is condemned as unfairly taking advantage of others' needs, language that is often associated with exploitation.[2]

But it isn't clear from these kinds of sentiments when a price increase amounts to price gouging or why, if at all, certain price increases following disasters are morally worrisome. Moreover, there are many reasons to think that price increases can create a net benefit for a community following a disaster. As one critic of anti-price gouging legislation puts it:

> Price to the left of the intersection of the supply-and-demand curve and you are guaranteed to vaporize whatever you are attempting to keep inexpensive. . . . The reason that gasoline is disappearing from service stations across the nation is because station owners aren't gouging with sufficient gusto. Whether out of misguided sense of kindness, concern about what politicians might think, fear of bad press, or the desire to keep customers happy, they are pricing below what the market would otherwise bear and, as a result, their inventory has disappeared. Now, how are the poor being helped by service stations closing down for lack of fuel? Gas at $6 a gallon, after all, is better than gas unavailable at any price. (Taylor 2005)

Price increases lead to rationing by consumers and encourage increased production of scarce goods. If the aim of anti-gouging legislation is to prevent vendors from profiting too much from a supply disruption, then achieving this aim may come at the cost of a swift return to normal market conditions.

From *Business Ethics Quarterly*, April 2009, pp. 275–293. Copyright © 2009 by *Business Ethics Quarterly*. Reprinted by permission of The Philosophy Documentation Center, publisher of *Business Ethics Quarterly*.

In this paper, I discuss what moral wrongs, if any, are most reasonably ascribed to accusations of price gouging. This discussion keeps in mind both practical and moral defenses of price gouging following disasters.[3] In the first section of this paper, I examine existing anti-gouging legislation for commonalities in their definitions of gouging. I then present arguments in favor of the permissibility of gouging, focusing on the economic benefits of price increases following disasters. In the third section I present a critique of gouging based on specific forms of a failure of respect for others. This critique is followed by a discussion of means for avoiding gouging in practice and responses to objections to my view. As I will argue, even when morally defensible anti-gouging legislation is not in place, individual vendors will have a duty not to gouge their customers. . . .

Price Gouging in the Law

At present, thirty-two states and the District of Columbia have passed some form of anti-gouging legislation. Although there is no federal anti-gouging law in the US, a bill targeting fuel price increases passed the House of Representatives in 2007. In order to develop a better sense of what actions raise worries about price gouging, I will briefly examine this body of legislation.

Anti-gouging legislation is typically triggered by the declaration of a state of emergency or disaster. This declaration may be made by the state governor, local officials, or even the President. In substantially fewer cases, anti-gouging legislation requires a declaration by public officials in addition to a declaration of emergency. The duration of the activation of anti-gouging controls can vary from the length of the declaration of a disaster to a fixed length of time or some mix of the two.[4]

Laws against price gouging limit price increases for goods during their period of activation. For the most part, price increases are allowed when they reflect increases in the cost of doing business following the disaster and, to some extent, changes in the market. For example, the Federal Trade Commission defined price gouging as occurring when "a firm's average monthly sales price for gasoline in a particular area is higher than for a previous month, *and* where such higher prices are not substantially attributable to *either* (1) increased costs, or (2) national or international market trends" (Federal Trade Commission 2006, 137). In many cases, these caps seek to factor in changes in the market and costs by allowing the price of goods to increase a certain percentage above the pre-disaster price. Otherwise, vague language prohibiting 'unconscionable' or 'gross' increases in prices is used.[5] At their most extreme, anti-gouging legislation may forbid *any* increase in the prices of goods beyond those justified by higher business costs. These more extreme restrictions are unusual and at present limited to Georgia, Louisiana, Mississippi, and Connecticut.[6]

Anti-gouging laws can be tied to all goods and services following activation of anti-gouging statutes[7] or limited to specific, essential goods. What counts as an essential good is often left undefined but can explicitly include dwelling units, gasoline, food, water, supplies for home repair, and pharmaceuticals.[8] Florida Statute 501.160, for example, states that following a state of emergency, it is unlawful "for a person or her or his agent or employee to rent or sell or offer to rent or sell at an unconscionable price within the area for which the state of emergency is declared, any essential commodity including, but not limited to, supplies, services, provisions, or equipment that is necessary for consumption or use as a direct result of the emergency."

Despite many broad commonalities in state anti-gouging legislation, this overview reveals four key areas of disagreement and vagueness in determining what constitutes price gouging. First, there is disagreement as to how much of a price increase, particularly beyond what can be justified by increases in business costs, is allowable. Second, state legislatures disagree as to whether prohibitions of price increases should be extended to all goods and services or limited only to certain exchanges, although most favor the latter. Third, when legislation is limited to certain exchanges, there is disagreement as to what goods and services should be covered. Fourth, and most importantly from the perspective of this paper, when anti-gouging legislation uses moral language to justify itself, this language tends to be vague.[9]

In Defense of Price Increases

Anti-gouging legislation and charges of price gouging are common. While the precise nature of the moral wrong associated with gouging is unclear, there is widespread agreement that *something* is wrong about these price increases. Yet, there are many reasons to think that price increases condemned as gouging are morally innocent at worst and, more often, create a positive and morally praiseworthy benefit for all concerned.

In a gouging situation following a disaster, both vendor and customer understand the exchange to be to their advantage. Since the good being exchanged is likely to be something essential to the well-being of the customer (e.g., food, water, shelter), the exchange is actually likely to provide proportionally greater utility to the customer than the vendor even at the higher than usual price. While the vendor may stand to clear a larger than normal profit as a result of the disaster, the essential nature of the goods mean that they will be of enormous, possibly even life saving, benefit to the consumer. Despite the harms to the consumer and possibly vendor as a result of the disaster, the high price exchange does no harm in itself when compared to the welfare of each person following the disaster. Rather, the exchange will provide the customer with essential goods that increase her welfare.

While disasters create a temporary increase in the pricing power of vendors, this shift can easily be explained and justified by the rules of the market. A disaster is likely to cause a reduction in essential supplies. . . .

Not only are price increases explainable as a result of the natural functioning of the market, it is argued, they serve a beneficial purpose. High prices for essential goods have the effect of helping the market to return to pre-disaster prices. These prices achieve a signaling effect for both vendors and consumers (Hayek 1945). The high prices charged by vendors will lure other suppliers into the market, quickly increasing supplies of essential goods. An increase in supplies will meet increased demand and help move prices toward pre-disaster levels. Without these price increases, vendors may lack both the information and motivation necessary to enter the post-disaster market and increase supplies.

Defenders of price gouging argue that higher prices also aid in the conservation of scarce goods by making it more likely that they will be purchased by those who place the greatest value on them. These high prices also tend to ensure that scarce essential goods will be used sparingly. While ice might be valuable to those seeking to keep their beer cold following a hurricane, higher prices will tend to ensure that those purchasing ice put it to more highly valued uses such as preserving medicine and scarce food. This efficiency of allocation is coupled with a rationing effect created by higher prices. When fuel prices spike, generators that might have been used to power the air conditioning in an entire house will instead be limited to cooling a single room. As a result, fuel supplies that would have been exhausted quickly at pre-disaster prices are now prolonged (Wall Street Journal 2005).

The promise of price increases following a disaster can also help increase supplies of essential goods prior to the event. If the disaster is foreseeable (as in the case of a hurricane), suppliers can pre-position goods in the area likely to be affected. The prospect of higher prices encourages such preemptive actions and acts in the long run to keep prices relatively low, meeting the needs of far more people than otherwise would have been the case.

Some extra profit following a disaster can also serve as a fair reward for the efforts and risks undertaken by vendors. Vendors of scarce goods may go to extraordinary lengths to get goods to the market following a disaster. A vendor might pre-position goods in a likely disaster area at considerable cost to himself and at considerable risk if the disaster destroys these stocks or strikes too far away for the supplies to be of use. . . .

Price Gouging and Respect for Others

If there is something morally wrong with price gouging, it is not that gouging causes direct harms or economic inefficiency. In fact, a critique of price gouging will need to confront the positive moral value of the efficiencies and rationing effect created by price increases.

As I have noted, many anti-gouging laws are limited to price increases on certain goods that are tied to basic human needs. I believe that this characteristic of anti-gouging legislation offers an important insight regarding what is morally objectionable about price gouging. As not all types of price increases trigger the worry about gouging, it is not price increases themselves that motivate this concern. Rather, I would like to argue, it is price increases that undermine equitable access to certain, essential goods that motivate the worry about price gouging.

Put another way, worries about price gouging are engaged when price increases cut off poor consumers from necessary goods, not when price increases are unfair. . . .

Consider that the language surrounding gouging typically focuses on the vulnerability created by the disaster and the desperation of consumers to meet their basic needs. As the Attorney General of Texas put it, following gouging accusations in the wake of hurricane Ike, "They took advantage of the fear and the needs of people who were evacuating the Gulf Coast region, and they jacked up prices" (Elliott 2008). Price hikes for gasoline following that same hurricane again focus on the absolute needs of consumers: "It's sad to think that merchants would take advantage of people who are already struggling to fill their gas tanks just to get from home to work or from home to church and back" (*Jackson Sun* 2008). . . . It is the desperation of individuals for essential goods, rather than simply the unfairness of the transaction, that motivates accusations of price gouging following a disaster.

Having located the wrongness of price gouging in access to essential goods, we can now say more about the duty that price gouging violates. To be specific, I would like to argue that price increases following a disaster can undermine equitable access to the goods essential to minimal human functioning. When price increases do so, they violate the norm of equal respect for persons. Respect for persons is often understood in terms of a duty to treat others as ends in themselves. More specifically, this respect is expressed both through recognizing that human animals are capable of forming and acting on a conception of the good life but need material support in order to do so (Hill 1991).[10]

Proponents of various ethical theories can agree that basic respect for human persons will entail two components: Negatively, we should not interfere with others as they live out their conception of the good life given reciprocal respect and non-interference. Positively, we should aid others in forming and living out their conception of the good life, particularly by ensuring that they have the minimal means of developing such a conception. An attitude of respect for others will be expressed through our actions, including non-interference, positive support, and other expressions of the equal value of all human persons (Anderson 1993).

At first glance, it would seem that placing limits on the functioning of the market through anti-gouging legislation would run counter to the goal of respecting others' freedom to pursue their conception of the good life. In the first place, I have discussed how price increases efficiently bring new supplies of essential goods into the market and help ration existing supplies. In this way, free markets serve as a means of supplying the goods essential to forming and acting on a conception of the good life.

Secondly, in their ideal form, markets carry their own value as institutions that protect and enlarge human freedom.[11] By offering a space in which consumers can freely negotiate, consummate, and exit exchanges, markets ensure that consumers are not beholden to any particular vendor in their pursuit of the good life.[12] Adam Smith specifically defends markets in terms of their historical role in undermining the oppressive feudal system of production (Satz 2007). . . . The moral concern that justifies the idealized institution of the market, then, is an interest in providing the material means to and institutional protection of individual freedom.

Conditions following a disaster can be highly non-ideal for a market, however, at least from the perspective of a stable balance between supply and demand. A disaster potentially results in a reduction of supply and spike in demand for some or all essential goods. While price increases reflect a new, post-disaster balance between supply and demand, over the short term this new equilibrium point can be particularly disruptive to the lives of the poorest members of a community. Until the pricing signals created by the new equilibrium increase supplies of essential goods, prices will remain high and supplies may be insufficient to meet demand. This gap between supply and demand is morally troubling because the goods in question are essential to minimal human functioning and may be out of reach for the poorest members of the affected community. While price increases in a free market represent one means of restoring supplies and rationing existing stocks of essential goods, anti-gouging legislation offers an alternative approach to this problem.

There are many good reasons to think that, following a disaster, an unfettered free market does not best serve the freedom-enhancing purpose by which it is morally justified. While unfettered price increases work toward *efficiently* promoting increases in the supply of essential goods following a disaster, the concern that motivates price gouging laws is that an unfettered market in these goods runs counter to the goal of *equity*, a key component of respect for persons. This failure of equity takes place in terms of the distribution of scarce essential goods within the affected community.[13]

While price increases can decrease consumption rates of essential goods, they do so at the cost of giving the wealthiest members of a community the greatest access to limited supplies. This access is created in two ways. First, and most obviously, wealthy persons will have greater financial means with which to bid on scarce resources when they have been located (Ramasastry 2005).[14] Second, these persons will likely have greater access to the information and transport needed to locate and reach scarce resources. In an idealized market, free competition lowers prices in order to put essential goods into the hands of all but the poorest members of a community. Following a disaster, free competition gives greater access to these goods to those who have the greatest resources within a community.

Under these conditions, the market does not act as the great equalizer and vehicle of individual freedom praised by Smith. Instead, for the period of time between the occurrence of the disaster and when the market again becomes competitive and prices normalize, the market serves to distribute scarce and essential goods on the basis of pre-existing privilege within a community. . . .

In the absence of anti-gouging legislation, we can also assess the behavior of individual vendors who have legally sanctioned opportunities to raise their prices on essential goods following a disaster. While legal, this behavior can be morally impermissible. All of us share a general duty to further the goal of access to essential goods for all persons. This duty is a form of a general duty of beneficence, where we are granted latitude in determining which needy persons to aid in this regard. Our relationships with others, however, can help specify this general duty (Reader 2003) (Kittay 1999) (Waldron 2003) (Snyder 2008). Following a disaster, a vendor's general duty to ensure others' access to essential goods can become more focused, targeting the members of her community who will vie for access to her supplies. The vendor's decision as to how to ration her limited supplies—whether by ability to pay for the goods or through some other, more equitable means—will have a direct impact on her customers' access to these goods. Should she choose to ration her goods according to ability to pay, then she will fail to discharge her duty of beneficence toward all those in her community in need of essential goods or, rather, privileging the wealthiest members of her community.

Of course, merchants normally set their prices at the highest point the market will bear with little moral condemnation. Why, then, would it be impermissible to do so following a disaster? In an idealized market, competition is established through hard bargaining—that is, seeking out the best terms of exchange for oneself. This bargaining takes place between people in roughly equal positions, where the consumer has the option to exit the exchange in search of better terms. Even when the exchange involves an essential good, the ability to select from multiple vendors and flexibility as to when the good is purchased preserves the consumer's option of exit from any given exchange. When functioning in this way, the institution of the market transforms the self-interested nature of hard-bargaining into a vehicle for generating efficiencies in the production and distribution of goods. At the same time, the market remains a venue in which to pursue one's own conception of the good life through the consumption and exchange of goods.

But these institutional protections are undermined when normal competition is disrupted by a disaster. When this happens, hard-bargaining has different implications. Competition, adequate supplies of essential goods, and flexibility as to when these goods are purchased all expand access to essential goods for all members of the community. When these conditions are disrupted, the self-interested motivation of hard bargaining is no longer limited by the institutional protections of a well-functioning market such as consumers' power of exit from the exchange. Instead, self-interest unconstrained by a well-functioning market fails to protect the access of the poorest members of the communities to the goods essential to minimal human functioning.

Following a disaster, then, a vendor who increases her prices in the face of inelastic demand and diminished supply will undercut access by the poorest members of her community to essential goods. In doing so, she will fail to demonstrate the value of equitable access to these goods for all members of her community. If the vendor's own livelihood has not been threatened by the disaster—through, for example, the destruction of supplies or damage to buildings—then these price increases serve merely as an opportunity for the vendor to reap unusual profits. Instead of discharging a specified duty of beneficence to all members of her community, with whom she now stands in a special relationship of dependence, the vendor merely looks to her own good. These profits can be compared to those accrued under a well-functioning market, where they are conjoined with efficiencies that are spread more evenly across the community through decreased prices and increased supplies.

In short, the market disruption brought on by a disaster can have two important effects from the perspective of price gouging. First, the loss of access to essential goods can create a pool of persons to whom the vendor is connected in a relationship of dependence and to whom the vendor has a special responsibility. Second, the institutional protections of an ideally functioning market can become undermined. If so, a vendor who chooses to charge the highest prices the market will bear and thereby distributes her goods according to ability to pay will fail to demonstrate equal respect for all members of her community. Taken together, these effects create the opportunity for price gouging by the vendor, even when anti-gouging legislation has not been enacted in her community. . . .

Avoiding Price Gouging in Practice

. . . Recall that state price gouging legislation is divided on what price increases were acceptable following a disaster and on what goods should be covered by the legislation. My account suggests that, for the vendor operating under conditions of uncertainty, equal respect for all members of a community will require: 1) Limited price increases beyond those justified by increases in costs and risk; and 2) Caps on purchases of essential goods in order to ration supplies of these goods. Neither of these restrictions should apply to persons selling non-essential goods. These guidelines will be most relevant when the pre-disaster market is reasonably successful at meeting the basic needs of all members of the community. Therefore, contextual factors make these guidelines defeasible.

Objections

Matt Zwolinski (2008) argues against both the effectiveness of price gouging legislation and the immorality of price increases that are typically condemned as gouging. His positive argument hinges largely on the benefits created by price increases, which I have largely granted in this paper.[15] In order to strengthen my argument as to the immorality of these price increases, I will respond to two of Zwolinski's central arguments. First, I will address the 'non-worseness claim' (NWC) that it cannot be morally worse to engage in a voluntary and mutually beneficial exchange than no exchange at all. Second, I will consider Zwolinski's argument that price increases do not exhibit a failure of respect for consumers.

Zwolinski asks how we can criticize vendors who engage in voluntary and mutually beneficial exchanges while we ignore those who do nothing to help the needy in disaster areas:

> On the one hand, to the extent that we hold that price gougers are guilty of mutually beneficial exploitation, we hold that they are acting wrongly even though their actions bring *some* benefit to disaster victims. On the other hand, many of *us* do *nothing* to relieve the suffering of most disaster victims, and we generally do not view ourselves as acting wrongly in failing to provide this benefit—or, at least, we do not view ourselves as acting *as* wrongly as price gougers. (Zwolinski 2008, 356–57)

This 'non-worseness claim' asks why we should condemn those who help bring needed supplies into disaster areas as 'gougers' when we do not condemn those who stay home, helping no one.[16] That is, how can it be morally worse to engage in a voluntary and mutually beneficial interaction than to do nothing at all?[17]

In response, I believe that we must take the long view when assessing the moral principles underlying our actions. Individual actions, such as charging high prices for essential goods or sitting on one's couch in response to a disaster, may not tell the full story as to one's responsiveness toward the basic needs of others. One is not required to respond to every disaster nor every needy person in order to live a morally praiseworthy life. However, a *pattern* of failure to respond to the needs of others can exhibit a greater level of indifference toward the basic needs of others than is exhibited through a single instance of price gouging.

Zwolinski is right to note that some of those who charge market clearing prices following a disaster might be motivated both by self-interest and the benefits created for some consumers (Zwolinski 2008, 337–68). These motives may be morally superior to those of the person motivated to enter the disaster zone purely by self-interest. My point is that the person who chooses not to enter the disaster zone may be motivated purely by self-interest or have other, morally laudable responses toward the basic needs of her fellow humans. As the non-gouger's duty of beneficence has not been specified in the way that, as I have argued, the gouger's duty has been specified, she retains leeway as to how she will discharge this duty. . . .

A second concern raised by Zwolinski also hinges on the positive consequences created by price gouging. Given that the exchanges I have been discussing are mutually beneficial and voluntary, Zwolinski questions whether placing limits on these exchanges is in keeping with respect for others:

> Exploitation might plausibly be argued to manifest a lack of respect for the personhood of the exploitee. But laws against price gouging both manifest and encourage similar or greater lack of respect. They manifest a lack of respect for both merchants and customers by preventing them from making the autonomous choice to enter into economic exchanges at the market-clearing price. They send the signal, in effect, that *your* decision that this exchange is in your best interest is unimportant, and that the law will decide for you what sorts of transactions you are allowed to enter into. (Zwolinski 2008, 352–53).

That is, if consumers are not forced into these exchanges—and in fact they desperately seek them out—how can it be consistent with respect for others' choices to rule them out of bounds?

I have argued that proper respect for the needs of others demands that vendors moderate their price increases and engage in non-price rationing. This argument does not hold that agreements between vendors and consumers at market clearing prices are coercive. Rather, vendors ought to limit their price increases and legislators ought to pass laws requiring vendors to do so. These restrictions aim to aid the entire post-disaster community while distributing essential goods more equitably. My claim is not that individual freedom is unimportant, but that the market may not support freedom equitably following a disaster.

Zwolinski defends his position by noting, "Price gougers treat their fellow human beings as traders, rather than as brothers and sisters in the Kingdom of Ends. But to treat someone as a trader is still a far cry more respectful than treating him as an object" (Zwolinski 2008, 359). Perhaps so, but I have argued that a disaster disrupts the market in a way that makes it *inappropriate* to treat one's fellow human beings as traders. When the market is functioning under normal conditions, it can be appropriate to treat one's fellow humans as traders in market transactions, especially in the presence of an adequate social safety net. This is so because the institution of the market creates a space in which self-interest and hard bargaining enhances the freedom of all persons. Following a disaster, however, the market fails to behave in this way over the short-term, pricing the poorest members of the community out of the market for essential goods.

Treating one's fellow humans as traders is appropriate under conditions where trading in the market enables efficient and reasonably equitable access to essential goods. The justification for treating others as traders, however, is not that persons are appropriately understood as purely self-interested actors who are disinterested as to others' capacity to obtain essential goods. Rather, treating others as traders is one way, in the setting of a well-functioning market, to help others to efficiently and reasonably equitably obtain those essential goods. The conditions where it is appropriate to treat others as traders can break down because trading is merely instrumentally valuable toward respecting others as vulnerable persons in need of support in order to engage in minimal human functioning. When market conditions change so that trading no longer serves to support reasonably equitable access to these goods and where other, more equitable options are available, then treating others as traders is inconsistent with respect for persons as rational but vulnerable agents.

A choice between market clearing and pre-disaster prices represents a false dichotomy. Instead, I have argued, price increases following a disaster should be limited to reflect changes in risks and business costs to the vendor and perhaps a small premium as well. These price increases should also be coupled with caps on purchases of essential goods by consumers. I have provided an argument for why we should attempt to adopt legislation that protects consumers in a post-disaster market and am optimistic that creative solutions to the shortcomings of existing legislation can be found.[18] However, I also grant the possibility that these policies cannot be reflected in price gouging legislation without being so detailed as to restrict efficient increases in supplies of essential goods or so flexible as to be capricious in their application, as Zwolinski charges.

But, if not, my argument still stands as a guide for the behavior of individual vendors whose actions can be more sensitive to local context. Raising prices on essential goods can fail to express appropriate respect for others. Even if it is not illegal to raise prices on essential goods following a disaster, I have argued that it can be immoral to do so. While on the macro level price gouging legislation might undermine the price signaling effect needed to address the needs of the community affected by the disaster, individual vendors can, and should, choose to constrain their prices to reasonable levels out of an interest in the basic needs of all those around them.

Conclusions

If my account of the wrongness of price gouging is correct, it supports three major conclusions. First, the moral wrongs associated with price gouging should be understood generally as failures of respect for others. Vendors who ration scarce essential goods according to ability to pay undercut the goal of equitable access to essential goods within their community. This failure of respect takes place in a setting where the vendor owes a specified duty of beneficence to her customers and alternative means of achieving price signaling (through modest price increases) and rationing (through purchasing caps) are available.

Second, price gouging is only possible in transactions involving some good essential to living a distinctly human life. Price increases for diamonds, for example, are not instances of price gouging under my account. Moral wrongs, such as unfairness, may accompany price increases for non-essential goods. These wrongs, however, are distinct from the wrongs I have ascribed to price gouging.

Finally, the potential for price gouging will depend on the extent and strength of non-market social institutions for distributing essential goods. If these institutions are in place prior to a disaster and survive that event, price gouging is unlikely to occur even if vendors freely raise their prices in the post-disaster market. Individuals are more highly susceptible to price gouging in communities where entitlements to essential goods are weak or non-existent. Therefore, the moral wrong of price gouging cannot be reduced merely to price increases for essential goods following a disaster, even if these prices cannot be justified by increased costs.

The general shape of anti-gouging legislation gives a good rule of thumb for avoiding gouging. Price gouging legislation should allow for price increases justified by changes in the costs and risks of doing business. Otherwise, price increases should be limited and vendors should be required to ration their goods by placing caps on the number of purchases of essential goods. These limits on the market should be triggered by declarations of a state of emergency and limited to essential goods. Price controls should be restricted to the area affected by the disaster rather than entire states (Rapp 2005/2006). If price gouging legislation along these lines should prove to be deeply impractical or has not been enacted in a community, vendors should still constrain their market transactions along these lines.

Many cases of what are sometimes popularly called gouging are not morally problematic under my account nor considered cases of gouging. We should expect price increases on many goods following a disaster and many, if not most, of these increases will be justified by increases in cost, supply disruptions, and increased risk. However, in the most egregious cases, price increases cannot be justified in these ways, giving justification to the charge of price gouging as representing a kind of moral wrong.

These observations depend on an account of price gouging as a kind of failure of respect for others, but I hope to have shown that this account tracks well with widespread intuitions as to when and why certain price increases are morally problematic while revealing where those intuitions are unjustified. In practice, determining whether gouging has taken place will require great attention to local context, as shaped by the goal of equitable access to goods that meet the essential needs of consumers.

Notes

1. I am grateful to Robert Leider, Maggie Little, Daniel Levine, Leigh Anne Palmer, David Skarbek, Justin Weinberg, and Matt Zwolinski for their extensive comments on earlier versions of this paper. I am also thankful to the participants in a presentation of an earlier version of this paper at the 2008 APA Pacific Division Annual Meeting.

2. For example, a proposed federal anti-gouging law bans "taking unfair advantage of the circumstances related to an energy emergency to increase prices unreasonably." See http://thomas.loc.gov/cgi-bin/bdquery/z?dl10:h.r.01252: (accessed May 28, 2008). New York's anti-gouging law (NY GEN BUS S 396-r) is justified by the need to prevent vendors "from taking unfair advantage of consumers during abnormal disruptions of the market." In broader terms, USA Today condemns gougers as 'Vultures' (McCarthy 2004). Similarly, Florida Governor Charlie Crist complained that "It is astounding to me, the level of greed that someone must have in their soul to be willing to take advantage of someone suffering in the wake of a hurricane" (Jacoby 2004, F11).

3. I will use the term 'disasters' to include any event that creates physical damage to a discrete area, disrupting the normal functioning of the market. These events include both natural disasters such as hurricanes and man-made disasters such as terrorist attacks.

4. For a helpful summary of US anti-gouging laws, see Skarbek & Skarbek 2008.

5. See, for example, Michigan (Mich. Stat. Ann. §445.903(z)), Missouri (15 CSR §60-8.030), and Texas (Tex. Bus & Com. Code §17.46(b)(27)).

6. See Geoffrey Rapp (2005/2006).

7. For example, California, Connecticut, the District of Columbia, Hawaii, and Mississippi make general prohibitions against price increases. California prohibits price increases generally for consumer goods and services (Cal. Pen. Code §396), Connecticut includes any item (Conn. Gen. Stat. §42-230), DC any merchandise or service (D.C. Code §28.4101 to 4102), Hawaii any commodity (Haw. Rev. Stat. §209-9), and Mississippi all goods and services (Miss. Code Ann. §75-24-25).

8. See generally the American Bar Association's summary of state legislation at: http://www.abanet.org/antitrust/at-committees/at-fe/pdf/price-gouging-statutes.pdf (accessed May 28, 2008).

9. When explicit justification for anti-gouging legislation is given, references to 'unfair' prices is most common. The language of unconscionable and gross price increases, drawn from the common law tradition, are frequent as well (Rapp 2005/2006).

10. The goods essential to minimal human functioning are supported through various non-essential goods. For this reason, I will also discuss non-essential goods like electrical generators, gasoline, and ice that are, in many

communities, instrumental to the durability of essential goods such as food, water, and adequate shelter. Insofar as the essential goods are relevant to the wrongness of gouging, these non-essential goods will be relevant as well.

11. Of course, disagreement will take place as to what corresponding regulatory environment best supports this freedom-enhancing function.

12. This point has been made by authors as diverse as Milton Friedman (1962) and Amartya Sen (1999).

13. There is a long history within Judeo-Christian and Islamic thought condemning excessive price increases against vulnerable populations. These restrictions are motivated by concerns about oppression of the weak. Consider, for example, Leviticus 25:14: "And if thou sell ought unto thy neighbor, or buyest ought of thy neighbor's hand, ye shall not oppress one another." More generally, see Brewer 2007, 1104–06.

14. In some cases, even wealthy persons following a disaster may not have the immediately available resources to afford price increases on essential goods. When referencing 'the wealthy' I intend those with the resources available to afford price increases rather than those with the greatest savings and assets within a community. My thanks to an anonymous reviewer for pointing out this ambiguity.

15. There is some disagreement on this point, however. Geoffrey Rapp (2005/2006, 553–59) argues that anti-gouging laws are economically justified in two ways. First, they help preserve hard currency reserves when a disaster or terrorist attack disrupts electronic payment systems such as ATMs. Second, they counteract the effects of pricing irrationality that prevent efficient pricing during market disruptions.

16. Zwolinski discusses price increases among vendors who bring goods into the post-disaster market whereas I have focused my discussion on vendors with goods already in the market. The risks and opportunity costs faced by outsiders may be different from those of locals, meaning that outsiders and locals may be justified in offering different prices for their goods based on different levels of risk and cost. I discuss the relevance of vendors' risks and costs to post-disaster prices in the previous section. The source of these goods, however, is not relevant to the basic moral wrong of price gouging.

17. Alan Wertheimer (1996, 289–93) describes the non-worseness claim as holding that an interaction Y between A and B cannot be morally worse than no interaction at all if Y makes both A and B better off when compared to a baseline of no interaction. In other words, the NWC denies the possibility that a mutually beneficial exploitative interaction can be morally worse than no interaction at all.

18. Reforms and standardization of existing legislation have been suggested. Anita Ramasastry (2005) argues that anti-gouging legislation should give clear guidance as which price increases are impermissible while allowing increases that reflect changes in costs and risks for vendors. See also, Page & Cho 2006.

Bibliography

Anderson, Elizabeth. 1993. *Value in ethics and economics*. Cambridge, MA: Harvard University Press.

Brewer, Michael. 2007. Planning disaster: Price gouging statutes and the shortages they create. *Brooklyn Law Review,* 72: 1101–37.

Elliott, Janet. 2008. Two hotels face lawsuits for raising rates. *The Houston Chronicle* (October 3).

Federal Trade Commission. 2006. *Investigation of gasoline price manipulation and post-Katrina gasoline price increases.* http://www.ftc.gov/reports/060518PublicGas olinePricesInvestigationReportFinal.pdf.

Friedman, Milton. 1962. *Capitalism and freedom.* Chicago: University of Chicago Press.

Hayek, Friedrich. 1945. The use of knowledge in society. *American Economic Review,* 35(4): 519–30.

Hill, Thomas. 1991. *Autonomy and self-respect.* New York: Cambridge University Press.

Jackson Sun. 2008. Go after those who may be price gouging. *The Jackson Sun* (September 17).

Kittay, Eva. 1999. *Love's labor: Essays on women, equality, and dependency.* New York: Routledge.

McCarthy, Michael. 2004. After the storm come the vultures. *USA Today* (August 20): 6B.

Nussbaum, Martha. 2000. *Women and human development.* New York: Cambridge University Press.

Page, Edward, & Cho, Min. 2006. Price gouging 101: A call to Florida lawmakers to perfect Florida's price gouging law, *Florida Bar Journal,* 80: 49–52.

Raghunathan, Abhi. 2005. South Florida shortages fuel black market. *St. Petersburg Times* (October 29): 1B.

Ramasastry, Anita. 2005. Assessing anti-price-gouging statutes in the wake of hurricane Katrina: Why they're necessary in emergencies, but need to be rewritten. *Findlaw* (September 15). Available at http://writ.news.findlaw.com/ ramasastry/20050916.html.

Rapp, Geoffrey. 2005/2006. Gouging: Terrorist attacks, hurricanes, and the legal and economic aspects of post-disaster price regulation. *Kentucky Law Journal,* 94: 535–60.

Reader, Soran. 2003. Distance, relationship and moral obligation. *The Monist,* 86: 367–81.

Rockoff, Hugh. 2002. Price controls. In David R. Henderson (Ed.), *The Concise Encyclopedia of Economics.* Indianapolis: Liberty Fund, Inc. Available at http:// www.econlib.org/library/Enc/PriceControls.html.

Rushing, J. Taylor. 2004. Storms stir up price gouging. *Florida Times-Union* (September 18): A-1.

Satz, Debra. 2007. Liberalism, economic freedom, and the limits of markets. *Social Philosophy and Policy,* 24: 120–40.

Sen, Amartya. 1992. *Inequality reexamined.* Cambridge, MA: Harvard University Press.

_____. 1999. *Development as freedom.* New York: Knopf.

Skarbek, Brian R., & Skarbek, David B. 2008. The price is right: Regulation, reputation, and recovery. *Dartmouth Law Journal,* 6(2): 235–76.

Snyder, Jeremy. 2008. Needs exploitation. *Ethical Theory and Moral Practice,* 11: 389–405.

Taylor, Jerry. 2005. Gouge on. *National Review Online* (September 2). http://www .nationalreview.com/comment/taylor200509022359.asp.

Treaster, Joseph. 2004. With storm gone, Floridians are hit with price gouging. *New York Times* (August 18): A1.

Waldron, Jeremy. 2003. Who is my neighbor?: Humanity and proximity. *The Monist,* 86: 333–54.

Wall Street Journal. 2005. In praise of 'gouging.' *Wall Street Journal* (September 7): A16.

Zwolinski, Matt. 2008. The ethics of price gouging. *Business Ethics Quarterly,* 18: 347–78.

Matt Zwolinski  **NO**

Price Gouging, Non-Worseness, and Distributive Justice

Price gouging tends to evoke from humane and decent people an immediate and overwhelming sense of repugnance.[1] Most people have a strong sense that price gouging involves a kind of predatory behavior—a ruthless satisfaction of individual greed at the expense of the vulnerable—and that it must therefore constitute a serious moral wrong. Indeed, recent research in moral psychology suggests that this kind of "gut" reaction against price gouging might be very deeply rooted in us indeed. Instinctive and powerful reactions against the exploitation of the vulnerable may have served our early ancestors well by promoting the cohesion and survival of the small groups in which they lived.[2] But while reliance on automatic emotional reactions might have worked well for our primitive ancestors, such reactions are of little help in coming to a sophisticated and subtle understanding of the many and varied questions bearing on the morality of price gouging.[3] For such an understanding requires us to do more than simply decide whether "price gouging" is "good" or "bad." It requires us to discriminate among the many forms price gouging can take—between, for instance, an established merchant's raising prices to cover increased costs of supplies and risk, and a low-level entrepreneur who is drawn by the lure of high profits to begin selling items for the first time in the wake of a disaster. And it requires us to discriminate between the many different kinds of moral evaluations we can make of price gouging—whether it ought to be morally permissible or impermissible; whether it is morally praiseworthy, morally blameworthy, or merely morally tolerable; whether we have good moral reasons to prohibit it by law or by social pressure; and so forth. Each of these questions in turn raises a host of differing and difficult subsidiary questions that require both careful empirical research and thoughtful philosophical analysis to fully address.

Fortunately, Jeremy Snyder's paper on the subject contains no shortage of precisely this sort of thoughtful analysis.[4] Although his conclusions differ in some ways from my own,[5] he nevertheless provides a carefully argued case for the immorality of price gouging, while at the same time demonstrating an admirable sensitivity to the many morally attractive features of a free-market price system. Still, in spite of its many strengths, there are some points at which Snyder's position is less clear or less well-defended than it might be. Rather than continuing to sing the praises of what is generally a very fine piece of work, then, I shall focus my comments on what I take to be two problematic areas of his paper—first, Snyder's rejection of the non-worseness claim appears to be based on a misunderstanding of the kind of moral objects to which that principle is meant to apply; and second, Snyder's appeal to considerations of distributive justice and equal respect for persons is flawed insofar as it rests on two false assumptions—that price gouging undermines equitable access to vital goods, and that a regime in which price gouging is banned promotes equitable access. I will conclude with some brief comments on how Snyder's evaluation of price gouging compares with my own.

1. The Non-Worseness Claim

One of Snyder's major objections to my argument stems from my use of the "nonworseness claim" (NWC) to defend price gouging against the charge that it is wrongfully exploitative. NWC, as I described it, holds that "in cases where A has a right not to transact with B, and where transacting with B is not worse for B than not transacting with B at all, then it cannot be seriously wrong for A to engage in this transaction, even if its terms are judged to be unfair by some external standard" (Zwolinski 2008: 357). If the NWC is true, then it is hard to see how standard cases of price gouging can be serious moral wrongs. After all, most of us would think that an individual who could sell generators to victims of a disaster but chose not to do so would be acting within his rights (even if we also believe that she would be acting less than fully virtuously), and it also seems clear (Snyder himself concedes this [Snyder 2009: 277–78]) that those who buy from price gougers at inflated prices are nevertheless better off as a result than they would have been had the transaction not taken place at all. So, since gouging someone is better for them than neglecting them, and we have a moral right to neglect them, must we not therefore have a moral right to gouge them as well? How could gouging possibly be worse than neglect?

Snyder takes issue with this argument by holding that it fails when "motivations are assessed through sets of actions rather than single, morally ambiguous actions" (Snyder 2009: 288). Price gougers might indeed be acting in ways that help their customers, Snyder concedes, but they might be doing so only out of the vicious motive to extract as much profit as possible out of people in desperate need. Of course, they *might* be doing it out of a sense of morally virtuous beneficence as well. We can't tell just by looking at one action in isolation. To determine whether a person is properly motivated by a responsiveness to the needs of others, we need to look at their pattern of action as a whole, and not just one isolated instance.

This reasoning seems correct, as far as it goes. But it is not clear what lesson Snyder thinks he can draw from it. At times, Snyder writes as though he is making a point about the *moral character* of the price gouger and what it takes to lead a "morally praiseworthy life" (Snyder 2009: 287). With this point I am in full agreement—indeed it is one which I tried to make myself in part five of my paper (Zwolinski 2008: 366–68). One's moral character is a matter of one's general disposition to see the needs of others as reason-giving and to respond appropriately to those reasons. And the act of price gouging is too morally ambiguous for us to read this disposition (or its absence) off of it. But NWC is not a thesis about moral character, it is a thesis about the wrongness of moral *acts*. And this is importantly different. Vicious people can perform morally permissible actions. Think, for instance, of Kant's shopkeeper who returns the correct change to a naïve customer *only* out of a selfish concern for his own reputation and long-term profit. If he could be sure he could steal a penny from a child's change and get away with it, he would, but prudence dictates restraint. Such a person has a bad moral character. But the act he is performing—giving the child back her correct change—is perfectly innocent. The distinction between these two moral assessments becomes clear, and especially important to recognize, when we think about their respective implications for third parties. If we see a person—vicious or innocent—performing a morally *impermissible* action then, all else being equal, we should try to stop him, either as individuals or perhaps through the collective institutions of the state. But there is no comparable reason for us to try to stop someone from doing that which it is morally permissible for her to do, even if the person doing it is morally vicious. Her moral viciousness might give us *other* kinds of reason for action. We might have reason to censure her and get her to see the intrinsic value of all persons. And, in the case of Kant's shopkeeper, we might be very hesitant to patronize her store for fear that circumstances in the future will *not* always tip the scales of self-interest toward the side of honesty. But we do not have reason to interfere with her performance of a morally permissible act, or even to morally condemn the act, though we might have reason to morally condemn the agent.

Thus, Snyder's concerns about NWC do not give us reason to prohibit price gouging, or even condemn it. For all his arguments show (correctly, I think) is that price gouging can sometimes be done by morally vicious people. They do not show that the act of price gouging itself is morally impermissible. And that is all that my use of NWC was ever meant to deny.

2. Distributive Justice

One of the most common criticisms of price gouging, and one which is central to Snyder's argument as I understand it, is that it leads to vital resources being distributed in a morally objectionable way. Because price gouging involves charging a higher than normal price for goods, it disadvantages those who are poor relative to those who are well off. According to Snyder, price gouging thus undermines equitable access to essential goods, and thereby manifests a lack of equal respect for persons (Snyder 2009: 280).

However, the claim that price gouging undermines equitable access to goods is problematic for two reasons. First, it is the *emergency* that undermines equitable access, not whatever price gouging may occur in response to that disaster. Prior to the emergency, there is generally a well-functioning market in food, water, and other vital goods that generally ensures that all who need these goods will be able to purchase them. Emergencies lead to either a sharp increase in the demand for, or a sharp decrease in the supply of, these goods, and it is *this fact* that undermines equitable access. When supply and demand are radically altered so that there are not enough goods to go around, *no* method of distribution will produce equitable access—at least not at levels sufficient to meet people's needs.[6] Some people will get the goods, and others will not.

This is true of all methods of distribution, including Snyder's proposed method involving legislatively imposed caps on both the price of essential goods and on the amount of those goods that any consumer can purchase. Such a method of distribution, Snyder says, "mimic[s] a lottery for essential goods, treating all persons as equally deserving of the goods essential to basic human functioning" (Snyder 2009: 285). But the lottery metaphor, while apt in its characterization of a system of this sort, is puzzling as a way of highlighting the alleged distributive justice of such a system. For a lottery has seemed to many—most memorably to John Rawls—the paradigm case of moral arbitrariness (Rawls 1971: 74). In a lottery, some will obtain goods, some will not, and the difference between the two is nothing more than brute luck. In Snyder's lottery-like system, people will likewise be divided into "Haves" and "Have-Nots," and the difference between them will be based on who manages to get in line before supplies run out. This may not be *entirely* a matter of luck—perhaps it gives an edge to the perceptive, or those with a lot of time on their hands to stand in line. But it can hardly be said to be a system that distributes in accordance with any characteristic of great moral significance.

Furthermore, the sense in which it can be said to be a system that treats people as "equals" is at best a highly attenuated one. Because the context in which such a system operates is one where demand greatly exceeds supply, it is highly unlikely that the result of such a system will be equal units of vital goods being distributed to each person. For non-divisible goods like generators and radios, there will simply be no alternative to some people getting the good while others go away empty-handed. Other goods like ice could theoretically be divided into equally sized units for each person. But such a proposal is rife with practical difficulties. What if the portions of the good, once equally divided, are too small to be of any practical use? A bag of 300 ice cubes equally divided among 300 people is almost infinitely less useful than the same bag of ice in one person's hands. How is the relevant 'community' among which equal distribution is to take place to be defined? How are shopkeepers to determine what an equal unit of the good should be? And, most significantly, what sort of restrictions are to be put on the use to which people's shares of the good may be put? Will people be allowed to sell their goods to others—even though this would be certain to undermine equitable access?[7] Or will such secondary markets be prohibited?

The only kind of equality that Snyder's system can hope to achieve, then, is equality of *opportunity* to access vital goods. But this too, on closer examination, turns out to be less satisfying from a moral perspective than we might have hoped for. For in reality, opportunity under Snyder's proposed system will *not* be equal. Even if the system runs perfectly, those who show up first to a vendor will have a better opportunity than those who show up later. And in reality, rationing systems like the one proposed are often subject to corruption that favors 'insiders'—those with a personal, religious, ethnic, or other connection to those with resources or the power to affect their distribution.[8] It is true that nothing in Snyder's proposed system directly makes access to vital goods contingent on wealth, so with respect to *that* variable opportunity may be said to be equal. But in reality, and with respect to other equally if not more arbitrary variables, opportunity will not be equal.

Finally, it is worth noting that while Snyder's proposed distributive mechanism seeks to mimic while improving upon the *allocative* function of prices, it makes *no* effort to mimic their equally if not more important *signaling* function.[9] Prices that increase and decline in response to changes in supply and demand are important not only to allocate scarce resources among competing uses, but to signal when too much or too little social resources are being invested in a particular activity. In particular, the high prices that vital goods like water, sandbags, and hotel rooms command in the wake of a disaster signal to entrepreneurs to provide *more* of these goods, and indicate that larger-than-normal profits can be made by doing so. Post-disaster high prices thus convey both the *information* that increased supply is needed, and the *incentive* to provide that additional supply. But in so doing, high prices provide their own best corrective—as profit-seeking entrepreneurs rush to reap the windfall profits that the radically altered balance of supply and demand makes possible, they increase supply and in doing so drive the price down to something approximating its pre-disaster equilibrium. This means that the window of opportunity during which price gouging can occur is narrow, *but only if individuals are free to set prices as they see fit.*

This point is crucial. No one, not even those of us who argue that price gouging is morally permissible, thinks that price gouging is unqualifiedly *good* in the sense of being something that would occur in an ideal world. Cases of price gouging occur in circumstances of desperate need and terrible suffering. And in the short run, price gouging is just one more allocative mechanism among others, with the result that some people's needs—often the needs of the poorest and most vulnerable—will go unmet. But policies and moral injunctions that prevent prices from rising freely in the wake of a disaster do not diminish the desperation of the short run; they simply make it harder to move past that short run into a period of recovery. This might not be the case if we could rely on all people to act on the principles of beneficence that Snyder enjoins. And indeed, one of the most heartening aspects of some of the recent natural disasters in the United States has been the extent to which beneficence *has* been effective in delivering vital goods and services to those who so desperately need them. But it is probably a permanent feature of the human condition that there will always be less beneficence to go around than is needed. And in such a condition we would do well to take as much advantage as we can of the market's ability to channel individual self-interest toward socially desirable ends. In some cases, as is demonstrated in the response of Wal-Mart and Home Depot to Hurricane Katrina, even narrow self-interest will not lead to price gouging, and this is a happy result.[10] But where it does, we should recognize that gouging ought to be tolerated not as an end in itself, but merely as a method of making a very bad short-run situation less bad (by conserving scarce resources and allocating them effectively) and also of making that short run as short as possible (by providing incentives to increase supply).

3. Conclusion

. . . Snyder's position is somewhat unclear. He states that some "price increases condemned as gouging are morally innocent at worst and, more often, create a positive and morally praiseworthy benefit for all concerned" (Snyder 2009: 277). They do this, he notes, in many of the ways I discussed in my own paper: they aid "in the conservation of scarce goods by making it more likely that they will be purchased by those who place the greatest value on them" (Snyder 2009: 278), they send signals which lead "other suppliers into the market, quickly increasing supplies of essential goods" (Snyder 2009: 278), they provide an incentive to merchants to "increase supplies of essential goods prior to the [disaster]" (Snyder 2009: 278), and they serve as a "fair reward for the efforts and risks undertaken by vendors" (Snyder 2009: 278). And Snyder seems to indicate that insofar as price increases are necessary to serve these morally praiseworthy goals, they are morally permissible, as when he writes that "price increases even beyond those justified by increased costs and risks can be justified" insofar as they increase supplies, encourage rationing, and discourage waste (Snyder 2009: 285).

The question this raises, then, is under what conditions price gouging *will not* be morally acceptable on Snyder's account. The only clue Snyder provides to an answer is that price increases will be unacceptable when they "undermine equitable access to certain, essential goods" (Snyder 2009: 279). But this is puzzling, since price increases can presumably serve the morally praiseworthy goals described above (e.g. increasing rationing, discouraging waste) while *at the same time* undermining the equitable access of individuals to those goods. Indeed, it seems likely that the only way that price increases *can* promote goals like allocative efficiency and signaling new supply is by undermining equitable access, since these price increases will operate in a context in which individuals will face dramatically different budget constraints. This suggests that we cannot hope for both equitable access and the morally attractive benefits of price increases, and it is not clear which of these Snyder's account counsels us to choose in the (possibly ubiquitous) cases of conflict.

. . . I favor the repeal of all laws prohibiting or regulating price gouging, whereas Snyder thinks some regulation is appropriate. . . . We both think, as far as I can tell, that current laws are a bad idea insofar as they prohibit many mutually beneficial exchanges that would not be objectionably exploitative. But Snyder does seem to suggest that there is some role for the legal regulation of price gouging, and that it will involve limiting permissible price increases to those necessary to promote allocative efficiency, signal new supply, and compensate for increased risk and costs to merchants (Snyder 2009: 285). . . . But as a proposal for the *legal regulation* of price gouging (or even the social regulation of price gouging in the forms of boycotts/social pressure), I have a serious problem. . . . The problem is that by Snyder's standard, it is virtually impossible to know whether any given price increase is moral or immoral.[11] What percentage price increase is necessary to encourage the optimal level of rationing among one's consumers? In trying to answer this question, the merchant at least has the advantage of observing the behavior of her customers and seeing who responds in what way to a certain rate of price increase. But how will the merchant know who *should* be buying less, and who *should* be buying more? How would legislators now this? And what hope does a merchant or a legislator have—even if she is lucky enough to have a PhD in econometrics—of predicting the level of price increase necessary to attract sufficient supply to where it is needed?[12]

Thus, even if Snyder's list of morally relevant criteria is complete, it is useless as a standard of regulation because we cannot ever know if we are satisfying it. My contention is that the best hope we have of finding a price that approximates the satisfaction of these criteria is to let that price emerge through the free choices of numerous individuals in the market. This, too, is an imperfect mechanism, since actual prices do not always and necessarily reflect a proper balance of supply and demand, nor do they even purport to approximate "fair rewards" for risk and effort. Market prices, in other words, are not a perfect measure of moral significance. My claim, though, is that given the constraints in knowledge faced by those who would be charged with regulating prices, reliance on market prices in post-disaster contexts does a better job at promoting our moral values than any feasible alternative mechanism.

Notes

1. For a discussion of the role of repugnance as a reaction to price gouging and other forms of market exchange, see Roth 2007: 43–44.

2. For an overview of the possible evolutionary origins of "deontic" moral intuitions, such as those which tend to be invoked against the permissibility of mutually beneficial exploitation, see Greene 2007; Haidt 2001; Prinz 2008.

3. They may also be less helpful in a world in which distant, impersonal relationships have replaced close-knit societies as the locus of interpersonal interaction, and in which the distant indirect and non-obvious effects of our actions have an increasingly great relative causal significance on human well-being as the direct and visible ones. On this point, see Hayek's discussion of the extended order in Hayek and Bartley 1988: chap. 1, but also the concluding sections of Greene 2007.

4. Snyder 2009.

5. See Zwolinski 2008. See also Zwolinski forthcoming.

6. Of course, one could guarantee equity of a sort with a policy that bans distribution of the good altogether. Such a policy, if effectively enforced, could result in each person getting an equitable share of nothing.

7. Here we face a problem similar to that illustrated by Robert Nozick's famous Wilt Chamberlain example (Nozick 1974: 160–64). The maintenance of an initially equal distribution will require either a prohibition on trades or continual redistribution. And since Snyder's proposal is not to

initially distribute *all* resources equally, but only to provide equal access to certain vital resources, the difficulty of maintaining equality will be even greater.

8. See, for a discussion, Alchian and Allen 1968: 95–99.

9. On this distinction, see Zwolinski 2008: 360–64.

10. Steven Horowitz has documented the response of the private sector to Hurricane Katrina, noting that in the two weeks following the disaster Wal-Mart shipped over 2500 truckloads of needed goods to Louisiana, a substantial portion of which was given away free. This quick response time was made possible by Wal-Mart's elaborate mechanisms for tracking storms before they hit in order to ensure that its stores are well stocked prior to the time that demand increases. Neither Home Depot nor Wal-Mart engaged in price gouging in the aftermath of Katrina. And while it is possible that this restraint was at least partly motivated by altruistic concerns, no doubt a large part of it was motivated by the recognition that their behavior during this highly public and emotionally charged disaster situation would affect consumers' future willingness to give them their business. For established retailers, post-disaster deals are but one move in a long series of iterated prisoners' dilemmas with customers, and in such contexts mutual cooperation is often the strategy best in accord with individual self-interest (Axelrod 1984). Or, as one Home Depot executive put it, "I can't think of a quicker way to lose customers than price gouging." See Horowitz 2008; Horowitz forthcoming.

11. The problem is that no individual or group of individuals has sufficient information to know what price would be necessary to satisfy the criteria Snyder sets out. This problem is essentially just a specific instance of the more general knowledge problem discussed by Friedrich Hayek in Hayek 1937, 1945, and elsewhere.

12. There is strong evidence that even well-trained economists are severely limited in their ability to predict how actual markets will respond to events like a change in the general price level, much less a change in the price charged by one particular merchant. See, for a discussion, Gaus forthcoming; Gaus 2007.

Bibliography

Alchian, A., and W. Allen. 1968. *University Economics,* 2nd ed. New York: Wadsworth.

Axelrod, R. 1984. *The Evolution of Cooperation.* New York: Basic Books.

Gaus, G. F. 2007. "Social Complexity and Evolved Moral Principles," in *Liberalism, Conservatism, and Hayek's Idea of Spontaneous Order,* ed. P. McNamara. London: Palgrave Macmillan.

_____. Forthcoming. "Is the Public Incompetent? Compared to Whom? About What?" *Critical Review.*

Greene, J. 2007. "The Secret Joke in Kant's Soul," in *Moral Psychology, Vol. 3: The Neuroscience of Morality: Emotion, Disease, and Development,* ed. W. Sinnott-Armstrong. Cambridge, Mass.: MIT Press.

Haidt, J. 2001. "The Emotional Dog and its Rational Tail: A Social Intuitionist Approach to Moral Judgment," *Psychological Review* 108: 814–34.

Hayek, F. A. 1937. "Economics and Knowledge," *Economica* 4: 33–54.

_____. 1945. "The Use of Knowledge in Society," *American Economic Review* 35(4): 519–30.

Hayek, F. A., and W. W. Bartley III. 1988. *The Fatal Conceit: The Errors of Socialism.* Chicago: University of Chicago Press.

Horowitz, S. 2008. *Making Hurricane Response More Effective: Lessons from the Private Sector and the Coast Guard During Katrina.* Washington, D.C.: Mercatus Center.

_____. Forthcoming. "Wal-Mart to the Rescue: Private Enterprise's Response to Hurricane Katrina," *The Independent Review* 13(4).

Nozick, R. 1974. *Anarchy, State, and Utopia.* New York: Basic Books.

Prinz, J. 2008. *The Emotional Construction of Morals.* Oxford: Oxford University Press.

Rawls, J. 1971. *A Theory of Justice,* 1st ed. Cambridge: Belknap Press.

Roth, A. 2007. "Repugnance as a Constraint on Markets," *Journal of Economic Perspectives* 21(3): 37–58.

Snyder, J. 2009. "What's the Matter with Price Gouging?" *Business Ethics Quarterly.* 19(2) (April): 275–93.

Zwolinski, M. 2008. "The Ethics of Price Gouging," *Business Ethics Quarterly* 18(3): 347–78.

_____. Forthcoming. "Price Gouging and Market Failure," in *New Essays on Philosophy, Politics & Economics: Integration and Common Research Projects,* ed. G. Gaus, J. Lamont, and C. Favor. Stanford, Calif.: Stanford University Press.

POSTSCRIPT

Is Price Gouging Wrong?

The first challenge in this issue is to isolate what it is about price gouging that seems wrong or at least unsavory. (For it is at least sometimes the case that our feelings about a subject are very hazy, or even not right at all, prior to our looking more closely into the matter.) In the present case, is there something problematic about the whole idea of a market? Or about a market after a disaster? Or about a market in essential goods? Or about a market in essential goods after a disaster? And, if this unsavory element can be more or less precisely located, can we eliminate it? Will the elimination be achieved through restrictions on the market or in some other way?

There are, indeed, so many questions that can be raised with respect to price gouging. One wonders to what extent price gouging is just a case of the market in action, or whether this is a case in which the market fails or collapses. How, if indeed at all, do we count the attitudes and motivations of the price gougers here? Is it their intention to make a profit, to exploit people, to take advantage of people or the situation? Even if all of them always had a bad intention behind what they did, are they not still bring need goods to where they are most needed? If there is a worry about rich people being able to pay the high charges of the price gougers, how exactly is this different from rich people being able to afford more and better goods even when there is no disaster? Should the presence of the disaster mean that rich people are no longer able to use their wealth? Would a distribution of goods by means of lottery make more sense? (Would a distribution of *wealth* by means of a lottery make sense?) This issue raises these and other questions and deeper issues about the just distribution of wealth and goods.

Resources for further reading include Frederic P. Miller, Agnes F. Vandome, and John McBrewster, eds., *Coercive Monopoly: Economics, Business Ethics, Contestable Market, Price Gouging, Murray Rothbard, Monopoly, Government-Granted Monopoly, Government Monopoly, Natural Monopoly* (Alphascript Publishing, 2010); Lambert H. Surhone, Mariam T. Tennoe, and Susan F. Henssonow, *Price Gouging* (Betascript Publishing, 2010); and Gerald Gaus, Christi Favor, and Julian Lamont, *Essays on Philosophy, Politics & Economics: Integration & Common Research Projects* (Stanford Economics and Finance, 2010).

ISSUE 11

Is Affirmative Action Fair?

YES: Albert G. Mosley, from "Affirmative Action: Pro," in Albert G. Mosley and Nicholas Capaldi, eds., *Affirmative Action: Social Justice or Unfair Preference?* (Rowman & Littlefield, 1996)

NO: Louis P. Pojman, from "The Case Against Affirmative Action," *International Journal of Applied Philosophy* (Spring 1998)

ISSUE SUMMARY

YES: Professor of philosophy Albert G. Mosley argues that affirmative action is a continuation of the history of black progress since the *Brown v. Board of Education* desegregation decision of 1954 and the Civil Rights Act of 1964. He defends affirmative action as a "benign use of race."

NO: Professor of philosophy Louis P. Pojman contends that affirmative action violates the moral principle that maintains that each person is to be treated as an individual, not as representative of a group. He stresses that individual merit needs to be appreciated and that respect should be given to each person on an individual basis.

Throughout history, women and minority groups have been discriminated against in the United States. However, it might be difficult for many of us today to appreciate the extent of past discrimination and the ways in which social, legal, and political institutions were discriminatory.

Slavery is probably the most blatant form of past racism. We know that people were bought and sold, but the words are so familiar that the realities they stand for may never rise to consciousness. Many particular events and experiences lie behind a simple word like *slavery*. For example, the importation of slaves to this country was illegal before slaveholding itself became so. When ships at sea bringing African slaves to America found themselves in danger of being confronted by the law, it was easy to do what smugglers on the high seas always do with their contraband: the blacks, chained together and weighted down, were dropped overboard. Even after the Civil War, blacks were denied the right to vote, to testify in court, to own land, or to make contracts. In many states, laws restricted blacks in every conceivable aspect of their lives, including education, employment, and housing.

With respect to discrimination against women, consider the following, written by U.S. Supreme Court justice Joseph Bradley in concurring with the Court's decision in *Bradwell v. Illinois* (1873) that the state of Illinois was justified in denying Myra Bradwell a license to practice law on the grounds that she was a woman:

> [T]he civil law, as well as nature herself, has always recognized a wide difference in the respective spheres and destinies of man and woman. Man is, or should be, woman's protector and defender. The natural and proper timidity and delicacy which belongs to the female sex evidently unfits it for many of the occupations of civil life. The constitution of the family organization, which is founded in the divine ordinance, as well as in the nature of things, indicates the domestic sphere as that which properly belongs to the domain and functions of womanhood. The harmony . . . of interests and views which belong . . . to the family institution is repugnant to the idea of a woman adopting a distinct and independent career from that of her husband. . . . The paramount destiny and mission of woman are to fulfill the noble and benign offices of wife and mother.

Such thoughts are rarely openly expressed these days, and segregation and discrimination do not have legal support. One wonders, though, how much attitudes have actually changed. The law can change, but old attitudes can persist, and they can even be preserved and passed down from generation to generation. Moreover, the results of past social injustices are with us today.

Some of the consequences of past discrimination are systemic rather than individual-based. However much *individuals* might reject certain attitudes and practices of the past, there will usually be some *systemic* problems that are not so easily eliminated. There are systemic consequences of racist and sexist practices in the professions, in housing, in education, in the distribution of wealth, etc. For example, even if previously "white only" schools take down their "white only" signs, and the individuals involved agree to accept applicants of any race, the school system itself would be left virtually unchanged from its segregationist days. The situation of white-only schools would systematically perpetuate itself. This is where many feel that affirmative action can step in and change the system.

Albert G. Mosley places controversies surrounding affirmative action in a historical context and considers the justification of affirmative action both from the "backward-looking" perspective of corrective justice and from the "forward-looking" perspective of the social distribution of harms and benefits. Louis P. Pojman explains what he means by the term *affirmative action*. He maintains that affirmative action requires us to practice *reverse discrimination*, to fail to treat people as individuals, and to undervalue merit.

YES

Albert G. Mosley

Affirmative Action: Pro

Legislative and Judicial Background

In 1941, Franklin Roosevelt issued Executive Order 8802 banning discrimination in employment by the federal government and defense contractors. Subsequently, many bills were introduced in Congress mandating equal employment opportunity but none were passed until the Civil Rights Act of 1964. The penalty for discrimination in Executive Order 8802 and the bills subsequently proposed was that the specific victim of discrimination be "made whole," that is, put in the position he or she would have held were it not for the discriminatory act, including damages for lost pay and legal expenses.

The contemporary debate concerning affirmative action can be traced to the landmark decision of *Brown v. Board of Education* (1954), whereby local, state, and federal ordinances enforcing segregation by race were ruled unconstitutional. In subsequent opinions, the Court ruled that state-mandated segregation in libraries, swimming pools, and other publicly funded facilities was also unconstitutional. In *Swann v. Charlotte-Mecklenburg* (1971), the Court declared that "in order to prepare students to live in a pluralistic society" school authorities might implement their desegregation order by deciding that "each school should have a prescribed ratio of Negro to White students reflecting the proportion for the district as a whole."[1] The ratio was not to be an inflexible one, but should reflect local variations in the ratio of Whites to Blacks. But any predominantly one-race school in a district with a mixed population and a history of segregation was subject to "close scrutiny." This requirement was attacked by conservatives as imposing a "racial quota," a charge that reverberates in the contemporary debate concerning affirmative action.

With the Montgomery bus boycotts of the mid-1950s, Blacks initiated an era of nonviolent direct action to publicly protest unjust laws and practices that supported racial discrimination. The graphic portrayals of repression and violence produced by the civil rights movement precipitated a national revulsion against the unequal treatment of African Americans. Blacks demanded their constitutional right to participate in the political process and share equal access to public accommodations, government-supported programs, and employment opportunities. But as John F. Kennedy stated in an address to Congress: "There is little value in a Negro's obtaining the right to be admitted to hotels and restaurants if he has no cash in his pocket and no job."[2]

From *Affirmative Action: Social Justice or Unfair Preference?* by Albert G. Mosley and Nicholas Capaldi, eds. (1996), pp. 1–3, 23–28, 44–48, 50. Copyright © 1996 by Rowman & Littlefield. Reprinted by permission.

Kennedy stressed that the issue was not merely eliminating discrimination, but eliminating as well the oppressive economic and social burdens imposed on Blacks by racial discrimination.[3] To this end, he advocated a weak form of affirmative action, involving eliminating discrimination and expanding educational and employment opportunities (including apprenticeships and on-the-job training). The liberal vision was that, given such opportunities, Blacks would move up the economic ladder to a degree relative to their own merit. Thus, a principal aim of the Civil Rights Act of 1964 was to effect a redistribution of social, political, and economic benefits and to provide legal remedies for the denial of individual rights.

The Civil Rights Act of 1964

The first use of the phrase "affirmative action" is found in Executive Order 10952, issued by President John F. Kennedy in 1961. This order established the Equal Employment Opportunity Commission (EEOC) and directed that contractors on projects funded, in whole or in part, with federal funds "take affirmative action to ensure that applicants are employed, and employees are treated during their employment, without regard to the race, creed, color, or national origin."

As a result of continuing public outrage at the level of violence and animosity shown toward Blacks, a stronger version of the Civil Rights Bill was presented to the Congress than Kennedy had originally recommended. Advocates pointed out that Blacks suffered an unemployment rate that was twice that of Whites and that Black employment was concentrated in semiskilled and unskilled jobs. They emphasized that national prosperity would be improved by eliminating discrimination and integrating Black talent into its skilled and professional workforce.[4]

Fewer Blacks were employed in professional positions than had the requisite skills, and those Blacks who did occupy positions commensurate with their skill level had half the lifetime earnings of Whites. Such facts were introduced during legislative hearings to show the need to more fully utilize and reward qualified Blacks throughout the labor force, and not merely in the unskilled and semiskilled sectors. . . .

Conceptual Issues

There are many interests that governments pursue—maximization of social production; equitable distribution of rights, opportunities, and services; social safety and cohesion; restitution—and those interests may conflict in various situations. In particular, governments as well as their constituents have a prima facie obligation to satisfy the liabilities they incur. One such liability derives from past and present unjust exclusionary acts depriving minorities and women of opportunities and amenities made available to other groups.

"Backward looking" arguments defend affirmative action as a matter of *corrective justice*, where paradigmatically the harmdoer is to make restitution to the harmed so as to put the harmed in the position the harmed most likely

would have occupied had the harm not occurred. An important part of making restitution is the acknowledgment it provides that the actions causing injury were unjust and such actions will be curtailed and corrected. In this regard Bernard Boxill writes:

> Without the acknowledgement of error, the injurer implies that the injured has been treated in a manner that befits him. . . . In such a case, even if the unjust party repairs the damage he has caused . . . nothing can be demanded on legal or moral grounds, and the repairs made are gratuitous. . . . [J]ustice requires that we acknowledge that this treatment of others can be required of us; thus, where an unjust injury has occurred, the injurer reaffirms his belief in the other's equality by conceding that repair can be demanded of him, and the injured rejects the allegation of his inferiority . . . by demanding reparation.[5]

This view is based on the idea that restitution is a basic moral principle that creates obligations that are just as strong as the obligations to maximize wealth and distribute it fairly.[6] If x has deprived y of opportunities y had a right not to be deprived of in this manner, then x is obligated to return y to the position y would have occupied had x not intervened; x has this obligation irrespective of other obligations x may have. . . .

[An] application of this principle involves the case where x is not a person but an entity, like a government or a business. If y was unjustly deprived of employment when firm F hired z instead of y because z was White and y Black, then y has a right to be made whole, that is, brought to the position he/she would have achieved had that deprivation not occurred. Typically, this involves giving y a position at least as good as the one he/she would have acquired originally and issuing back pay in the amount that y would have received had he/she been hired at the time of the initial attempt.

Most critics of preferential treatment acknowledge the applicability of principles of restitution to individuals in specific instances of discrimination. The strongest case is where y was as or more qualified than z in the initial competition, but the position was given to z because y was Black and z was White.[7] Subsequently, y may not be as qualified for an equivalent position as some new candidate z', but is given preference because of the past act of discrimination by F that deprived y of the position he or she otherwise would have received.

Some critics have suggested that, in such cases, z' is being treated unfairly. For z', as the most qualified applicant, has a right not to be excluded from the position in question purely on the basis of race; and y has a right to restitution for having unjustly been denied the position in the past. But the dilemma is one in appearance only. For having unjustly excluded y in the past, the current position that z has applied for is not one that F is free to offer to the public. It is a position that is already owed to y, and is not available for open competition. Judith Jarvis Thomson makes a similar point:

> suppose two candidates [A and B] for a civil service job have equally good test scores, but there is only one job available. We could decide

between them by coin-tossing. But in fact we do allow for declaring for A straightway, where A is a veteran, and B is not. It may be that B is a non-veteran through no fault of his own. . . . Yet the fact is that B is not a veteran and A is. On the assumption that the veteran has served his country, the country owes him something. And it is plain that giving him preference is not an unjust way in which part of that debt of gratitude can be paid.[8]

In a similar way, individual Blacks who have suffered from acts of unjust discrimination are owed something by the perpetrator(s) of such acts, and this debt takes precedence over the perpetrator's right to use his or her options to hire the most qualified person for the position in question.

Many White males have developed expectations about the likelihood of their being selected for educational, employment, and entrepreneurial opportunities that are realistic only because of the general exclusion of women and non-Whites as competitors for such positions. Individuals enjoying inflated odds of obtaining such opportunities because of racist and sexist practices are recipients of an "unjust enrichment."

Redistributing opportunities would clearly curtail benefits that many have come to expect. And given the frustration of their traditional expectations, it is understandable that they would feel resentment. But blocking traditional expectations is not unjust if those expectations conflict with the equally important moral duties of restitution and just distribution. It is a question, not of "is," but of "ought": not "Do those with decreased opportunities as a result of affirmative action feel resentment?" but "Should those with decreased opportunities as a result of affirmative action feel resentment?". . .

Since Title VII [of the Civil Rights Act of 1964] protects bona fide seniority plans, it forces the burden of rectification to be borne by Whites who are entering the labor force rather than Whites who are the direct beneficiaries of past discriminatory practices. Given this limitation placed on affirmative action remedies, the burden of social restitution may, in many cases, be borne by those who were not directly involved in past discriminatory practices. But it is generally not true that those burdened have not benefited at all from past discriminatory practices. For the latent effects of acts of invidious racial discrimination have plausibly bolstered and encouraged the efforts of Whites in roughly the same proportion as it inhibited and discouraged the efforts of Blacks. Such considerations are also applicable to cases where F discriminated against y in favor of z, but the make-whole remedy involves providing compensation to y rather than y. This suggests that y is an *undeserving beneficiary* of the preferential treatment meant to compensate for the unjust discrimination against y, just as z above appeared to be the innocent victim forced to bear the burden that z benefited from. Many critics have argued that this misappropriation of benefits and burdens demonstrates the unfairness of compensation to groups rather than individuals. But it is important that the context and rationale for such remedies be appreciated.

In cases of "egregious" racial discrimination, not only is it true that F discriminated against a particular Black person y, but F's discrimination advertised a general disposition to discriminate against any other Black person who might seek such positions. The specific effect of F's unjust discrimination was that y was refused a position he or she would otherwise have received. The latent (or dispositional) effect of F's unjust discrimination was that many Blacks who otherwise would have sought such positions were discouraged from doing so. Thus, even if the specific y actually discriminated against can no longer be compensated, F has an obligation to take affirmative action to communicate to Blacks as a group that such positions are indeed open to them. After being found in violation of laws prohibiting racial discrimination, many agencies have disclaimed further discrimination while in fact continuing to do so.[9] In such cases, the courts have required the discriminating agencies to actually hire and/or promote Blacks who may not be as qualified as some current White applicants until Blacks approach the proportion in F's labor force they in all likelihood would have achieved had F's unjust discriminatory acts not deterred them.

Of course, what this proportion would have been is a matter of speculation. It may have been less than the proportion of Blacks available in the relevant labor pool from which applicants are drawn if factors other than racial discrimination act to depress the merit of such applicants. This point is made again and again by critics. Some, such as Thomas Sowell, argue that cultural factors often mitigate against Blacks meriting representation in a particular labor force in proportion to their presence in the pool of candidates looking for jobs or seeking promotions.[10] Others, such as Michael Levin, argue that cognitive deficits limit Blacks from being hired and promoted at a rate proportionate to their presence in the relevant labor pool.[11] What such critics reject is the assumption that, were it not for pervasive discrimination and overexploitation, Blacks would be equally represented in the positions in question. What is scarcely considered is the possibility that, were it not for racist exclusions, Blacks might be over rather than under represented in competitive positions.

Establishing Blacks' presence at a level commensurate with their proportion in the relevant labor market need not be seen as an attempt to actualize some valid prediction. Rather, given the impossibility of determining what level of representation Blacks would have achieved were it not for racist discrimination, the assumption of proportional representation is the only *fair* assumption to make. This is not to argue that Blacks should be maintained in such positions, but their contrived exclusion merits an equally contrived rectification.[12]

Racist acts excluding Blacks affected particular individuals, but were directed at affecting the behavior of the group of all those similar to the victim. Likewise, the benefits of affirmative action policies should not be conceived as limited in their effects to the specific individuals receiving them. Rather, those benefits should be conceived as extending to all those identified with the recipient, sending the message that opportunities are indeed available to qualified Black candidates who would have been excluded in the past. . . .

Forward-Looking Justifications of Affirmative Action

. . . [Some] have defended preferential treatment but denied that it should be viewed as a form of reparation. This latter group rejects "backward looking" justifications of affirmative action and defends it instead on "forward-looking" grounds that include distributive justice, minimizing subordination, and maximizing social utility.

Thus, Ronald Fiscus argues that backward-looking arguments have distorted the proper justification for affirmative action policies.[13] Backward-looking arguments depend on the paradigm of traditional tort cases, where a specific individual x has deprived another individual y of a specific good t through an identifiable act a, and x is required to restore y to the position y would have had, had a not occurred. But typically, preferential treatment requires that x (rather than x) restore y' (instead of y) with a good t' that y' supposedly would have achieved had y not been deprived of t by x. The displacement of perpetrator (x' for x) and victim (y' for y) gives rise to the problem of (1) White males who are innocent of acts having caused harm nonetheless being forced to provide restitution for such acts; and (2) Blacks who were not directly harmed by those acts nonetheless becoming the principal beneficiaries of restitution for those acts. . . .

Fiscus argues that the backward-looking argument reinforces the perception that preferential treatment is unfair to innocent White males, and so long as this is the case, both the courts and the public are likely to oppose strong affirmative action policies such as quotas, set-asides, and other preferential treatment policies.

In contrast, Fiscus recommends that preferential treatment be justified in terms of distributive justice, which as a matter of equal protection, "requires that individuals be awarded the positions, advantages, or benefits they would have been awarded under fair conditions," that is, conditions under which racist exclusion would not have precluded Blacks from attaining "their deserved proportion of the society's important benefits." Conversely, "distributive justice also holds that individuals or groups may not claim positions, advantages, or benefits that they would not have been awarded under fair conditions."[14] These conditions jointly prohibit White males from claiming an unreasonable share of social benefits and protects White males from having to bear an unreasonable share of the redistributive burden.

Fiscus takes the position that any deviation between Blacks and Whites from strict proportionality in the distribution of current goods is evidence of racism. Thus, if Blacks were 20 percent of a particular population but held no positions in the police or fire departments, that is indicative of past and present racial discrimination. . . .

Because the Equal Protection Clause of the Fourteenth Amendment protects citizens from statistical discrimination on the basis of race, the use of race as the principal reason for excluding certain citizens from benefits made available to other citizens is a violation of that person's constitutional rights. This was one basis for [Alan] Bakke's suit against the UC-Davis medical school's

16 percent minority set-aside for medical school admission. There were eighty-four seats out of the one hundred admission slots that he was eligible to fill, and he was excluded from competing for the other sixteen slots because of his race. On the basis of the standard criteria (GPA, MCAT scores, etc.), Bakke argued that he would have been admitted before any of the Black applicants admitted under the minority set-aside. He therefore claimed that he was being excluded from the additional places available because he was White.

Currently, Blacks have approximately 3.25 times fewer physicians than would be expected given their numbers in the population. Native Americans have 7 times fewer physicians than what would have been expected if intelligent, well-trained, and motivated Native Americans had tried to become physicians at the same rate as did European Americans.

For Fiscus, the underrepresentation of African and Native Americans among physicians and the maldistribution of medical resources to minority communities is clearly the effect of generations of racist exclusions. . . . Not only are qualified members of the oppressed group harmed by . . . prejudice, but even more harmed are the many who would have been qualified but for injuries induced by racial prejudice.

For Fiscus, individuals of different races would have been as equally distributed in the social body as the molecules of a gas in a container and he identifies the belief in the inherent equality of races with the Equal Protection Clause of the Fourteenth Amendment.[15] In a world without racism, minorities would be represented among the top one hundred medical school applicants at UC-Davis in the same proportion as they were in the general population. Accordingly, because Bakke did not score among the top eighty-four Whites, he would not have qualified for admission. Thus, he had no right to the position he was contesting, and indeed if he were given such a position in lieu of awarding it to a minority, Bakke would be much like a person who had received stolen goods. "Individuals who have not personally harmed minorities may nevertheless be prevented from reaping the benefits of the harm inflicted by the society at large."[16]

Justice O'Connor has voiced skepticism toward the assumption that members of different races would "gravitate with mathematical exactitude to each employer or union absent unlawful discrimination."[17] She considers it sheer speculation as to "how many minority students would have been admitted to the medical school at Davis absent past discrimination in educational opportunities."[18] I likewise consider it speculative to assume that races would be represented in every area in proportion to their proportion of the general population. But because it is impossible to reasonably predict what that distribution would have been absent racial discrimination, it is not mere speculation but morally fair practice to assume that it would have been the same as the proportion in the general population. Given the fact of legally sanctioned invidious racism against Blacks in U.S. history, the burden of proof should not be on the oppressed group to prove that it would be represented at a level proportionate to its presence in the general population. Rather, the burden of proof should be on the majority to show why its overrepresentation among the most well off is not the result of unfair competition imposed by racism.

We are morally obligated to assume proportional representation until there are more plausible reasons than racism for assuming otherwise. . . .

Thus, it should be the responsibility of the Alabama Department of Public Safety to show why no Blacks were members of its highway patrol as of 1970, even though Blacks were 25 percent of the relevant workforce in Alabama. It should be the responsibility of the company and the union to explain why there were no Blacks with seniority in the union at the Kaiser plant in Louisiana, although Blacks made up 39 percent of the surrounding population. Likewise, it should be the responsibility of the union to explain why no Blacks had been admitted to the Sheet Metal Workers' Union in New York City although minorities were 29 percent of the available workforce. If no alternative explanations are more plausible, then the assumption that the disparity in representation is the result of racism should stand.

The question should not be whether White males are innocent or guilty of racism or sexism, but whether they have a right to inflated odds of obtaining benefits relative to minorities and women. A White male is innocent only up to the point where he takes advantage of "a benefit he would not qualify for without the accumulated effects of racism. At that point he becomes an accomplice in, and a beneficiary of, society's racism. He becomes the recipient of stolen goods."[19] . . .

Cass Sunstein also argues that the traditional compensation model based on the model of a discrete injury caused by one individual (the tort-feasor or defendant) and suffered by another individual (the plaintiff) is inadequate to capture the situation arising from racial and sexual discrimination.[20] With the traditional tortlike model, the situation existing prior to the injury is assumed to be noncontestable, and the purpose of restitution is to restore the injured party to the position that party would have occupied if the injury had not occurred. But in cases where the injury is not well defined, where neither defendant nor plaintiff are individuals connected by a discrete event, and where the position the injured party would have occupied but for the injury is unspecifiable, then in such cases dependence on the traditional model of compensatory justice is questionable.[21]

In contrast to the position taken by Fiscus, Sunstein argues that the claim that affirmative action and preferential treatment is meant to put individuals in the position they would have occupied had their groups not been subject to racial and sexual discrimination is nonsensical: "What would the world look like if it had been unaffected by past discrimination on the basis of race and sex? . . . the question is unanswerable, not because of the absence of good social science, but because of the obscure epistemological status of the question itself."[22]

Affirmative action must be justified in terms of alternative conceptions of the purpose of legal intervention, and Sunstein recommends instead the notion of "risk management" (intended to offset increased risks faced by a group rather than compensate the injuries suffered by a particular individual) and the "principle of nonsubordination" (whereby measures are taken to reverse a situation in which an irrelevant difference has been transformed by legally sanctioned acts of the state into a social disadvantage). The notion of risk management is meant to apply to cases where injuries are "individually small but collectively large" so that pursuing each case individually would be too costly both in terms of time and effort.[23] In such cases, those harmed may be unable to establish a direct causal link between their injuries and the plaintiff's actions. Thus, a person who develops a certain type of cancer associated with a toxin produced by a particular company might have developed that condition even in the absence of the company's negligent behavior. At most, they can argue that the company's actions caused an increased risk of injury, rather than any specific instance of that injury.

Harms suffered in this way systematically affect certain groups with higher frequency than other groups, without it being possible to establish causal links between the injuries of specific plaintiffs and the actions of the defendant. Regulatory agencies should be designed to address harms that are the result of increased risks rather than of a discrete action.[24] One of their principal aims should be not to compensate each injured party (and only injured parties), "but instead to deter and punish the risk-creating behavior" by redistributing social goods.[25] . . .

The principle of nonsubordination is meant to apply to cases where the existing distribution of wealth and opportunities between groups are the result of law rather than natural attributes.[26] The purpose of affirmative action from a forward-looking perspective should be to end social subordination and reverse the situation in which irrelevant differences have been, through social and legal structures, turned into systematic disadvantages operative in multiple spheres that diminish participation in democratic forms of life.[27] . . .

> affirmative action does not appear an impermissible 'taking' of an antecedent entitlement. Because the existing distribution of benefits and burdens between Blacks and Whites and men and women is not natural . . . and because it is in part a product of current laws and practices having discriminatory effects, it is not decisive if some Whites and men are disadvantaged as a result.[28]

A central question in the debate over affirmative action is the extent to which racial classifications are important in accomplishing the goal of relieving the subordinate status of minorities and women. Given the aim of improving safety in transportation, classifying people in terms of their race is rationally irrelevant, while classifying them in terms of their driving competency, visual acuity, and maturity is essential. On the other hand, given the aim of improving health care in Black neighborhoods, classifying applicants for medical school in terms of their race is, in addition to their academic and clinical abilities, a very relevant factor.

To illustrate, African Americans, Hispanics, and Native Americans make up 22 percent of the population but represent only 10 percent of entering medical students and 7 percent of practicing physicians. A number of studies have shown that underrepresented minority physicians are more likely than their majority counterparts to care for poor patients and patients of similar ethnicity. Indeed, "each ethnic group of patients was more likely to be cared for by a physician of their own ethnic background than by a physician of another ethnic background."[29] This suggests that sociocultural factors such as language, physical identity, personal background, and experiences are relevant factors in determining the kinds of communities in which a physician will establish a practice. If this is the case, then the race of a medical school applicant would be an important factor in providing medical services to certain underrepresented communities. Thus, while there might be some purposes for which race is irrelevant, there might be other purposes in which race is important (though perhaps not necessary) for achieving the end in view.[30] The remedy targets Blacks as a group because racially discriminatory practices were directed against Blacks as a group.[31]

. . . Preferential treatment programs are meant to offset the disadvantages imposed by racism so that Blacks are not forced to bear the principal costs of that error.

. . . To condemn polices meant to correct for racial barriers as themselves erecting barriers is to ignore the difference between action and reaction, cause and effect, aggression and self-defense. . . .

Conclusion

Racism was directed against Blacks whether they were talented, average, or mediocre, and attenuating the effects of racism requires distributing remedies similarly. Affirmative action policies compensate for the harms of racism (overt and institutional) through antidiscrimination laws and preferential policies. Prohibiting the benign use of race as a factor in the award of educational, employment and business opportunities would eliminate compensation for past and present racism and reinforce the moral validity of the status quo, with Blacks overrepresented among the least well off and underrepresented among the most well off.

It has become popular to use affirmative action as a scapegoat for the increased vulnerability of the White working class. But it should be recognized that the civil rights revolution (in general) and affirmative action (in particular) has been beneficial, not just to Blacks, but also to Whites (e.g., women, the disabled, the elderly) who otherwise would be substantially more vulnerable than they are now.

Affirmative action is directed toward empowering those groups that have been adversely affected by past and present exclusionary practices. Initiatives to abolish preferential treatment would inflict a grave injustice on African Americans, for they signal a reluctance to acknowledge that the plight of African Americans is the result of institutional practices that require institutional responses.

Notes

1. Kent Greenawalt, *Discrimination and Reverse Discrimination* (New York: Alfred A. Knopf, 1983), 129 ff.

2. Kathanne W. Greene, *Affirmative Action and Principles of Justice* (New York: Greenwood Press, 1989), 22.

3. Kennedy stated: "Even the complete elimination of racial discrimination in employment—a goal toward which this nation must strive—will not

put a single unemployed Negro to work unless he has the skills required."
Greene, *Affirmative Action*, 23.

4. Greene, *Affirmative Action*, 31.

5. Bernard Boxill, "The Morality of Reparation" in *Social Theory and Practice*, 2,
   no. 1, Spring 1972: 118–119. It is for such reasons that welfare programs are
   not sufficient to satisfy the claims of Blacks for restitution. Welfare programs
   contain no admission of the unjust violation of rights and seek merely to
   provide the basic means for all to pursue opportunities in the future.

6. I am presuming that most of us would recognize certain primae facie
   duties such as truth telling, promise keeping, restitution, benevolence,
   justice, nonmalficience as generally obligatory. See W. D. Ross, *The Right
   and the Good* (Oxford: Clarendon Press, 1930).

7. Even in the case where y was only as qualified as z, a fair method of choice
   between candidates should produce an equitable distribution of such positions between Blacks and Whites in the long run if not in the short.

8. Judith Jarvis Thompson, *Philosophy and Public Affairs*, 2 (Summer 1973):
   379–380.

9. *Sheet Metal Workers v. EEOC* (1986); *United States v. Paradise* (1987).

10. Thomas Sowell, *Ethnic America* (New York: Basic Books, 1981); *Preferential
    Policies: An International Perspective* (New York: William Morrow, 1990); For a
    recent critique of Sowell's position, see Christopher Jencks, *Rethinking Social
    Policy: Race, Poverty, and the Underclass* (New York: Harper, 1993), chap. 1.

11. Michael Levin, "Race, Biology, and Justice" in *Public Affairs Quarterly*, 8, no. 3
    (July 1994). There are many good reasons for skepticism regarding the validity
    of using IQ as a measure of cognitive ability. See *The Bell Curve Wars* ed. Steven
    Fraser (New York: Basic Books, 1995); *The Bell Curve Debate*, ed. by Russell
    Jacoby and Naomi Glauberman (New York: Times Books, 1995); Allan Chase,
    The Legacy of Malthus (Urbana: University of Illinois Press, 1980); Steven J.
    Gould, *The Mismeasure of Man* (New York: Norton, 1981); R. C. Lewontin, S.
    Rose, L. J. Kamin, *Not in Our Genes* (New York: Pantheon Books, 1984).

12. See Robert Fullinwider, *The Reverse Discrimination Controversy: A Moral and
    Legal Analysis* (Totowa, N.J.: Rowman & Littlefield, 1980), 117. Ronald
    Fiscus, *The Constitutional Logic of Affirmative Action* (Durham, N.C.: Duke
    University Press, 1992).

13. Ronald J. Fiscus, *The Constitutional Logic of Affirmative Action* (Durham,
    N.C.: Duke University Press, 1992).

14. Fiscus, *Constitutional Logic*, 13.

15. Fiscus, *Constitutional Logic*, 20–26.

16. Fiscus, *Constitutional Logic*, 38.

17. *Sheet Metal Workers v. EEOC*, 478 US 421, 494 (1986); Fiscus, *Constitutional
    Logic*, 42.

18. *City of Richmond v. J. A. Croson Co.*, 109 S.Ct. at 724 (1989); Fiscus, *Constitu-
    tional Logic*, 42.

19. Fiscus, *Constitutional Logic*, 47. With regard to the problem of so-called
    "undeserving beneficiaries" of affirmative action Fiscus writes: "When the
    rightful owner of stolen goods cannot be found, the law . . . may or may
    not award possession to the original but wrongful claimant; but if it does

not, if it awards possession to a third party whose claim is arguable, the original claimant cannot justifiably feel morally harmed. And the government's action cannot be said to be arbitrary unless it awards the goods to an individual whose claim is even less plausible than that of the original claimant" (49).

20. Cass Sunstein, "Limits of Compensatory Justice" in *Nomos* 33, *Compensatory Justice*, ed. John Chapman (New York: New York University Press, 1991), 281–310.

21. "It is not controlling and perhaps not even relevant that the harms that affirmative action attempts to redress cannot be understood in the usual compensatory terms. . . . [T]he nature of the problem guarantees that the legal response cannot take the form of discrete remedies for discrete harms" (Sunstein, "Limits," 297).

22. Sunstein, "Limits," 303.

23. The orientation of the EEOC toward investigating individual cases of alleged discrimination is one explanation of its extraordinary backlog of over 80,000 cases. This orientation precludes it from focusing on systemic practices that affect many individuals, and instead forces it to expend resources dealing with particular instances. See "The EEOC: Pattern and Practice Imperfect" by Maurice Munroe in *Yale Law and Policy Review*, 13, no. 2, (1995): 219–80.

24. Sunstein, "Limits," 292.

25. Sunstein, "Limits," 289.

26. "The current distribution of benefits and burdens as between blacks and whites and women and men is not part of the state of nature but a consequence of past and present social practices" (Sunstein, "Limits," 294).

27. See also Thomas H. Simon, *Democracy and Social Justice* (Lanham, Md.: Rowman & Littlefield, 1995), chap. 5.

28. Sunstein, "Limits," 306.

29. Gang Xu, Sylvia Fields, et al., "The Relationship between the Ethnicity of Generalist Physicians and Their Care for Underserved Populations," Ohio University College of Osteopathic Medicine, Athens, Ohio, 10.

30. Of course, we may ask whether the use of race is necessary for the achievement of the end in view or whether it is one among alternative ways of achieving that end. For instance, it might be possible to induce doctors to practice in Black neighborhoods by providing doctors, irrespective of their race, with suitable monetary incentives. But given the importance of nonmonetary factors in physician-patient relationships, it is doubtful that purely monetary rewards would be sufficient to meet the needs of underserved populations.

31. Remedial action based on the imbalance between blacks in the available work force and their presence in skilled jobs categories presumes that imbalance is caused by racial discrimination. This assumption has been challenged by many who cite cultural and cognitive factors that might equally be the cause of such imbalances. See Thomas Sowell, *Markets and Minorities* (New York: Basic Books, 1981); Richard Herrenstein and Charles Murray, *The Bell Curve* (New York: The Free Press, 1994). This literature has itself been subject to critique: for Sowell, see Christopher Jencks, *Rethinking Social Policy* (New York: Harper, 1993); for Herrenstein and Murray, see *The Bell Curve Wars*, ed. Steven Fraser (New York: Basic Books, 1995).

Louis P. Pojman  **NO**

The Case Against Affirmative Action

Let us agree that despite the evidences of a booming economy, the poor are suffering grievously, with children being born into desperate material and psychological poverty; for them the ideal of "equal opportunity for all" is a cruel joke. Many feel that the federal government has abandoned its guarantee to provide the minimum necessities for each American, so that the pace of this tragedy seems to be worsening daily. In addition to this, African-Americans have a legacy of slavery and unjust discrimination to contend with, and other minorities have also suffered from injustice. Women have their own peculiar history of being treated unequally in relevant ways. What is the answer to this national problem? Is it increased welfare? More job training? More support for education? Required licensing of parents to have children? Negative income tax? More support for families or for mothers with small children? All of these have merit and should be part of the national debate. But, my thesis is, however tragic the situation may be (and we may disagree on just how tragic it is), one policy is *not* a legitimate part of the solution and that is *reverse, unjust discrimination* against young white males. Strong Affirmative Action, which implicitly advocates reverse discrimination, while no doubt well intentioned, is morally heinous, asserting, by implication, that *two wrongs make a right*.

The *Two Wrongs Make a Right* Thesis goes like this: Because *some* Whites once enslaved some Blacks, the descendants of those slaves (some of whom now may enjoy high incomes and social status) have a right to opportunities and offices over better qualified Whites who had nothing to do with either slavery or the oppression of Blacks (and who may even have suffered hardship comparable to that of poor Blacks). In addition, Strong Affirmative Action creates a new Hierarchy of the Oppressed: Blacks get primary preferential treatment, women second, Native Americans third, Hispanics fourth, Handicapped fifth, and Asians sixth and so on until White males, no matter how needy or well qualified, must accept the leftovers. . . .

Before analyzing arguments concerning Affirmative Action, I must define my terms.

By *Weak Affirmative Action* I mean policies that will increase the opportunities of disadvantaged people to attain social goods and offices. It includes such things as dismantling of segregated institutions, widespread advertisement to groups not previously represented in certain privileged positions,

From *International Journal of Applied Philosophy,* vol. 12, Spring 1998, pp. 97–115. Copyright © 1998 by Philosophy Documentation Center. Reprinted by permission.

special scholarships for the disadvantaged classes (e.g., the poor, regardless of race or gender), and even using diversity or under-representation of groups with a history of past discrimination as a tie breaker when candidates for these goods and offices are relatively equal. The goal of *Weak Affirmative Action* is equal opportunity to compete, not equal results. We seek to provide each citizen regardless of race or gender a fair chance to the most favored positions in society. . . .

By *Strong Affirmative Action* I mean preferential treatment on the basis of race, ethnicity or gender (or some other morally irrelevant criterion), discriminating in favor of underrepresented groups against overrepresented groups, aiming at roughly equal results. *Strong Affirmative Action* is *reverse discrimination*. It says it is right to do wrong to correct a wrong. This is the policy currently being promoted under the name of *Affirmative Action*, so I will use that term or "AA" for short throughout this essay to stand for this version of affirmative action. I will not argue for or against the principle of *Weak Affirmative Action*. Indeed, I think it has some moral weight. *Strong Affirmative Action* has none, or so I will argue.

This essay concentrates on AA policies with regard to race, but the arguments can be extended to cover ethnicity and gender. I think that if a case for Affirmative Action can be made it will be as a corrective to racial oppression. I will examine eight arguments regarding AA. The first six will be *negative*, attempting to show that the best arguments for Affirmative Action fail. The last [two] will be *positive* arguments for policies opposing Affirmative Action:

A Critique of Arguments for Affirmative Action

The Need for Role Models

This argument is straightforward. We all have need of role models, and it helps to know that others like us can be successful. We learn and are encouraged to strive for excellence by emulating our heroes and "our kind of people" who have succeeded.

In the first place it's not clear that role models of one's own racial or sexual type are necessary (let alone sufficient) for success. One of my heroes was Gandhi, an Indian Hindu, another was my grade school science teacher, Miss DeVoe, and another Martin Luther King, behind whom I marched in Civil Rights demonstrations. More important than having role models of one's "own type" is having genuinely good people, of whatever race or gender, to emulate. Our common humanity should be a sufficient basis for us to see the possibility of success in people of virtue and merit. To yield to the demand, however tempting it may be, for "role-models-just-like-us" is to treat people like means not ends. . . .

The Compensation Argument

The argument goes like this: blacks have been wronged and severely harmed by whites. Therefore white society should compensate blacks for the injury caused them. Reverse discrimination in terms of preferential hiring, contracts, and scholarships is a fitting way to compensate for the past wrongs.[1]

This argument actually involves a distorted notion of compensation. Normally, we think of compensation as owed by a specific person A to another person B whom A has wronged in a specific way C. For example, if I have stolen your car and used it for a period of time to make business profits that would have gone to you, it is not enough that I return your car. I must pay you an amount reflecting your loss and my ability to pay. If I have made $5,000 and only have $10,000 in assets, it would not be possible for you to collect $20,000 in damages—even though that is the amount of loss you have incurred. . . .

On the face of it, demands by blacks for compensation do not fit the usual pattern. Southern States with Jim Crow laws could be accused of unjustly harming blacks, but it is hard to see that the United States government was involved in doing so. Much of the harm done to blacks was the result of private discrimination, not state action. . . . Furthermore, it is not clear that all blacks were harmed in the same way or whether some were *unjustly* harmed or harmed more than poor whites and others (e.g., short people). Finally, even if identifiable blacks were harmed by identifiable social practices, it is not clear that most forms of Affirmative Action are appropriate to restore the situation. The usual practice of a financial payment seems more appropriate than giving a high level job to someone unqualified or only minimally qualified. . . .

Still, there may be something intuitively compelling about compensating members of an oppressed group who are minimally qualified. Suppose that the Hatfields and the McCoys are enemy clans and some youths from the Hatfields go over and steal diamonds and gold from the McCoys, distributing it within the Hatfield economy. Even though we do not know which Hatfield youths did the stealing, we would want to restore the wealth, as far as possible, to the McCoys. One way might be to tax the Hatfields, but another might be to give preferential treatment in terms of scholarships and training programs and hiring to the McCoys.

This is perhaps the strongest argument for Affirmative Action, and it may well justify some weaker versions of AA, but it is doubtful whether it is sufficient to justify strong versions with quotas and goals and time tables in skilled positions. There are at least two reasons for this. First, we have no way of knowing how many people of any given group would have achieved some given level of competence had the world been different. . . . Secondly, the normal criterion of competence is a strong prima facie consideration when the most important positions are at stake. There are three reasons for this: (1) treating people according to their merits respects them as persons, as ends in themselves, rather than as means to social ends (if we believe that individuals possess a dignity which deserves to be respected, then we ought to treat that individual on the basis of his or her merits, not as a mere instrument for social policy); (2) society has given people expectations that if they attain certain levels of excellence they will be awarded appropriately; and (3) filling the most important positions with the best qualified is the best way to ensure efficiency in job-related areas and in society in general. These reasons are not absolutes.

They can be overridden.[2] But there is a strong presumption in their favor, so that a burden of proof rests with those who would overrride them. . . .

The Argument for Compensation from Those Who Innocently Benefitted from Past Injustice

Young White males as innocent beneficiaries of unjust discrimination against blacks and women have no grounds for complaint when society seeks to level the tilted field. They may be innocent of oppressing blacks, other minorities, and women, but they have unjustly benefitted from that oppression or discrimination. So it is perfectly proper that less qualified women and blacks be hired before them.

The operative principle is: He who knowingly and willingly benefits from a wrong must help pay for the wrong. Judith Jarvis Thomson puts it this way. "Many [white males] have been direct beneficiaries of policies which have downgraded blacks and women . . . and even those who did not directly benefit . . . had, at any rate, the advantage in the competition which comes of the confidence in one's full membership [in the community] and of one's right being recognized as a matter of course."[3] That is, white males obtain advantages in self respect and self-confidence deriving from a racist/sexist system which denies these to blacks and women.

Here is my response to this argument: As I noted in the previous section, compensation is normally individual and specific. If A harms B regarding x, B has a right to compensation from A in regards to x. If A steals B's car and wrecks it, A has an obligation to compensate B for the stolen car, but A's son has no obligation to compensate B. Furthermore, if A dies or disappears, B has no moral right to claim that society compensate him for the stolen car— though if he has insurance, he can make such a claim to the insurance company. Sometimes a wrong cannot be compensated, and we just have to make the best of an imperfect world. . . .

The Diversity Argument

It is important that we learn to live in a pluralistic world, learning to get along with those of other races, conditions, and cultures, so we should have schools and employment situations as fully integrated as possible. . . . Diversity is an important symbol and educative device. Thus, proponents of AA argue, preferential treatment is warranted to perform this role in society.

Once again, there is some truth in these concerns. Diversity of ideas challenges us to scrutinize our own values and beliefs. . . . Diversity may expand our moral horizons. But, again, while we can admit the value of diversity, it hardly seems adequate to override the moral requirement to treat each person with equal respect. *Diversity for diversity's sake is moral promiscuity*, since it obfuscates rational distinctions, undermines treating individuals as ends, treating them, instead as mere means (to the goals of social engineering), and, furthermore, unless those hired are highly qualified, the diversity factor threatens to become a fetish. . . .

There may be times when diversity may seem to be "crucial" to the well-being of a diverse community, such as for a police force. Suppose that White policemen tend to overreact to young Black males and the latter group distrusts White policemen. Hiring more less qualified Black policemen, who would relate better to these youth, may have overall utilitarian value. But such a move, while we might make it as a lesser evil, could have serious consequences in allowing the demographic prejudices to dictate social policy. A better strategy would be to hire the best police, that is, those who can perform in [a] disciplined, intelligent manner, regardless of their race. A White policeman must be able to arrest a Black burglar, even as a Black policeman must be able to arrest a White rapist. The quality of the police man or woman, not their race or gender, is what counts.

On the other hand, if a Black policeman, though lacking some of the formal skills of the White policeman, really is able to do a better job in the Black community, this might constitute a case of merit, not Affirmative Action. As Stephen Kershnar points out, this is similar to the legitimacy of hiring Chinese men to act as undercover agents in Chinatown.[4]

The Equal Results Argument

Some philosophers and social scientists hold that human nature is roughly identical, so that on a fair playing field the same proportion from every race and ethnic group and both genders would attain to the highest positions in every area of endeavor. It would follow that any inequality of results itself is evidence for inequality of opportunity.

> History is important when considering governmental rules like Test 21 because low scores by blacks can be traced in large measure to the legacy of slavery and racism: segregation, poor schooling, exclusion from trade unions, malnutrition, and poverty have all played their roles. Unless one assumes that blacks are naturally less able to pass the test, the conclusion must be that the results are themselves socially and legally constructed, not a mere given for which law and society can claim no responsibility.
>
> The conclusion seems to be that genuine equality eventually requires equal results. Obviously blacks have been treated unequally throughout U.S. history, and just as obviously the economic and psychological effects of that inequality linger to this day, showing up in lower income and poorer performance in school and on tests than whites achieve. Since we have no reason to believe that differences in performance can be explained by factors other than history, equal results are a good benchmark by which to measure progress made toward genuine equality. (John Arthur, *The Unfinished Constitution* [Belmont, CA: Wadsworth Publishing Co, 1990], p. 238)

. . . Albert G. Mosley develops a similar argument. "Establishing Blacks' presence at a level commensurate with their proportion in the relevant labor market need not be seen as an attempt to actualize some valid prediction.

Rather, given the impossibility of determining what level of representation Blacks would have achieved were it not for racial discrimination, the assumption of proportional representation is the only *fair* assumption to make. This is not to argue that Blacks should be maintained in such positions, but their contrived exclusion merits equally contrived rectification."[5]. . . However, Arthur [and] Mosley . . . fail even to consider studies that suggest that there are innate differences between races, sexes, and groups. If there are genetic differences in intelligence, temperament, and other qualities within families, why should we not expect such differences between racial groups and the two genders? Why should the evidence for this be completely discounted?

Mosley's reasoning is as follows: Since we don't know for certain whether groups proportionately differ in talent, we should presume that they are equal in every respect. So we should presume that if we were living in a just society, there would be roughly proportionate representation in every field (e.g., equal representation of doctors, lawyers, professors, carpenters, airplane pilots, basketball players, and criminals). Hence, it is only fair—productive of justice—to aim at proportionate representation in these fields.

But the logic is flawed. Under a situation of ignorance we should not presume equality or inequality of representation—but conclude that we *don't know* what the results would be in a just society. Ignorance doesn't favor equal group representation any more than it favors unequal group representation. It is neutral between them . . .

The "No One Deserves His Talents" Argument Against Meritocracy

According to this argument, the competent do not deserve their intelligence, their superior character, their industriousness, or their discipline; therefore they have no right to the best positions in society; therefore it is not unjust to give these positions to less (but still minimally) qualified blacks and women. In one form this argument holds that since no one deserves anything, society may use any criteria it pleases to distribute goods. The criterion most often designated is social utility. Versions of this argument are found in the writings of John Arthur, John Rawls, Bernard Boxill, Michael Kinsley, Ronald Dworkin, and Richard Wasserstrom. Rawls writes, "No one deserves his place in the distribution of native endowments, any more than one deserves one's initial starting place in society. The assertion that a man deserves the superior character that enables him to make the effort to cultivate his abilities is equally problematic; for his character depends in large part upon fortunate family and social circumstances for which he can claim no credit. The notion of desert seems not to apply to these cases."[6] Michael Kinsley is even more adamant:

> Opponents of affirmative action are hung up on a distinction that seems more profoundly irrelevant: treating individuals versus treating

groups. What is the moral difference between dispensing favors to people on their "merits" as individuals and passing out society's benefits on the basis of group identification?

Group identifications like race and sex are, of course, immutable. They have nothing to do with a person's moral worth. But the same is true of most of what comes under the label "merit." The tools you need for getting ahead in a meritocratic society—not all of them but most: talent, education, instilled cultural values such as ambition—are distributed just as arbitrarily as skin color. They are fate. The notion that people somehow "deserve" the advantages of these characteristics in a way they don't "deserve" the advantage of their race is powerful, but illogical.[7]

It will help to put the argument in outline form.

1. Society may award jobs and positions as it sees fit as long as individuals have no claim to these positions.
2. To have a claim to something means that one has earned it or deserves it.
3. But no one has earned or deserves his intelligence, talent, education or cultural values which produce superior qualifications.
4. If a person does not deserve what produces something, he does not deserve its products.
5. Therefore better qualified people do not deserve their qualifications.
6. Therefore, society may override their qualifications in awarding jobs and positions as it sees fit (for social utility or to compensate for previous wrongs).

So it is permissible if a minimally qualified black or woman is admitted to law or medical school ahead of a white male with excellent credentials or if a less qualified person from an "underutilized" group gets a professorship ahead of an eminently better qualified white male. Sufficiency and underutilization together outweigh excellence.

My response: Premise 4 is false. To see this, reflect that just because I do not deserve the money that I have been given as a gift (for instance) does not mean that I am not entitled to what I get with that money. If you and I both get a gift of $100 and I bury mine in the sand for 5 years while you invest yours wisely and double its value at the end of five years, I cannot complain that you should split the increase 50/50 since neither of us deserved the original gift. . . .

But there is no good reason to accept the argument against [moral] desert. We do act freely and, as such, we are responsible for our actions. We deserve the fruits of our labor, reward for our noble feats and punishment for our misbehavior.[8]

We have considered six arguments for Affirmative Action and have found no compelling case for Strong AA and only one plausible argument (a version of the compensation argument) for Weak AA. We must now turn to the arguments against Affirmative Action to see whether they fare any better.

Arguments Against Affirmative Action

Affirmative Action Requires Discrimination Against a Different Group

Weak AA weakly discriminates against new minorities, mostly innocent young white males, and Strong Affirmative Action strongly discriminates against these new minorities. . . . [T]his discrimination is unwarranted, since, even if some compensation to blacks were indicated, it would be unfair to make innocent white males bear the whole brunt of the payments. . . . [I]t is poor white youth who become the new pariahs on the job market. The children of the wealthy have little trouble getting into the best private grammar schools and, on the basis of superior early education, into the best universities, graduate schools, managerial and professional positions. Affirmative Action simply shifts injustice, setting Blacks, Hispanics, Native Americans, Asians and women against young white males, especially ethnic and poor white males. It makes no more sense to discriminate in favor of a rich Black or female who had the opportunity of the best family and education available against a poor White, than it does to discriminate in favor of White males against Blacks or women. It does little to rectify the goal of providing equal opportunity to all. . . .

Respect for persons entails that we treat each person as an end in him or herself, not simply as a means to be used for social purposes. What is wrong about discrimination against Blacks is that it fails to treat Black people as individuals, judging them instead by their skin color not their merit. What is wrong about discrimination against women is that it fails to treat them as individuals, judging them by their gender, not their merit. What is equally wrong about *Affirmative Action* is that it fails to treat White males with dignity as individuals, judging them by *both their race and gender*, instead of their merit. *Current Strong Affirmative Action* is both racist and sexist. . . .

An Argument from the Principle of Merit

Traditionally, we have believed that the highest positions in society should be awarded to those who are best qualified. Rewarding excellence both seems just to the individuals in the competition and makes for efficiency. Note that one of the most successful acts of racial integration, the Brooklyn Dodgers's recruitment of Jackie Robinson in the late 40s, was done in just this way, according to merit. If Robinson had been brought into the major league as a mediocre player or had batted .200 he would have been scorned and sent back to the minors where he belonged.

As mentioned earlier, merit is not an absolute value, but there are strong *prima facie* reasons for awarding positions on that basis, and it should enjoy a weighty presumption in our social practices.

. . . We generally want the best to have the best positions. . . . Only when little is at stake do we weaken the standards and content ourselves with sufficiency (rather than excellence)—there are plenty of jobs where "sufficiency" rather than excellence is required. Perhaps we have even come to feel that medicine or law or university professorships are so routine that they can be performed by minimally qualified people—in which case AA has a place.

Note! no one is calling for quotas or proportional representation of *under-utilized* groups in the National Basketball Association where blacks make up 80% of the players. But, surely, if merit and merit alone reigns in sports, should it not be valued at least as much in education and industry?

The case for meritocracy has two pillars. One pillar is a deontological argument which holds that we ought to treat people as ends and not merely means. By giving people what they deserve as *individuals*, rather than as members of *groups*, we show respect for their inherent worth. . . .

The second pillar for meritocracy is utilitarian. In the end, we will be better off by honoring excellence. We want the best leaders, teachers, policemen, physicians, generals, lawyers, and airplane pilots that we can possibly produce in society. So our program should be to promote equal opportunity, as much as is feasible in a free market economy, and reward people according to their individual merit.[9]

Conclusion

Let me sum up my discussion. The goal of the Civil Rights movement and of moral people everywhere has been justice for all, including equal opportunity. The question is: how best to get there. Civil Rights legislation removed the unjust legal barriers, opening the way towards equal opportunity, but it did not tackle the deeper causes that produce differential results. Weak Affirmative Action aims at encouraging minorities to strive for excellence in all areas of life, without unduly jeopardizing the rights of majorities. The problem of Weak Affirmative Action is that it easily slides into Strong Affirmative Action where quotas, "goals and timetables," "equal results"—in a word—*reverse discrimination*—prevail and are forced onto groups, thus promoting mediocrity, inefficiency, and resentment. Furthermore, AA aims at the higher levels of society—universities and skilled jobs, but if we want to improve our society, the best way to do it is to concentrate on families, children, early education, and the like, so all are prepared to avail themselves of opportunity. Affirmative Action, on the one hand, is too much, too soon and on the other hand, too little, too late. . . .

Martin Luther said that humanity is like a man mounting a horse who always tends to fall off on the other side of the horse. This seems to be the case with Affirmative Action. Attempting to redress the discriminatory iniquities of our history, our well-intentioned social engineers now engage in new forms of discriminatory iniquity and thereby think that they have successfully mounted the horse of racial harmony. They have only fallen off on the other side of the issue.[10]

Notes

1. For a good discussion of this argument see B. Boxill, "The Morality of Reparation," in *Social Theory and Practice* 2:1 (1972) and Albert G. Mosley in his and Nicholas Capaldi, *Affirmative Action; Social Justice or Unfair Preference?* (Rowman and Littlefield, 1996), pp. 23–27.

2. Merit sometimes may be justifiably overridden by need, as when parents choose to spend extra earnings on special education for their disabled child rather than for their gifted child. Sometimes we may override merit for utilitarian purposes. E.g., suppose you are the best shortstop on a baseball team but are also the best catcher. You'd rather play shortstop, but the manager decides to put you at catcher because, while your friend can do an adequate job at [shortstop], no one else is adequate at catcher. It's permissible for you to be assigned the job of catcher. Probably, some expression of appreciation would be due you.

3. Judith Jarvis Thomson, "Preferential Hiring," in Marshall Cohen, Thomas Nagel and Thomas Scanlon, eds., *Equality and Preferential Treatment* (Princeton: Princeton University Press, 1977).

4. Stephen Kershnar pointed this out in written comments (December 22, 1997).

5. See Mosley, op cit., p. 28, and Bernard Boxill, *Blacks and Social Justice* (Rowman & Littlefield, 1984), whom Mosley quotes in his article, also defends this position.

6. John Rawls, *A Theory of Justice* (Harvard University Press, 1971), p. 104. See Bernard Boxill, "The Morality of Preferential Hiring," *Philosophy and Public Affairs* 7:3 (1983).

7. Michael Kinsley, "Equal Lack of Opportunity," *Harper's* (June 1983).

8. My point does not depend on any particular theory of free will. One is reminded of Nozick's point that Rawls' professed aim of articulating the enormous worth of each individual seems contrary to the reductive determinism in his natural lottery argument.

9. For further discussion of this point see my "Equality and Desert," *Philosophy* 72 (1997).

10. Some of the material in this essay appeared in "The Moral Status of Affirmative Action," *Public Affairs Quarterly* 6:2 (1992). I have not had space to consider all the objections to my position or discuss the issue of freedom of association which, I think, should be given much scope in private but not in public institutions. Barbara Bergmann (*In Defense of Affirmative Action* [New York: Basic Books, 1996], pp. 122–25) and others argue that we already offer preferential treatment for athletes and veterans, especially in university admissions, so being consistent, we should provide it for women and minorities. My answer is that I am against giving athletic scholarships, and I regard scholarships to veterans as a part of a contractual relationship, a reward for service to one's country. But I distinguish entrance programs from actual employment. I don't think that veterans should be afforded special privilege in hiring practice, unless it be as a tiebreaker.

   I should also mention that my arguments from merit and respect apply more specifically to public institutions than private ones, where issues of property rights and freedom of association carry more weight.

POSTSCRIPT

Is Affirmative Action Fair?

That racial discrimination and sexual discrimination have existed in the United States is a matter of historical record and beyond dispute. But the question remains, What follows for us here and now?

Opponents of affirmative action say that nothing at all follows, except perhaps that we might be more careful and vigilant about allowing any form of discrimination, including modern forms of reverse discrimination.

Proponents of strong affirmative action say that although these views might *look* fair and aim to *be* fair, they are not fair. Just preventing discrimination without taking positive action to improve minorities' positions in society would simply freeze an unfairly established status quo. As American society is now, blacks are not represented in professions, in graduate schools, in business boardrooms, or in positions of social and political leadership in a way that is consistent with their numbers in the population. This is not for lack of interest or ability; it is a legacy of social injustice. To insist that we now freeze this status quo and proceed "fairly," on a case-by-case basis, will guarantee that the white-biased social momentum will continue for at least the foreseeable future. Advocates of affirmative action want to eradicate the effects of past discrimination and to put an end to the bias in momentum as soon as possible. They call for active measures to achieve this.

Sources that are relevant to this issue include Gertrude Ezorsky, *Racism and Justice: The Case for Affirmative Action* (Cornell University Press, 1991); Andrew Kull, *The Colorblind Constitution* (Harvard University Press, 1992); Bernard R. Boxhill, *Blacks and Social Justice*, rev. ed. (Rowman & Littlefield, 1992); Andrew Hacker, *Two Nations: Black and White, Separate, Hostile, Unequal* (Scribner, 1992); Stanley Fish, "Reverse Racism, or How the Pot Got to Call the Kettle Black," *The Atlantic Monthly* (November 1993); Steven M. Cahn, ed., *Affirmative Action and the University* (Temple University Press, 1993); Carl Cohen, *Naked Racial Preference: The Case Against Affirmative Action* (Madison Books, 1995); Ralph R. Reiland, "Affirmative Action or Equal Opportunity?" *Regulation* (vol. 18, 1995), pp. 19–23; and Steven M. Cahn, ed., *The Affirmative Action Debates*, 2d ed. (Routledge, 2002).

Other sources on this controversial policy are George E. Curry, ed., *The Affirmative Action Debate* (Addison-Wesley, 1996); Richard F. Thomasson, Faye J. Crosby, and Sharon D. Herzberger, *Affirmative Action: The Pros and Cons of Policy and Practice* (University Press of America, 1996); John David Skrentny, *The Ironies of Affirmative Action: Politics, Culture, and Justice in America* (University of Chicago Press, 1996); Robert Emmett Long, ed., *Affirmative Action* (H. W. Wilson, 1996); Barbara Bergmann, *In Defense of Affirmative Action* (Basic Books, 1996); Terry Eastland, *Ending Affirmative Action: The Case for Colorblind*

Justice (Basic Books, 1996); Jewelle Taylor Gibbs, *Color of Justice: Rodney King, O. J. Simpson, and Race in America* (Jossey-Bass, 1996); K. Anthony Appiah and Amy Gutmann, *Color Conscious: The Political Morality of Race* (Princeton University Press, 1996); David Theo Goldberg, *Racial Subjects: Writing on Race in America* (Routledge, 1997); Michael Levin, *Why Race Matters: Race Differences and What They Mean* (Greenwood Publishing Group, 1997); Abigail Thernstrom and Stephen Thernstrom, *America in Black and White: One Nation, Indivisible* (Simon & Schuster, 1997); Peter Skerry, "The Strange Politics of Affirmative Action," *Wilson Quarterly* (Winter 1997); Francis J. Beckwith, Todd E. Jones, eds., *Affirmative Action: Social Justice or Reverse Discrimination?* (Prometheus Books, 1997); Glenn C. Loury, "How to Mend Affirmative Action," *The Public Interest* (Spring 1997); Charles R. Lawrence III and Mari Matsuda, *We Won't Go Back: Making the Case for Affirmative Action* (Houghton Mifflin, 1997); David K. Shipler, *A Country of Strangers: Blacks and Whites in America* (Alfred A. Knopf, 1997); Lincoln Caplan, *Up Against the Law: Affirmative Action and the Supreme Court* (Century Foundation, 1997); Jim Sleeper, *Liberal Racism* (Viking Penguin, 1997); "Racism and the Law: The Legacy and Lessons of Plessy," a special issue of *Law and Philosophy* (May 1997); "The Affirmative Action Debate," a special issue of *Report From the Institute for Philosophy and Public Policy* (Winter–Spring 1997); Bryan K. Fair, *Notes of a Racial Caste Baby: Color Blindness and the End of Affirmative Action* (New York University Press, 1997); John Davis Skrentny, "Affirmative Action: Some Advice for the Pundits," *American Behavioral Scientist* (April 1998); *Focus on Law Studies* (Spring 1998) (this entire issue concerns affirmative action); Matt Cavanagh, *Against Equality of Opportunity* (Clarendon Press, 2002); Samuel Leiter and William M. Leiter, *Affirmative Action in Antidiscrimination Law and Policy: An Overview and Synthesis* (State University of New York Press, 2002); Charles V. Dale, *Affirmative Action Revisited* (Nova Science Publishers, 2002); and Fred L. Pincus, *Reverse Discrimination: Dismantling the Myth* (Lynne Rienner Publishers, 2003).

A concise account of civil rights history (including the birth of the phrase "affirmative action") is Hugh Davis Graham, *Civil Rights and the Presidency: Race and Gender in American Politics, 1960–1972* (Oxford University Press, 1992). Another useful historical account is Paul D. Moreno, *From Direct Action to Affirmative Action: Fair Employment Law and Policy in America, 1933–1972* (Louisiana State University Press, 1999). The position that affirmative action policies are necessary for women is defended by Susan D. Clayton and Faye J. Crosby, *Justice, Gender and Affirmative Action* (University of Michigan Press, 1992).

ISSUE 12

Should the Death Penalty Be Abolished?

YES: Michael Welch, from *Punishment in America: Social Control and the Ironies of Imprisonment* (Sage, 1999)

NO: Ernest van den Haag, from "The Death Penalty Once More," *U.C. Davis Law Review* (Summer 1985)

ISSUE SUMMARY

YES: Criminologist Michael Welch argues that the death penalty encourages murder and is applied in a biased and mistake-laden way to growing groups of people. Much of the recent popular support of capital punishment is due to ignorance of the facts.

NO: Professor of law Ernest van den Haag argues that the death penalty is entirely in line with the U.S. Constitution and that although studies of its deterrent effect are inconclusive, the death penalty is morally justified and should not be abolished.

Since punishment involves the intentional infliction of harm upon another person, and since the intentional infliction of harm is generally wrong, the idea of punishment itself is somewhat problematic. Punishment requires some strong rationale if it is not to be just another form of wrongdoing; capital punishment requires an especially strong rationale.

Consider some actual cases of capital punishment: Socrates was tried in ancient Athens and condemned to die (by drinking poison) for not believing in the gods of the state and for corrupting young people. In 1977 a princess and her lover were executed (by firing squad and beheading, respectively) in Saudi Arabia for adultery. Also in 1977 Gary Gilmore insisted that he receive the death penalty and was executed by a firing squad in Utah for murder.

Justification for capital punishment usually comes down to one of two different lines of reasoning. One is based on the idea of justice, the other on the idea of deterrence.

Justice, it is said, demands that certain criminal acts be paid for by death. The idea is that some people deserve death and have to pay for their criminal acts with their lives.

There are several objections to this view. One of the most important of these focuses on the idea of a person "paying" for a crime by death (or even in some other way). What concept of "paying" is being used here? It does not seem like an ordinary case of paying a debt. It seems to be a kind of vengeance, as when one person says to another "I'll make you pay for that," meaning "I'll make you suffer for that." Yet one of the ideas behind state-inflicted punishment is that it is supposed to be very official, even bureaucratic, and it is designed to eliminate private vendettas and personal vindictiveness. The state, in a civilized society, is not supposed to be motivated by revenge or vindictiveness. The state's only intent is to support law and order and to protect its citizens from coming to harm at the hands of wrongdoers.

The other major line of reasoning in support of capital punishment is based on the idea of deterrence. According to this view, capital punishment must be retained in order to deter criminals and potential criminals from committing capital crimes. An old joke reflects this view: A Texan tells a visitor that in the old days the local punishment for horse-stealing was hanging. The visitor is shocked. "You used to hang people just for taking horses?" "Nope," says the Texan, "horses never got stolen."

Unlike the argument about "paying," the logic behind deterrence is supposed to be intuitively easy to understand. However, assertions concerning deterrence do not seem to be clearly borne out by actual statistics and empirical evidence.

Your intuition may support the judgment that the death penalty deters crime, but the empirical evidence is not similarly uniform and clear, and in some cases the evidence even points to the opposite conclusion. (For example, some people may be more likely to murder an innocent victim if they are reasonably certain of achieving their own death and perhaps some notoriety.) Or consider the example of the failure of deterrence that occurred in England when public hanging was the punishment for the crime of pickpocketing. Professional pickpockets, undeterred by the activity on the gallows, circulated among the crowd of spectators, aware that a good time to pick pockets was when everyone's attention was focused on something else—in this case, when the rope tightened around the neck of the convicted pickpocket.

Further thought about this matter of deterrence raises more questions. Consider this scenario: Two men get into an argument while drinking, and one pulls a gun and shoots the other, who dies. Do we suppose that this killer is even aware of the punishment for murder when he acts? Would he be deterred by the prospect of capital punishment but be willing to shoot if the punishment were only 20 years or life in prison?

In the following selection, Michael Welch argues for the abolition of the death penalty. He refers to its brutalizing effects and to a host of difficulties involving who actually receives the punishment. Then Ernest van den Haag argues against its abolition, discussing the constitutionality, possible deterrent effect, and moral justification of the death penalty.

YES

Michael Welch

The Machinery of Death: Capital Punishment and the Ironies of Social Control

Mechanical terms abound in criminal justice, connoting efficiency, stability, and equilibrium. Consider, for instance, the depiction of criminal justice as a *system* with law *enforcement*. Even critics rely on mechanical metaphors while describing criminal justice as a social control *apparatus* whose *mechanisms* function as *tools* of the ruling class (Lynch & Groves, 1989; Welch, 1996a, 1996b). Contributing to this lexicon, Justice Harry A. Blackmun referred to capital punishment as a *machinery* of death (also see Harlow, Matas, & Rocamora, 1995). The momentum behind executions has increased dramatically since the late 1970s due to several social forces, including political pandering to—and manipulation of—public opinion, the expansion of capital crimes, and the reduction of appeals, which hastens executions. . . .

The efficiency of the machinery of death has been streamlined recently in accordance with the principles of Frederick Taylor's "scientific management."[1] For example, in Arkansas, a triple execution was carried out in 1997 (the second of its kind since capital punishment was resumed). It has been said by prison officials that "such multiple executions minimize overtime costs and reduce stress on prison employees" (Kuntz, 1997, p. E-7). . . .

Although the death penalty is portrayed by its supporters as a precise, reliable, and necessary armament of criminal justice, in reality this machinery of death has proven to be imprecise, unreliable, and reckless. Opponents criticize capital punishment for perpetuating injustice because it is fraught with errors, contradictions, and various ironies. . . . [Here,] we apply Marx's (1981) notions of escalation, nonenforcement, and covert facilitation to capital punishment to illuminate its contradictions. In addition to exploring how the machinery of death produces counterdeterrent effects, creates new categories of violators and victims, and falsely convicts the innocent, we shall remain mindful of the significance of racism and classism in shaping the patterns of executions.

Escalation

. . . [Escalation] implies that "by taking enforcement action, authorities unintentionally encourage rule breaking" (Marx, 1981, p. 222). In this analysis of capital punishment, murder is one type of rule breaking we shall examine;

thus, it is argued that executions not only fail to deter homicide but, ironically, promote violence. To support this claim, there is an emerging body of research documenting that capital punishment may indeed have counterdeterrent effects.

Brutalization Versus Deterrence

Despite the volume of empirical studies demonstrating that there is *no* conclusive evidence linking deterrence with capital punishment, the myth persists. Walker (1994) characterized the myth of deterrence as a crime control theology, a belief that resembles a religious conviction more than an intellectual position because it rests on faith rather than on facts. But the issue is not whether the death penalty offers greater deterrence than no penalty at all—of course it does. Rather, the issue is whether the death penalty deters more than other severe penalties, such as life imprisonment without parole. . . .

Proponents of deterrence theory argue that publicizing executions is a necessary component of capital punishment because it is through such publicity that the tough "law and order" message of death sentences is widely communicated. Conversely, a competing theory about publicized executions has challenged the notion of deterrence. Brutalization theory suggests that publicized executions not only fail to deter violence but, paradoxically, increase it. To appreciate fully brutalization theory, we must deconstruct the central element of deterrence theory, namely the assumption that potential killers are restrained from committing murder because they *identify* with those who have been executed. Brutalization theory suggests that *some* persons, rather than identifying with the condemned, identify with the executioner (Bowers & Pierce, 1980). It is crucial here to return to the principal message inherent in capital punishment: Those who commit heinous crimes *deserve* to die. Supporting this perspective, advocates of the death penalty view executions as a "public service" performed by the state, ridding society of its despicable members.

According to brutalization theory, however, publicized executions create an *alternative identification process* that promotes imitation, not deterrence. Bowers and Pierce (1980) found an increase in homicides soon after well-publicized executions, suggesting that some murderers liken their victims to the condemned. This finding was presented as evidence of a counterdeterrent effect (also see Bailey, 1983, 1998; Bowers, 1988; Cochran, Chamlin, & Seth, 1994; Decker & Kohfeld, 1990; Forst, 1983; King, 1978). It is important to emphasize that Bowers and Pierce specified that the brutalization effect has an impact on individuals who are prone to violence, not persons who are generally nonviolent; in such cases, the publicized execution reinforces the belief that lethal vengeance is justified. Executions devalue human life and "demonstrate that it is appropriate to kill those who have gravely offended us" (Bowers & Pierce, 1980, p. 456). In the context of social control, evidence engendered by brutalization studies supports the claim that capital punishment produces an ironic and escalating effect by promoting, rather than deterring, murder.

The Creation of New Categories and Net Widening

. . .

Juvenile Offenders

Increasingly, the application of the death penalty has expanded to include juveniles. Although eight states do not specify a minimum age at which the death penalty may be imposed, 14 states and the federal system require a minimum age of 18, and 16 states indicate an age of eligibility between 14 and 17 (Snell, 1996; see Table 1). In 1997, California Governor Pete Wilson reported

Table 1

Minimum Age Authorized for Capital Punishment, 1996

Age 16 or Less	Age 17	Age 18	None Specified
Alabama (16)	Georgia	California	Arizona
Arkansas (14)[a]	New Hampshire	Colorado	Idaho
Delaware (16)	North Carolina[b]	Connecticut[c]	Montana
Florida (16)	Texas	Federal system	Louisiana
Indiana (16)		Illinois	Pennsylvania
Kentucky (16)		Kansas	South Carolina
Mississippi (16)[d]		Maryland	South Dakota[e]
Missouri (16)		Nebraska	Utah
Nevada (16)		New Jersey	
Oklahoma (16)		New Mexico	
Virginia (14)[f]		New York	
Wyoming (16)		Ohio	
		Oregon	
		Tennessee	
		Washington	

Source: Snell (1997, p. 5).

Note: Reporting by states reflects interpretations by state attorney general offices and may differ from previously reported ages.
a. See Arkansas Code Ann. 9-27-318(b)(1)(Repl. 1991).
b. The age required is 17 unless the murderer was incarcerated for murder when a subsequent murder occurred; then the age may be 14.
c. See Conn. Gen. Stat. 53a-46a(g)(1).
d. The minimum age defined by statute is 13, but the effective age is 16, based on a Mississippi Supreme Court decision.
e. Juveniles may be transferred to adult court. Age can be a mitigating factor.
f. The minimum age for transfer to adult court is 14 by statute, but the effective age for a capital sentence is 16, based on interpretation of a U.S. Supreme Court decision by the state attorney general's office.

that he would consider a state law allowing executions of 14-year olds, and Cruz M. Bustamante said he might support executions for "hardened criminals" as young as 13 (Verhovek, 1998, p. A-7). Texas State Representative Jim Pitts in 1998 proposed the death penalty for 11-year-old killers. Pitts reasoned: "This is a drastic step. . . . But some of the kids are growing up today, they just aren't the 'Leave it to Beaver' kids that I grew up with" (Verhovek, 1998, p. A-7). Reacting to the 1998 Arkansas schoolyard killings, Pitts argued that the state needs to "send a message to our kids that they can't do these kinds of crimes" (Verhovek, 1998, p. A-7).

Mentally Handicapped Offenders

The new categories of offenders eligible for the death penalty also include the emotionally and mentally handicapped. Although in recent memory the U.S. Supreme Court has prohibited the execution of emotionally disturbed capital defendants (*Ford v. Wainwright,* 1986; Miller & Radelet, 1993; Paternoster, 1991), such restrictions have been not been uniformly enforced. In 1995, Varnall Weeks, a convicted murderer diagnosed by psychiatric experts as a paranoid schizophrenic, was executed in Alabama. Weeks was clearly disturbed: Living in a maze of delusions, he believed that "he would come back to life as a giant flying tortoise that would rule the world" (Bragg, 1995, p. 7). At one of his hearings, Weeks described himself as God, wore a domino on a band around his shaved head, and responded to the court's question with a "rambling discourse on serpents, cybernetics, albinos, Egyptians, the Bible, and reproduction. . . . [He also] sat in his cell naked in his own feces, mouthing senseless sounds" (Shapiro, 1995, p. A-29). Although prosecution and defense acknowledged that he suffered from paranoid schizophrenia, the courts contended that he was sane enough to be executed. The U.S. Supreme Court unanimously rejected his appeal. To date, legislators and the courts have not established a consistent or humane definition of how sane or competent a capital defendant needs to be in order to be executed.

Whereas the death penalty for mentally ill murderers is characterized by inconsistent court rulings, there are no such obstacles interfering with the execution of mentally retarded capital defendants (those scoring below 70 on a standardized intelligence test). It has been speculated that throughout history, mildly retarded offenders have been commonly executed but that their level of intelligence was never known to the courts because such tests were not conducted. Today, defendants are routinely administered intelligence tests; thus, the courts are fully aware of the defendant's level of intelligence. In 1989, the High Court ruled in *Penry v. Lynaugh* that states have the right to execute mentally retarded persons convicted of capital murder.

Critics point out that executing mentally retarded (even mildly retarded) offenders raises serious moral and ethical issues, especially because mental retardation constitutes a serious liability affecting every dimension of that person's life. "Many individuals who are sentenced to death and executed in this country have mental retardation" (Harlow et al., 1995, p. 1; Reed, 1993). Persons with mental retardation are quite susceptible to suggestion and have serious difficulty in logic, planning, and understanding consequences. With this in mind, Professor of Special Education Ruth Luckasson asked, "Can you imagine anyone easier to execute?" (quoted in Harlow et al., 1995, p. 1). Luckasson added, "I have seen people with mental retardation sitting in their own capital trials, with their lives at stake, who had absolutely no understanding of what was going on" (quoted in Harlow et al., 1995, p. 1). In 1992, Bill Clinton, then governor of Arkansas, refused to halt the execution of Ricky Ray Rector, who had blown away part of his brain in a suicide attempt just after he had killed a police officer. At the time of his trial, Rector was so mentally retarded that "he did not understand that death was permanent" (Ridgeway, 1994, p. 23). On the day of his death, he told his lawyer that "he planned to vote for Mr. Clinton that November" (Shapiro, 1995, p. A-29) and asked the guards to "save his dessert for a snack before bedtime" (Terry, 1998, p. 22).

In 1995, Mario Marquez was executed by the state of Texas after being convicted of double murder and rape. Marquez, a grade-school dropout with an IQ of 65, was the 10th of 16 children born to a migrant farmworker. As a child, he was beaten with a horsewhip by his father and abandoned to the streets and a life of drug abuse at the age of 12. During the trial, Marquez asked his lawyer "if he [Marquez] was going to have a good job when he goes to heaven" and wanted his lawyer to tell him "if he could get a job being a gardener, or taking care of animals" (Hentoff, 1995, p. 30). . . .

In sum, capital punishment generates an escalating, counterdeterrent effect because, by taking enforcement action (i.e., performing executions), authorities unintentionally encourage a type of rule breaking, namely homicide. The irony of this form of social control is supported by brutalization research. To reiterate, a particularly important analytic element of escalation is the creation of new categories of violators and victims. Such categories are the products of legislation, driven by relentless political pandering to the public on crime. Not only do these self-serving political activities widen the net of capital punishment, but they tend to snare violators—juveniles, the mentally handicapped, the emotionally disturbed—who paradoxically become vulnerable victims of an overzealous criminal justice apparatus.

Nonenforcement

. . . [Nonenforcement] constitutes another irony of social control in that authorities, by taking no enforcement action, intentionally permit rule breaking (Marx, 1981). Arguably one of the more tragic examples of nonenforcement can be found in America's history of vigilante "justice," particularly lynching. Authorities deliberately encouraged these travesties of justice by refusing to impose sanctions on persons who carried them out. In addition, many of these incidents of nonenforcement were motivated by racism, in that blacks served as convenient scapegoats.

Contemporary examinations of racism and the death penalty should not neglect the history of formal (executions) and informal (lynchings) penalties imposed on black defendants and suspects. Following the Civil War, black codes were *formally* established to perpetuate the economic subordination of former slaves. Such codes employed harsher penalties for crimes committed by blacks and led to a disproportionate number of black executions. *Informally*, black men also were subject to lynching (illegal execution) by vigilante mobs. Bowers (1984) reported that in the 1890s there were more lynchings (1,540) than legal executions (1,098). Though lynchings gradually declined, nearly 2,000 illegal executions occurred in the early part of the 20th century: Between 1900 and 1909 there were 885 reported lynchings, between 1910 and 1919, 621 lynchings, and in the 1920s, 315 (Bowers, 1984; also see Brundage, 1993; Jackson, 1996; Tolnay & Beck, 1992, 1994).[2]

Nowadays, a long-standing criticism of the death penalty is that despite efforts to guard against arbitrariness (as enumerated in *Gregg v. Georgia*, 1976), it continues to be administered in ways that are racially biased. Casual observers of the death penalty controversy might assume that the death penalty is racially discriminatory because black murderers, compared to white murderers, are disproportionately sentenced to death. This assumption, however, would be too simplistic. To clarify the extent of racism evident in the death penalty, one must look at the race of the victim as well as the race of the offender. In the United States, approximately half of those murdered each year are black. However, since 1977, about 85% of capital defendants who have been executed had killed a white person, whereas only 11% had murdered a black person (Baldus, Woodworth, & Pulaski, 1990). Research continues to demonstrate that killers of whites are more likely than killers of blacks to be sentenced to death: Paternoster (1983) revealed that blacks who kill whites have a 4.5 times greater chance of facing the death penalty than blacks who kill blacks. When the race of the victim is ignored, the chances of blacks' and whites' receiving a death sentence are almost equal. Furthermore, Keil and Vito (1989) found that when controlling for seriousness of the murder (in Kentucky), "Prosecutors were more likely to seek the death penalty in cases in which blacks killed whites and . . . juries were more likely to sentence to death blacks who killed whites" (p. 511). Baldus et al. (1990) concluded that when the murder victim was white, the chance of a death penalty was roughly doubled in certain kinds of cases: in particular, those cases catalogued as "middle-ground" incidents in which the victim was killed during the commission of a felony (e.g., homicide during a robbery).[3] In a recent study on racial disparities in capital punishment, Baldus (in press) reported that in Philadelphia, black defendants in murder cases are four times more likely than other defendants to be sentenced to death, even when the circumstances of the killings are the same (see Butterfield, 1998). . . .

The racial bias in capital punishment should be viewed as another irony of social control, especially in the realm of nonenforcement. Given that only 11% of all executions involve capital defendants convicted of killing a black person, there is the appearance that the lives of white victims are more valuable than black victims. From 1977 to 1995, 88 black men were executed for murdering whites, whereas only 2 white men have been executed for killing blacks (Eckholm, 1995). To date, Texas—the all-time leader of executions with 404 at year end 1996—has never executed *anyone* for killing a black person. . . .

Incidentally, in Virginia in 1998, Louis Ceparano pleaded guilty to burning alive a black man, Garnett P. Johnson, and chopping off his head with an ax. Ceparano was one of two white men accused of soaking Johnson with gasoline and subjecting him to racial slurs, then setting fire to him. Ceparano was spared the death penalty and received two consecutive life terms without possibility of parole ("White Man Pleads Guilty," 1998).

Advocates who believe that the death penalty can be modified to eliminate its racial bias (van den Haag & Conrad, 1983) are likely to encounter an even greater irony. Because in most murders, the assailant and the victim are of the same race, eliminating the disparity linked to the race of the victim would be likely to result in a higher proportion of blacks sentenced to death.

> If killers of black people were executed at the rate of killers of whites, many more blacks would receive death sentences. If, on the other hand, killers of whites were executed at the same rate as killers of blacks, many whites would be spared. (Eckholm, 1995, p. B-4)

The history of black lynchings in America serves as a reminder of egregious acts of nonenforcement that authorized and perpetuated the racist practice of unlawful executions. Nowadays, incidents of nonenforcement are not as clear-cut and obvious. Admittedly, it is unlikely that authorities *intentionally* encourage lethal violence against blacks. Still, executions remain significantly patterned by the race of the victim, thereby suggesting that in the eyes of the state, white murder victims are inherently more valuable than their black counterparts. Thus, racial disparities in capital punishment contradict fundamental principles of justice in a democratic society.

Covert Facilitation

Although sentencing disparities according to the race of murder victims violate basic ideals of fairness, such contradictions are compounded when innocent people are falsely convicted, and worse, executed. False convictions in capital crimes may be the result of error, wrongdoing, or a combination of the two. Whereas the former serves as evidence of an imperfect criminal justice system, the latter reveals an insidious side of the machinery of death. The deliberate prosecution of innocent people typically emerges in the form of covert facilitation: hidden or deceptive enforcement action in which authorities intentionally encourage rule breaking (Marx, 1981). In this context, *rule breaking* refers to wrongdoing by the prosecutors and police that is encouraged by the state for the purpose of securing capital convictions, even if the suspect is innocent (e.g., framing a suspect, prosecutorial misconduct, allowing perjured testimony). Cases of false conviction shed additional light on racism and classism because people of color and the impoverished are more vulnerable to these miscarriages of justice.

Capital punishment experts have long speculated that numerous innocent persons have been convicted, and in some instances, executed; still, a general understanding of such injustices was previously based on anecdotal and unsystematic research. Then, in 1987, Hugo Bedau and Michael Radelet published a systematic study of 350 defendants believed to have been wrongly convicted in capital (or potential capital) cases between the years 1900 and 1985. It is important to note that Bedau and Radelet did not simply include any case that appeared suspect. Rather, they applied strict standards of miscarriages of justice and accepted cases only on the basis of *overwhelming* evidence that an innocent person had been falsely convicted. In an expanded volume of their work, Radelet, Bedau and Putnam released *In Spite of Innocence: Erroneous Convictions in Capital Cases* (1992), cataloguing 416 cases of falsely convicted capital defendants between 1900 and 1991. Approximately one-third of these defendants were sentenced to death, and the authors persuasively documented 23 cases in which innocent people were executed. Most of the remaining defendants, though initially trapped in the machinery of justice, fortunately escaped execution. Radelet et al. referred to them as the lucky ones. Nevertheless, they still experienced years of incarceration along with the agony of uncertainty; consequently, their lives were virtually ruined (also see Dieter, 1997; Huff, Rattner, & Sagarin, 1996).

Covert facilitation is commonly found in the most egregious cases of false convictions, and as we shall see, racism and classism also permeate many such travesties of justice. Consider Walter McMillian, who, after spending 6 years on Alabama's death row, was released in 1993. Upon further scrutiny, different prosecutors conceded that the state had withheld evidence from his lawyers and had relied on perjured testimony to falsely convict McMillian. In a case that fits the "middle-ground" category of homicide, Ronda Morrison, an 18-year-old white female clerk, was murdered by a black male during a robbery in Monroeville, Alabama—coincidentally, the home town of Harper Lee, author of *To Kill a Mockingbird* (1960), a story of race and justice in the Jim Crow South. While being interrogated in connection to another killing, Ralph Myers, an ex-con with a lengthy criminal record, accused McMillian of murdering Morrison. In an unusual move, McMillian was assigned to death row before his trial. After a one-and-a-half day trial, McMillian was convicted on the testimony of three witnesses, including that of Myers and another criminal suspect. The defense lawyer called a dozen witnesses who each testified that McMillian was at home the day of the murder, socializing with friends at a fish fry. The prosecution offered no physical evidence linking McMillian to the murder; thus, critics insist that the trial was driven by racism. It was well known that McMillian was dating a white woman and that one of his sons had married a white woman; both McMillian and his attorney believed that these interracial relationships motivated the prosecution (Dieter, 1997).

The Alabama Bureau of Investigation eventually discredited the prosecution's case against McMillian. All three witnesses recanted their testimony, and Myers also reported that he was pressured by law officers to accuse McMillian. The case emerged at a time when federal appeals for capital defendants were becoming increasingly restricted, a reminder of how flawed—and corrupt—the machinery of death can be. Bryan Stevenson, McMillian's attorney, said, "It's clear that he had nothing to do with this crime. There are other folks in prison who don't have the money or the resources or the good fortune to have folks come in and help them" (Applebome, 1993, p. B-11).

In another recent case, all charges were dropped against three black men who were incarcerated in an Illinois prison from 1978 to 1996 for a double murder they did not commit. Dennis Williams spent much of that sentence waiting on death row, as did Verneal Jimerson, a fourth black inmate whose charges were dismissed a month earlier. Their case not only underscores the flaws of the criminal justice system but sheds additional light on the controversy over the restriction of federal death penalty appeals recently affirmed by the U.S. Supreme Court. The reduction of federal appeals for capital defendants is expected to cut in half the time between conviction and execution (from approximately 8 to 4 years). Richard C. Dieter, director of the Death Penalty Information Center, warns that these restrictions mean that the length of appeals would "fall well below the average time it takes to discover new evidence of innocence. . . . This rush to get on with the death penalty by shortening the appeals process will raise the danger of executing innocent people" (Terry, 1996, p. A-14).

The case against Williams, Jimerson, and their codefendants, Willie Rainge and Kenneth Williams, stems from the murder of a white couple in suburban Chicago in 1978, but new DNA evidence, witness recantations, and a jailhouse confession led to their release. Cook County State's Attorney Jack O'Malley said his office was trying to determine how the original investigation "got derailed and why it is the wrong people were charged" (Terry, 1996, p. A-14). To this, Dennis Williams quickly responded *racism*: "The police just picked up the first young black men they could and that was it. . . . They didn't care if we were guilty or innocent. . . . We are victims of this crime too" (Terry, 1996, p. A-14). In a strange turn of events, Jimerson had been previously released when the only witness connecting him to the crime recanted; later, in a deal to get released from prison, the witness changed her testimony again. Jimerson was then rearrested, convicted, and sentenced to die. Jimerson and his codefendants believe they were indeed *framed* by the prosecution.

Contrary to popular belief, capital cases often are not meticulously litigated. Indigent defendants assigned court-appointed attorneys stand a good chance of being consumed by the machinery of death. . . .

Although the term *presumed innocence* rings of democratic notions of justice, many prosecutors smugly overlook its importance. Even Edwin R. Meese, while serving as U.S. Attorney General, stated that "suspects who are innocent of a crime should [have the right to have lawyer present during police questioning]. But the thing is, you don't have many suspects who are innocent of a crime. That's contradictory. If a person is innocent of a crime, he is not a uspect" ("Attorney General Speaks," 1985, p. 67). . . .

[The] concept covert facilitation is useful in analyzing the complex ironies of capital punishment. From this perspective, we can look beyond *honest* mistakes occurring in capital cases and examine activities that are truly pernicious. In these cases, capital defendants not only face a flawed criminal justice process but also risk being falsely convicted by unethical prosecutors willing to frame suspects to advance their political aspirations. Again, minorities, the impoverished, and the mentally handicapped remain easy targets of covert facilitation.

Conclusion

Despite clear and compelling evidence that the system of capital punishment has glaring biases and errors, its popularity continues to rise. Approximately 80% of the U.S. population favors the death penalty for offenders convicted of first-degree murder (Moore, 1994), and this level of support is the highest since 1936 (Bohm, 1991).[4] Researchers have found, however, that Americans are greatly misinformed about capital punishment (Bohm, 1991, 1996; Bowers, 1993). Ironically, then, the enormous public support for the death penalty is based, not on a sophisticated understanding of the facts, but on beliefs rooted in popular myths of criminal justice.

[Here] we explored the machinery of death as it pertains to the ironies of social control, namely escalation, nonenforcement, and covert facilitation. To summarize, [we] confronted significant contradictions apparent in American capital punishment. The United States is the only Western industrialized democracy to execute offenders, and this practice continues to violate contemporary standards of decency, especially the execution of juveniles and the mentally retarded. Contradictions also are found in the death penalty's failure to offer a deterrent effect, protect the community (including police; Bailey & Peterson, 1987), eliminate racial and socioeconomic biases, and ensure that innocent people are not falsely convicted or executed. In addition, the death penalty is confounded by several other problems that reveal deep structural contradictions in the social control apparatus, including financial costs, the alliance between the state and certain physicians and psychiatrists who facilitate the execution protocol, and the recent restriction of appeals, all of which paradoxically make errors more likely. . . .

The nation's enthusiasm for the death penalty has become a "fatal attraction" insofar as its contradictions and ironies lead to a self-defeating form of social control. In addition to producing a counterdeterrent effect (i.e., brutalization), a greater commitment to capital punishment creates more categories of violators (and victims), resulting in a higher volume of death sentences. A greater commitment to expediting capital cases by eliminating appeals also means more mistakes are likely to occur.[5] In the end, capital punishment policy is reckless and unjust—especially for people of color, the impoverished, and the mentally handicapped.

Notes

1. Frederick Taylor (1856–1915) promoted the "efficiency movement" in managing the industrial workforce, emphasizing the optimum use of time and motion.

2. A discussion of racism and the death penalty ought to include references to *racial hoaxes* in which black men are easily targeted as criminal suspects. Consider the cases of Charles Stuart, Susan V. Smith, and Jesse Anderson, all of whom committed premeditated murder and falsely reported to police that their crimes were the acts of a black man (Russell, 1998; Welch, 1996a).

3. Baldus et al. (1990) showed that disparities in the death penalty are more clearly understood by classifying murders into three types. The first category includes crimes of passion and killings in barroom brawls; these rarely draw the death penalty. The second category includes grisly murders such as mass and serial killings; these are typically sanctioned by capital punishment, regardless of race. However, racial disparities most commonly arise in the third category, known as "middle-ground" incidents in which homicide occurs during the commission of a felony (e.g., armed robbery); in this type of murder, the race of the victim is a crucial factor in determining the penalty. The killing of a white victim under these circumstances, especially when the perpetrator is black, has the highest chance of drawing capital punishment.

4. Researchers also conclude that the support for the death penalty may not be as deep as the polls suggest. When given the choice between favoring the death penalty and life imprisonment with absolutely no possibility of parole, support for the death penalty drops to less than half (Bohm, 1991, 1996; Bowers, 1993; Gallup & Newport, 1991; McGarrell & Sandys, 1996).

5. Opponents of the death penalty are alarmed and enraged over Congress's passing of the Anti-Terrorism and Effective Death Penalty Act of 1996, which sharply limits the prisoner's ability to file more than one habeas corpus petition. In 1996, Congress also voted to stop funding ($20 million) the Post-Conviction Defender Organizations that have played a vital role in representing death row inmates. In reaction to this move and to Congress's curtailing of federal habeas corpus protections, the American Bar Association in 1997 called for the suspension of the death penalty until the system is changed to afford adequate due process ("A Lawyerly Cry of Conscience," 1997). Regarding the defender's program, the *New York Times* editorialized, "It deserves to live. A Congress committed to the death penalty cannot in good conscience deny competent legal counsel. Abolishing the Defender Organizations harms the causes of economy, speed, and justice" ("Shortchanging Inmates," 1995, p. A-32).

References

Applebome, P. (1993, March 3). Alabama releases man held on death row for six years. *New York Times*, pp. A-1, B-11.

Attorney General speaks. (1985, October 14). *U.S. News and World Report*, p. 67.

Bailey, W. C. (1983). Disaggregation in deterrence and death penalty research: The case of murder in Chicago. *Journal of Criminal Law and Criminology, 74*, 827–859.

Bailey, W. C. (1998). Deterrence and brutalization, and the death penalty. *Criminology, 36*, 711–734.

Bailey, W. C., & Peterson, R. D. (1987). Police killings and capital punishment: The post-Furman period. *Criminology, 25*, 1–26.

Baldus, D. (in press). The death penalty in black and white: Who lives, who dies, who decides. *Cornell Law Review*.

Baldus, D., Woodworth, G., & Pulaski, C. (1990). *Equal justice and the death penalty: A legal and empirical analysis*. Boston: Northeastern University Press.

Bohm, R. (1991). American death penalty opinion, 1936–1986: A critical examination of the Gallup polls. In R. Bohm (Ed.), *The death penalty in America: Current research* (pp. 113–145). Cincinnati, OH: Anderson.

Bohm, R. (1996). Understanding and changing public support for capital punishment. *Corrections Now, 1*(1), 1–4.

Bowers, W. J. (1984). *Legal homicide: Death as punishment in America, 1864–1982*. Boston: Northeastern University Press.

Bowers, W. J. (1988). The effect of execution is brutalization, not deterrence. In K. Hass & J. Inciardi (Eds.), *Challenging capital punishment: Legal and social science approaches* (pp. 49–90). Newbury Park, CA: Sage.

Bowers, W. J. (1993). Capital punishment and contemporary values: People's misgivings and the court's misperceptions. *Law and Society Review, 27*, 157–175.

Bowers, W. J., & Pierce, G. (1980). Deterrence or brutalization: What is the effect of executions. *Crime and Delinquency, 26*, 453–484.

Bragg, R. (1995, May 13). A killer racked by delusions dies in Alabama's electric chair. *New York Times*, p. 7.

Brundage, W. (1993). *Lynching in the New South: Georgia and Virginia, 1880–1930*. Champaign: University of Illinois Press.

Butterfield, F. (1998, June 7). New study adds to evidence of bias in death sentences. *New York Times*, p. 20.

Cochran, J. K., Chamlin, M., & Seth, M. (1994). Deterrence or brutalization? An impact assessment of Oklahoma's return to capital punishment. *Criminology, 32*, 107–134.

Decker, S., & Kohfeld, C. (1990). The deterrent effect of capital punishment in the five most active execution states: A time series analysis. *Criminal Justice Review, 15*, 173–191.

Dieter, R. (1997). *Innocence and the death penalty: The increasing danger of executing the innocent*. Washington, DC: Death Penalty Information Center.

Eckholm, E. (1995, February 25). Studies find death penalty tied to race of the victims. *New York Times*, pp. B-1, B-2.

Ford v. Wainwright, 477 U.S. 699 (1986).

Forst, B. (1983). Capital punishment and deterrence: Conflicting evidence? *Journal of Criminal Law and Criminology, 74*, 927–942.

Gallup, A., & Newport, F. (1991, June). Death penalty support remains strong. *Gallup Monthly Report*, No. 321, pp. 3–5.

Gregg v. Georgia, 428 U.S. 153 (1976).

Harlow, E., Matas, D., & Rocamora, J. (1995). *The machinery of death: A shocking indictment of capital punishment in the United States*. New York: Amnesty International.

Hentoff, N. (1995, February 21). Executing the retarded in our name. *Village Voice*, pp. 30–31.

Huff, C. R., Rattner, A., & Sagarin, E. (1996). *Convicted but innocent: Wrongful conviction and public policy*. Thousand Oaks, CA: Sage.

Jackson, J. (1996). *Legal lynching: Racism, injustice, and the death penalty.* New York: Marlowe.

Keil, T., & Vito, G. (1989). Race, homicide severity, and application of the death penalty: A consideration of the Barnett Scale. *Criminology, 27,* 511–536.

King, D. (1978). The brutalization effect: Execution publicity and the incidence of homicide in South Carolina. *Social Forces, 57,* 683–687.

Kuntz, T. (1997, January 12). Banality, nausea, triple execution: Guards on inmates' final hours. *New York Times,* p. E-7.

A lawyerly cry of conscience. (1997, February 22). *New York Times,* p. 20.

Lee, H. (1960). *To kill a mockingbird.* New York: HarperCollins.

Lynch, M., & Groves, W. B. (1989). *A primer in radical criminology.* New York: Harrow & Heston.

Marx, G. (1981). Ironies of social control: Authorities as contributors to deviance through escalation, nonenforcement, and covert facilitation. *Social Problems, 28,* 221–233.

McGarrell, E. F., & Sandys, M. (1996). Misperception of public opinion toward capital punishment: Examining the spuriousness explanation of death penalty support. *American Behavioral Scientist, 39,* 500–513.

Miller, K., & Radelet, M. (1993). *Executing the mentally ill: The criminal justice system and the case of Alvin Ford.* Newbury Park, CA: Sage.

Moore, D. W. (1994, September). Majority advocate death penalty for teenage killers. *Gallup Poll Monthly,* No. 321, pp. 2–5.

Paternoster, R. (1983). Race of the victim and location of crime: The decision to seek the death penalty in South Carolina. *Journal of Criminal Law and Criminology, 74,* 754–785.

Paternoster, R. (1991). *Capital punishment in America.* New York: Lexington.

Penry v. Lynaugh, 57 U.S.L.W. 4958 (1989).

Radelet, M., Bedau, H., & Putnam, C. (1992). *In spite of innocence: Erroneous convictions in capital cases.* Boston: Northeastern University Press.

Reed, E. (1993). *The Penry penalty: Capital punishment and offenders with mental retardation.* Landam, MD: University Press of America.

Ridgeway, J. (1994, October 11). Slaughterhouse justice: Race, poverty, and politics: The essential ingredients for a death penalty conviction. *Village Voice,* pp. 23–24.

Russell, K. (1998). *The color of crime: Racial hoaxes, white fear, black protectionism, police aggression and other macroaggressions.* New York: New York University Press.

Shapiro, A. (1995, May 11). An insane execution. *New York Times,* p. A-29.

Shortchanging inmates on death row. (1995, October 13). *New York Times,* p. A-32.

Snell, T. (1997). *Capital punishment 1996.* Washington, DC: Bureau of Justice Statistics.

Terry, D. (1996, July 3). After 18 years in prison, 3 are cleared of murders. *New York Times,* p. A-14.

Terry, D. (1998, April 12). Jury to decide if condemned man comprehends his fate. *New York Times,* p. 22.

Tolnay, S., & Beck, E. (1994). Lethal social control in the South: Lynchings and executions between 1880 and 1930. In G. Bridges & M. Myers (Eds.), *Inequality, crime, and social control* (pp. 176–194). Boulder, CO: Westview.

van den Haag, E., & Conrad, J. (1983). *The death penalty: A debate.* New York: Plenum.

Verhovek, S. (1998, April 18). Texas legislator proposes the death penalty for murderers as young as 11. *New York Times,* p. A-7.

Walker, S. (1994). *Sense and nonsense about crime and drugs: A policy guide* (3rd ed.). Belmont, CA: Wadsworth.

Welch, M. (1996a). *Corrections: A critical approach.* New York: McGraw-Hill.

Welch, M. (1996b). Critical criminology, social justice, and an alternative view of incarceration. *Critical Criminology: An International Journal, 7*(2), 43–58.

White man pleads guilty to killing a black man. (1998, May 31). *New York Times,* p. 22.

Ernest van den Haag

 **NO**

The Death Penalty Once More

People concerned with capital punishment disagree on essentially three questions: (1) Is it constitutional? (2) Does the death penalty deter crime more than life imprisonment? (3) Is the death penalty morally justifiable?

Is the Death Penalty Constitutional?

The fifth amendment, passed in 1791, states that "no person shall be deprived of life, liberty, or property, without due process of law." Thus, with "due process of law," the Constitution authorizes depriving persons "of life, liberty or property." The fourteenth amendment, passed in 1868, applies an identical provision to the states. The Constitution, then, authorizes the death penalty. It is left to elected bodies to decide whether or not to retain it.

The eighth amendment, reproducing almost verbatim a passage from the English Bill of Rights of 1689, prohibits "cruel and unusual punishments." This prohibition was not meant to repeal the fifth amendment since the amendments were passed simultaneously. "Cruel" punishment is not prohibited unless "unusual" as well, that is, new, rare, not legislated, or disproportionate to the crime punished. Neither the English Bill of Rights, nor the eighth amendment, hitherto has been found inconsistent with capital punishment.

Evolving Standards

Some commentators argue that, in *Trop v. Dulles,* the Supreme Court indicated that "evolving standards of decency that mark the progress of a maturing society" allow courts to declare "cruel and unusual," punishments authorized by the Constitution. However, *Trop* was concerned with expatriation, a punishment that is not specifically authorized by the Constitution. The death penalty is. *Trop* did not suggest that "evolving standards" could de-authorize what the Constitution repeatedly authorizes. Indeed, Chief Justice Warren, writing for the majority in *Trop,* declared that "the death penalty . . . cannot be said to violate the constitutional concept of cruelty."[1] Furthermore, the argument based on "evolving standards" is paradoxical: the Constitution would be redundant if current views, enacted by judicial fiat, could supersede what it plainly says. If "standards of decency" currently invented or evolved could, without formal amendment, replace or repeal the standards authorized by the Constitution, the Constitution would be superfluous.

It must be remembered that the Constitution does not force capital punishment on the population but merely authorizes it. Elected bodies are left to decide whether to use the authorization. As for "evolving standards," how could courts detect them without popular consensus as a guide? Moral revelations accepted by judges, religious leaders, sociologists, or academic elites, but not by the majority of voters, cannot suffice. The opinions of the most organized, most articulate, or most vocal might receive unjustified deference. Surely the eighth amendment was meant to limit, but was not meant to replace, decisions by the legislative branch, or to enable the judiciary [to] do what the voters won't do.[2] The general consensus on which the courts would have to rely could be registered only by elected bodies. They favor capital punishment. Indeed, at present, more than seventy percent of the voters approve of the death penalty. The state legislatures reflect as much. Wherefore, the Supreme Court, albeit reluctantly, rejected abolition of the death penalty by judicial *fiat*. This decision was subsequently qualified by a finding that the death penalty for rape is disproportionate to the crime,[3] and by rejecting all mandatory capital punishment.

Caprice

Laws that allowed courts too much latitude to decide, perhaps capriciously, whether to actually impose the death penalty in capital cases also were found unconstitutional. In response, more than two-thirds of the states have modified their death penalty statutes, listing aggravating and mitigating factors, and imposing capital punishment only when the former outweigh the latter. The Supreme Court is satisfied that this procedure meets the constitutional requirements of non-capriciousness. However, abolitionists are not.

In *Capital Punishment: The Inevitability of Caprice and Mistake,*[4] Professor Charles Black contends that the death penalty is necessarily imposed capriciously, for irremediable reasons. If he is right, he has proved too much, unless capital punishment is imposed more capriciously now than it was in 1791 or 1868, when the fifth and fourteenth amendments were enacted. He does not contend that it is. Professor Black also stresses that the elements of chance, unavoidable in all penalizations, are least tolerable when capital punishment is involved. But the irreducible chanciness inherent in human efforts does not constitutionally require the abolition of capital punishment, unless the framers were less aware of chance and human frailty than Professor Black is. (I shall turn to the moral as distinguished from the legal bearing of chanciness anon.)

Discrimination

Sociologists have demonstrated that the death penalty has been distributed in a discriminatory pattern in the past: black or poor defendants were more likely to be executed than equally guilty others. This argues for correction of the distributive process, but not for abolition of the penalty it distributes, unless constitutionally excessive maldistribution ineluctably inheres in the penalty.

There is no evidence to that effect. Actually, although we cannot be sure that it has disappeared altogether, discrimination has greatly decreased compared to the past.[5]

However, recently the debate on discrimination has taken a new turn. Statistical studies have found that, *ceteris paribus,* a black man who murders a white has a much greater chance to be executed than he would have had, had his victim been black.[6] This discriminates against black *victims* of murder: they are not as fully, or as often, vindicated as are white victims. However, although unjustified per se, discrimination against a class of victims need not, and here does not, amount to discrimination against their victimizers. The pattern discriminates *against* black murderers of whites and *for* black murderers of blacks. One may describe it as discrimination for, or discrimination against, just as one may describe a glass of water as half full or half empty. Discrimination against one group (here, blacks who kill whites) is necessarily discrimination in favor of another (here, blacks who kill blacks).

Most black victims are killed by black murderers, and a disproportionate number of murder victims is black. Wherefore the discrimination in favor of murderers of black victims more than offsets, numerically, any remaining discrimination against other black murderers.[7]

Comparative Excessiveness

Recently lawyers have argued that the death penalty is unconstitutionally disproportionate if defendants, elsewhere in the state, received lesser sentences for comparable crimes. But the Constitution only requires that penalties be appropriate to the gravity of the crime, not that they cannot exceed penalties imposed elsewhere. Although some states have adopted "comparative excessiveness" reviews, there is no constitutional requirement to do so.

Unavoidably, different courts, prosecutors, defense lawyers, judges and juries produce different penalties even when crimes seem comparable. Chance plays a great role in human affairs. Some offenders are never caught or convicted, while others are executed; some are punished more than others guilty of worse crimes. Thus, a guilty person, or group of persons, may get away with no punishment, or with a light punishment, while others receive the punishment they deserve. Should we let these others go too, or punish them less severely? Should we abolish the penalty applied unequally or discriminatorily?[8]

The late Justice Douglas suggested an answer to these questions:

> A law that . . . said that blacks, those who never went beyond the fifth grade in school, those who made less than $3,000 a year, or those who were unpopular or unstable should be the only people executed [would be wrong]. A law which in the overall view reaches that result in practice has no more sanctity than a law which in terms provides the same.[9]

Justice Douglas' answer here conflates an imagined discriminatory law with the discriminatory application of a non-discriminatory law. His imagined law would be inconsistent with the "equal protection of the laws" demanded by the fourteenth amendment, and the Court would have to invalidate it *ipso facto*. But discrimination caused by uneven application of non-discriminatory death penalty laws may be remedied by means other than abolition, as long as the discrimination is not intrinsic to the laws.

Consider now, albeit fleetingly, the moral as distinguished from the constitutional bearing of discrimination. Suppose guilty defendants are justly executed, but only if poor, or black and not otherwise. This unequal justice would be morally offensive for what may be called tautological reasons:[10] if any punishment for a given crime is just, then a greater or lesser punishment is not. Only one punishment can be just for all persons equally guilty of the same crime.[11] Therefore, different punishments for equally guilty persons or group members are unjust: some offenders are punished more than they deserve, or others less.

Still, equality and justice are not the same. "Equal justice" is not a redundant phrase. Rather, we strive for two distinct ideals, justice and equality. Neither can replace the other. We want to have justice and, having it, we want to extend it equally to all. We would not want equal injustice. Yet, sometimes, we must choose between equal injustice and unequal justice. What should we prefer? Unequal justice is justice still, even if only for some, whereas equal injustice is injustice for all. If not every equally guilty person is punished equally, we have unequal justice. It seems preferable to equal injustice—having no guilty person punished as deserved.[12] Since it is never possible to punish equally all equally guilty murderers, we should punish, as they deserve, as many of those we apprehend and convict as possible. Thus, even if the death penalty were inherently discriminatory—which is not the case—but deserved by those who receive it, it would be morally just to impose it on them. If, as I contend, capital punishment is just and not inherently discriminatory, it remains desirable to eliminate inequality in distribution, to apply the penalty to all who deserve it, sparing no racial or economic class. But if a guilty person or group escaped the penalty through our porous system, wherein is this an argument for sparing others?

If one does not believe capital punishment can be just, discrimination becomes a subordinate argument, since one would object to capital punishment even if it were distributed equally to all the guilty. If one does believe that capital punishment for murderers is deserved, discrimination against guilty black murderers and in favor of equally guilty white murderers is wrong, not because blacks receive the deserved punishment, but because whites escape it.

Consider a less emotionally charged analogy. Suppose traffic police ticketed all drivers who violated the rules, except drivers of luxury cars. Should we abolish tickets? Should we decide that the ticketed drivers of nonluxury cars were unjustly punished and ought not to pay their fines? Would they become innocent of the violation they are guilty of because others have not been ticketed? Surely the drivers of luxury cars should not be exempted. But the fact that they were is no reason to exempt drivers of nonluxury cars as well. Laws could never be applied if the escape of one person, or group, were accepted as ground for not punishing another. To do justice is primarily to punish as deserved, and only secondarily to punish equally.

Guilt is personal. No one becomes less guilty or less deserving of punishment because another was punished leniently or not at all. That justice does not catch up with all guilty persons understandably is resented by those caught. But it does not affect their guilt. If some, or all, white and rich murderers escape the death penalty, how does that reduce the guilt of black or poor murderers, or make them less deserving of punishment, or deserving of a lesser punishment?

Some lawyers have insisted that the death penalty is distributed among those guilty of murder as though by a lottery and that the worst may escape it.[13] They exaggerate, but suppose one grants the point. How do those among the guilty selected for execution by lottery become less deserving of punishment because others escaped it? What is wrong is that these others escaped, not that those among the guilty who were selected by the lottery did not.

Those among the guilty actually punished by a criminal justice system unavoidably are selected by chance, not because we want to so select them, but because the outcome of our efforts largely depends on chance. No murderer is punished unless he is unlucky enough both to be caught and to have convinced a court of his guilt. And courts consider evidence not truth. They find truth only when the evidence establishes it. Thus they may have reasonable doubts about the guilt of an actually guilty person. Although we may strive to make justice as equal as possible, unequal justice will remain our lot in this world. We should not give up justice, or the death penalty, because we cannot extend it as equally to all the guilty as we wish. If we were not to punish one offender because another got away because of caprice or discrimination, we would give up justice for the sake of equality. We would reverse the proper order of priorities.

Is the Death Penalty More Deterrent Than Other Punishments?

Whether or not the death penalty deters the crimes it punishes more than alternative penalties—in this case life imprisonment with or without parole—has been widely debated since Isaac Ehrlich broke the abolitionist ranks by finding that from 1933–65 "an additional execution per year . . . may have resulted on the average in seven or eight fewer murders."[14] Since his article appeared, a whole cottage industry devoted to refuting his findings has arisen.[15] Ehrlich, no slouch, has been refuting those who refuted him.[16] The result seems inconclusive.[17] Statistics have not proved conclusively that the death penalty does or does not deter murder more than other penalties.[18] Still, Ehrlich has the merit of being the first to use a sophisticated statistical analysis to tackle the problem, and of defending his analysis, although it showed deterrence. (Ehrlich started as an abolitionist.) His predecessors cannot be accused of mathematical sophistication. Yet the academic community uncritically accepted their abolitionist results. I myself have no contribution to make to the mathematical analyses of deterrent effects. Perhaps this is why I have come to believe that they may becloud the issue, leading us to rely on demonstrable deterrence as though decisive.

Most abolitionists believe that the death penalty does not deter more than other penalties. But most abolitionists would abolish it, even if it did.[19] I have discussed this matter with prominent abolitionists such as Charles Black, Henry Schwarzchild, Hugo Adam Bedau, Ramsey Clark, and many others. Each told me that, even if every execution were to deter a hundred murders, he would oppose it. I infer that, to these abolitionist leaders, the life of every murderer is more valuable than the lives of a hundred prospective victims, for these abolitionists would spare the murderer, even if doing so would cost a hundred future victims their lives.

Obviously, deterrence cannot be the decisive issue for these abolitionists. It is not necessarily for me either, since I would be for capital punishment on grounds of justice alone. On the other hand, I should favor the death penalty for murderers, if probably deterrent, or even just possibly deterrent. To me, the life of any innocent victim who might be spared has great value; the life of a convicted murderer does not. This is why I would not take the risk of sacrificing innocents by not executing murderers.

Even though statistical demonstrations are not conclusive, and perhaps cannot be, I believe that capital punishment is likely to deter more than anything else. They fear most death deliberately inflicted by law and scheduled by the courts. Whatever people fear most is likely to deter most. Hence, I believe that the threat of the death penalty may deter some murderers who otherwise might not have been deterred. And surely the death penalty is the only penalty that could deter prisoners already serving a life sentence and tempted to kill a guard, or offenders about to be arrested and facing a life sentence. Perhaps they will not be deterred. But they would certainly not be deterred by anything else. We owe all the protection we can give to law enforcers exposed to special risks.

Many murders are "crimes of passion" that, perhaps, cannot be deterred by any threat. Whether or not they can be would depend on the degree of passion; it is unlikely to be always so extreme as to make the person seized by it totally undeterrable. At any rate, offenders sentenced to death ordinarily are guilty of premediated murder, felony murder, or multiple murders. Some are rape murderers, or hit men, but, to my knowledge, no one convicted of a "crime of passion" is on death row. Whatever the motive, some prospective offenders are not deterrable at all, others are easily deterred, and most are in between. Even if only some murders were, or could be, deterred by capital punishment, it would be worthwhile. . . .

Almost all convicted murderers try to avoid the death penalty by appeals for commutation to life imprisonment. However, a minuscule proportion of convicted murderers prefer execution. It is sometimes argued that they murdered for the sake of being executed, of committing suicide via execution. More likely, they prefer execution to life imprisonment. Although shared by few, this preference is not irrational per se. It is also possible that these convicts accept the verdict of the court, and feel that they deserve the death penalty for the crimes they committed, although the modern mind finds it hard to imagine such feelings. But not all murderers are ACLU humanists. . . .

Is the Death Penalty Moral?

Miscarriages

Miscarriages of justice are rare, but do occur. Over a long enough time they lead to the execution of some innocents.[20] Does this make irrevocable punishments morally wrong? Hardly. Our government employs trucks. They run over innocent bystanders more frequently than courts sentence innocents to death. We do not give up trucks because the benefits they produce outweigh the harm, including the death of innocents. Many human activities, even quite trivial ones, forseeably cause wrongful deaths. Courts may cause fewer wrongful deaths than golf. Whether one sees the benefit of doing justice by imposing capital punishment as moral, or as material, or both, it outweighs the loss of innocent lives through miscarriages, which are as unintended as traffic accidents.

Vengeance

Some abolitionists feel that the motive for the death penalty is an un-Christian and unacceptable desire for vengeance. But though vengeance be the motive, it is not the purpose of the death penalty. Doing justice and deterring crime are the purposes, whatever the motive. Purpose (let alone effect) and motive are not the same.

The Lord is often quoted as saying "Vengeance is mine." He did not condemn vengeance. He merely reserved it to Himself—and to the government. For, in the same epistle He is also quoted as saying that the ruler is "the minister of God, a revenger, to execute wrath upon him that doeth evil." The religious notion of hell indicates that the biblical God favored harsh and everlasting punishment for some. However, particularly in a secular society, we cannot wait for the day of judgment to see murderers consigned to hell. Our courts must "execute wrath upon him that doeth evil" here and now.

Charity and Justice

Today many religious leaders oppose capital punishment. This is surprising, because there is no biblical warrant for their opposition. The Roman Catholic Church and most Protestant denominations traditionally have supported capital punishment. Why have their moral views changed? When sharing secular power, the churches clearly distinguished between justice, including penalization as deserved, a function of the secular power, and charity, which, according to religious doctrine, we should feel for all those who suffer for whatever reasons. Currently, religious leaders seem to conflate justice and charity, to conclude that the death penalty and, perhaps, all punishment, is wrong because uncharitable. Churches no longer share secular power. Perhaps bystanders are more ready to replace justice with charity than are those responsible for governing.

Human Dignity

Let me return to the morality of execution. Many abolitionists believe that capital punishment is "degrading to human dignity" and inconsistent with the "sanctity of life." Justice Brennan, concurring in *Furnam,* stressed these phrases repeatedly.[21] He did not explain what he meant.

Why would execution degrade human dignity more than life imprisonment? One may prefer the latter; but it seems at least as degrading as execution. Philosophers, such as Immanuel Kant and G. F. W. Hegel, thought capital punishment indispensable to redeem, or restore, the human dignity of the executed. Perhaps they were wrong. But they argued their case, whereas no one has explained why capital punishment degrades. Apparently those who argue that it does degrade dignity simply define the death penalty as degrading. If so, degradation (or dehumanization) merely is a disguised synonym for their disapproval. Assertion, reassertion, or definition, do not constitute evidence or argument, nor do they otherwise justify, or even explain, disapproval of capital punishment.

Writers, such as Albert Camus, have suggested that murderers have a miserable time waiting for execution and anticipating it.[22] I do not doubt that. But punishments are not meant to be pleasant. Other people suffer greatly waiting for the end, in hospitals, under circumstances that, I am afraid, are at least as degrading to their dignity as execution. These sufferers have not deserved their suffering by committing crimes, whereas murderers have. Yet, murderers suffer less on death row, unless their consciences bother them.

Lex Talionis

Some writers insist that the suffering the death penalty imposes on murderers exceeds the suffering of their victims. This is hard to determine, but probably true in some cases and not in other cases. However, the comparison is irrelevant. Murderers are punished, as are all offenders, not just for the suffering they caused their victims, but for the harm they do to society by making life insecure, by threatening everyone, and by requiring protective measures. Punishment, ultimately, is a vindication of the moral and legal order of society and not limited by the *Lex Talionis,* meant to limit private retaliation for harms originally regarded as private.

Sanctity of Life

We are enjoined by the Declaration of Independence to secure life. How can this best be achieved? The Constitution authorizes us to secure innocent life by taking the life of murderers, so that any one who deliberately wants to take an innocent life will know that he risks forfeiting his own. The framers did not think that taking the life of a murderer is inconsistent with the "sanctity of life" which Justice Brennan champions. He has not indicated why they were wrong.[23]

Legalized Murder?

Ever since Cesare Bonesana, Marchese di Beccaria, wrote *Dei Delitti e Delle Pene,* abolitionists have contended that executing murderers legitimizes murder by doing to the murderer what he did to his victim. Indeed, capital punishment retributes, or pays back the offender. Occasionally we do punish offenders by doing to them what they did to their victims. We may lock away a kidnapper who wrongfully locked away his victim, and we may kill the murderer who wrongfully killed his victim. To lawfully do to the offender what he unlawfully did to his victim in no way legitimizes his crime. It legitimizes (some) killing, and not murder. An act does not become a crime because of its physical character, which, indeed, it may share with the legal punishment, but because of its social, or, better, antisocial, character—because it is an unlawful act.

Severity

Is the death penalty too severe? It stands in a class by itself. But so does murder. Execution is irreparable. So is murder. In contrast, all other crimes and punishments are, at least partly or potentially, reparable. The death penalty thus is congruous with the moral and material gravity of the crime it punishes.[24]

Still, is it repulsive? Torture, however well deserved, now is repulsive to us. But torture is an artifact. Death is not, since nature has placed us all under sentence of death. Capital punishment, in John Stuart Mills' phrase, only "hastens death"—which is what the murderer did to his victim. I find nothing repulsive in hastening the murderer's death, provided it be done in a nontorturous manner. Had he wished to be secure in his life, he could have avoided murder.

To believe that capital punishment is too severe for any act, one must believe that there can be no act horrible enough to deserve death.[25] I find this belief difficult to understand. I should readily impose the death penalty on a Hitler or a Stalin, or on anyone who does what they did, albeit on a smaller scale.

Conclusion

The death penalty has become a major issue in public debate. This is somewhat puzzling, because quantitatively it is insignificant. Still, capital punishment has separated the voters as a whole from a small, but influential, abolitionist elite. There are, I believe, two reasons that explain the prominence of the issue.

First, I think, there is a genuine ethical issue. Some philosophers believe that the right to life is equally imprescriptible for all, that the murderer has as much right to live as his victim. Others do not push egalitarianism that far. They believe that there is a vital difference, that one's right to live is lost when one intentionally takes an innocent life, that everyone has just the right to one life, his own. If he unlawfully takes that of another he, *eo ipso,* loses his own right to life.

Second, and perhaps as important, the death penalty has symbolic significance. Those who favor it believe that the major remedy for crime is punishment. Those who do not, in the main, believe that the remedy is anything but punishment. They look at the causes of crime and conflate them with compulsions, or with excuses, and refuse to blame. The majority of the people are less sophisticated, but perhaps they have better judgment. They believe that everyone who can understand the nature and effects of his acts is responsible for them, and should be blamed and punished, if he could know that what he did was wrong. Human beings are human because they can be held responsible, as animals cannot be. In that Kantian sense the death penalty is a symbolic affirmation of the humanity of both victim and murderer.

Notes

1. 356 U.S. 99 (1958).

2. The courts have sometimes confirmed the obsolescence of non-repealed laws or punishments. But here they are asked to invent it.

3. In *Coker v. Georgia,* 433 U.S. 584, 592 (1977), the Court concluded that the eighth amendment prohibits punishments that are "'excessive' in relation to the crime committed." I am not sure about this disproportion. However, threatening execution would tempt rapists to murder their victims who, after all, are potential witnesses. By murdering their victims, rapists would increase their chances of escaping execution without adding to their risk. Therefore, I agree with the court's conclusion, though not with its argument.

4. C. BLACK, CAPITAL PUNISHMENT: THE INEVITABILITY OF CAPRICE AND MISTAKE (2d ed. 1981).

5. Most discrimination occurred in rape cases and was eliminated when the death penalty for rape was declared unconstitutional.

6. For a survey of the statistical literature, see, e.g., Bowers, *The Pervasiveness of Arbitrariness and Discrimination under Post-*Furman *Capital Statutes,* 74 J. CRIM. L. & CRIMINOLOGY 1067 (1983). His article is part of a "Symposium on Current Death Penalty Issues" compiled by death penalty opponents.

7. Those who demonstrated the pattern seem to have been under the impression that they had shown discrimination against black murderers. They were wrong. However, the discrimination against black victims is invidious and should be corrected.

8. The capriciousness argument is undermined when capriciousness is conceded to be unavoidable. But even when capriciousness is thought reducible, one wonders whether releasing or retrying one guilty defendant, because another equally guilty defendant was not punished as much, would help reduce capriciousness. It does not seem a logical remedy.

9. *Furman v. Georgia,* 408 U.S. 238, 256 (1971) (Douglas, J., concurring).

10. I shall not consider here the actual psychological motives that power our unending thirst for equality.

11. If courts impose different punishments on different persons, we may not be able to establish in all cases whether the punishment is just, or (it amounts to the same) whether the different persons were equally guilty of the same crime, or whether their crimes were identical in all relevant respects. Thus, we may not be able to tell which of two unequal punishments is just. Both may be, or neither may be. Inequality may not entail more injustice than equality, and equality would entail justice only if we were sure that the punishment meted out was the just punishment.

12. Similarly, it is better that only some innocents suffer undeserved punishment than that all suffer it equally.

13. It would be desirable that all of the worst murderers be sentenced to death. However, since murderers are tried in different courts, this is unlikely. Further, sometimes the testimony of one murderer is needed to convict another, and cannot be obtained except by leniency. Morally, and legally it is enough that those sentenced to death deserve the penalty for their crimes, even if others, who may deserve it as much, or more, were not sentenced to death.

14. Ehrlich, *The Deterrent Effect of Capital Punishment: A Question of Life or Death*, 65 AM. ECON. REV. 397, 414 (1975).

15. *See, e.g.*, Baldus & Cole, *A Comparison of the Work of Thorsten Sellin and Isaac Ehrlich on the Deterrent Effect of Capital Punishment*, 85 YALE L. J. 170 (1975); Bowers & Pierce, *Deterrence or Brutalization: What Is the Effect of Executions?*, 26 CRIME & DELINQ. 453 (1980); Bowers & Pierce, *The Illusion of Deterrence in Isaac Ehrlich's Research on Capital Punishment*, 85 YALE L. J. 187 (1975).

16. Ehrlich, *Fear of Deterrence*, 6 J. LEGAL STUD. 293 (1977); Ehrlich & Gibbons, *On the Measurement of the Deterrent Effect of Capital Punishment and the Theory of Deterrence*, 6 J. LEGAL STUD. 35 (1977).

17. At present there is no agreement even on whether the short run effects of executions delay or accelerate homicides. *See* Phillips, *The Deterrent Effect of Capital Punishment: New Evidence on an Old Controversy*, 86, AM. J. SOC. 139 (1980).

18. As stated in *Gregg v. Georgia*, 428 U.S. 153, 185 (1976), "Although some of the studies suggest that the death penalty may not function as a significantly greater deterrent than lesser penalties, there is no convincing empirical evidence either supporting or refuting this view."

19. Jeffrey Reiman is an honorable exception. *See* Reiman, *Justice, Civilization, and the Death Penalty: Answering van den Haag*, 14 PHIL. & PUB. AFF. 115 (1985).

20. Life imprisonment avoids the problem of executing innocent persons to some extent. It can be revoked. But the convict also may die in prison before his innocence is discovered.

21. "[T]he Cruel and Unusual Punishments Clause prohibits the infliction of uncivilized and inhuman punishments. The State, even as it punishes, must treat its members with respect for their intrinsic worth as human beings." *Furman v. Georgia*, 408 U.S. 238, 270 (1972) (Brennan, J., concurring). "When we consider why [certain punishments] have been condemned, . . . we realize that the pain involved is not the only reason. The true significance of these punishments [that have been condemned] is that they treat members of the human race as nonhumans, as objects to be toyed with and discarded." *Id.* at 272–73.

> In determining whether a punishment comports with human dignity, we are aided also by a second principle inherent in the Clause—that the State must not arbitrarily inflict a severe punishment. This principle derives from the notion that the State does not respect human dignity when, without reason, it inflicts upon some people a severe punishment that it does not inflict upon others.

Id. at 274. "Death is truly an awesome punishment. The calculated killing of a human being by the State involves, by its very nature, a denial of the executed person's humanity." *Id.* at 290. "In comparison to all other punishments today, then, the deliberate extinguishment of human life by the State is uniquely degrading to human dignity." *Id.* at 291.

22. In *Reflections on the Guillotine*, Camus stated that "[t]he parcel [the condemned person] is no longer subject to the laws of chance that hang over the living creature but to mechanical laws that allow him to foresee accurately the day of his beheading. . . . The Greeks, after all, were more humane with their hemlock." A. CAMUS, RESISTANCE, REBELLION AND DEATH 175, 202 (1960).

23. "Sanctity of life" may mean that we should not take, and should punish taking innocent life: "*homo homini res sacra.*" In the past this meant that we should take the life of a murderer to secure innocent life, and stress its sacredness. Justice Brennan seems to mean that the life of the murderer should be sacred too—but no argument is given for this premise.

24. Capital punishment is not inconsistent with *Weems v. United States,* 217 U.S. 349 (1910), which merely held that punishment cannot be excessive, that is, out of proportion to the gravity of the crime. Indeed, if life imprisonment suffices for anything else, it cannot be appropriate for murder.

25. The notion of deserving is strictly moral, depending exclusively on our sense of justice, unlike the notion of deterrence, which depends on the expected factual consequences of punishment. Whilst deterrence alone would justify most of the punishments we should impose, it may not suffice to justify all those punishments that our sense of justice demands. Wherefore criminal justice must rest on desert as well as deterrence, to be seen as morally justified.

POSTSCRIPT

Should the Death Penalty Be Abolished?

The argument is sometimes made that even if capital punishment is not a deterrent (or, more radically, even if capital punishment actually encourages crime), justice demands that certain criminals be executed. For example, former Nazis who killed many innocent people are today tracked down and brought to trial. Usually, these are elderly men who have lived many years without killing anyone. If the death penalty is demanded for these people, would this demand receive support from the deterrence line of reasoning? Probably not. First, these people have already stopped killing and so do not need to be deterred. Second, should we suppose that executing them will deter potential future Nazis, Aryan supremacists, and other racists from murder? More likely, in these cases, the argument is that these former Nazis should die for what they have done as a matter of justice.

A special issue for Americans is whether or not the death penalty is constitutional—in particular, whether or not it is cruel and unusual punishment. In a series of important legal cases (including *Furman v. Georgia,* 1972, and *Gregg v. Georgia,* 1976), the U.S. Supreme Court found that capital punishment *as then applied* was indeed unconstitutional. The main problem was that a lack of explicit standards in applying the death penalty gave much room for discretion, which in turn allowed prejudice and racism to hide behind legality. But the Court allowed the development of procedures of administering capital punishment that did not violate the Constitution.

One of the major points on which Welch and van den Haag seem to differ is over the extent to which we can separate and correct the bias, error, and other negative features to which Welch draws our attention from the death penalty itself. Van den Haag would argue that all the negative features that Welch has identified can be addressed without the moral acceptability of the death penalty being brought into question. Welch would probably respond that the moral acceptability of the death penalty is not its moral acceptability in an ideal world but in the real world that we live in.

Much has been written about the death penalty. Useful recent sources are Mark Grossman, *Encyclopedia of Capital Punishment* (ABC-CLIO, 1998); Hugo Bedau and Paul Cassell, eds., *Debating the Death Penalty: Should America Have Capital Punishment?* (Oxford University Press, 2004); and Bill Kurtis, *The Death Penalty on Trial: Crisis in American Justice* (Public Affairs, 2004).

ISSUE 13

Is Torture Ever Justified?

YES: Mirko Bagaric and Julie Clarke, from "Not Enough Official Torture in the World?" *University of San Francisco Law Review* (Spring 2005)

NO: Philip E. Devine, from "What's Wrong with Torture?" *International Philosophical Quarterly*, vol. 49 (September 2009)

ISSUE SUMMARY

YES: Bagaric and Clarke remind us, first of all, that torture, although prohibited by international law, is nevertheless widely practiced. A rational examination of torture and a consideration of hypothetical (but realistic) cases show that torture is justifiable in order to prevent great harm. Torture should be regulated and carefully practiced as an information-gathering technique in extreme cases.

NO: Philosopher Philip E. Devine argues for an absolute (or virtually absolute) position against torture. Devine suggests that the wrongness of torture and the repugnance that we feel toward it ultimately go beyond any moral theory. In addition, the examination of extreme cases should not inform our general thought about these and other matters.

This is a question that might not even have arisen in a serious way if it were not for current events and the War on Terrorism. Actually, philosophers had been talking about questions like this before 9/11, but only in a purely hypothetical way. No one anticipated that seemingly crazy ideas about buildings being blown up in New York and thousands of people being killed would actually become a reality. But times have changed. And the question is now asked as a reflection of the times. Yet, to ask the question does not mean that one is considering torture as a possibility. For some of those who address this very question—Philip Devine, for example—would insist that the answer is no and would further insist that in this day of terrorism one of the important values that distinguishes us from the terrorists is that our answer should be that torture is absolutely out of the question. We should not try to imagine situations or conditions under which we torture people. So, on this view, we should not try to "draw a line," for one side of the line will be the side where torture is justified. Part of what we would be doing is determining an area in which we believed that torture is justified. But, in order to stay faithful to a negative answer to the issue question, we should not define any such area. Opponents of the view that torture is never justified might construct various scenarios. Suppose, for example, that there was a ticking bomb that was hidden in a secret location and was set to go off at a certain time and would be sure to kill hundreds or thousands of innocent people. And suppose that the authorities had in their custody an individual who had detailed information about the bomb, including its location and the time it was set to go off. If this person were unwilling to disclose the information voluntarily, would torture be justified? After all, so much is at stake. If that one person were tortured, the very lives of a great many innocent people lie in the balance. How, it might be asked, could his well-being outweigh theirs?

The opponents of torture would probably respond that the question of torturing the person does not really have to do with his well-being at all, but rather with our own actions. The imagined scenario seems to suggest that so much is (potentially) at stake that we must be prepared to torture people. If so, we can't lay claim to ideas about human rights, the sacredness of life, etc. For example, if we really are going to be prepared to torture people, we have to have trained torturers who know how to do their job well. Even in the imagined "ticking bomb" scenario, the innocent people wouldn't be saved if we used an incompetent torturer who bungled the job and did something that resulted in the person's death—in which case we'd never find out any information about the ticking bomb. But the torturer has to cause some serious pain nevertheless. Proponents of torture seem to need someone who is a trained torturer, someone who is not doing this for the first time. So one question is whether we should initiate action now to produce such people in case they might be used. In the first reading, Bagaric and Clarke argue that torture is already being practiced widely—although unmonitored and "underground." Their idea is to acknowledge it, endorse it to some extent, but draw lines. In the second reading, Philip Devine does not wish to condone torture at all. On his view, our attitude toward torture as something repugnant is not an attitude that we should not lose.

YES

Mirko Bagaric
and Julie Clarke

Not Enough Official Torture in the World? The Circumstances in Which Torture Is Morally Justifiable

Recent events stemming from the "war on terrorism" have highlighted the prevalence of torture, both as an interrogation technique and as a punitive measure. Torture is almost universally deplored. It is prohibited by international law and is not officially sanctioned by the domestic laws of any state. The formal prohibition against torture is absolute—there are no exceptions to it. This is not only pragmatically unrealistic, but unsound at a normative level. Despite the absolute ban on torture, it is widely used. Contrary to common belief, torture is not the preserve of despot military regimes in third world nations. For example, there are serious concerns regarding the treatment by the United States of senior Al Qaeda leader Khalid Shaikh Mohammad. There is also irrefutable evidence that the United States tortured large numbers of Iraqi prisoners, as well as strong evidence that it tortured prisoners at Guantanamo Bay prison in Cuba, where suspected Al Qaeda terrorists are held. More generally Professor Alan Dershowitz has noted, "[C]ountries all over the world violate the Geneva Accords [prohibiting torture]. They do it secretly and hypothetically, the way the French did it in Algeria."

Dershowitz has also recently argued that torture should be made lawful. His argument is based on a harm minimization rationale from the perspective of victims of torture. He said, "Of course it would be best if we didn't use torture at all, but if the United States is going to continue to torture people, we need to make the process legal and accountable." Our argument goes one step beyond this. We argue that torture is indeed morally defensible, not just pragmatically desirable. The harm minimization rationale is used to supplement our argument.

While a "civilized" community does not typically condone such conduct, this Article contends that torture is morally defensible in certain circumstances, mainly when more grave harm can be avoided by using torture as an interrogation device. The pejorative connotation associated with torture should be abolished. A dispassionate analysis of the propriety of torture indicates that it is morally justifiable. At the outset of this analytical discussion, this Article requires readers to move from the question of

From *University of San Francisco Law Review,* vol. 39, Spring 2005, pp. 581–616. Copyright © 2005 by University of San Francisco Law Review. Reprinted by permission.

whether torture is *ever* defensible to the issue of the circumstances in which it is morally permissible.

Consider the following example: A terrorist network has activated a large bomb on one of hundreds of commercial planes carrying over three hundred passengers that is flying somewhere in the world at any point in time. The bomb is set to explode in thirty minutes. The leader of the terrorist organization announces this intent via a statement on the Internet. He states that the bomb was planted by one of his colleagues at one of the major airports in the world in the past few hours. No details are provided regarding the location of the plane where the bomb is located. Unbeknown to him, he was under police surveillance and is immediately apprehended by police. The terrorist leader refuses to answer any questions of the police, declaring that the passengers must die and will do so shortly.

Who in the world would deny that all possible means should be used to extract the details of the plane and the location of the bomb? The answer is not many. The passengers, their relatives and friends, and many in society would expect that all means should be used to extract the information, even if the pain and suffering imposed on the terrorist resulted in his death.

Although the above example is hypothetical and is not one that has occurred in the real world, the force of the argument cannot be dismissed on that basis. As C.L. Ten notes, "fantastic examples" that raise fundamental issues for consideration, such as whether it is proper to torture wrongdoers, play an important role in the evaluation of moral principles and theories. These examples sharpen contrasts and illuminate the logical conclusions of the respective principles to test the true strength of our commitment to the principles. Thus, fantastic examples cannot be dismissed summarily merely because they are "simply" hypothetical.

Real life is, of course, rarely this clear cut, but there are certainly scenarios approaching this degree of desperation, which raise for discussion whether it is justifiable to inflict harm on one person to reduce a greater level of harm occurring to a large number of blameless people. Ultimately, torture is simply the sharp end of conduct whereby the interests of one agent are sacrificed for the greater good. As a community, we are willing to accept this principle. Thus, although differing in degree, torture is no different in nature from conduct that we sanction in other circumstances. It should be viewed in this light.

Given this, it is illogical to insist on a blanket prohibition against torture. Therefore, the debate must turn to the circumstances when torture is morally appropriate. This is the topic of this Article.

International law defines torture as severe pain and suffering, generally used as an interrogation device or as a punitive measure. This Article focuses on the use of torture as an interrogation device and poses that the device is only permissible to prevent significant harm to others. In these circumstances, there are five variables relevant in determining whether torture is permissible and the degree of torture that is appropriate. The variables are (1) the number of lives at risk; (2) the immediacy of the harm; (3) the availability of other means to acquire the information; (4) the level of wrongdoing of the agent; and (5) the likelihood that the agent actually does possess the relevant information.

This Article analyzes the meaning of torture and the nature and scope of the legal prohibition against torture [and] examines whether torture is morally defensible. It is argued that torture is no different than other forms of morally permissible behavior and is justifiable on a utilitarian ethic. It is also argued that, on close reflection, torture is also justifiable against a backdrop of a non-consequentialist rights-based ethic, which is widely regarded as prohibiting torture in all circumstances. Thus, the Article concludes that torture is morally justifiable in rare circumstances, irrespective of which normative theory one adopts. [We] examine the circumstances in which torture is justifiable. Finally, [we] debunk the argument that torture should not be legalized because it will open the floodgates to more torture.

Torture: Reality and Legal Position

The Law on Torture

Pursuant to international law, "torture" is defined as:

> Any act by which severe pain or suffering, whether physical or mental, is intentionally inflicted on a person for such purposes as obtaining from him or a third person information or a confession, punishing him for an act he or a third person has committed or is suspected of having committed, or intimidating or coercing him or a third person, or for any reason based on discrimination of any kind, when such pain or suffering is inflicted by or at the instigation of or with the consent or acquiescence of a public official or other person acting in an official capacity. It does not include pain or suffering arising only from, inherent in or incidental to lawful sanctions.

Torture is prohibited by a number of international documents. It is also considered to carry a special status in customary international law, that of *jus cogens,* which is a "peremptory norm" of customary international law. The significance of this is that customary international law is binding on all states, even if they have not ratified a particular treaty. At the treaty level, there are both general treaties that proscribe torture and specific treaties banning the practice.

In terms of general treaties, torture is prohibited by a number of international and regional treaties. . . .

The rigidity of the rule against torture is exemplified by the fact that it has a non-derogable status in human rights law. That is, there are no circumstances in which torture is permissible. This prohibition is made clear in Article 2(2) of the U.N. Convention Against Torture, which states, "No exceptional circumstances whatsoever, whether a state of war or a threat of war, internal political instability or any other public emergency, may be invoked as a justification of torture." Thus, the right not to be tortured is absolute. . . .

This absolute prohibition is frequently highlighted by Amnesty International and other human rights organizations. For example, Amnesty International states, "The law is unequivocal—torture is absolutely prohibited in all circumstances. . . . The right to be free from torture is absolute. It cannot be denied to anyone in any circumstances."

Torture is also prohibited as a war crime, pursuant to humanitarian law. In addition, torture is considered to be a crime against humanity when the acts are perpetrated as part of a widespread or systematic attack against a civilian population, whether or not they are committed in the course of an armed conflict.

The Reality of Torture

As with many legal precepts, the black letter law must be considered against the context of reality. As this part shows, various forms of torture are used despite the legal prohibition of it.

1. Forms of Torture

As is noted by Dershowitz, torture comes in many different forms and intensities:

> Torture is a continuum and the two extremes are on the one hand torturing someone to death—that is torturing an enemy to death so that others will know that if you are caught, you will be caused excruciating pain—that's torture as a deterrent. . . . At the other extreme, there's non-lethal torture which leaves only psychological scars. The perfect example of this is a sterilised needle inserted under the fingernail, causing unbearable pain but no possible long-term damage. These are very different phenomena. What they have in common of course is that they allow the government physically to come into contact with you in order to produce pain.

Various methods of torture have and continue to be applied in a multitude of countries. The most common methods are beating, electric shock, rape and sexual abuse, mock execution or threat of death, and prolonged solitary confinement. Other common methods include sleep and sensory deprivation, suspension of the body, "shackling interrogees in contorted painful positions" or in "painful stretching positions," and applying pressure to sensitive areas, such as the "neck, throat, genitals, chest and head."

2. The Benefits of Torture: An Effective Information Gathering Device

The main benefit of torture is that it is an excellent means of gathering information. Humans have an intense desire to avoid pain, no matter how short term, and most will comply with the demands of a torturer to avoid the pain. Often even the threat of torture alone will evoke cooperation. To this end, Dershowitz cites a recent kidnapping case in Germany in which the son of a distinguished banker was kidnapped. The eleven-year-old boy had been missing for three days. The police had in their custody a man they were convinced had perpetrated the kidnapping. The man was taken into custody after being seen collecting a ransom that was paid by the boy's family. During seven hours of interrogation the man "toyed" with police, leading them to one false location after another. After exhausting all lawful means of interrogation, the deputy commissioner of the Frankfurt police instructed his officers, in writing, that they could try to extract information "by means of the infliction of pain, under medical supervision and subject to prior warning." Ten minutes after the warning was given the suspect told the police where the boy was; unfortunately the boy was already dead, having been killed shortly after the kidnapping.

3. The Widespread Use of Torture

a. Torture Around the World   Despite the contemporary abhorrence against it, dozens of countries continue to use torture. A study of 195 countries and territories by Amnesty International between 1997 and mid-2000 found reports of torture or ill-treatment by state officials in more than 150 countries and in more than seventy countries that torture or ill-treatment was reported as "widespread or persistent." It is also clear that torture is not limited to military regimes in third world nations. Amnesty International recently reported that in 2003 it had received reports of torture and ill-treatment from 132 countries, including the United States, Canada, Japan, France, Italy, Spain, and Germany. . . .

The Circumstances in Which Torture Is Acceptable

The only situation where torture is justifiable is where it is used as an information gathering technique to avert a grave risk. In such circumstances, there are five variables relevant in determining whether torture is permissible and the degree of torture that is appropriate. The variables are (1) the number of lives at risk; (2) the immediacy of the harm; (3) the availability of other means to acquire the information; (4) the level of wrongdoing of the agent; and (5) the likelihood that the agent actually does possess the relevant information. Where (1), (2), (4) and (5) rate highly and (3) is low, all forms of harm may be inflicted on the agent—even if this results in death.

The Harm to Be Prevented

The key consideration regarding the permissibility of torture is the magnitude of harm that is sought to be prevented. To this end, the appropriate measure is the number of lives that are likely to be lost if the threatened harm is not alleviated. Obviously, the more lives that are at stake, the more weight that is attributed to this variable.

Lesser forms of threatened harm will not justify torture. Logically, the right to life is the most basic and fundamental of all human rights—non-observance of it would render all other human rights devoid of meaning. Every society has some prohibition against taking life, and "the intentional taking of human life is . . . the offence which society condemns most strongly." The right to life is also enshrined in several international covenants. For example, Article 2 of the European Convention on Human Rights (which in essence mirrors Article 6 of the International Covenant on Civil and Political Rights) provides that "everyone's right to life shall be protected by law. No one shall be deprived of his life intentionally save in the execution of a sentence of a court following his conviction of a crime for which this penalty is provided by law."

Torture violates the right to physical integrity, which is so important that it is only a threat to the right to life that can justify interference with it. Thus, torture should be confined to situations where the right to life is imperiled.

Immediacy of Harm and Other Options to Obtain Information

Torture should only be used as a last resort and hence should not be utilized where there is time to pursue other avenues of forestalling the harm. It is for this reason that torture should only be used where there is no other means to obtain the relevant information. Thus, where a terrorist has planted a bomb on a plane, torture will not be permissible where, for example, video tapes of international airports are likely to reveal the identity of the plane that has been targeted.

The Likelihood of Knowledge or Guilt

As a general rule torture should normally be confined to people that are responsible in some way for the threatened harm. This is not, however, invariably the case. People who are simply aware of the threatened harm, that is "innocent people," may in some circumstances also be subjected to torture.

Regardless of the guilt of the agent, it is most important that torture is only used against individuals who actually possess the relevant information. It will be rare that conclusive proof is available that an individual does, in fact, possess the required knowledge; for example, potential torturees will not have been through a trial process in which their guilt has been established. This is not a decisive objection, however, to the use of torture. The investigation and trial process is simply one means of distinguishing wrongdoers from the innocent. To that end, it does not seem to be a particularly effective process. There are other ways of forming such conclusions. One is by way of lie-detector tests. The latest information suggests that polygraphs are accurate about eighty to ninety per cent of the time. There has been little empirical research done to ascertain the number of innocent people who are ultimately convicted of criminal offenses. As one example, however, research carried out in the United Kingdom for the Royal Commission on Criminal Justice suggests that up to eleven percent of people who plead guilty claim innocence. The wrongful acquittal rate would no doubt be even higher than this.

Moreover, it is important to note that even without resort to polygraphs there will be many circumstances where guilt or relevant knowledge is patently obvious. A clear example is where a person makes a relevant admission that discloses information that would only be within the knowledge of the wrongdoer. Another example occurred in the recent German kidnapping case, referred to earlier, where the man in custody had been witnessed collecting a ransom and had indicated to the police that the kidnapped boy was still alive. Where lesser forms of evidence proving guilt are available, the argument in favor of torture is lower.

The Formula

Incorporating all these considerations, the strength of the case in favor of torture can be mapped as follows:

$$\frac{W + L + P}{T \times O}$$

Where:

- W = whether the agent is the wrongdoer
- L = the number of lives that will be lost if the information is not provided
- P = the probability that the agent has the relevant knowledge
- T = the time available before the disaster will occur ("immediacy of the harm")
- O = the likelihood that other inquiries will forestall the risk

W is a weighting that is attributable to whether the agent has had any direct connection with the potential catastrophe. Where the person is responsible for the incident—for example, planted or organized the bomb—more emphasis should be attached. Where the agent is innocent and has simply stumbled on the relevant information—for example, she saw the bomb being planted or overheard the plan to plant the bomb—this should be reduced by a certain amount. The prohibition against inflicting harm on the innocent is certainly strong, but it is not inviolable.

Torture should be permitted where the application of the variables exceeds a threshold level. Once beyond this level, the higher the figure the more severe the forms of torture that are permissible. There is no bright line that can be drawn concerning the point at which the "torture threshold" should be set. More precision can, however, be obtained by first ascribing unit ranges to each of the above variables (depending on their relative importance), then applying the formula to a range of hypothetical situations, and then making a judgment about the numerical point at which torture is acceptable.

There is obviously a degree of imprecision attached to this process and considerable scope for discussion and disagreement regarding the *exact* weight that should be attached to each variable. It is important to emphasize, however, that this is not an argument against our proposal. Rather it is a signal for further discussion and refinement. This is a call that we are confident other commentators will take up. The purpose of this Article is not to set in stone the full range of circumstances where torture is justifiable. Our aim is more modest—to convince readers that torture is justifiable in some circumstances and to set out the variables that are relevant to such an inquiry.

Regulation Better Than Prohibition

In addition to the moral argument for torture as an interrogation device, Dershowitz has argued that torture should be legalized for harm minimization reasons. Dershowitz has pushed for the introduction of "a torture warrant," which would place a "heavy burden on the government to demonstrate by factual evidence the necessity to administer this horrible, horrible technique of torture." He further adds:

> I think that we're much, much better off admitting what we're doing or not doing it at all. I agree with you, it will much better if we never did it. But if we're going to do it and subcontract and find ways of circumventing, it's much better to do what Israel did. They were the only country in the world ever directly to confront the issue, and it led to a supreme court decision, as you say, outlawing torture, and yet Israel has been criticized all over the world for confronting the issue directly. Candor and accountability in a democracy is very important. Hypocrisy has no place.

The obvious counter to this is the slippery slope argument. "If you start opening the door, making a little exception here, a little exception there, you've basically sent the signal that the ends justify the means," resulting in even more torture. The slippery slope argument is often invoked in relation to acts that in themselves are justified, but which have similarities with objectionable practices, and urges that in morally appraising an action we must not only consider its intrinsic features but also the likelihood of it being used as a basis for condoning similar, but in fact relevantly different undesirable practices. The slippery slope argument in the context of torture holds that while torture might be justified in the extreme cases, legalizing it in these circumstances will invariably lead to torture in other less desperate situations.

This argument is not sound in the context of torture. First, the floodgates are already open—torture is widely used, despite the absolute legal prohibition against it. It is, in fact, arguable that it is the existence of an unrealistic absolute ban on torture that has driven torture "beneath the radar screen of accountability" and that the legalization of torture in very rare circumstances would, in fact, reduce the instances of torture because of the increased level of accountability.

Second, there is no evidence to suggest that the *lawful* violation of fundamental human interests will necessarily lead to a violation of fundamental rights where the pre-conditions for the activity are clearly delineated and controlled. Thus, in the United States the use of the death penalty has not resulted in a gradual extension of the offenses for which people may be executed or an erosion in the respect for human life. Third, promulgating the message that the "means justifies the ends [sometimes]" is not inherently undesirable. Debate can then focus on the precise means and ends that are justifiable.

Conclusion

The absolute prohibition against torture is morally unsound and pragmatically unworkable. There is a need for measured discussion regarding the merits of torture as an information gathering device. This would result in the legal use of torture in circumstances where there are a large number of lives at risk in the immediate future and there is no other means of alleviating the threat. While none of the recent high profile cases of torture appear to satisfy these criteria, it is likely that circumstances will arise in the future where torture is legitimate and desirable. A legal framework should be established to properly accommodate these situations.

Philip E. Devine  **NO**

What's Wrong with Torture?

It is hard to believe that we are sitting here talking about torture.

—Dana Priest[1]

On 8 March 2008 President Bush vetoed a bill forbidding torture by the CIA. An attempt to override his veto failed in the House of Representatives three days later. Thus a moral issue that many people thought had been settled, at last so far as public discourse is concerned, is with us, very likely for the duration.

Torture is pain or suffering inflicted for its own sake or as means to an end. Surgery without anesthetics is not torture because the pain inflicted is an unintended side effect. Corporal punishments such as caning, if they do not do permanent damage, might be morally preferable to imprisonment for long periods, and in that case I would not regard them as torture.

But torture does not only inflict pain upon its victim; it also dehumanizes him or her.[2] On any reasonable definition, torture involves not only the infliction of pain but also of fear and bodily shame. Some forms of torture involve outrage to a person's religious or ideological identity. The reported flushing of a copy of the *Qur'an* in the presence of a pious Muslim at Guantánamo Bay (roughly comparable to the defiling of the Sacrament in the presence of a pious Catholic) is an example of this sort of torture.

Torture also dehumanizes the perpetrators. We have every reason to believe that it contributes to a downward spiral of retaliation, and therefore to the collapse of whatever vestiges of civilization may remain into utter barbarism. And the information gained by torture is not reliable since someone under torture will tell his or her tormentors whatever they want to hear. Hence, if it is not possible, in an imperfect world, to abolish torture altogether, it should be limited as much as possible, and in no case receive public approval. As Elaine Scarry puts it,

> The best way to preserve the future from "our enemies" is to reaffirm each day the blanket prohibition of torture, and to work with newspapers, human rights groups, and investigative bodies to document and hold those who torture accountable for their acts. [3] . . .

From *International Philosophical Quarterly*, September 2009. Copyright © 2009 by Philosophy Documentation Center. Reprinted by permission.

One question that we expect a definition of "torture" to answer is how to draw the line between forms of coercive interrogation that are legitimate under extreme circumstances and torture, against which we want to maintain at least a virtually absolute prohibition. (A virtually absolute prohibition has exceptions, but these are so rare that they need and should not be mentioned in moral teaching.)[4] The European Court on Human Rights has identified interrogation methods that, though they fall short of torture in the full sense, are nonetheless prohibited.[5] The expression *torture lite,* which has been coined to cover such behavior,[6] should make us shudder, but the concept still poses complex problems for moral judgment. (For the record, waterboarding is not torture lite in my view.) European courts have also held that the suffering of people on death row renders capital punishment tantamount to torture.[7] Judge Richard Posner has concluded: "What is involved in using the word [torture] is picking out a point along a continuum where the observer's queasiness turns to revulsion."[8] On the other hand, the reluctance of officials to admit that what they are authorizing is torture, or their insistence that it is at most torture lite, does testify to a continuing conviction that torture, real torture, is wrong.[9]

Second, the stock view of torture relies heavily on what Leon Kass calls "the wisdom of repugnance."[10] Such expressions as "warped" and "unnatural" give voice to the deliverances of this wisdom. Many contemporary intellectuals, however, distrust our moral sense as it applies to concrete issues in difficult situations. Green eggs and ham, we are told, may turn out to be delicious—and the point has wide application beyond culinary matters.[11] . . .

It is . . . perilous to rely on shared "gut" responses to defend a prohibition on torture, especially of those people whom many political actors regard as moral outlaws.[12] (This is a stronger contention than disapproval of terrorism on moral or political grounds.)[13] No one has any right to be surprised when the supposedly liberal mainstream media, shortly after the terrorist attacks of 11 September 2001, began to inform us that it was "time to think about torture."[14] . . .

Torture Defended

Jeremy Bentham provides a classic formulation of the "ticking bomb" argument, though his argument does not mention bombs:

> Suppose an occasion to arise, in which a suspicion is entertained . . . that at this very time a considerable number of individuals are actually suffering, by illegal violence inflictions equal in intensity to those which if inflicted by the hand of justice, would universally be spoken of under the name of torture. For the purpose of rescuing from torture these hundred innocents, should any scruple be made of applying equal or superior torture, to extract the requisite information from the mouth of one criminal, who having it in his power to make known the place where at this time the enormity was practising or about to be practised, should refuse to do so?[15]

Michael Levin applies this argument to the contemporary situation:

> Suppose a terrorist has hidden an atomic bomb on Manhattan Island, which will detonate on July 4 unless. . . . If the only way to save [the] lives [of the people there] is to subject the terrorist to the most excruciating possible pain, what grounds can there be for not doing so? . . . Once you concede that torture is justified in extreme cases, you have admitted that the decision to use torture is a matter of balancing innocent lives against the means needed to save them. . . . The line demarcating the legitimate use of torture can be drawn. Torture only the obviously guilty, and only for the sake of saving innocents, and the line between US and THEM will remain clear.[16]

Hence, he argues that torture of terrorists is in general legitimate, when used by an otherwise legitimate government to save innocent lives.

We have every reason to question the general form of Levin's argument. He starts with an extreme case and moves from it to a general permission. Other arguments of this form are standard in the polemical literature. . . . What makes these arguments work, despite their apparent badness, is the difficulty of maintaining a firm line between the permissible and the impermissible once a well-established prohibition has been displaced. Those who deride the slippery slope argument when used defensively find it a very useful offensive weapon.

Whatever moral rules we may accept, as individuals or as a society, there will be occasional cases where everything but the rule itself seems to speak for a violation. These cases, while they may arise in private life, are more common in politics where horrifying consequences on a large scale are a real possibility. But they are unlikely to arise for torture since there is always a palpable reason for abstaining, unless one has excluded the victim from common humanity before proceeding.

. . . My concern is what moral principles should inform our laws and public policies, including the training of our servicemen and women. As David Luban asks, "Should we create a professional cadre of trained torturers? . . . Should there be a medical sub-specialty of torture doctors, who ensure that captives do not die before they talk?"[17] I am concerned, in short, with any policy that might normalize torture as a practice, not with the possibility of an unusual situation in which all moral bets are off. . . .

Even if torture is permissible under some circumstances, it still does not follow, contra Levin's second proposition, that the question of its legitimacy is merely one of balancing goods and evils in a quasi-utilitarian fashion. The social value of the rule, over and above the pain and suffering caused the victim of torture and his friends and family, is a vital consideration. In the words of the Israeli Supreme Court, "[t]his is the destiny of a democracy, as all means are not acceptable to it, and not all means employed by its enemies are open to it."[18]

Levin's third proposition is the crux of his argument. Everything depends on a hardening of the "the line between *us* and *them*," in a context in which, as Levin himself admits, "'clear guilt' is difficult to define."[19] Though not all Muslims are terrorists (or defenders of terrorism) and not all terrorists (or defenders of terrorism) are Muslim, under the pressure of politics such distinctions get lost. The West has experienced, and has every reason to fear, the sort of society that rests on a need for absolute distinctions between *them* and *us*.

The stock case for torture therefore fails. But establishing that conclusion is not the same thing as establishing, in positive terms, the wrongness of torture, or finding principles to distinguish torture from forms of rough treatment possibly legitimate in extreme circumstances.

Torture and Theory

Ethical and social theory has a limited role in the discussion of moral issues. Few people are thoroughgoing utilitarians, and even the most conventional people are not conventionalists in the sense of Bradley or of Hobbes. Moreover, the application of moral theories to real cases displays their malleability.[20] Nonetheless, examining their implications may shed some light on the issue.

Conventionalism

Conventional morality is the result of a tacit agreement among its adherents and of their converging and mutually reinforcing moral emotions.[21] Laws, customs, and codes of professional ethics independent of civil law,[22] as well as the "gut" feelings of my readers, are witnesses to conventional morality.

Torture is a violation of both American and international law—law that was supported, at least until recently, by a degree of moral consensus difficult to obtain about any other issue. The participation of doctors and nurses in torture is a violation of established principles of medical ethics.[23] The Eighth Amendment's prohibition on cruel and unusual punishments trumps any statute or executive policy to the contrary. The United Nations Convention is categorical: "No exceptional circumstances, whether in a state of war of threat of war, internal political instability or other public emergency, may be invoked as a justification of torture."[24] Even the lenient treatment of torturers acting in good faith runs afoul of the Convention's provision that "each State Party shall make these offenses punishable by appropriate penalties that take into account their grave nature."[25] . . .

That torture is evil is as conventional a moral judgment as one can hope to find. But conventional morality everywhere allows that acts that it finds distasteful may sometimes be necessary. For if society is the author of the moral law, then the needs of society—and in particular those of the society to which the agent or evaluator belongs—take precedence over those of any individual. And the judge of those needs, both as a matter of fact and as a matter of value, is society itself through its acknowledged leaders. Moral minorities can and do attempt to pressure or persuade the majority to accept their views but cannot hold, as a matter of secular morality, that they are right even if society persistently rejects their arguments. Nor can one hold, in conventionalist terms, that there are things that one may not do to a person whatever the circumstances (including the judgment of one's society).

Hence, the verdict of conventional morality on torture is that of Jean Bethke Elshtain:

> Few "moral imperatives make such sense on a large scale"—referring to the prohibition against torture—"but breakdown so dramatically in the particular." When you put a microscope above the word "torture" and peer through it, you see a teeming mass of possibilities, prohibitions, complexities, legalities, and ethical perils.[26]

Doing better than this requires going beyond convention.

Liberal Political Philosophy

In contrast with the debates concerning the *Miranda* warnings,[27] torture is not a left-right, conservative-liberal or Democratic-Republican issue in contemporary America.[28] Luban[29] cites William Safire as a conservative opponent of torture and Senator Schumer of Connecticut as a liberal defender. On the other hand, arch-conservative Patrick Buchanan has defended torture on utilitarian grounds,[30] while liberal Antony Lewis approvingly cites Jacobo Timmerman: "You cannot start down that road."[31] The strongest cases against torture strike a centrist note. Colonel Morris Davis, chief prosecutor for the military commissions at Guantánamo Bay from 2005 to 2007, writes: "We either do stuff like that or we do not. It is in our national interest to restore our reputation for the latter."[32]

    I here address the issue in terms of the broad liberal ideology, held by nearly everyone in America, regardless of his political persuasion otherwise. Liberal political philosophy looks for a mean between authoritarianism and anarchism, and for that reason concentrates on limiting the power of the state. Thus it attempts to impose limits on what the majority may do to the minority, usually on strictly secular grounds. The liberal tradition is reflected in such official definitions of *torture* as the following: "any act by which severe pain or suffering, whether physical or mental, is intentionally inflicted on a person . . . when such pain or suffering is inflicted by or at the instigation of or with the acquiescence of a public official or other person acting in an official capacity."[33] (Much, of course, depends on how we read "severe.")

. . .

Kantianism

The Kantian tradition supports a form of liberalism that holds that torture is wrong, whatever the conventions of society, because it is a violation of human dignity. . . . Kant also holds that it is wrong to treat a human being as a mere means. . . .

Utilitarianism

The most obvious objection to the torture of human beings is that it inflicts intense suffering upon its victim, including both physical pain and the "higher pains" of dread, anguish, and self-disgust,[34] as well as many long-term disabling effects. Many torture victims report that these effects are such as to destroy any hope of communication or shared experience.[35] For a utilitarian, however, the torture of a human being is at root no different from the torture of an animal. For most people, however, though cruelty to animals is wrong, but the rules are different from those concerning human beings.[36]

People whom no one calls softies endorse the key premise of the utilitarian argument against interrogational torture—that the information it produces is unreliable. Hobbes writes:

> Also accusations upon torture are not to be reputed as testimonies. For torture is to be used merely as a means of conjecture and light, in the further examination and search for truth; and what in that case is confessed tendeth to the ease of him that is tortured, not to the informing of the torturers, and therefore ought not to have the credit of sufficient testimony; for whether he deliver himself by true or false accusation, he does it by the right of preserving his own life.[37]

A retired Marine general observes that "different kinds of interrogation techniques, most specifically those that are gentle but persistent, that cause a detainee to gain confidence in his interrogator and so forth, usually produce better information."[38] In short, there is a reputable utilitarian case against torture that may suffice for some argumentative purposes. Colonel Davis points out another consequentialist argument against torture: "During the Persian Gulf war in 1991, the Iraqi armed forces surrendered by the tens of thousands because they believed Americans would treat them humanely."[39] . . .

Virtue Ethics

The effect of torture on the torturer and his likely behavior toward others outside official contexts are of persistent concern to opponents of the practice. Even Admiral Mayoga, a participant in Argentina's 'dirty war,' said, "The day we stop condemning torture—although we tortured—the day we become insensitive to mothers who lose their guerilla sons—even though they are guerillas—is the day we stop being human beings."[40]

The underlying picture here is that of a normative human nature that is distorted by certain kinds of action and of "gut" responses that support this judgment even when circumstances might require us to act against it. . . .

Natural Law

Thomas Aquinas neither defended nor opposed torture, though church legislation of 1252 and 1259 authorized those forms that "did not imperil life or limb."[41] Despite such troubling precedents, and the behavior of some priests and bishops on the ground,[42] Roman Catholic authority now says all the right things about torture. The Second Vatican Council summarily condemns "torments inflicted on body or mind" along with a host of other contemporary practices such as abortion and euthanasia.[43] Pope John Paul II cites this passage as establishing exceptionless prohibitions against torture, among other things, without attention to the question why these prohibitions and not others have this character.[44] The pope holds that the existence of absolute norms, though perhaps not all the examples cited, is a deliverance of reason. The Catechism of Catholic Church adds a (not very useful) definition: "'Torture' . . . uses physical or moral violence to extract confessions, punish the guilty, frighten opponents, or satisfy hatred" and regrets the prior acceptance of such practices by church authority.[45]

I take these judgments as results of rational reflection on shared human experience—in other words, of natural law—rather than an appeal to faith or revelation. (Religious responses to torture will depend on the particular features of the tradition in question. In the Christian case, such responses invoke the figure of the crucified Lord.) Yet the attempt to give theoretical substance to this judgment has lagged far behind the firmness with which it is asserted. One prominent and rigorous moral theologian does not even discuss torture, though he implicitly condemns those forms of it that involve mutilation or sexual assault:[46]

Torture, besides being degrading to the torturer is an assault on the entire person of the victim, not on one or more of some list of basic goods. Torturers strip their victims of their humanity, whether because the victim is thought subhuman already, as in penal torture, or for the sake of some further end, as in interrogational torture. (In practice, these forms of assault blend.) The degradation imposed on the victims of torture has at least four aspects.

First, severe physical pain occupies the entire consciousness and blocks out the higher human capacities.

Second, sexual assault reduces a person to his or her bodily parts and functions.

Third, assaults on a person's belief system undermine the terms in which he or she defines his or her humanity: those hostile to Islam should realize that the pertinent alternative is not Christian faith or secular liberalism, but nihilism.

Finally, the aim of interrogational torture is to get its victims to betray their deeply held moral and political commitments, as well as their personal and group loyalties. Men and women who do such things become hateful in their own eyes as well as those of their former associates. . . .

Conclusion

No theoretical argument can fit the horror that torture evokes in many of us. We want to say that such behavior is not only wrong but also unthinkable. Connor Gearty's remarks that proposals to legalize torture are like "reacting to a series of police killings with proposals to reform the law of homicide as to sanction officially approved pre-trial executions."[47]

Torture is important for social and political philosophy because its victim is a social outsider in two different ways. He or she is an outsider already, either on ethnic or ideological grounds, or because accused of a crime so reprobated by authority that, whatever contrary official professions may be in place, the maxim *guilty because accused* informs practice. A man suspected of terrorism is far more likely to be tortured if his name is "Mohammed" than if it is "Timothy." The point of declaring Afghanistan a failed state is to strip its citizens of protection under international law by rendering them stateless. "Prisoner of war" is an honorable legal status to which not all persons in captivity are entitled.[48] . . .

Notes

1. Bert Neuborne et al., "Torture: The Road to Abu Ghraib and Beyond," in *The Torture Debate in America,* ed. Karen J. Greenberg (Cambridge UK: Cambridge Univ. Press, 2006), p. 15.

2. Pronouns arc a problem. Both men and women are tortured, and such torture often takes the form of an assault on their sexuality or sexual role. Hence I find the use of the common gender "she" for torture victims not only a bit of unfortunate academic argot but also in questionable taste. See, for example, David Sussman, "What's Wrong with Torture?" *Philosophy and Public Affairs* 3 (2005): 1. Nicholas Wolterstorff, *Justice* (Princeton NJ: Princeton Univ. Press, 2008), also shows a tendency to use "she" for victims (and not only of torture). I therefore accept the awkwardness of using "he or she" for torture victims; otherwise I use the common gender *he* for persons whose sex is unknown.

3. Scarry, "Five Errors in the Reasoning of Alan Dershowitz," in *Torture: A Collection,* ed. Sanford Levinson (Oxford UK: Oxford Univ. Press, 2004), pp 289–90.

4. On this distinction, see Philip E. Devine, *Natural Law Ethics* (Westport CT: Greenwood, 2000), chap. 12.

5. *Ireland* v. *United Kingdom* (1978) 2 EHRR 25.

6. This phrase is due to Mark Bowden, "The Dark Art of Interrogation," *Atlantic Monthly* 292 (2003): 51. For discussion, see Jean Bethke Elshtain, "Reflections on the Problem of 'Dirty Hands,'" in Levinson, *Torture,* pp. 85–87.

7. *Sering* v. *United Kingdom and Germany,* 11 EHRR 439 (1989), *Pratt* v. *Attorney General for Jamaica,* 1 All E.R.769 (Privy Council, 1993). I am indebted to Richard C. Dieter, "The Death Penalty and Human Rights," http://www.deathpenalty.org/Oxfordpaper.pdf (accessed December 29, 2007), for these references.

8. Richard Posner, "Torture, Terrorism, and Interrogation," in Levinson, *Torture,* p. 291.

9. I owe this point to George Rutherglen.

10. See Kass, "The Wisdom of Repugnance," *New Republic* 216 (1997): 17.

11. Ann Norton, *Leo Strauss and the Politics of Empire* (New Haven CT: Yale Univ. Press, 2004), pp. 81–82.

12. On terrorists as moral outlaws, see Alfred Louch, "Terrorism is Immoral," excerpted from "Terrorism: The Immorality of Belief," *Terrorism: Religious and Secular Justifications,* ed. David C. Rapaport and Jonah Alexander (Cambridge UK: Cambridge Univ. Press, 1989), in *Ethics for Modern Life,* sixth edition, ed. Raziel Abelson and Marie-Louise Friquegnon (Boston MA: Bedford/St. Martin's, 2003), p. 547

13. For a defense of this judgment, see Philip E. Devine and Robert J. Rafalko, "On Terror," *Annals* 463 (1982): 39.

14. Jonathan Alter, *Newsweek* (November 5, 2001): 45.

15. Bentham Mss. Box 74b., p. 429 (May 27, 1804), quoted in John Alan Cohan, "Torture and the Necessity Doctrine," *Valparaiso University Law Review* 41 (2007): 1587, 1590–91.

16. Levin, "The Case for Torture," http://people.brandeis.edu/~teuber/torture.html, accessed September 18, 2007.

17. David Luban, "Liberalism, Torture and the Ticking Bomb," *University of Virginia Law Review* 91 (2005): 1425, 1445, 1446. This essay is reprinted in Greenberg, *The Torture Debate,* essay 1.

18. Israeli Supreme Court, ¶39, pp. 180–81.

19. Levin, "The Case for Torture."

20. See Philip E. Devine, "Theory and Practice in Ethics" in *Moral Theory and Moral Judgments in Medical Ethics,* ed. Baruch A. Brody (Dordrecht, Holland: Kluwer Academic, 1988), pp. 213–23.

21. See Philip E. Devine, "The Structure of Conventional Morality," *International Philosophical Quarterly* 45 (2005): 243.

22. As Steven H. Miles, M.D., *Oath Betrayed* (New York NY: Random House, 2006), p. xii, rightly insists.

23. See ibid. esp. pp. 31–40.

24. United Nations Convention against Torture and Other Inhuman and Degrading Acts (1987, ratified with reservations by the United States, 1994), art. 2 ¶2. Selected articles of the pertinent United Nations Convention are reprinted in Sanford Levinson, "Contemplating Torture," in Levinson, *Torture,* pp. 40–42.

25. United Nations Convention, art. 4 ¶2. This article is seldom if ever put into effect. Levinson, "Contemplating Torture," p. 36.

26. Elshtain, "Reflections," p. 86, quoting Bowden, "The Dark Art," p. 70.

27. For a short discussion of this debate, see Jerome H. Schlonick, "American Interrogation" in Levinson, *Torture,* pp. 114–16.

28. Political labels are dreadful. At this point in my argument I follow popular usage without suggesting that it has any deep significance.

29. Luban, "Liberalism," p. 1426.

30. Patrick Buchanan, "The Case for Torture," *World Net Daily* (March 10, 2003). I am indebted to Giuseppe Butera for this reference, and for that to Colonel Davis below.

31. In Neuborne et al., "Torture," p. 18.

32. Davis, "Unforgivable Behavior, Inadmissible Evidence," *New York Times* (February 17, 2008).

33. United Nations Convention, art. 1 ¶1.

34. Barrie Paskins, "Torture and Philosophy," *Proceedings of the Aristotelian Society* Supp. 52 (1978): 165.

35. See the references collected in Sussman, "What's Wrong with Torture?" p. 1 n1.

36. For discussion, see Philip E. Devine, "The Moral Basis of Vegetarianism," *Philosophy* 53 (1978): 481.

37. Hobbes, *Leviathan,* chap. 14. On the history underlying Hobbes's judgment, see John H. Langbein, "The Legal History of Torture" in Levinson, *Torture,* pp. 93–104.

38. Interview with General Joseph Hoar, "Iraq, Afghanistan, and the Gonzalez Nomination," *Executive Intelligence Review* 32 (2005); http://www.larouchepub.com/other/interviews/205/3202general hoar.html (accessed September 27, 2007). The references to Hobbes and Hoar are due to Michael O'Neill.

39. Davis, "Unforgivable Behavior."

40. Quoted in Levinson, "Contemplating Torture," p. 23.

41. John Finnis, *Aquinas* (Oxford UK: Oxford Univ. Press, 1998), p. 293 n. c.

42. See Mark Osiel, "The Mental State of Torturers," in Levinson, *Torture,* pp. 132–36.

43. Vatican Council II, *Pastoral Constitution on the Modern World* (*Gaudium et Spes*) (1965), §27. This and the two following references following are from Finnis, *Aquinas.*

44. John Paul II, *The Splendor of Truth* (*Veritatis Splendor*) §80.

45. *Catechism of the Catholic Church* (Liguori MD: Liguori Publications 1994), ¶2297 (quoted), ¶2298.

46. Germain Grisez, *The Way of the Lord Jesus,* vol. 2 (Quincy IL: Franciscan Press, 1983), chap. 8, "Life, Health, and Bodily Integrity," esp. Q. G. See §1,¶c, on mutilation and §2, on sexual assault.

47. Gearty, "Legalizing Torture—with a Little Help from our Friends," *Index on Censorship: 1/05: Torture—a User's Manual,* available at www.indexonline.org/en/news/articles/2005/international-legitimizing-torture-with-a-li.shtml. Cited in Brecher, *Torture and the Ticking Bomb,* p. ix.

48. As Andrew McCarthy points out in, "Torture: Thinking about the Unthinkable," in Greenberg, *The Torture Debate,* p. 100.

POSTSCRIPT

Is Torture Ever Justified?

Bagaric and Clarke first remind us that torture is a widespread reality. Just because treaties are signed and international agreements are made, we should not assume that there is no torture (or that what little torture there may be is practiced only by rogue states, dictators, international pariahs, etc.). To this, however, there may be two sorts of responses. One is to seek to get a handle on torture, to regulate it in some way, so that the harm is reduced. Think of a somewhat similar response to the situation in which hard drugs are a social problem: Here a harm reduction strategy may involve the distribution of clean needles. The problem isn't solved in such a way that it no longer exists. Rather, the harm that may result—for example, the transmission of HIV—is minimized. Another type of response is to reinforce the prohibition of torture and not to regulate it. On this view, the occurrence of torture is not something that we have to take into account and come to grip with—it is considered to be in a category like crime: We know that it goes on, but we don't want to *regulate* it. We want to *stamp it out.* We try as hard as we can to prevent others from torturing, but we have ultimate control only over our own actions, not theirs. So the first move in stamping it out is that we ourselves do not practice it. One problem is that this second approach leaves an opening for "the bad guys" to act in ways that we say and show by our actions that we will not act. So, if we follow this path, some will say that we are really being negligent of our duty, for we have to protect and take care of those near and dear to us. We have to protect innocent people from "the bad guys." Here, we face one of the major problems in politics: How to act right in a world in which other people do not act right. For, in the end, this is the kind of world that we live in—the real world, rather than an ideal world.

Further resources on torture are Sanford Levinson, *Torture: A Collection* (Oxford University Press, new edition, 2006); Karen J. Greenberg, *The Torture Debate in America* (Cambridge University Press, 2005); Alfred W. McCoy, *A Question of Torture: CIA Interrogation, from the Cold War to the War on Terror* (American Empire Project) (Owl Books, reprint edition, 2007); Jennifer K. Harbury, *Truth, Torture, and the American Way: The History and Consequences of U.S. Involvement in Torture* (Beacon Press, 2005); Karen J. Greenberg and Joshua L. Dratel, eds., *The Torture Papers: The Road to Abu Ghraib* (Cambridge University Press, 2005); Darius Rejali, *Torture and Democracy* (Princeton University Press, 2007); James E. White, *Contemporary Moral Problems: War, Terrorism, and Torture,* 3rd ed. (Wadsworth Publishing, 2008); Darius Rejali, *Torture and Democracy* (Princeton University Press, 2009); and David Cole, *Torture Memos: Rationalizing the Unthinkable* (The New Press, 2009).

ISSUE 14

Is Physician-Assisted Suicide Wrong?

YES: Richard Doerflinger, from "Assisted Suicide: Pro-Choice or Anti-Life?" *Hastings Center Report* (January/February 1989)

NO: David T. Watts and Timothy Howell, from "Assisted Suicide Is Not Voluntary Active Euthanasia," *Journal of the American Geriatrics Society* (October 1992)

ISSUE SUMMARY

YES: Admitting that religiously based grounds for the wrongness of killing an innocent person are not convincing to many people, Doerflinger argues on mainly secular grounds having to do with inconsistencies in the arguments of supporters of physician-assisted suicide. He examines the idea of autonomy, and the tendency for something like physician-assisted suicide to spread once it becomes initially accepted in a limited way.

NO: Watts and Howell first claim that it is very important to distinguish between *assisted suicide* and *voluntary active euthanasia*. Basically, the first of these is suicide or killing oneself; the second involves being killed by someone else (e.g., a physician). Watts and Howell argue that most of the opposition to physician-assisted suicide turns out to be really opposition to voluntary active euthanasia; furthermore, they argue that physician-assisted suicide would not have the dire consequence that its opponents predict.

The initial situation here is that someone—usually a terminally ill patient—wishes to die and requests physician assistance. (After all, the doctor knows what drugs will do the job, and there have been cases of laypeople botching a suicide attempt and ending up alive but paralyzed.) But a physician who agrees to this request seems to be going against all his or her training and experience (including the Hippocratic Oath and a career devoted to the preservation of life and health). Not only that but, according to the ordinary understanding of murder (as well according to the legal definition and most religious views), to participate in purposely bringing about the death of an innocent person would be murder. (It is no defense to a charge of murder that the victim asked you to do it—contrast the case of killing in self-defense where such killing is indeed a defense against the charge of murder, and is generally considered not to be wrong anyway.)

Consider one particular case that was reported a few years ago. A physicist who had long been exposed to X-rays in his scientific practice had cancer. The disease was at an advanced stage. During the course of the cancer, the physicist had lost his left hand and two of the fingers on the right hand; he had lost other body parts as well; and he had lost his sight. Hospitalized, and in great pain, he was given about a year to live. He was not able to kill himself and begged his brothers to kill him. The first two brothers refused. But the third brother agreed, brought a gun to the hospital, and shot his dying brother.

Many people would be quite sympathetic in a case like this, but nevertheless warn us of a slippery slope. If we allow physician-assisted suicide, it might be said, the policy would expand. Even if we grant that in fact a case like the physicist is the most appropriate case for physician-assisted suicide, most cases won't be like that. What about a physicist who lapses into a coma and can't express his wishes? Or a person who is still at the early stages of some fatal disease and is not in great pain at the moment, but has nothing to look forward to but death? What about a great athlete who wants to die because he now finds himself confined to a wheelchair? What about elderly people who request that they be killed through physician-assisted suicide because they are not well and do not wish to be "a burden" on their offspring? Perhaps family members who wish to inherit something (rather than see it go for fruitless medical expenses) and will subtly get the message across to their aged relatives that "it's time to go"? The list goes on. The problem, opponents to physician-assisted suicide might say, is that once you begin to allow this in some cases, it's easy to begin sliding down a slippery slope and ending up with results that are not at all what was desired in the first place.

In the following essays, Richard Doerflinger first argues that physician-assisted suicide is wrong and that the whole idea of there being such a thing as "rational suicide" is flawed. Then David Watts and Timothy Howell distinguish between various categories of euthanasia and suicide, and conclude that there really are cases of rational suicide and that physician-assisted suicide is not necessarily wrong.

YES

Richard Doerflinger

Assisted Suicide: Pro-Choice or Anti-Life?

The intrinsic wrongness of directly killing the innocent, even with the victim's consent, is all but axiomatic in the Jewish and Christian worldviews that have shaped the laws and mores of Western civilization and the self-concept of its medical practitioners. This norm grew out of the conviction that human life is sacred because it is created in the image and likeness of God, and called to fulfillment in love of God and neighbor.

With the pervasive secularization of Western culture, norms against euthanasia and suicide have to a great extent been cut loose from their religious roots to fend for themselves. Because these norms seem abstract and unconvincing to many, debate tends to dwell not on the wrongness of the act as such but on what may follow from its acceptance. Such arguments are often described as claims about a "slippery slope," and debate shifts to the validity of slippery slope arguments in general.

Since it is sometimes argued that acceptance of assisted suicide is an outgrowth of respect for personal autonomy, and not lack of respect for the inherent worth of human life. I will outline how autonomy-based arguments in favor of assisting suicide do entail a statement about the value of life. I will also distinguish two kinds of slippery slope argument often confused with each other, and argue that those who favor social and legal acceptance of assisted suicide have not adequately responded to the slippery slope claims of their opponents.

Assisted Suicide versus Respect for Life

Some advocates of socially sanctioned assisted suicide admit (and a few boast) that their proposal is incompatible with the conviction that human life is of intrinsic worth. Attorney Robert Risley has said that he and his allies in the Hemlock Society are "so bold" as to seek to "overturn the sanctity of life principle" in American society. A life of suffering, "racked with pain," is "not the kind of life we cherish."[1]

Others eschew Risley's approach, perhaps recognizing that it creates a slippery slope toward practices almost universally condemned. If society is to help terminally ill patients to commit suicide because it agrees that death is

From *Hastings Center Report,* Special Supplement, vol. 19, no. 1, January/February 1989, pp. 16–19. Copyright © 1989 by The Hastings Center. Reprinted by permission of the publisher and author.

objectively preferable to a life of hardship, it will be difficult to draw the line at the seriously ill or even at circumstances where the victim requests death.

Some advocates of assisted suicide therefore take a different course, arguing that it is precisely respect for the dignity of the human person that demands respect for individual freedom as the noblest feature of that person. On this rationale a decision as to when and how to die deserves the respect and even the assistance of others because it is the ultimate exercise of self-determination—"ultimate" both in the sense that it is the last decision one will ever make and in the sense that through it one takes control of one's entire self. What makes such decisions worthy of respect is not the fact that death is chosen over life but that it is the individual's own free decision about his or her future.

Thus Derek Humphry, director of the Hemlock Society, describes his organization as "pro-choice" on this issue. Such groups favor establishment of a constitutional "right to die" modeled on the right to abortion delineated by the U.S. Supreme Court in 1973. This would be a right to choose *whether or not* to end one's own life, free of outside government interference. In theory, recognition of such a right would betray no bias toward choosing death.

Life versus Freedom

This autonomy-based approach is more appealing than the straight-forward claim that some lives are not worth living, especially to Americans accustomed to valuing individual liberty above virtually all else. But the argument departs from American traditions on liberty in one fundamental respect.

When the Declaration of Independence proclaimed the inalienable human rights to be "life, liberty, and the pursuit of happiness," this ordering reflected a long-standing judgment about their relative priorities. Life, a human being's very earthly existence, is the most fundamental right because it is the necessary condition for all other worldly goods including freedom; freedom in turn makes it possible to pursue (without guaranteeing that one will attain) happiness. Safeguards against the deliberate destruction of life are thus seen as necessary to protect freedom and all other human goods. This line of thought is not explicitly religious but is endorsed by some modern religious groups:

> The first right of the human person is his life. He has other goods and
> some are more precious, but this one is fundamental—the condition of
> all the others. Hence it must be protected above all others.[2]

On this view suicide is not the ultimate exercise of freedom but its ultimate self-contradiction: A free act that by destroying life, destroys all the individual's future earthly freedom. If life is more basic than freedom, society best serves freedom by discouraging rather than assisting self-destruction. Sometimes one must limit particular choices to safeguard freedom itself, as when American society chose over a century ago to prevent people from selling themselves into slavery even of their own volition.

It may be argued in objection that the person who ends his life has not truly suffered loss of freedom, because unlike the slave he need not continue to exist under the constraints of a loss of freedom. But the slave does have some freedom, including the freedom to seek various means of liberation or at least the freedom to choose what attitude to take regarding his plight. To claim that a slave is worse off than a corpse is to value a situation of limited freedom less than one of no freedom whatsoever, which seems inconsistent with the premise of the "pro-choice" position. Such a claim also seems tantamount to saying that some lives (such as those with less than absolute freedom) are objectively not worth living, a position that "pro-choice" advocates claim not to hold.

It may further be argued in objection that assistance in suicide is only being offered to those who can no longer meaningfully exercise other freedoms due to increased suffering and reduced capabilities and lifespan. To be sure, the suffering of terminally ill patients who can no longer pursue the simplest everyday tasks should call for sympathy and support from everyone in contact with them. But even these hardships do not constitute total loss of freedom of choice. If they did, one could hardly claim that the patient is in a position to make the ultimate free choice about suicide. A dying person capable of making a choice of that kind is also capable of making less monumental free choices about coping with his or her condition. This person generally faces a bewildering array of choices regarding the assessment of his or her past life and the resolution of relationships with family and friends. He or she must finally choose at this time what stance to take regarding the eternal questions about God, personal responsibility, and the prospects of a destiny after death.

In short, those who seek to maximize free choice may with consistency reject the idea of assisted suicide, instead facilitating all choices *except* that one which cuts short all choices.

In fact proponents of assisted suicide do *not* consistently place freedom of choice as their highest priority. They often defend the moderate nature of their project by stating, with Derek Humphry, that "we do not encourage suicide for any reason except to relieve unremitting suffering." It seems their highest priority is the "pursuit of happiness" (or avoidance of suffering) and not "liberty" as such. Liberty or freedom of choice loses its value if one's choices cannot relieve suffering and lead to happiness; life is of instrumental value, insofar as it makes possible choices that can bring happiness.

In this value system, choice as such does not warrant unqualified respect. In difficult circumstances, as when care of a suffering and dying patient is a great burden on family and society, the individual who chooses life despite suffering will not easily be seen as rational, thus will not easily receive understanding and assistance for this choice.

In short, an unqualified "pro-choice" defense of assisted suicide lacks coherence because corpses have no choices. A particular choice, that of death, is given priority over all the other choices it makes impossible, so the value of choice as such is not central to the argument.

A restriction of this rationale to cases of terminal illness also lacks logical force. For if ending a brief life of suffering can be good, it would seem that ending a long life of suffering may be better. Surely the approach of the California "Humane and Dignified Death Act"—where consensual killing of a patient expected to die in six months is presumably good medical practice, but killing the same patient a month or two earlier is still punishable as homicide—is completely arbitrary.

Slippery Slopes, Loose Cannons

Many arguments against sanctioning assisted suicide concern a different kind of "slippery slope": Contingent factors in the contemporary situation may make it virtually inevitable in practice, if not compelling at the level of abstract theory, that removal of the taboo against assisted suicide will lead to destructive expansions of the right to kill the innocent. Such factors may not be part of euthanasia advocates' own agenda; but if they exist and are beyond the control of these advocates, they must be taken into account in judging the moral and social wisdom of opening what may be a Pandora's box of social evils.

To distinguish this sociological argument from our dissection of the conceptual *logic* of the rationale for assisted suicide, we might call it a "loose cannon" argument. The basic claim is that socially accepted killing of innocent persons will interact with other social factors to threaten lives that advocates of assisted suicide would agree should be protected. These factors at present include the following:

The psychological vulnerability of elderly and dying patients. Theorists may present voluntary and involuntary euthanasia as polar opposites; in practice there are many steps on the road from dispassionate, autonomous choice to subtle coercion. Elderly and disabled patients are often invited by our achievement-oriented society to see themselves as useless burdens on younger, more vital generations. In this climate, simply offering the *option* of "self-deliverance" shifts a burden of proof, so that helpless patients must ask themselves why they are *not* availing themselves of it. Society's offer of death communicates the message to certain patients that they *may* continue to live if they wish but the rest of us have no strong interest in their survival. Indeed, once the choice of a quick and painless death is officially accepted as rational, resistance to this choice may be seen as eccentric or even selfish.[3]

The crisis in health care costs. The growing incentives for physicians, hospitals, families, and insurance companies to control the cost of health care will bring additional pressures to bear on patients. Curt Garbesi, the Hemlock Society's legal consultant, argues that autonomy-based groups like Hemlock must "control the public debate" so assisted suicide will not be seized upon by public officials as a cost-cutting device. But simply basing one's own defense of assisted suicide on individual autonomy does not solve the problem. For in the economic sphere also, offering the option of suicide would subtly shift burdens of proof.

Adequate health care is now seen by at least some policymakers as a human right, as something a society owes to all its members. Acceptance of assisted suicide as an option for those requiring expensive care would not only offer health care providers an incentive to make that option seem attractive—it would also demote all other options to the status of strictly private choices by the individual. As such they may lose their moral and legal claim to public support—in much the same way that the U.S. Supreme Court, having protected abortion under a constitutional "right of privacy," has quite logically denied any government obligation to provide public funds for this strictly private choice. As life-extending care of the terminally ill is increasingly seen as strictly elective, society may become less willing to appropriate funds for such care, and economic pressures to choose death will grow accordingly.

Legal doctrines on "substituted judgment." American courts recognizing a fundamental right to refuse life-sustaining treatment have concluded that it is unjust to deny this right to the mentally incompetent. In such cases the right is exercised on the patient's behalf by others, who seek either to interpret what the patient's own wishes might have been or to serve his or her best interests. Once assisted suicide is established as a fundamental right, courts will almost certainly find that it is unjust not to extend this right to those unable to express their wishes. Hemlock's political arm, Americans Against Human Suffering, has underscored continuity between "passive" and "active" euthanasia by offering the Humane and Dignified Death Act as an amendment to California's "living will" law, and by including a provision for appointment of a proxy to choose the time and manner of the patient's death. By such extensions our legal system would accommodate nonvoluntary, if not involuntary, active euthanasia.

Expanded definitions of terminal illness. The Hemlock Society wishes to offer assisted suicide only to those suffering from terminal illnesses. But some Hemlock officials have in mind a rather broad definition of "terminal illness." Derek Humphry says "two and a half million people alone are dying of Alzheimer's disease."[4] At Hemlock's 1986 convention, Dutch physician Pieter Admiraal boasted that he had recently broadened the meaning of terminal illness in his country by giving a lethal injection to a young quadriplegic woman—a Dutch court found that he acted within judicial guidelines allowing euthanasia for the terminally ill, because paralyzed patients have difficulty swallowing and could die from aspirating their food at any time.

The medical and legal meaning of terminal illness has already been expanded in the United States by professional societies, legislatures, and courts in the context of so-called passive euthanasia. A Uniform Rights of the Terminally Ill Act proposed by the National Conference of Commissioners on Uniform State Laws in 1986 defines a terminal illness as one that would cause the patient's death in a relatively short time if life-preserving treatment is *not* provided—prompting critics to ask if all diabetics, for example, are "terminal" by definition. Some courts already see comatose and vegetative states as "terminal" because they involve an inability to swallow that will lead to death unless artificial feeding is instituted. In the *Hilda Peter* case, the New Jersey Supreme Court declared that the traditional state interest in "preserving life" referred only to "cognitive and sapient life" and not to mere "biological" existence, implying that unconscious patients are terminal, or perhaps as good as dead, so far as state interests are concerned. Is there any reason to think that American law would suddenly resurrect the older, narrower meaning of "terminal illness" in the context of *active* euthanasia?

Prejudice against citizens with disabilities. If definitions of terminal illness expand to encompass states of severe physical or mental disability, another social reality will increase the pressure on patients to choose death: long-standing prejudice, sometimes bordering on revulsion, against people with disabilities. While it is seldom baldly claimed that disabled people have "lives not worth living," able-bodied people often say they could not live in a severely disabled state or would prefer death. In granting Elizabeth Bouvia a right to refuse a feeding tube that preserved her life, the California Appeals Court bluntly stated that her physical handicaps led her to "consider her existence meaningless" and that "she cannot be faulted for so concluding." According to disability rights expert Paul Longmore, in a society with such attitudes toward the disabled, "talk of their 'rational' or 'voluntary' suicide is simply Orwellian newspeak."[5]

Character of the medical profession. Advocates of assisted suicide realize that most physicians will resist giving lethal injections because they are trained, in Garbesi's words, to be "enemies of death." The California Medical Association firmly opposed the Humane and Dignified Death Act, seeing it as an attack on the ethical foundation of the medical profession.

Yet California appeals judge Lynn Compton was surely correct in his concurring opinion in the *Bouvia* case, when he said that a sufficient number of willing physicians can be found once legal sanctions against assisted suicide are dropped. Judge Compton said this had clearly been the case with abortion, despite the fact that the Hippocratic Oath condemns abortion as strongly as it condemns euthanasia. Opinion polls of physicians bear out the judgment that a significant number would perform lethal injections if they were legal.

Some might think this division or ambivalence about assisted suicide in the medical profession will restrain broad expansions of the practice. But if anything, Judge Compton's analogy to our experience with abortion suggests the opposite. Most physicians still have qualms about abortion, and those who perform abortions on a full-time basis are not readily accepted by their colleagues as paragons of the healing art. Consequently they tend to form their own professional societies, bolstering each other's positive self-image and developing euphemisms to blunt the moral edge of their work.

Once physicians abandon the traditional medical self-image, which rejects direct killing of patients in all circumstances, their new substitute self-image may require ever more aggressive efforts to make this killing more widely practiced and favorably received. To allow killing by physicians in certain circumstances may create a new lobby of physicians in favor of expanding medical killing.

The human will to power. The most deeply buried yet most powerful driving force toward widespread medical killing is a fact of human nature: Human beings are tempted to enjoy exercising power over others; ending another person's life is the ultimate exercise of that power. Once the taboo against killing has been set aside, it becomes progressively easier to channel one's aggressive instincts into the destruction of life in other contexts. Or as James Burtchaell has said: "There is a sort of virginity about murder; once one has violated it, it is awkward to refuse other invitations by saying, 'But that would be murder!'"[6]

Some will say assisted suicide for the terminally ill is morally distinguishable from murder and does not logically require termination of life in other circumstances. But my point is that the skill and the instinct to kill are more easily turned to other lethal tasks once they have an opportunity to exercise themselves. Thus Robert Jay Lifton has perceived differences between the German "mercy killings" of the 1930s and the later campaign to annihilate the Jews of Europe, yet still says that "at the heart of the Nazi enterprise . . . is the destruction of the boundary between healing and killing."[7] No other boundary separating these two situations was as fundamental as this one, and thus none was effective once it was crossed. As a matter of historical fact, personnel who had conducted the "mercy killing" program were quickly and readily recruited to operate the killing chambers of the death camps.[8] While the contemporary United States fortunately lacks the anti-Semitic and totalitarian attitudes that made the Holocaust possible, it has its own trends and pressures that may combine with acceptance of medical killing to produce a distinctively American catastrophe in the name of individual freedom.

These "loose cannon" arguments are not conclusive. All such arguments by their nature rest upon a reading and extrapolation of certain contingent factors in society. But their combined force provides a serious case against taking the irreversible step of sanctioning assisted suicide for any class of persons, so long as those who advocate this step fail to demonstrate why these predictions are wrong. If the strict philosophical case on behalf of "rational suicide" lacks coherence, the pragmatic claim that its acceptance would be a social benefit lacks grounding in history or common sense.

References

1. Presentation at the Hemlock Society's Third National Voluntary Euthanasia Conference, "A Humane and Dignified Death," September 25–27, 1986, Washington, DC. All quotations from Hemlock Society officials are from the proceedings of this conference unless otherwise noted.
2. Vatican Congregation for the Doctrine of the Faith, *Declaration on Procured Abortion* (1974), para. 11.
3. I am indebted for this line of argument to Dr. Eric Chevlen.
4. Denis Herbstein, "Campaigning for the Right to Die," *International Herald Tribune*, 11 September 1986.
5. Paul K. Longmore, "Elizabeth Bouvia, Assisted Suicide and Social Prejudice," *Issues in Law & Medicine* 3:2 (1987), 168.
6. James T. Burtchaell, *Rachel Weeping and Other Essays on Abortion* (Kansas City: Andrews & McMeel, 1982), 188.
7. Robert Jay Lifton, *The Nazi Doctors: Medical Killing and the Psychology of Genocide* (New York: Basic Books, 1986), 14.
8. Yitzhak Rad, *Belzec, Sobibor, Treblinka* (Bloomington, IN: Indiana University Press, 1987), 11, 16–17.

David T. Watts
and Timothy Howell

 **NO**

Assisted Suicide Is Not Voluntary Active Euthanasia

Ongoing developments continue to spotlight the controversial issues of voluntary active euthanasia and assisted suicide. In November 1991, Washington State's Initiative 119, which would have allowed physicians, in certain circumstances, to aid terminally ill patients' dying, was defeated by 56% to 44%.[1] Dr. Jack Kevorkian assisted in the suicides of two non-terminally ill women in October 1991, leading to the suspension of his Michigan medical license.[2] Murder charges were later brought against Kevorkian by a grand jury. In New Hampshire, a bill has been introduced which would allow physicians to assist patients' suicides but not perform active euthanasia.[3, 4]

Such developments highlight some of the confusion emerging from discussions of voluntary active euthanasia (V.A.E.) and assisted suicide. A significant source of confusion has been the tendency to join these concepts or even to consider them synonymous. For example, the AGS Position Statement on V.A.E. and a recent article by Teno and Lynn in the *Journal of the American Geriatrics Society* both reject easing restrictions on V.A.E. and assisted suicide while making arguments *only* against euthanasia.[5, 6] The National Hospice Organization also opposes euthanasia and assisted suicide, but it, too, appears to blur the distinction between them in stating that "euthanasia encompasses . . . in some settings, physician-assisted suicide."[7] Others appear to use the terms euthanasia and assisted suicide synonymously in arguing against both.[8]

In contrast, the AMA Ethics and Health Policy Counsel argues against physician-assisted suicide and distinguishes this from euthanasia.[9] The AMA Council on Ethical and Judicial Affairs also acknowledges there is "an ethically relevant distinction between euthanasia and assisted suicide that makes assisted suicide a more attractive option." Yet it then goes on to assert that "the ethical concerns about physician-assisted suicide are similar to those of euthanasia since both are essentially interventions intended to cause death."[10]

In order to weigh and appreciate the merits of the different arguments for and against V.A.E. and physician-assisted suicide, it is critical that appropriate distinctions be made. For example, we believe the arguments made in the references cited above and by others[11, 12] against euthanasia are telling. However, we find that these same arguments are substantially weaker when used against assisted suicide. And while we agree with the AMA Council on Ethical and

From *Journal of the American Geriatrics Society,* vol. 40, no. 10, October 1992, pp. 1043–1046. Copyright © 1992 by American Geriatrics Society. Reprinted by permission of Wiley-Blackwell.

Judicial Affairs that an ethically relevant distinction exists between euthanasia and assisted suicide, we think it is important to distinguish further between different forms of assisted suicide. Only by doing so can we begin to sort out some of the apparent confusion in attitudes toward these issues. We caution our readers that the literature on this topic, while growing, remains preliminary, with little empirical research yet completed.[13] Our arguments, however, are philosophical in nature and do not ultimately stand or fall on empirical data.

Definitions

Voluntary active euthanasia: Administration of medications or other interventions intended to cause death at a patient's request.

Assisted suicide: Provision of information, means, or direct assistance by which a patient may take his or her own life. Assisted suicide involves several possible levels of assistance: *providing information,* for example, may mean providing toxicological information or describing techniques by which someone may commit suicide; *providing the means* can involve written prescriptions for lethal amounts of medication; supervising or *directly aiding* includes inserting an intravenous line and instructing on starting a lethal infusion.

These levels of assistance have very different implications. Providing only information or means allows individuals to retain the greatest degree of control in choosing the time and mode of their deaths. Physician participation is only indirect. This type of limited assistance is exemplified by the widely reported case of Dr. Timothy Quill, who prescribed a lethal quantity of barbiturates at the request of one of his patients who had leukemia.[14] By contrast, supervising or directly aiding is the type of physician involvement characterizing the case of Dr. Jack Kevorkian and Janet Adkins. Adkins was a 54-year-old woman with a diagnosis of Alzheimer-type dementia who sought Kevorkian's assistance in ending her life. Dr. Kevorkian inserted an intravenous catheter and instructed Mrs. Adkins on activating a lethal infusion of potassium following barbiturate sedation, a process personally monitored by Kevorkian.[15] This form of assisted suicide carries significant potential for physician influence or control of the process, and from it there is only a relatively short step to physician initiation (i.e., active euthanasia). We therefore reject physician-supervised suicide for the arguments commonly made against V.A.E., namely, that legalization would have serious adverse consequences, including potential abuse of vulnerable persons, mistrust of physicians, and diminished availability of supportive services for the dying.[6, 7, 10–12] We find each of these arguments, however, insufficient when applied to more limited forms of physician-assisted suicide (i.e., providing information or means).

Will Assisted Suicide Lead to Abuse of Vulnerable Persons?

A major concern is that some patients will request euthanasia or assisted suicide out of convenience to others.[6, 9] It is certainly possible that a patient's desire to avoid being a burden could lead to such a request. With euthanasia, there is danger that a patient's request might find too ready acceptance. With assisted suicide, however, the ultimate decision, and the ultimate action, are the patient's, not the physician's. This places an important check and balance on physician initiation or patient acquiescence in euthanasia. As the AMA Council on Ethical and Judicial Affairs acknowledges, a greater level of patient autonomy is afforded by physician-assisted suicide than by euthanasia.[10]

Culturally or socially mediated requests for assisted suicide would remain a significant concern. Patients might also request aid in suicide out of fear, pain, ambivalence, or depression.[16] The requirement that patients commit the ultimate act themselves cannot alone provide a sufficient safeguard. It would be incumbent on physicians to determine, insofar as possible, that requests for assisted suicide were not unduly influenced and that reversible conditions were optimally treated. As to how physicians might respond to such requests, data from the Netherlands indicate that about 75% of euthanasia requests in that country are refused.[17] It is our impression that most requests for assisted suicide, therefore, appear to represent opportunities for improved symptom control. We believe most serious requests would likely come from patients experiencing distressing symptoms of terminal illness.[18] By opening the door for counseling or treatment of reversible conditions, requests for assisted suicide might actually lead to averting some suicides which would have otherwise occurred.

Another concern regarding euthanasia is that it could come to be accepted without valid consent and that such a practice would more likely affect the frail and impoverished. The Remmelink Commission's investigation of euthanasia in the Netherlands appeared to justify such concerns in estimating that Dutch physicians may have performed 1,000 acts of involuntary euthanasia involving incompetent individuals.[19] But while euthanasia opens up the possibility of invalid consent, with assisted suicide consent is integral to the process. Because the choice of action clearly rests with the individual, there is substantially less likelihood for the abuse of assisted suicide as a societal vehicle for cost containment. And there is little basis for assuming that requests for assisted suicide would come primarily from frail and impoverished persons. Prolonged debilitation inherent in many illnesses is familiar to an increasing number of patients, family members, and health professionals. Such illnesses represent a greater financial threat to the middle- and upper-middle class, since the poor and disenfranchised have less to spend down to indigency. Thus, we suspect requests to assisted suicide might actually be more common from the educated, affluent, and outspoken.

Patients diagnosed with terminal or debilitating conditions are often vulnerable. We agree that such patients might request assisted suicide out of fear of pain, suffering, or isolation, and that too ready acceptance of such requests could be disastrous. Yet, we believe that patients' interests can be safeguarded by requirements for persistent, competent requests as well as thorough assessments for conditions, such as clinical depression, which could be reversed, treated, or ameliorated. Foley recently outlined an approach to the suicidal cancer patient.[20] We share her view that many such patients' requests to terminate life are altered by the availability of expert, continuing hospice services.

We concur with Foley and others in calling for the wider availability of such services,[5, 6] so that requests for assisted suicide arising from pain, depression, or other distressing symptoms can be reduced to a minimum.

Would Assisted Suicide Undermine Trust Between Patients and Physicians?

The cardinal distinction between V.A.E. and assisted suicide is that V.A.E. is killing by physicians, while suicide is self-killing. Prohibiting both euthanasia and physician-supervised suicide (i.e., with direct physician involvement) should diminish worries that patients might have about physicians wrongly administering lethal medicine. At present, physician-patient trust is compromised by widespread concern that physicians try too hard to keep dying patients alive. The very strength of the physician-patient relationship has been cited as a justification for physician involvement in assisted suicide.[21]

A number of ethicists have expressed concern that both euthanasia and assisted suicide, if legalized, would have a negative impact on the way society perceives the role of physicians.[6, 9, 11, 12] Limited forms of assisted suicide, however, have been viewed more positively.[22] Public and professional attitudes appear to be evolving on this issue. A 1990 Gallup poll found that 66% of respondents believed someone in great pain, with "no hope of improvement," had the moral right to commit suicide; in 1975 the figure was 41%.[23] A panel of distinguished physicians has stated that it is not immoral for a physician to assist in the rational suicide of a terminally ill person.[24] The recent publication of a book on techniques of committing or assisting suicide evoked wide interest and significant support for the right of people to take control of their dying.[25] For a significant segment of society, physician involvement in assisted suicide may be welcomed, not feared. Furthermore, while relatively few might be likely to seek assistance with suicide if stricken with a debilitating illness, a substantial number might take solace knowing they could request such assistance.

There is another argument raised against V.A.E. that we believe also falters when used to object to assisted suicide. It has been maintained that prohibiting euthanasia forces physicians to focus on the humane care of dying patients, including meticulous attention to their symptoms.[6, 18] This argument implies that physicians find it easier to relieve the suffering of dying patients by ending their lives rather than attempting the difficult task of palliating their symptoms. But for some patients, the suffering may not be amenable to even the most expert palliation. Even in such instances, some argue that limited forms of assisted suicide should be prohibited on the grounds that not to forbid them would open the door for more generalized, less stringent applications of assisted suicide.

To us, this "slippery slope" argument seems to imply that the moral integrity of the medical profession must be maintained, even if at the cost of prolonged, unnecessary suffering by at least some dying patients. We believe such a posture is itself inhumane and not acceptable. It contradicts a fundamental principle that is an essential ingredient of physician-patient trust: that patient comfort should be a primary goal of the physician in the face of incurable illness. Furthermore, by allowing limited physician involvement in assisted suicide, physicians can respect both the principle of caring that guides them and the patients for whom caring alone is insufficient. We concede that there is another alternative: terminally ill patients who cannot avoid pain while awake may be given continuous anesthetic levels of medication.[6] But this is exactly the sort of dying process we believe many in our society want to avoid.

Will Assisted Suicide and Euthanasia Weaken Societal Resolve to Increase Resources Allocated to Care of the Dying?

This argument assumes that V.A.E. and assisted suicide would both be widely practiced, and that their very availability would decrease tangible concern for those not choosing euthanasia or suicide. However, euthanasia is rarely requested even by terminal cancer patients.[6] In the Netherlands, euthanasia accounts for less than 2% of all deaths.[17] These data suggest that even if assisted suicide were available to those with intractable pain or distressing terminal conditions, it would likely be an option chosen by relatively few. With assisted suicide limited to relatively few cases, this argument collapses. For with only a few requesting assisted suicide, the vast number of patients with debilitating illnesses would be undiminished, and their numbers should remain sufficient to motivate societal concern for their needs. Furthermore, to withhold assisted suicide from the few making serious, valid requests would be to subordinate needlessly the interests of these few to those of the many. Compounding their tragedy would be the fact that these individuals could not even benefit from any increase in therapeutic resources prompted by their suffering, insofar as their conditions are, by definition, not able to be ameliorated.

Conclusion

We have argued that assisted suicide and voluntary active euthanasia are different and that each has differing implications for medical practice and society. Further discussion should consider the merits and disadvantages of each, a process enhanced by contrasting them. We have further argued that different forms of assisted suicide can be distinguished both clinically and philosophically. Although some may argue that all forms of assisted suicide are fundamentally the same, we believe the differences can be contrasted as starkly as a written prescription and a suicide machine.

We do not advocate ready acceptance of requests for suicide, nor do we wish to romanticize the concept of rational suicide.[26] In some situations, however, where severe debilitating illness cannot be reversed, suicide may represent a rational choice. If this is the case, then physician assistance could make the process more humane. Along with other geriatricians, we often face dilemmas involving the management of chronic illnesses in late life. We believe we can best serve our patients, and preserve their trust, by respecting their desire for autonomy, dignity, and quality, not only of life, but of dying.

References

1. Caplan A. Patient rights measure needs push from Bush. Wis State J November 13, 1991, p 11A.

2. Holyfield J. Doctor who helped suicides has his license suspended. Wis State J November 21, 1991, p 5A.

3. Beresford L., ed. Euthanasia movement may be helping spur new additional attention to pain relief. Hospice News Serv 1992;3:1–3.

4. Anonymous. New Hampshire: Lawmakers file suicide bill. Wis State J November 13, 1991, p 3A.

5. AGS Public Policy Committee. Voluntary active euthanasia. J Am Geriatr Soc 1991;39:826.

6. Teno J. Lynn J. Voluntary active euthanasia: The individual case and public policy. J Am Geriatr Soc 1991;39:827–830.

7. National Hospice Organization. Statement of the National Hospice Organization Opposing the Legalization of Euthanasia and Assisted Suicide. Arlington, VA: National Hospice Organization, 1991.

8. Travis R. Two arguments against euthanasia (letter). Gerontologist 1991; 31:561–562.

9. Orentlicher D. Physician participation in assisted suicide. JAMA 1989; 262; 1844–1845 .

10. AMA. Report of the Council on Ethical and Judicial Affairs: Decisions Near the End of Life. Chicago, IL: American Medical Association. 1991.

11. Singer PA. Should doctors kill patients? Can Med Assoc J 1988; 138:1001–1001.

12. Singer PA, Siegler M. Euthanasia—a critique. N Engl J Med 1990; 322: 1881–1883.

13. Watts DT, Howell T, Priefer BA. Geriatricians' attitudes toward assisting suicide of dementia patients. J Am Geriatr Soc 1992, September 40:878–885.

14. Quill TE. Death and dignity: A case of individualized decision making. N Engl J Med 1991;324:691–694.

15. Cassel CK, Meier DE. Morals and moralism in the debate over euthanasia and assisted suicide. N Engl J Med 1990;323:750–752.

16. Jackson DL, Youngner S. Patient autonomy and "death with dignity": Some clinical caveats. N Engl J Med 1979;301:404–408.

17. Van der Maas PJ, Van Delden JJM, Pijnenborg L. Looman CWN. Euthanasia and other medical decisions concerning the end of life. Lancet 1991; 338:669–74.

18. Palmore EB. Arguments for assisted suicide (letter). Gerontologist 1991; 31:854.

19. Karel R. Undertreatment of pain, depression needs to be addressed before euthanasia made legal in U.S. Psychiatric News. December 20, 1991, pp 5, 13, 23.

20. Foley KM. The relationship of pain and symptom management to patient requests for physician-assisted suicide. J Pain Symptom Manag 1991; 6:289–297.

21. Jecker NS. Giving death a hand. When the dying and the doctor stand in a special relationship. J Am Geriatr Soc 1991;39:831–835.

22. American College of Physicians ACP to DA, Grand Jury: Dr. Quill acted "humanely." ACP Observer, September, 1991, p 5.

23. Ames K. Wilson L. Sawhill R et al. Last rights. Newsweek August 26, 1991, pp 40–41.

24. Wanzer SH, Federman DD, Adelstein SJ et al. The physician's responsibility toward hopelessly ill patients: A second look. N Engl J Med 1989;320:844–849.

25. Humphry D. Final Exit: The Practicalities of Self-Deliverance and Assisted Suicide for the Dying. Eugene, OR: The Hemlock Society (distributed by Carol Publishing, Secaucus, NJ). 1991.

26. Conwell Y, Caine ED. Rational suicide and the right to die: Reality and myth. N Engl J Med 1991;325:1100–1103.

POSTSCRIPT

Is Physician-Assisted Suicide Wrong?

We normally understand that physician-assisted suicide, if adopted as a matter of policy, will bring with it certain regulations and safeguards. Clearly, just asking a physician for assistance is not going to be sufficient. Even ordinary people are sometimes depressed, and it is understandable that people with a serious illness are even more likely to be depressed. So, at a minimum, people who request physician-assisted suicide would have to be screened for depression.

Moreover, as Watts and Howell explain, levels of physician-assistance can vary from merely providing information, writing prescriptions, and so on, all the way up to the methods practiced by Dr. Kevorkian, including the use of his "suicide machines." In fact, while much of the public gets its ideas about what physician-assisted suicide is from Dr. Kevorkian, most proponents of physician-assisted suicide regard what he does as an example of what can happen if we *don't* have regulations and safeguards in place.

It is sometimes difficult for young and healthy people to imagine themselves at the end of life. But some people will have lived through their own relatives' deaths. And the very fact that we are all going to die—although no one knows the exact circumstances and whether we will go peacefully or in pain—makes this a real issue for all of us. The uncertainty that exists might make some people lean toward the side of the issue that provides the greater scope for leeway, allowing some provision for physician-assisted suicide, perhaps as a sort of "insurance" that may not even be needed.

Some of the opposition to the idea of physician-assisted suicide might come from a general repulsion against taking life. This is a good reaction to have. But it doesn't mean that the reaction is a substitute for judgment. Likewise, some of the opposition might come from a negative association of this with the Nazis. Again, the negative reaction is good one. What is required here though is an ability to get past purely emotional responses and mental associations. What we need are reasons and careful thinking.

Further resources on this issue can be found in James H. Ondrey, *Physician-Assisted Suicide* (Greenhaven Press, 2006); Gerald Dworkin, R.G. Frey, and Sissela Bok, *Euthanasia and Physician-Assisted Suicide (For and Against)* (Cambridge University Press, 2005); and Ian Dowbiggin, *A Merciful End: The Euthanasia Movement in Modern America* (Oxford University Press, 2007).

Perhaps of unique interest is Derek Humphry's *Final Exit: The Practicalities of Self-Deliverance and Assisted Suicide for the Dying,* 3rd ed. (Delta, 2003). This book was written by a founder of the Hemlock Society (now merged into the Compassion & Choices organization); the book contains useful information and is also a practical "how-to" guide so that "self-deliverance" (suicide) can be successfully achieved.

Internet References . . .

Animal Rights and Vegetarianism

http://www.peta.org/
http://ar.vegnews.org/Animal_Rights.html

Human Beings and Other Species

*N*owadays we recognize that human beings are part of nature and that we share the planet with other species. In former times, human beings and nature were thought to be two entirely different things. Even then, it was realized of course that we shared the planet with other species, but there was little or no question that eating their meat was morally acceptable. Now that we have become accustomed to seeing animals as fellow inhabitants of the natural world, the question arises about our proper relation to them.

• Does Morality Require Vegetarianism?

ISSUE 15

Does Morality Require Vegetarianism?

YES: Michael Allen Fox, from "Why We Should Be Vegetarians," *International Journal of Applied Philosophy* (vol. 20, no. 2, 2006)

NO: Holmes Rolston III, from *Environmental Ethics: Duties to and Values in the Natural World* (Temple University Press, 1988)

ISSUE SUMMARY

YES: Michael Allen Fox believes that the common practice of eating meat is something that we need to apply critical thinking to. He argues that if we care about pain, suffering, and death, and if we are to live up to the demands of justice, then we should take responsibility for our diets and become vegetarians.

NO: Environmental thinker Holmes Rolston III maintains that meat eating by humans is a natural part of the ecosystem. He states that it is important that animals do not suffer needlessly, but it would be a mistake to think that animals, like humans, are members of a culture. Rolston concludes that people too readily project human nature on animal nature.

This issue comes about because humans are rational beings and, at least to some extent, we are able to control our actions. Many other living things eat meat but are not rational beings. Lions, for example, eat meat—but a male lion will often kill all the lion cubs of his new mate, which would certainly seem by human standards to be unreasonable. The idea that we are just following nature when we eat meat may not exactly be true, say many who recognize that some animal behaviors are not to be used as models by people. Instead we must pick and choose the behaviors that we follow.

Moreover, unlike lions, most people do not *have* to eat meat in order to survive. Indeed, some entire cultures are vegetarian. Individual vegetarians can be found in other cultures as well, for example, in American culture. On the other hand, in American culture the practice of meat eating is the norm and is quite widespread—just look at all the McDonald's and Burger Kings!

As a justification for eating meat, some conclude that it is not quite right to say that we are just doing what the other living things do—for we do not follow animal behavior if we think it would be wrong to do so. But if meat eating is a cultural practice, then, like any other cultural practice, it should be subject to rational judgment and moral critique. We know that in the past, many socially accepted practices have been condoned at the time they were practiced but later found to be morally wanting. We can look back now in amazement at the practice of slavery in the South in the early part of the 1800s or the way great poverty was ignored in Victorian England while some people lived lives of luxury. One wonders, "How could people *do* that?" Could it be that future generations will look back at the Americans who thought nothing of consuming Big Macs and likewise wonder, "How could people *do* that?"

Many find the basic problem with meat eating to be the conditions under which animals that are raised for food live. The people who eat meat bring about these deplorable conditions, some argue, because high consumer demand dictates that the supermarkets are well stocked with meat, that fast food outlets sell meat, and therefore make it easier to obtain a meal with meat than one without. Animal husbandry is big business, and it is big business because the customers demand the product. Because of this huge demand, it can be said that many people look the other way when farmers raise animals under conditions that many vegetarians find appalling.

In the following selections, Michael Allen Fox argues that morality does in fact require vegetarianism. He emphasizes the ideas of caring, justice, and living responsibly. Rather than simply accepting cultural norms blindly, we need to subject them—in this case, the widespread practice of meat eating—to critical analysis. Holmes Rolston III then maintains that the human consumption of meat is part of our human interaction with the natural (as opposed to the cultural) environment. He asserts that it is important that animals do not suffer needlessly, of course, but it would be a mistake to think that animals are members of a culture in the same way that human beings belong to a culture. People too readily project human nature on animal nature, he contends.

YES

Michael Allen Fox

Why We Should Be Vegetarians

Introduction

Presenting the ethics of vegetarianism often arouses heated responses because it challenges the norm of meat eating most people subscribe to. This norm is associated with many symbols and rituals and has a lengthy history (Douglas 1975; Twigg 1983; Adams 1991; Fiddes 1991; Fox 1999b). These associations make the norm difficult to dislodge, and imbue it with considerable inertia. But vegetarianism also taps into the uneasiness and guilt-feelings many meat eaters harbor today, as is evident in hostile and defensive responses to vegetarian practices and arguments, ridicule, and frequent demands that vegetarians justify their "deviant" outlook. Vegetarianism is therefore commonly placed in a defensive position: on it rests the onus of showing that meat eating is unnecessary, environmentally unsustainable, wrong, and so on. This essay presents an ethical rationale for vegetarianism that is straightforward in its appeal, and has the additional aim of destabilizing the default position in favor of meat eating. The argument developed here does not rely upon either a specifically utilitarian view (like that of Peter Singer) or a rights-centred theory (like that of Tom Regan), but originates instead in observations that are fundamental to ethical thinking in a more general sense. Against this background, I offer a vigorous ethical argument for vegetarianism that is grounded in considerations of caring and justice. In addition, the relatively new issue of "responsible meat eating" will be examined, and the inadequacies of this concept exposed. I conclude that only by being vegetarians can we consistently honor what ethics is based upon, and by doing so, minimize the harm we cause by our lifestyle choices. What follows represents just a small part of the overall case for vegetarianism, which is presented in detail elsewhere (Wynne-Tyson 1979; Stephens 1994; Hill 1996; Fox 1999b).

Facing and Avoiding the Food Issue

Everyone who is concerned about making the world a better place in which to live must consider, among other things, the food he or she eats. Why? Because food does not come from nowhere, and how people obtain it has always been an indicator of the way they have chosen to live, of what they value, of their

From *International Journal of Applied Philosophy,* vol. 20, no. 2, 2006, pp. 295–310. Copyright © 2006 by Philosophy Documentation Center. Reprinted by permission.

attitudes toward life, each other, and nature in general. I believe most of us today are concerned about the state of the world; and not only this: most of us are concerned about our health. Therefore, we should be doubly concerned about what we eat.

But somehow these concerns often fall by the wayside, failing to translate into an examination of dietary choices. For some—perhaps most in the Western world, and an increasing number in the non-Western world—it seems to be enough to declare simply: "I love my meat and wouldn't think of giving it up," or: "I've heard the arguments against meat eating, but I'm still a carnivore." These responses exemplify an unreflective approach to life, however, and one that a philosopher must therefore question. I do not plan to go into the health-centred reasons for affirming that a diet that does not rely on meat is healthier than one that does. The largest study ever undertaken on this subject was conducted by Cornell University scientists in the People's Republic of China and Taiwan (Campbell and Campbell 2004). According to their findings, plant-based diets are significantly healthier in numerous respects than meat-based ones. Many other studies have confirmed this result in various sample groups. Thus, there would appear to be reason enough to choose being a vegetarian for health (that is, prudential) reasons alone. But there are additional and compelling reasons that can help us make this decision.

The most important among these has to do with the consequences of eating meat for nonhuman animals (see Singer and Mason 2006). First, note the expression just used: "nonhuman animals." We customarily forget or don't even consider that humans are animals too; we just refer to "animals" as all those other things that from time to time we may think resemble us in certain respects or behaviors but that, we comfort ourselves into believing, are not *really* all that much like us. Animals are those lesser beings that don't matter, or don't matter very much at any rate. They are those beings that work for us, serve our needs, and give up their lives for us. And generally we download an abundance of our problems onto them. For example, we experiment on them in order (we suppose) to improve our lives, as if *their* lives had no independent value—to the animals themselves (and perhaps in objective terms as well). We violate their habitats in order to achieve important but also entirely trivial objectives. We make them into slaves of our obsession with commodities and profits. If, on the other hand, we practice thinking of ourselves as animals too, a quite different perspective emerges. Now we enable ourselves to perceive continuity between humans and nonhumans rather than a false and untenable dichotomy. Now we can release the capacity to understand that other beings of value exist besides ourselves; that they have their own purposes independent of ours; experience pain and suffering; and have a will to live. Historically, there have always been voices to express these ideas, but they have been in the minority and have been ignored or marginalized. This is no longer the case. Anyone who is at all aware of new ideas about nonhuman animals—about their intelligence, communication skills, social life, sophisticated behaviors, and evolutionary proximity to us (Pepperberg 1999; Savage-Rumbaugh et al. 2000; Griffin 2001; Rendell and Whitehead 2001; de Waal and Tyack 2003; Linden 2003)—has to face the task of thinking through the complexities of our troubled relationship with them.

I referred above to the consequences for nonhuman animals of turning them into meat for human consumption. The obvious ones are: (1) pain and suffering, and (2) death. The level at which the meat industry inflicts these harms on sentient beings defies belief. Steven M. Wise reports that: "the sheer number of nonhuman animals whom we kill . . . is beyond understanding. More than 300 mammals and birds are killed [in the U.S. alone] each time your heart beats. The number triples for the rest of the world. In the United States, more than 10 billion are slaughtered annually just for food" (Wise 2002: 9). It is easy to see why we call the economic sector that generates these statistics "the meat industry"; but we could just as well label it "the torture and indiscriminate killing industry," because that is a more accurate description. It is difficult to explain why any normal person would not recoil in horror before this unending and insatiable carnage. Today, domesticated nonhuman animals, as they always have been, are purposely bred for eventual slaughter. They are genetically fashioned, selected, carefully confined, nourished, and often chemically enhanced for the ultimate goal of turning them into the products that satisfy people's taste preferences. Nowhere in this process is it ever considered whether our taste preferences can only, or best, be met in this manner, let alone whether our nutritional requirements must be so addressed.

People tend to compartmentalize their relationships with, and responses to, animals (Fox 1999b, chap. 3), so that pets receive lavish affection while domesticated livestock are merely expendable things, regarded for the most part in a purely instrumental manner, and often allowed to languish in miserable conditions. Furthermore, the process by which farmed animals become or yield food for human consumption is removed from view and also from thought by the meat-production system and its Image-makers.[1] Meat, as a prized commodity having considerable cultural and symbolic meaning and value, exercises a strong hold on our imagination, emotions, and desire. Inasmuch as this valuation rests on associations that go beyond our conscious control, it resists being analyzed and deconstructed, and this resistance helps prevent us from seeing connections between our professed belief in humaneness and kindness toward animals, on the one hand, and the brutality that brings meat to our tables, on the other. Failing to make connections likewise subverts the motivation to bring about changes in our dietary attitudes and practices. While philosophical examination can dislodge ethical prejudices against taking animals' moral status seriously, it requires a reorientation of both thought and feeling to allow natural sentiments of compassion and caring to embrace nonhuman creatures.

Animals' Pain and Suffering, and Why It Matters

. . . Why should anyone care about the suffering of nonhuman animals? First of all, why should anyone care about pain and suffering, period? The reason is that pain and suffering hurt; they are "aversive stimuli," or experiences that have a negative impact, are disvalued by us, and we seek to avoid if at all possible. No other reason can be offered: we care about our own pain and suffering because we don't like it and it adversely affects our well-being. I am not denying the obvious here—that pain and suffering are part of life, and that they are sometimes offset by a greater good. What I am talking about is *gratuitous* pain and suffering, which are caused by malice, cruelty, or carelessness, and *unjustified* pain and suffering, which are not outweighed by a greater good. As I shall argue below, the benefits of meat eating do not amount to a greater good that can mitigate or neutralize the harm done to the animals we rear and slaughter for food.

Now, why should we care about other people's pain and suffering, especially if we don't even know them? Again, the answer is: "Because it hurts, they don't like it, and it harms their well-being." To this, the response may be: "So what?" But if someone says, "So what?" then there's nothing else we can offer by way of persuasion. Harming others is bad because it's harmful, and what's harmful is bad. This is a circular statement, to be sure; but the reason is precisely that it is meant to convey a self-evident truth, not an argument. Anyone who refuses to accept that we should not harm others (who are demonstrably like oneself in relevant respects) simply because they don't want to be harmed, is unlikely to be persuaded by a different sort of appeal, or indeed by any appeal at all. We call people like this "amoral" or "sociopaths" or "psychopaths."

Are we, then, like sociopaths in a certain arena of our lives, if we don't care about hurting nonhuman animals? Well, maybe so, in an important sense. But the point here is not to engage in name-calling or laying on guilt-trips. Rather, it's to realize that nonhuman animals can be hurt, that it matters to them, and therefore, should matter to us.[2] I won't try to prove that nonhuman animals can experience pain and suffering. As I noted earlier, this has been confirmed many times over by the evidence. The biggest breakthrough we can make in our thinking about this matter, it seems to me, is to acknowledge that *it makes no difference what kind of creature we're talking about; if it can feel pain and suffer, such pain and suffering matter.* Jeremy Bentham put this view forward more than two centuries ago. Here, I refer to his famous and frequently quoted remark about sentient nonhuman animals. Bentham says, "The question is not, Can they *reason*? nor Can they *talk*? but, Can they *suffer*?" (Bentham 1789: chap. 19, sec. 1). It is relatively easy today to get utilitarians to accept this outlook. But Bentham's insight has a wider appeal, and those who hold different ethical views from his can nonetheless relate to what he is saying with equal facility.[3] Whether pain and suffering are bad in and of themselves or because of their consequences for our well-being (or both) is not really crucial. What *does* count is that they are sometimes harmful, and that beings who have these experiences seek relief from them. In this ethically important respect, humans and nonhuman animals are alike, and justice, as Aristotle observed long ago, means treating like beings alike.[4] Just treatment is to be understood as fair or deserving treatment. If nonhuman animals are like humans in respect to their experiences of pain and suffering, then so far as it is possible to do so, they should be treated alike. What this means in actual practice is not always easy to determine, since it is difficult to compare different beings' mental states with any degree of precision; but an accurate estimate is not always all that hard to arrive at either. In the case of animal pain and suffering, we have ample evidence to go on, as already stated. This evidence entails simply that we should try to avoid gratuitously or unjustifiably causing such hurtful, harmful feelings when (a) it is within our power to do so, and (b) the sacrifice this requires of us is minimal. And the most obvious way in which to apply this principle of conduct to nonhuman animals is to avoid committing direct or indirect acts—such as buying meat to eat—that violate their well-being in the way I have described.

The production of meat is not the only cause of gratuitous and/or unjustified pain and suffering in nonhumans, to be sure; but it is overwhelmingly the main source of the negative impacts we visit on other conscious, sentient creatures. And we can choose to be on the side of either causing or preventing this kind of pain and suffering. Again, whether we are utilitarians or not, we should care about the amount of pain and suffering in the world, and do what we can to make the world less, rather than more, full of these aversive experiences. Surely, this is what we try to do when we give to charities, help those in need, look after people in distress, and so on. We help nonhuman animals when they are the victims of wanton cruelty; why would we not choose to help them escape from the effects of cruel practices that form a more deliberately planned, systemic part of their lives as well? To many people, the answer is obvious: we *would* and *do* choose to help, and we *should* do so. Others evidently need persuasion on this point. While it is the philosopher's job to try to frame a rational appeal, it is often a more complex type of approach that enables us to change our minds. This is why I have invoked the notion of caring in this essay in order to broaden the case I am making in such a way that it links up with the sorts of feelings that are an essential part of our moral orientation. We need to pause for a moment, however, to consider more carefully what "caring" means.

Caring

To say that *a* cares about *b* may entail one (or both) of two things: *a* feels liking or affection toward *b*; *a* wants to look after or seriously respond to the needs or condition of *b*, in order to contribute to *b*'s welfare. I wish to focus here on *b* (some people do not like animals particularly well, and in any case, liking should not be a precondition for taking up a proper ethical attitude toward a being). It has been argued that: "What establishes a moral obligation to care for someone else is the existence of, or potential for, a relation between oneself and the other, or else the potential for growth in one's relation with the other."[5] I think that this claim is incorrect, because it states at best a sufficient condition for caring, and may just single out a possible (and obviously desirable) side effect of it. Certainly, there can be and is unrequited caring; and someone may feel a caring form of connectedness with other beings that are totally unaware of the carer's existence. Nor are we necessarily aware of the positive outcome of our caring (if there is any) in every case. Caring about another living thing springs from the fundamental sensibilities of sympathy, empathy, and compassion, and it is these that underpin a moral obligation to care. As for the benefits of caring, just as virtue is its own reward, so too does caring lead to inner contentment and personal growth that are not dependent upon reciprocity from the object of care. Furthermore, although unrelated to our present subject, there are other kinds of caring that don't involve reciprocity in principle, or else only do so in an indirect sense: one may care, for example, about the fate of inanimate entities such as natural formations or artworks.

I have said above that caring derives from basic moral sensibilities. "Compassion," etymologically, means "suffering with." The fact that compassion is a pretty nearly universal attribute of humans is indisputable. It exists and manifests itself even in the most jaded, cruel, and evil persons (think of the "Birdman of Alcatraz," who could only relate to stray birds, and whose nuturing of them transformed his life for the better, one might even say, "redeemed" it). The full meaning of "compassion" involves an acute awareness of another's suffering plus the wish to relieve it. We may speculate that, while the origin of compassion is innate, this sensibility (or moral emotion) is cognitively reinforced by an awareness of shared needs; an appreciation of and respect for (valorizing of) the other's independent life and welfare; and, in relation to nonhuman animals, a sense of our evolutionary continuity with them, and our shared interest in survival and flourishing. When I stated earlier that sentient nonhumans, like us, experience pain and suffering, have their own purposes, and display a will to live, I had in mind the kind of enhancement of compassion through knowledge just explained, which might be expected to positively regulate our behavior toward them.

"Sympathy" (etymologically: "feeling with") signifies resonant feeling occasioned in oneself by another's feelings, which one experiences at the same time as the other is having them. "Empathy" (etymologically: "feeling inside") conveys the sense of being able to understand and share another's feelings. Thus, empathy has a more cognitive element than sympathy; it suggests a deeper appreciation of others' affective states. The relationship between compassion, sympathy, and empathy, then, seems to be as follows: sympathy, modified by cognition, leads (or may lead) to empathy, which in turn yields compassion as a form of active involvement wherein one feels the imperative "I must do something" in order to remedy or ameliorate the situation of the other. This does not necessarily imply that only sympathy is an inborn response, for I think humans are too complex for us to make such a bald assertion. Perhaps it's best to say that we have the innate capacity for developing compassion as I have described it, and leave the matter there. . . .

Justice Considerations

One objection that may arise at this point comes from a utilitarian perspective. This is that the amount of pleasure or satisfaction humans derive from eating meat outweighs the amount of animal pain and suffering we cause in the process. Now aside from the fact that balancing benefits and harms in this way is notoriously difficult—even within the human sphere—I want to suggest that such a line of argument is a non-starter. The reason is that the beneficiaries of meat eating are humans and the recipients of harm are nonhumans. I am not talking here merely about the issue of comparing and balancing the experiences of members of different species. Rather, I have in mind an ethically more critical issue, namely, that of weighing benefits to one class of beings against costs to another class of beings. And this seems to me to involve considerations of justice. We can look at this issue in two ways. First, if we consider the experiences of nonhuman animals to be of a comparable character to those of humans, then it has to be manifestly true that the gustatory pleasures of humans cannot outweigh the amount of pain and suffering caused to animals by the process of obtaining these pleasures. At a very basic level, it seems reasonable to assume that the pain and suffering of meat production matter more to the creatures we choose to eat, for only our most rare gustatory experiences are either intensely or sublimely pleasurable (and these are, in any case, of very short duration), whereas the harms experienced by food animals are often agonizing and protracted. Furthermore, the average meat eater is (usually indirectly) responsible for the pain and suffering of scores of nonhuman animals during his or her lifetime. The aggregated pain and suffering of these creatures undoubtedly outweighs the pleasure of one human by a high degree. Finally, if nonhuman animals have an interest in their own well-being in the manner I have suggested, then this surely very basic interest must outweigh the nonbasic interest of humans in eating meat. (Meat eating is a nonbasic interest because for the vast majority of human beings there are alternative food sources capable of providing all of our nutritional needs.[6] And the alternatives can easily generate pleasurable experiences that are at least equal in value to those that meat eaters forfeit by giving up meat.[7])

The second way of looking at the justice issue is to note simply that in weighing human interests against those of nonhumans, we are comparing apples and oranges. That is, we are trying to rationalize something we prefer by shifting the effects of it onto a different class of beings that have no say in the matter and are powerless to resist our actions. This is the same model that fits acts of enslavement, exploitation of children, experimenting on other humans without their consent, and so on. . . .

The Killing of Animals as a Harm

Thus far, I have limited my remarks to pain and suffering. But there is also the matter of causing animals' deaths. Eating meat is essentially tied to killing, unlike many other forms of harm. . . .

Perhaps we should pause to consider here whether death *is* a harm for sentient nonhuman animals, and *why*. I think it is, and that the reasons for saying so are easy to grasp. These are that: (1) such animals show every sign of preferring to live when their lives are threatened, as when we bring them to slaughter; (2) they clearly have pleasurable experiences (or, in human terms, experiences that are of value to them); and (3) each has an identifiable welfare or state of well-being it strives to preserve. For any being that meets these criteria, death is a harm. Hence, death is a harm to livestock animals. An observation from the Jain tradition of India sums this up quite well: "A wise man should be neither glad nor angry, for he should know and consider the happiness of all things. . . . For nothing is inaccessible to death, and all beings are fond of themselves; they love pleasure and hate pain; they shun destruction and cling to life. They long to live. To all things life is dear" (Basham 1954:293). . . .

Many billions of nonhuman animals are consumed worldwide every year. This translates into many billions of deaths that are unnecessary from a nutritional point of view and that violate the justice principle stated earlier. It would seem that only a deformed, desensitized mind could declare that gratuitous, unjustified, human-caused pain and suffering on a very large scale, as in the food industry, do not matter, or are mitigated by aggregated, minor benefits to ourselves. And it is difficult to understand how widely practiced, institutionalized cruelty *of any kind* can contribute to creating decent and just societies and a nonviolent world order. These are the sorts of overarching issues that reflection on our eating habits makes us confront, and they are as important as any in ethics. What seems at first to be a minor affair, and one that concerns taste preferences alone—what we eat—thus turns into a much more significant matter. We are all responsible for the level of harm and violence that we have the ability to reduce or eliminate, and not to do so when we can, without risk to ourselves, and with only minor inconvenience, is negligent behavior we should correct.

Another objection often heard is that we could acquire our meat from smaller-scale producers, such as organic and free range farms, and operations that practice more "humane" methods of transportation and slaughter. Those who run this kind of facility often slaughter their own livestock, which is at least better than placing this burden upon someone else and distancing oneself from the act, as most meat eaters do. (We'll revisit this point later on.) But this improvement does not cancel out the fact that unnecessary killing is the final step in the process, no matter what the scale; nor can pain and suffering be completely eliminated along the way. In any event, many nonhuman animals reared on smaller farms will also end up at large commercial slaughterhouses. And the fact remains that they live equally artificially abbreviated lives in these circumstances. Finally, it is impossible to imagine how the growing demand for meat, by an increasing world population of humans conditioned to eating it and regarding it as high-status food, can be sustained at all, let alone being supplied by small, independent producers (Durning and Brough 1995; Tilston 2004).

At the outset, I posed three questions about the conditions under which meat is produced for human consumption: Why should I care? What can I do? and Will my choices make a difference? The first and second have been answered. Each of us should care because pain and suffering are inherently bad kinds of conscious experiences, no matter to whom or to what they occur. Causing gratuitous or unjustified pain and suffering is wrong. We should all be concerned to avoid being the agents of wrongdoing when circumstances permit. This leads to the second question. What each of us can do in order to avoid causing pain and suffering to nonhuman animals is first and foremost to stop eating meat. . . .

Taking Responsibility for Our Diets

[Y]ou may [say], "*I* don't cause gratuitous, unjustified pain and suffering to nonhuman animals or kill them for trivial or any other reasons. I may eat them, but *other people* are the ones who do these cruel things." True; but as we all know, demand creates supply, and for that reason, each of us must take responsibility for the food production system that depends upon his or her eating preferences. We are habituated to not confronting the consequences of our actions in large areas of life. We prefer to leave the decisions and actions to others, who act on our behalf, and often we avoid both awareness and accountability thereby—as in their own ways so do these others who do the dirty work for us. We are too used to seeing meat arrive magically, as it were, on our grocery shelves and in butcher shops as just "cuts," already wrapped in plastic or waiting to be wrapped in paper—as disembodied parts of living beings from which we remove ourselves in thought and action (Adams 1991). Taking responsibility for our food means understanding fully where it comes from and how it is obtained; that we have a crucial, if indirect, role in these things; and that we need to act morally in light of this knowledge. . . .

Choosing Vegetarianism as a Way of Life

What the foregoing discussion reveals are two central facts about vegetarianism: (1) that it is a committed, caring response to injustice; and therefore (2) that it represents more than a peculiar taste preference or a matter of lifestyle or fashion, but is, instead, part of a comprehensive outlook on how we ought to live. In short, vegetarianism is an ethical way of life. It follows that choosing to be a vegetarian involves developing a sense of responsibility that reaches beyond the human sphere. It entails an appreciation of the kinship between living beings, as well as a decision to make a serious effort at minimizing the amount of harm that flows from our eating preferences and practices. None of us is or ever could be morally perfect, but we all have different alternatives before us among which to choose; and those acts that contribute to lessening the levels of violence and agony in the world are surely to be preferred to those that do not. Again, this is not an endorsement of utilitarianism, but merely an ethical truism. The difficult part is not getting ourselves to agree to this idea; it is getting ourselves to accept that vegetarianism is part of the strategy needed to translate the idea into reality.

I think enough has been said to make it clear that a commitment to vegetarianism is ethically compelling. However, no one should conclude that I am making grandiose claims on behalf of vegetarianism. It isn't an answer to all the world's problems, only one essential aspect of that answer. We might think of it this way: by being vegetarians, we become part of the solution to global injustice rather than part of the problem of it. Again, this seems a manifestly preferable position to be in. This brings me back to a point I made earlier: that the rewards of doing what is right should come from within us. Being committed to making the world a more just and caring place, and to an outlook that helps promote non-violence, contributes to a more satisfying sense of purpose and of self, I would argue, and therefore, has a lot to do with positive personal development. So a change in diet, which to begin with looked like a big, unpleasant sacrifice, really turns out not to be so at all; and vegetarianism, which may appear, on first encounter, like some kind of self-punishing asceticism that assumes a condescending moral vantage-point, is really something quite different in character and very worthwhile in terms of its consequences. Does anything more need to be offered by way of incentives? You be the judge.[8]

Endnotes

1. This is true in general, especially in relation to slaughterhouses, which, in the past century, have been moved away from large urban centres like Chicago to more remote rural areas. But some things aren't so easily hidden from view. My sister recently drove across the U.S. and reported that in Kansas, cattle by the thousands can be seen, mile after mile, standing ankle-deep in their own excrement. The foul smell is completely penetrating and cannot be escaped even in a motel room.

2. For extended discussion on what it means to care about animals' well-being, see Donovan and Adams, eds. (1996).

3. Indeed, the point can be expressed in the form of a valid (and I think sound) logical argument.

   P1 Any sentient living being naturally seeks to avoid or escape from pain and suffering.

   P2 Any sentient living being that engages in such behavior shows that pain and suffering matter to it.

   P3 Humans and many nonhumans are sentient living beings.

   C1 Humans and many nonhumans are beings that naturally seek to avoid or escape from pain and suffering and to which pain and suffering matter.

   P4 If pain and suffering matter to a sentient living being, then they matter morally.

   C2 For both humans and many nonhumans, pain and suffering matter morally.

   P5 If something matters morally, it must be taken into account in our decisions leading to action.

   C3 The pain and suffering of nonhuman animals, like that of humans, must be taken into account in our decisions leading to action.

4. Aristotle (1995), bk. III, chap. 9: 103: "justice is considered to mean equality. It does mean equality—but for those who are equal, and not for all." Of course, for Aristotle, nonhuman animals were inferior beings that had no moral status; but so were various classes of human beings (women, slaves, non-Athenians). And justice for him was a function of one's contribution to society. Nevertheless, we may borrow his notion of justice for our purposes and apply it more broadly and consistently than he was prepared to do.

5. This criterion is attributed to Nel Noddings by Taylor (2003:79).

6. Exceptions include indigenous peoples who live in environments where meat (including fish) is the only food source. Kathryn Paxton George

argues for a much wider range of exceptions (George, 2000), but her case rests on nutritional data that are controversial.

7. The additional pleasure derived from the knowledge that one has got off the food animal exploitation treadmill is also significant.

8. I would like to thank Lesley McLean and Elliot Cohen for helpful comments on earlier drafts of this essay. Previous versions have also been presented at philosophy seminars in Australia (University of New England) and Taiwan (National Central University and National Chung Cheng University). I wish to express my appreciation to these audiences for their feedback.

Bibliography

Adams, Carol J. 1991. *The Sexual Politics of Meat: A Feminist-Vegetarian Critical Theory*. New York: Continuum.

Basham, A. L. 1954. *The Wonder That Was India: A Survey of the Culture of the Indian Subcontinent before the Coming of the Muslims*. New York: Grove Press.

Bentham, Jeremy. 1789. *An Introduction to the Principles of Morals and Legislation*. London: T. Payne.

Campbell, T. Colin, and Thomas M. Campbell. 2004. *The China Study*. Dallas: BenBella Books.

De Waal, F. B. M., and P. L. Tyack. 2003. *Animal Social Complexity: Intelligence, Culture, and Individualized Societies*. Cambridge, MA: Harvard University Press.

Douglas, Mary. 1975. "Deciphering a Meal." In Mary Douglas. *Implicit Meanings: Essays in Anthropology*. London and Boston: Routledge & Kegan Paul. Pp. 249–75.

Durning, Alan T., and Holly B. Brough. 1995. "Animal Farming and the Environment." In *Just Environments: Intergenerational, International and Interspecies Issues,* ed. David E. Cooper and Joy A. Palmer. London and New York: Routledge. 149–64.

Fiddes, Nick. 1991. *Meat: A Natural Symbol.* New York: Routledge.

Fox, Michael Allen. 1999b. *Deep Vegetarianism.* Philadelphia: Temple University Press.

Griffin, Donald R. 2001. *Animal Minds: Beyond Cognition to Consciousness.* Chicago: University of Chicago Press.

Hill, John Lawrence. 1996. *The Case for Vegetarianism: Philosophy for a Small Planet.* Lanham, MD: Rowman Littlefield.

Linden, Eugene. 2003. *The Octopus and the Orangutan: New Tales of Animal Intrigue, Intelligence, and Ingenuity.* New York: Plume.

Pepperberg, Irene. 1999. *The Alex Studies: Cognitive and Communicative Abilities of Grey Parrots.* Cambridge, MA: Harvard University Press.

Rendell, Luke, and Hal Whitehead. 2001. "Culture in Whales and Dolphins." *Behavioral and Brain Sciences,* 24: 309–24, 373–82.

Savage-Rumbaugh, Sue, W. M. Fields, and J. Taglialatela. 2000. "Ape Consciousness—Human Consciousness: A Perspective Informed by Language and Culture." *American Zoologist,* 40: 910–21.

Singer, Peter, and Jim Mason. 2006. *The Way We Eat: Why Our Food Choices Matter.* Emmaus, PA: Rodale Books. (Simultaneously published by Text Publishing in Australia under the title *The Ethics of What We Eat.*)

Stephens, William O. 1994. "Five Arguments for Vegetarianism." *Philosophy in the Contemporary World,* 1: 25–39.

Tilston, John. 2004. *How to Explain Why You're Vegetarian to Your Dinner Guests.* Victoria, BC: Trafford.

Twigg, J. 1983. "Vegetarianism and the Meanings of Meat." In *The Sociology of Food and Eating: Essays on the Sociological Significance of Food,* ed. A. Murcott. Aldershot, Hampshire: Gower. 18–30.

Wise, Steven M. 2002. *Unlocking the Cage: Science and the Case for Animal Rights.* Oxford: Perseus. (Simultaneously published by Perseus in the United States under the title *Drawing the Line.*)

Wynne-Tyson, John. 1979. *Food for a Future: The Complete Case for Vegetarianism.* London: Centaur Press; New York: Universe Books.

Holmes Rolston III

 **NO**

Higher Animals: Duties to Sentient Life

Domestic and Hunted Animals

Domestic Food Animals

Animal agriculture is tangential to an environmental ethic, yet there is a carry-over connecting the one to the other. Domestic animals are breeds, no longer natural kinds. They are "living artifacts,"[1] kept in culture for so long that it is often not known precisely what their natural progenitors were. They fit no environmental niche; the breeding of them for traits that humans desire has removed them from the forces of natural selection. Without human interest in these animals they would soon cease to exist. Most domestic breeds would go extinct; a few might revert to feral conditions; fewer still might resettle homeostatically into environmental niches. Most feral forms, unchecked by predators, competitors, and diseases, are misfits that cause heavy environmental degradation.

But domestic animals cannot enter the culture that maintains them. By all behavioral evidence, sheep, cows, and pigs are oblivious to the economy for which they are reared, much less to the cultural context of the persons who care for them. They cannot live in the world ethically, cognitively, and critically in those superior human ways. Pet dogs may join the life of the family, enthusiastically eating hot dogs at a picnic; nevertheless, pets are not in culture. Although food animals are taken out of nature and transformed by culture, they remain uncultured in their sentient life, cultural objects that cannot become cultural subjects. They live neither in nature nor in culture but in the peripheral rural world. Meanwhile, they can suffer.

This *is* the case, descriptive of their condition. What *ought* to be? . . . [W]e recognize the wild condition from which such animals were once taken and recognize also that they can neither return to the wild nor enter cultural subjectivity. Although tamed, they can have horizons, interests, goods no higher than those of wild subjectivity, natural sentience. They ought to be treated, by the homologous, baseline principle, with no more suffering than might have been their lot in the wild, on average, adjusting for their modified capacities to care for themselves. In taking an interest in them, humans have assumed a responsibility for them. (Whether modern industrial farming introduces suffering in excess of ecological norms will have to be investigated elsewhere.)

By a weaker (but significant) hedonist principle, domestic animals ought to be spared pointless suffering, but they have no claim to be spared innocent suffering. The killing and the eating of animals, when they occur in culture, are still events in nature; they are ecological events, no matter how superimposed by culture. Humans are claiming no superiority or privilege exotic to nature. Analogous to predation, human consumption of animals is to be judged by the principles of environmental ethics, not those of interhuman ethics. We step back from culture into agriculture, toward the wild, and fit the ecological pattern. What *is* in nature may not always imply *ought* (and it may seldom do so in interhuman ethics), but *ought* in environmental ethics seldom negates what *is* in wild nature. Humans eat meat, and meat-eating is a natural component of ecosystems, one to which we do not object in nature nor try to eliminate from our cultural interactions with nature.

A troop of half a dozen chimpanzees, our nearest relatives, will kill and eat about a hundred medium-sized animals a year. Hunter-gatherer cultures are the earliest known, and when agricultural cultures replace them, humans have no duty to cease to be omnivores and become herbivores. They might elect to become vegetarians, perhaps on grounds of more efficient food production or better nutrition, but they have no duty to sentient life to do so.

A characteristic argument for vegetarianism runs as follows:

1. Pain is a bad thing, whether in humans or in animals.
2. Humans (at least most of them) can live nutritiously without causing animal pain.
3. It is immoral for humans to kill and eat humans, causing them pain.
4. Food animals suffer pain, similarly to the way humans do, if killed and eaten.
5. There are no morally relevant differences between humans and food animals.
6. It is immoral for humans to kill and eat animals, causing them pain.

Appealing to sentiment and logically attractive in its charitable egalitarianism, such argument fails to distinguish between nature and culture, between environmental ethics and interhuman ethics. We simply see ourselves in fur. But there are morally relevant differences that distinguish persons in culture from food animals in agriculture, where quasi-ecosystemic processes remain. Whether or not there are differences in pain thresholds between sheep and humans, the value destruction when a sheep is eaten is far less, especially since the sheep have been bred for this purpose and would not otherwise exist. Because animals cannot enter culture, they do not suffer the *affliction* (a heightened, cognitively based pain, distinct from physical pain) that humans would if bred to be eaten.

Chickens can live in ignorant bliss of their forthcoming slaughter (until the moment of execution); persons in such a position could not, because they are in the world culturally and critically. Even if such a fate could be kept secret from persons, the value destruction in their killing would still be greater. The fact that there are twilight zones (humans who are pre-persons or failed persons) does not challenge the existence of morally relevant class differences. In recognizing the human superiority, nothing should be subtracted from the natural condition of animals. But we have no strong duty to deny their original ecology, and only a weaker duty to make their lot better by avoiding pointless pain.

It is not "unfair" or "unjust" to eat a pig. Even an alligator that eats humans is not being unfair or unjust (although humans will be reprehensible if they do not try to prevent it). Humans in their eating habits follow nature; they can and ought to do so. But humans do not eat other humans because such events interrupt culture; they destroy those superior ways in which humans live in the world. The eating of other humans, even if this were shown to be an event in nature, would be overridden by its cultural destructiveness. Cannibalism destroys interpersonal relations. But in nature no such relations obtain, or can obtain. (Human cannibalism has been rare and virtually always a cultural event with religious overtones, not a natural event.)

It may be objected that the differences in rules for those with superior gifts means here that the only moral animals should refuse to participate in the meat-eating phase of their ecology, just as they refuse to play the game merely by the rules of natural selection. Humans do not look to the behavior of wild animals as an ethical guide in other matters (marriage, truth-telling, promise-keeping, justice, charity). Why should they justify their dietary habits by watching what animals do? But these other matters are affairs of culture. Marriage, truth-telling, promise-keeping, justice, charity—these are not events at all in spontaneous nature. They are person-to-person events. By contrast, eating is omnipresent in spontaneous nature; humans eat because they are in nature, not because they are in culture. Eating animals is not an event between persons but a human-to-animal event, and the rules for it come from the ecosystems in which humans evolved and which they have no duty to remake. Humans, then, can model their dietary habits on their ecosystems, but they cannot and should not model their interpersonal justice or charity on ecosystems.

It may seem that while animals are not to be treated like persons in all respects, both they and persons have about equally the capacity to feel pain, and so both ought to be treated equally in this relevant respect involving the pain-pleasure scale. But this is not the only relevant scale, because it does not catch the full scale of value destructions at stake. The eating of persons would destroy cultural values, which the eating of animals does not. The eating of animals, though it does destroy values, reallocates such values when humans gain nutrition and pleasure at the sacrifice of animal lives in a manner wholly consistent with the operation of the natural ecosystem in which such animals were once emplaced and are still quasi-placed in their agricultural stations. Different rules do apply to persons, to persons in exchange with persons, and even to persons in exchange with nature. These rules do require that animals' lives count morally, but they do not require humans to deny their ecology and replace it with a charity or justice appropriate to culture.

Sentience in nature and sentience in culture are not really the same thing, despite their common physiology and origin. Sentience in nature belongs with food chains and natural selection; sentience in culture has been transformed into another gestalt, that of self-reflective personality and moral agency. Eating an animal implies no disrespect for animal life . . . ; to the contrary, it respects that ecology. Eating a person would disrupt personal life as set in a cultural pattern; it would reduce personal life to the level of animal life in an ecology. It insults persons to treat them as food objects by the criteria of animal ecology; persons may and must treat nonhuman lives as food objects, but it respects animals to treat them so.

Pain is a bad thing in humans or in animals. But this fools us until we distinguish between intrinsic and instrumental pain. Instrumental pain has contributory reference to further goods; intrinsic pain has no such reference. Intrinsic pain is a bad thing, absolutely; but only instrumental pain is characteristic of nature, where intrinsic pain is a nonfunctional anomaly. Pain is routinely instrumental in ecological defenses, captures, and transfers of goods, and the pains imposed in agriculture are homologous. They are not intrinsic pains; they must be judged in their instrumentality and with no presumption against innocent suffering.

Enjoying pleasure and escaping pain are of value, and evolutionary ecosystems are full of devices for accomplishing both. But much pain remains, and much thwarted pleasure. In nature, the pain-pleasure axis is not the only spectrum of value; indeed, it is not the highest value in either human or nonhuman life. It might be said, for instance, that knowing the meaning of life is more important for humans than leading a painless life, that a life with courage and sacrificial charity in it, which requires the presence of some pain, is a richer life than one without it. Similarly, the evolution of a world with carnivorous mammals, primates, humans, and culture is a richer world than one without them, and the presence of pain seems to have been necessary for such evolution. In that sense, advanced values are frequently built on suffering.

Perhaps it is not merely the pain but the indignity of domestication that is deplorable. A gazelle is pure wild grace, but a cow is a meat factory, pure and simple; a cow might even suffer less than a gazelle but be greatly disgraced. Cows cannot know they are disgraced, of course, and the capture of values in nature is not undignified. A lioness destroys a gazelle, and there is nothing unworthy here. Likewise, in domestication, humans parallel ecosystems and capture agriculturally the values in a cow. There is nothing undignified in this event, even though the once-natural values in the cow, like those in the gazelle, have to be destroyed by the predator.

Although we have defended eating animals as a primary, natural event, we have also said, secondarily, that there is an obligation to avoid pointless pain. Consider, for instance, the following case. There are more than 2,000,000 Muslims in Britain; the Jewish community numbers nearly 400,000. Muslims still practice animal sacrifice; a sheep or goat is sacrificed during a feast concluding a month of fasting, and often at the birth of a child. The animal is sacrificed to Allah, and the meat is eaten and enjoyed. Though Jews no longer practice animal sacrifice as they did in former times, they require their meat to be kosher, slaughtered according to religious ritual. Modern secular abattoirs stun animals with a massive blow or an electric shock before butchering them, and this is thought to be more humane. But it makes the animal unacceptable to Jews and Muslims, who must sever the major blood vessels of an unblemished animal. About 1,500,000 sheep and goats and 100,000 cattle are slaughtered by Jews and Muslims each year.

Animal rights activists have pressed to require stunning, and a government report finds that religious methods of slaughter result in a degree of suffering and distress that does not occur in a properly stunned animal. Muslims and Jews have joined forces to defend their practices.[2] But the additional pain that their methods impose, no longer necessary, cannot be interpreted in the context of ecology; it is pain inflicted for culture-based reasons. Unblemished animals make better sacrifices to God; they enhance religious cleanliness. This pain is ecologically pointless; it has point only culturally and, by the account given here, is not justified. This pain is not homologous; it is superfluous. Perhaps both Jews and Muslims can reach reformed religious convictions, in which respect for animal life overrides their previous concepts of cleanliness, or where the mercy of God prohibits pointless suffering.

Notes

1. J. Baird Callicott, "Animal Liberation: A Triangular Affair," *Environmental Ethics 2,* 1980, p. 330.
2. Karen DeYoung, "Ritual Slaughter Sparks Debate," *Washington Post,* 27 December 1985, pp. A19–20.

POSTSCRIPT

Does Morality Require Vegetarianism?

Traditionally, there has been no question with regard to the morality of eating meat. There is no law against it; it is widely practiced; and it is supported by the biblical idea that God gave people animals to eat, and specifically placed people in dominion over animals. So it is to some extent a great change in the moral climate that this question is even being raised at all.

It is partly due to the views of pioneering environmental thinkers such as Rolston that people have begun to think seriously about the place of human beings within the larger biological environment. This naturally leads to questions about animals and human beings and their relationship.

Of course, there is another biblical injunction to the effect that people should exercise stewardship over God's creation. It is, however, not clear how this is to fit in with the other biblical idea (above). Michael Allen Fox's ideas about caring seem to fit closer to the idea of stewardship than they do to the idea of dominion.

From a religious perspective, we might remember that there are millions of people who base vegetarianism on religion. And from a purely cultural perspective, we know that, as widely accepted as meat eating is in our own culture, some cultures practice vegetarianism.

Part of the difficulty for us in coming to grips with moral questions in this area stems from our dual role in nature. On the one hand, we use reason to stand apart from nature; on the other hand, reason tells us that we are part of nature. But even if we think of ourselves as part of nature, this does not solve our problem. For now, we have to think again (as we did in the introduction to this issue) and use reason to decide whether we should be like the lions, who hunt and kill animals to eat, or whether such killing and eating—even if culturally traditional for us—should be left behind.

A classic work in this field is Peter Singer, *Animal Liberation* (New York Review of Books, 1990). Bernard E. Rollin, in *Farm Animal Welfare: Social, Bioethical, and Research Issues* (Iowa State University Press, 1995), and Howard F. Lyman, in *Mad Cowboy: Plain Truth from the Cattle Rancher Who Won't Eat Meat* (Scribner, 1998), address the conditions under which animals are raised for food, and Lyman in particular is critical of the negative impact that this has on human beings. Carol J. Adams, in *The Sexual Politics of Meat: A Feminist-Vegetarian Critical Theory,* 10th anniversary ed. (Continuum Pub Group, 1999), argues that meat eating is connected with male dominance. Also relevant are Craig B. Stanford et al., eds., *Meat-Eating and Human Evolution* (Oxford University Press, 2001); Eric Schlosser, *Fast Food Nation: The Dark Side of the*

All-American Meal (Harper-Collins, 2002); Matthew Scully, *Dominion: The Power of Man, the Suffering of Animals, and the Call to Mercy* (St. Martin's Press, 2002); Charles Patterson, *Eternal Treblinka: Our Treatment of Animals and the Holocaust* (Lantern Books, 2002); Steve F. Sapontzis, *Food for Thought: The Debate over Eating Meat* (Prometheus Books, 2004); Lyle Munro, *Confronting Cruelty: Moral Orthodoxy and the Challenge of the Animal Rights Movement* (Brill Academic, 2005); and Josephine Donovan and Carol Adams, eds., *The Feminist Care Tradition in Animal Ethics* (Columbia University Press, 2007).

Internet References . . .

Why College Athletes Should Be Paid

The following two articles advocate for paying college athletes.

www.nytimes.com/2012/01/01/magazine/lets-start-paying-college-athletes.html?_r=1&ref=magazine

http://online.wsj.com/article/SB10001424053111904060604576572752351110850.html

Why College Athletes Should Not Be Paid

In this site, the NCAA explains why college athletes should not be paid.

www.ncaa.org/wps/wcm/connect/public/NCAA/Issues/Why+student-athletes+are+not+paid+to+play

Genetically Modified Foods Defined

This site defines genetically modified foods (GMFs) and gives the background and issues concerning GMFs.

http://en.wikipedia.org/wiki/Genetically_modified_food

The World Health Organization on GMFs

This World Health Organization site answers 20 questions on genetically modified foods.

www.who.int/foodsafety/publications/biotech/20questions/en/

Other Moral Issues

*T*he question whether college athletes should be paid is one that is not a legal question and does not fit easily into the other categories in this book. Nevertheless, in recent years it has seemed more and more strange that college althletes, who make possible so much wealth and income for their school, their coaches, etc., are not allowed to share in any of that wealth or income for themselves. On the other hand, we cherish the model of the student athlete, the amateur participant in college athletics. If it can seem strange that these athletes are not allowed to share in the wealth that they make possible, it can also seem strange that colleges and universities, long regarded as existing in a place apart, a place of learning and scholarship, would now pay their student athletes to play college sports and thus become strong actors in the commercial world.

Finally, the great technological advances that have made such strides in the areas of physical objects (including computers, and even electrons and pixels) have also come to biological organisms and genes. But the stakes can be much higher in the biological case—since we ourselves are part of the ecosystem and (could) put genetically modified foods (GMFs) into our own bodies. Accordingly, a high level of safety is required.

- Should College Athletes Be Paid?
- Is It Right to Produce Genetically Modified Food?

ISSUE 16

Should College Athletes Be Paid?

YES: **Taylor Branch**, from "The Shame of College Sports," *The Atlantic Monthly* (October 2011)

NO: **Seth Davis**, from "Should College Athletes Be Paid? Why, They Already Are," *Sports Illustrated* (September 21, 2011)

ISSUE SUMMARY

YES: Taylor Branch argues that college athletics is big business, and everyone involved is allowed a share of the wealth—except for the students who make it all possible. So-called "student athletes" are exploited. The phrase "student athletes" is itself a cop-out.

NO: Seth Davis addresses Branch's article directly, but he denies much of Branch's case. College sports, he says, are not big business; most teams lose money for their colleges. To think that college athletes, such as football players, come away empty-handed is simply false. For one thing, they receive an education (which itself could be valued at about $200,000 in tuition). They also receive training, coaching, and special tutoring.

One of the most striking things about college athletics—and here I'm mainly talking about "revenue sports" such as football—is that while a lot of money is involved—for coaches, for broadcasting rights, etc.—none of this money is allowed to flow to the athletes who make it all possible. This may immediately be thought to be an unfair exploitation of the players. Directly clashing with this, however, is the idea of the amateur—in this case, the unpaid student athlete. The student athletes play for their school, for the love of the game, for glory, and for bragging rights. Of course, a lucrative contract in the National Football League (NFL) is also possible, and may be a strong motivator for some players. Nevertheless, the requirements for remaining an amateur athlete are quite stringent. Suppose I am a football star at my school. Not only must I receive no money in that capacity, that is, not only must I receive no money for my actual playing on the field, but I also must receive no money from the sale of my image, my football memorabilia, etc. Note that *others* are able to make money from things like video games that include my image, but I can't do so without losing my amateur status.

But now, let's look closer at the situation. (And the closer we look, the more complicated we find things becoming.) The NFL won't allow a player to sign unless he is 3 years out of high school. (Such a player is not *required* to go to college, although most do; the main impact of the rule is to disallow recent high school graduates from entering the NFL.) In fact, one argument against college players being paid at the "market rate" is that there is no market for most of the players anyway, since they are not yet 3 years out of high school. And when it comes to choosing a college, the athlete must not accept any "gifts" from strong football boosters at the college, nor can immediate relatives accept such "gifts," even though boosters might want to give them. The student athlete must rather carefully avoid profiting from his position if he is to maintain his National Collegiate Athletic Association (NCAA) amateur status.

On the other hand, the student athlete gains in many ways that are difficult to quantify—and also in some ways that do have financial value. For one thing, the athlete may get a full scholarship (while nonathlete students may incur student loans of many thousands of dollars). The athlete may be given early enrollment in courses (since the whole team has to be ready to practice together at certain specified times), and special tutoring and study hall hours. He also gains experience working with top-notch coaches and other athletes who most likely play at a level that is far superior to what he knew in high school. It is impossible to put a price-tag on this. So the college athlete may benefit from an education that he would not otherwise have had, while not incurring any student debt, and he also benefits from the training and experience that goes along with playing the game he loves at a high level.

If we still believe that college athletes should be paid, then we have to face some complications. Just who exactly will be paid—all athletes, in all sports, in all conferences? Will the paid athletes all receive the same pay? Moreover, how will they be paid? Who will pay them? It may be, for example, that the college would pay them. On the other hand, it may be that they will be allowed to profit from the sale of their image, or jerseys with their name and number, or through sponsorships and endorsements. As it stands, of course, all of these payments would be out-of-bounds for an NCAA amateur. But we are thinking about changing the rules.

In the readings that follow, Taylor Branch, Pulitzer Prize–winning author, examines the history and the current state of the NCAA. He concludes that college athletes ought to be paid. But Seth Davis, writing in the next piece, emphasizes the idea that college athletes are already being paid (or being greatly benefited). Adding paychecks to the benefit package is simply not necessary.

The Shame of College Sports

"**I'**m not hiding," Sonny Vaccaro told a closed hearing at the Willard Hotel in Washington, D.C., in 2001. "We want to put our materials on the bodies of your athletes, and the best way to do that is buy your school. Or buy your coach."

Vaccaro's audience, the members of the Knight Commission on Intercollegiate Athletics, bristled. These were eminent reformers—among them the president of the National Collegiate Athletic Association, two former heads of the U.S. Olympic Committee, and several university presidents and chancellors. The Knight Foundation, a nonprofit that takes an interest in college athletics as part of its concern with civic life, had tasked them with saving college sports from runaway commercialism as embodied by the likes of Vaccaro, who, since signing his pioneering shoe contract with Michael Jordan in 1984, had built sponsorship empires successively at Nike, Adidas, and Reebok. Not all the members could hide their scorn for the "sneaker pimp" of schoolyard hustle, who boasted of writing checks for millions to everybody in higher education.

"Why," asked Bryce Jordan, the president emeritus of Penn State, "should a university be an advertising medium for your industry?"

Vaccaro did not blink. "They shouldn't, sir," he replied. "You sold your souls, and you're going to continue selling them. You can be very moral and righteous in asking me that question, sir," Vaccaro added with irrepressible good cheer, "but there's not one of you in this room that's going to turn down any of our money. You're going to take it. I can only offer it."

William Friday, a former president of North Carolina's university system, still winces at the memory. "Boy, the silence that fell in that room," he recalled recently. "I never will forget it." Friday, who founded and co-chaired two of the three Knight Foundation sports initiatives over the past 20 years, called Vaccaro "the worst of all" the witnesses ever to come before the panel.

But what Vaccaro said in 2001 was true then, and it's true now: corporations offer money so they can profit from the glory of college athletes, and the universities grab it. In 2010, despite the faltering economy, a single college athletic league, the football-crazed Southeastern Conference (SEC), became the first to crack the billion-dollar barrier in athletic receipts. The Big Ten pursued closely at $905 million. That money comes from a combination of ticket sales, concession sales, merchandise, licensing fees, and other sources—but the great bulk of it comes from television contracts.

Educators are in thrall to their athletic departments because of these television riches and because they respect the political furies that can burst from a locker room. "There's fear," Friday told me when I visited him on the University of North Carolina campus in Chapel Hill last fall. As we spoke, two giant construction cranes towered nearby over the university's Kenan Stadium, working on the latest $77 million renovation. (The University of Michigan spent almost four times that much to expand its Big House.) Friday insisted that for the networks, paying huge sums to universities was a bargain. "We do every little thing for them," he said. "We furnish the theater, the actors, the lights, the music, and the audience for a drama measured neatly in time slots. They bring the camera and turn it on." Friday, a weathered idealist at 91, laments the control universities have ceded in pursuit of this money. If television wants to broadcast football from here on a Thursday night, he said, "we shut down the university at 3 o'clock to accommodate the crowds." He longed for a campus identity more centered in an academic mission.

The United States is the only country in the world that hosts big-time sports at institutions of higher learning. This should not, in and of itself, be controversial. College athletics are rooted in the classical ideal of *Mens sana in corpore sano*—a sound mind in a sound body—and who would argue with that? College sports are deeply inscribed in the culture of our nation. Half a million young men and women play competitive intercollegiate sports each year. Millions of spectators flock into football stadiums each Saturday in the fall, and tens of millions more watch on television. The March Madness basketball tournament each spring has become a major national event, with upwards of 80 million watching it on television and talking about the games around the office water cooler. ESPN has spawned ESPNU, a channel dedicated to college sports, and Fox Sports and other cable outlets are developing channels exclusively to cover sports from specific regions or divisions.

With so many people paying for tickets and watching on television, college sports has become Very Big Business. According to various reports, the football teams at Texas, Florida, Georgia, Michigan, and Penn State—to name just a few big-revenue football schools—each earn between $40 million and $80 million in profits a year, even after paying coaches multimillion-dollar salaries. When you combine so much money with such high, almost tribal, stakes—football boosters are famously rabid in their zeal to have their alma mater win—corruption is likely to follow.

Scandal after scandal has rocked college sports. In 2010, the NCAA sanctioned the University of Southern California after determining that star running back Reggie Bush and his family had received "improper benefits" while he played for the Trojans. (Among other charges, Bush and members of his family were alleged to have received free airfare and limousine rides, a car, and a rent-free home in San Diego, from sports agents who wanted Bush as a client.) The Bowl Championship Series stripped USC of its 2004 national title, and Bush returned the Heisman Trophy he had won in 2005. Last fall, as Auburn University football stormed its way to an undefeated season and a national championship, the team's star quarterback, Cam Newton, was dogged by allegations that his father had used a recruiter to solicit up to $180,000 from Mississippi State in exchange for his son's matriculation there after junior college in 2010. Jim Tressel, the highly successful head football coach of the Ohio State Buckeyes, resigned last spring after the NCAA alleged he had feigned ignorance of rules violations by players on his team. At least 28 players over the course of the previous nine seasons, according to *Sports Illustrated*, had traded autographs, jerseys, and other team memorabilia in exchange for tattoos or cash at a tattoo parlor in Columbus, in violation of NCAA rules. Late this summer, Yahoo Sports reported that the NCAA was investigating allegations that a University of Miami booster had given millions of dollars in illicit cash and services to more than 70 Hurricanes football players over eight years.

The list of scandals goes on. With each revelation, there is much wringing of hands. Critics scold schools for breaking faith with their educational mission, and for failing to enforce the sanctity of "amateurism." Sportswriters denounce the NCAA for both tyranny and impotence in its quest to "clean up" college sports. Observers on all sides express jumbled emotions about youth and innocence, venting against professional mores or greedy amateurs.

For all the outrage, the real scandal is not that students are getting illegally paid or recruited, it's that two of the noble principles on which the NCAA justifies its existence—"amateurism" and the "student-athlete"—are cynical hoaxes, legalistic confections propagated by the universities so they can exploit the skills and fame of young athletes. The tragedy at the heart of college sports is not that some college athletes are getting paid, but that more of them are not. . . .

Fans and educators alike recoil from this proposal as though from original sin. Amateurism is the whole point, they say. Paid athletes would destroy the integrity and appeal of college sports. Many former college athletes object that money would have spoiled the sanctity of the bond they enjoyed with their teammates. I, too, once shuddered instinctively at the notion of paid college athletes.

But after an inquiry that took me into locker rooms and ivory towers across the country, I have come to believe that sentiment blinds us to what's before our eyes. Big-time college sports are fully commercialized. Billions of dollars flow through them each year. The NCAA makes money, and enables universities and corporations to make money, from the unpaid labor of young athletes.

Slavery analogies should be used carefully. College athletes are not slaves. Yet to survey the scene—corporations and universities enriching themselves on the backs of uncompensated young men, whose status as "student-athletes" deprives them of the right to due process guaranteed by the Constitution—is to catch an unmistakable whiff of the plantation. Perhaps a more apt metaphor is colonialism: college sports, as overseen by the NCAA, is a system imposed by well-meaning paternalists and rationalized with hoary sentiments about caring for the well-being of the colonized. But it is, nonetheless, unjust. The NCAA, in its zealous defense of bogus principles, sometimes destroys the dreams of innocent young athletes.

The NCAA today is in many ways a classic cartel. Efforts to reform it—most notably by the three Knight Commissions over the course of 20 years—have, while making changes around the edges, been largely fruitless. The time has come for a major overhaul. And whether the powers that be like it or not, big changes are coming. Threats loom on multiple fronts: in Congress, the courts, breakaway athletic conferences, student rebellion, and public disgust. Swaddled in gauzy clichés, the NCAA presides over a vast, teetering glory.

Founding Myths

From the start, amateurism in college sports has been honored more often in principle than in fact; the NCAA was built of a mixture of noble and venal impulses. . . .

For nearly 50 years, the NCAA, with no real authority and no staff to speak of, enshrined amateur ideals that it was helpless to enforce. (Not until 1939 did it gain the power even to mandate helmets.) In 1929, the Carnegie Foundation made headlines with a report, "American College Athletics," which concluded that the scramble for players had "reached the proportions of nationwide commerce." Of the 112 schools surveyed, 81 flouted NCAA recommendations with inducements to students ranging from open payrolls and disguised booster funds to no-show jobs at movie studios. Fans ignored the uproar, and two-thirds of the colleges mentioned told *The New York Times* that they planned no changes. In 1939, freshman players at the University of Pittsburgh went on strike because they were getting paid less than their upperclassman teammates.

Embarrassed, the NCAA in 1948 enacted a "Sanity Code," which was supposed to prohibit all concealed and indirect benefits for college athletes; any money for athletes was to be limited to transparent scholarships awarded solely on financial need. Schools that violated this code would be expelled from NCAA membership and thus exiled from competitive sports.

This bold effort flopped. Colleges balked at imposing such a drastic penalty on each other, and the Sanity Code was repealed within a few years. The University of Virginia went so far as to call a press conference to say that if its athletes were ever accused of being paid, they should be forgiven, because their studies at Thomas Jefferson University were so rigorous.

The Big Bluff

In 1951, the NCAA seized upon a serendipitous set of events to gain control of intercollegiate sports. First, the organization hired a young college dropout named Walter Byers as executive director. A journalist who was not yet 30 years old, he was an appropriately inauspicious choice for the vaguely defined new post. He wore cowboy boots and a toupee. He shunned personal contact, obsessed over details, and proved himself a bureaucratic master of pervasive, anonymous intimidation. Although discharged from the Army during World War II for defective vision, Byers was able to see an opportunity in two contemporaneous scandals. In one, the tiny College of William and Mary, aspiring to challenge football powers Oklahoma and Ohio State, was found to be counterfeiting grades to keep conspicuously pampered players eligible. In the other, a basketball point-shaving conspiracy (in which gamblers paid players to perform poorly) had spread from five New York colleges to the University of Kentucky, the reigning national champion, generating tabloid "perp" photos of gangsters and handcuffed basketball players. The scandals posed a crisis of credibility for collegiate athletics, and nothing in the NCAA's feeble record would have led anyone to expect real reform.

But Byers managed to impanel a small infractions board to set penalties without waiting for a full convention of NCAA schools, which would have been inclined toward forgiveness. Then he lobbied a University of Kentucky dean—A. D. Kirwan, a former football coach and future university president—not to contest the NCAA's dubious legal position (the association had no actual authority to penalize the university), pleading that college sports must do something to restore public support. His gambit succeeded when Kirwan reluctantly accepted a landmark precedent: the Kentucky basketball team would be suspended for the entire 1952–53 season. Its legendary coach, Adolph Rupp, fumed for a year in limbo.

The Kentucky case created an aura of centralized command for an NCAA office that barely existed. At the same time, a colossal misperception gave Byers leverage to mine gold. Amazingly in retrospect, most colleges and marketing experts considered the advent of television a dire threat to sports. Studies found that broadcasts reduced live attendance, and therefore gate receipts, because some customers preferred to watch at home for free. Nobody could yet imagine the revenue bonanza that television represented. With clunky new TV sets proliferating, the 1951 NCAA convention voted 161–7 to outlaw televised games except for a specific few licensed by the NCAA staff.

All but two schools quickly complied. The University of Pennsylvania and Notre Dame protested the order to break contracts for home-game television broadcasts, claiming the right to make their own decisions. Byers objected that such exceptions would invite disaster. The conflict escalated. Byers brandished penalties for games televised without approval. Penn contemplated seeking antitrust protection through the courts. Byers issued a contamination notice, informing any opponent scheduled to play Penn that it would be punished for showing up to compete. In effect, Byers mobilized the college world to isolate the two holdouts in what one sportswriter later called "the Big Bluff."

Byers won. Penn folded in part because its president, the perennial White House contender Harold Stassen, wanted to mend relations with fellow schools in the emerging Ivy League, which would be formalized in 1954. When Notre Dame also surrendered, Byers conducted exclusive negotiations with the new television networks on behalf of every college team. Joe Rauh Jr., a prominent civil-rights attorney, helped him devise a rationing system to permit only 11 broadcasts a year—the fabled Game of the Week. Byers and Rauh selected a few teams for television exposure, excluding the rest. On June 6, 1952, NBC signed a one-year deal to pay the NCAA $1.14 million for a carefully restricted football package. Byers routed all contractual proceeds through his office. He floated the idea that, to fund an NCAA infrastructure, his organization should take a 60 percent cut; he accepted 12 percent that season. (For later contracts, as the size of television revenues grew exponentially, he backed down to 5 percent.) Proceeds from the first NBC contract were enough to rent an NCAA headquarters, in Kansas City.

Only one year into his job, Byers had secured enough power and money to regulate all of college sports. Over the next decade, the NCAA's power grew along with television revenues. Through the efforts of Byers's deputy and chief lobbyist, Chuck Neinas, the NCAA won an important concession in the Sports Broadcasting Act of 1961, in which Congress made its granting of a precious antitrust exemption to the National Football League contingent upon the blackout of professional football on Saturdays. Deftly, without even mentioning the NCAA, a rider on the bill carved each weekend into protected broadcast markets: Saturday for college, Sunday for the NFL. The NFL got its antitrust exemption. Byers, having negotiated the NCAA's television package up to $3.1 million per football season—which was higher than the NFL's figure in those early years—had made the NCAA into a spectacularly profitable cartel.

"We Eat What We Kill"

The NCAA's control of college sports still rested on a fragile base, however: the consent of the colleges and universities it governed. For a time, the vast sums of television money delivered to these institutions through Byers's deals made them willing to submit. But the big football powers grumbled about the portion of the television revenue diverted to nearly a thousand NCAA member schools that lacked major athletic programs. They chafed against cost-cutting measures—such as restrictions on team size—designed to help smaller schools. "I don't want Hofstra telling Texas how to play football," Darrell Royal, the Longhorns coach, griped. By the 1970s and '80s, as college football games delivered bonanza ratings—and advertising revenue—to the networks, some of the big football schools began to wonder: Why do we need to have our television coverage brokered through the NCAA? Couldn't we get a bigger cut of that TV money by dealing directly with the networks?

Byers faced a rude internal revolt. The NCAA's strongest legions, its big football schools, defected en masse. Calling the NCAA a price-fixing cartel that siphoned every television dollar through its coffers, in 1981 a rogue consortium of 61 major football schools threatened to sign an independent contract with NBC for $180 million over four years.

With a huge chunk of the NCAA's treasury walking out the door, Byers threatened sanctions, as he had against Penn and Notre Dame three decades earlier. But this time the universities of Georgia and Oklahoma responded with an antitrust suit. "It is virtually impossible to overstate the degree of our resentment . . . of the NCAA," said William Banowsky, the president of the University of Oklahoma. In the landmark 1984 *NCAA v. Board of Regents of the University of Oklahoma* decision, the U.S. Supreme Court struck down the NCAA's latest football contracts with television—and any future ones—as an illegal restraint of trade that harmed colleges and viewers. Overnight, the NCAA's control of the television market for football vanished. Upholding Banowsky's challenge to the NCAA's authority, the Regents decision freed the football schools to sell any and all games the markets would bear. Coaches and administrators no longer had to share the revenue generated by their athletes with smaller schools outside the football consortium. "We eat what we kill," one official at the University of Texas bragged.

A few years earlier, this blow might have financially crippled the NCAA—but a rising tide of money from basketball concealed the structural damage of the Regents decision. During the 1980s, income from the March Madness college basketball tournament, paid directly by the television networks to the NCAA, grew tenfold. The windfall covered—and then far exceeded—what the organization had lost from football.

Still, Byers never forgave his former deputy Chuck Neinas for leading the rebel consortium. He knew that Neinas had seen from the inside how tenuous the NCAA's control really was, and how diligently Byers had worked to prop up its Oz-like façade. During Byers's tenure, the rule book for Division I athletes grew to 427 pages of scholastic detail. His NCAA personnel manual banned conversations around water coolers, and coffee cups on desks, while specifying exactly when drapes must be drawn at the NCAA's 27,000-square-foot headquarters near Kansas City (built in 1973 from the proceeds of a 1 percent surtax on football contracts). It was as though, having lost control where it mattered, Byers pedantically exerted more control where it didn't.

After retiring in 1987, Byers let slip his suppressed fury that the ingrate football conferences, having robbed the NCAA of television revenue, still expected it to enforce amateurism rules and police every leak of funds to college players. A lethal greed was "gnawing at the innards of college athletics," he wrote in his memoir. When Byers renounced the NCAA's pretense of amateurism, his former colleagues would stare blankly, as though he had gone senile or, as he wrote, "desecrated my sacred vows." But Byers was better positioned than anyone else to argue that college football's claim to amateurism was unfounded. Years later, as we will see, lawyers would seize upon his words to do battle with the NCAA.

Meanwhile, reformers fretted that commercialism was hurting college sports, and that higher education's historical balance between academics and athletics had been distorted by all the money sloshing around. News stories revealed that schools went to extraordinary measures to keep academically incompetent athletes eligible for competition, and would vie for the most-sought-after high-school players by proffering under-the-table payments. In 1991, the first Knight Commission report, "Keeping Faith With the Student Athlete," was published; the commission's "bedrock conviction" was that university presidents must seize control of the NCAA from athletic directors in order to restore the preeminence of academic values over athletic or commercial ones. In response, college presidents did take over the NCAA's governance. But by 2001, when the second Knight Commission report ("A Call to Action: Reconnecting College Sports and Higher Education") was issued, a new generation of reformers was admitting that problems of corruption and commercialism had "grown rather than diminished" since the first report. Meanwhile the NCAA itself, revenues rising, had moved into a $50 million, 116,000-square-foot headquarters in Indianapolis. By 2010, as the size of NCAA headquarters increased yet again with a 130,000-square-foot expansion, a third Knight Commission was groping blindly for a hold on independent college-athletic conferences that were behaving more like sovereign pro leagues than confederations of universities. . . .

The Myth of the "Student-Athlete"

Today, much of the NCAA's moral authority—indeed much of the justification for its existence—is vested in its claim to protect what it calls the "student-athlete." The term is meant to conjure the nobility of amateurism, and the precedence of scholarship over athletic endeavor. But the origins of the "student-athlete" lie not in a disinterested ideal but in a sophistic formulation designed, as the sports economist Andrew Zimbalist has written, to help the NCAA in its "fight against workmen's compensation insurance claims for injured football players."

"We crafted the term student-athlete," Walter Byers . . . wrote, "and soon it was embedded in all NCAA rules and interpretations." The term came into play in the 1950s, when the widow of Ray Dennison, who had died from a head injury received while playing football in Colorado for the Fort Lewis A&M Aggies, filed for workmen's-compensation death benefits. Did his football scholarship make the fatal collision a "work-related" accident? Was he a school employee, like his peers who worked part-time as teaching assistants and bookstore cashiers? Or was he a fluke victim of extracurricular pursuits? Given the hundreds of incapacitating injuries to college athletes each year, the answers to these questions had enormous consequences. The Colorado Supreme Court ultimately agreed with the school's contention that he was not eligible for benefits, since the college was "not in the football business."

The term *student-athlete* was deliberately ambiguous. College players were not students at play (which might understate their athletic obligations), nor were they just athletes in college (which might imply they were professionals). That they were high-performance athletes meant they could be forgiven for not meeting the academic standards of their peers; that they were students meant they did not have to be compensated, ever, for anything more than the cost of their studies. *Student-athlete* became the NCAA's signature term, repeated constantly in and out of courtrooms.

Using the "student-athlete" defense, colleges have compiled a string of victories in liability cases. On the afternoon of October 26, 1974, the Texas Christian University Horned Frogs were playing the Alabama Crimson Tide in Birmingham, Alabama. Kent Waldrep, a TCU running back, carried the ball on a "Red Right 28" sweep toward the Crimson Tide's sideline, where he was met by a swarm of tacklers. When Waldrep regained consciousness, Bear Bryant, the storied Crimson Tide coach, was standing over his hospital bed. "It was like talking to God, if you're a young football player," Waldrep recalled.

Waldrep was paralyzed: he had lost all movement and feeling below his neck. After nine months of paying his medical bills, Texas Christian refused to pay any more, so the Waldrep family coped for years on dwindling charity.

Through the 1990s, from his wheelchair, Waldrep pressed a lawsuit for workers' compensation. (He also, through heroic rehabilitation efforts, recovered feeling in his arms, and eventually learned to drive a specially rigged van.

"I can brush my teeth," he told me last year, "but I still need help to bathe and dress.") His attorneys haggled with TCU and the state worker-compensation fund over what constituted employment. Clearly, TCU had provided football players with equipment for the job, as a typical employer would—but did the university pay wages, withhold income taxes on his financial aid, or control work conditions and performance? The appeals court finally rejected Waldrep's claim in June of 2000, ruling that he was not an employee because he had not paid taxes on financial aid that he could have kept even if he quit football. (Waldrep told me school officials "said they recruited me as a student, not an athlete," which he says was absurd.)

The long saga vindicated the power of the NCAA's "student-athlete" formulation as a shield, and the organization continues to invoke it as both a legalistic defense and a noble ideal. Indeed, such is the term's rhetorical power that it is increasingly used as a sort of reflexive mantra against charges of rabid hypocrisy. . . .

In theory, the NCAA's passion to protect the noble amateurism of college athletes should prompt it to focus on head coaches in the high-revenue sports—basketball and football—since holding the top official accountable should most efficiently discourage corruption. The problem is that the coaches' growing power has rendered them, unlike their players, ever more immune to oversight. According to research by Charles Clotfelter, an economist at Duke, the average compensation for head football coaches at public universities, now more than $2 million, has grown 750 percent (adjusted for inflation) since . . . 1984; that's more than 20 times the cumulative 32 percent raise for college professors. For top basketball coaches, annual contracts now exceed $4 million, augmented by assorted bonuses, endorsements, country-club memberships, the occasional private plane, and in some cases a negotiated percentage of ticket receipts. (Oregon's ticket concessions netted former football coach Mike Bellotti an additional $631,000 in 2005.)

The NCAA rarely tangles with such people, who are apt to fight back and win. When Rick Neuheisel, the head football coach of the Washington Huskies, was punished for . . . gambling (in a March Madness pool, as it happened), he sued the NCAA and the university for wrongful termination, collected $4.5 million, and later moved on to UCLA. When the NCAA tried to cap assistant coaches' entering salary at a mere $16,000, nearly 2,000 of them brought an antitrust suit, *Law v. NCAA*, and in 1999 settled for $54.5 million. Since then, salaries for assistant coaches have commonly exceeded $200,000, with the top assistants in the SEC averaging $700,000. In 2009, Monte Kiffin, then at the University of Tennessee, became the first assistant coach to reach $1 million, plus benefits.

The late Myles Brand, who led the NCAA from 2003 to 2009, defended the economics of college sports by claiming that they were simply the result of a smoothly functioning free market. He and his colleagues deflected criticism about the money saturating big-time college sports by focusing attention on scapegoats; in 2010, outrage targeted sports agents. Last year *Sports Illustrated* published "Confessions of an Agent," a firsthand account of dealing with high-strung future pros whom the agent and his peers courted with flattery, cash, and tawdry favors. Nick Saban, Alabama's head football coach, mobilized his peers to denounce agents as a public scourge. "I hate to say this," he said, "but how are they any better than a pimp? I have no respect for people who do that to young people. None."

Saban's raw condescension contrasts sharply with the lonely penitence from Dale Brown, the retired longtime basketball coach at LSU. "Look at the money we make off predominantly poor black kids," Brown once reflected. "We're the whoremasters."

"Picayune Rules"

NCAA officials have tried to assert their dominion—and distract attention from the larger issues—by chasing frantically after petty violations. Tom McMillen, a former member of the Knight Commission who was an All-American basketball player at the University of Maryland, likens these officials to traffic cops in a speed trap, who could flag down almost any passing motorist for prosecution in kangaroo court under a "maze of picayune rules." The publicized cases have become convoluted soap operas. At the start of the 2010 football season, A. J. Green, a wide receiver at Georgia, confessed that he'd sold his own jersey from the Independence Bowl the year before, to raise cash for a spring-break vacation. The NCAA sentenced Green to a four-game suspension for violating his amateur status with the illicit profit generated by selling the shirt off his own back. While he served the suspension, the Georgia Bulldogs store continued legally selling replicas of Green's No. 8 jersey for $39.95 and up.

A few months later, the NCAA investigated rumors that Ohio State football players had benefited from "hook-ups on tatts"—that is, that they'd gotten free or underpriced tattoos at an Ohio tattoo parlor in exchange for autographs and memorabilia—a violation of the NCAA's rule against discounts linked to athletic personae. The NCAA Committee on Infractions imposed five-game suspensions on Terrelle Pryor, Ohio State's tattooed quarterback, and four other players (some of whom had been found to have sold their Big Ten championship rings and other gear), but did permit them to finish the season and play in the Sugar Bowl. (This summer, in an attempt to satisfy NCAA investigators, Ohio State voluntarily vacated its football wins from last season, as well as its Sugar Bowl victory.) A different NCAA committee promulgated a rule banning symbols and messages in players' eyeblack—reportedly aimed at Pryor's controversial gesture of support for the pro quarterback Michael Vick, and at Bible verses inscribed in the eyeblack of the former Florida quarterback Tim Tebow.

The moral logic is hard to fathom: the NCAA bans personal messages on the bodies of the players, and penalizes players for trading their celebrity status for discounted tattoos—but it codifies precisely how and where commercial insignia from multinational corporations can be displayed on college players, for the financial benefit of the colleges. Last season, while the NCAA investigated him and his father for the recruiting fees they'd allegedly sought, Cam Newton compliantly wore at least 15 corporate logos—one on his jersey, four on his helmet visor, one on each wristband, one on his pants, six on his shoes, and one on the headband he wears under his helmet—as part of Auburn's $10.6 million deal with Under Armour. . . .

"They Want to Crush These Kids"

Academic performance has always been difficult for the NCAA to address. Any detailed regulation would intrude upon the free choice of widely varying schools, and any academic standard broad enough to fit both MIT and Ole Miss would have little force. From time to time, a scandal will expose extreme lapses. In 1989, Dexter Manley, by then the famous "Secretary of Defense" for the NFL's Washington Redskins, teared up before the U.S. Senate Subcommittee on Education, Arts, and Humanities, when admitting that he had been functionally illiterate in college.

Within big-time college athletic departments, the financial pressure to disregard obvious academic shortcomings and shortcuts is just too strong. In the 1980s, Jan Kemp, an English instructor at the University of Georgia, publicly alleged that university officials had demoted and then fired her because she refused to inflate grades in her remedial English courses. Documents showed that administrators replaced the grades she'd given athletes with higher ones, providing fake passing grades on one notable occasion to nine Bulldog football players who otherwise would have been ineligible to compete in the 1982 Sugar Bowl. (Georgia lost anyway, 24–20, to a University of Pittsburgh team led by the future Hall of Fame quarterback Dan Marino.) When Kemp filed a lawsuit against the university, she was publicly vilified as a troublemaker, but she persisted bravely in her testimony. Once, Kemp said, a supervisor demanding that she fix a grade had bellowed, "Who do you think is more important to this university, you or Dominique Wilkins?" (Wilkins was a star on the basketball team.) Traumatized, Kemp twice attempted suicide.

In trying to defend themselves, Georgia officials portrayed Kemp as naive about sports. "We have to compete on a level playing field," said Fred Davison, the university president. During the Kemp civil trial, in 1986, Hale Almand, Georgia's defense lawyer, explained the university's patronizing aspirations for its typical less-than-scholarly athlete. "We may not make a university student out of him," Almand told the court, "but if we can teach him to read and write, maybe he can work at the post office rather than as a garbage man when he gets through with his athletic career." This argument backfired with the jurors: finding in favor of Kemp, they rejected her polite request for $100,000, and awarded her $2.6 million in damages instead. (This was later reduced to $1.08 million.) Jan Kemp embodied what is ostensibly the NCAA's reason for being—to enforce standards fairly and put studies above sports—but no one from the organization ever spoke up on her behalf. . . .

The debates and commissions about reforming college sports nibble around the edges—trying to reduce corruption, to prevent the "contamination" of athletes by lucre, and to maintain at least a pretense of concern for academic integrity. Everything stands on the implicit presumption that preserving amateurism is necessary for the well-being of college athletes. But while amateurism—and the free labor it provides—may be necessary to the preservation of the NCAA, and perhaps to the profit margins of various interested corporations and educational institutions, what if it doesn't benefit the athletes? What if it hurts them?

"The Plantation Mentality"

"Ninety percent of the NCAA revenue is produced by 1 percent of the athletes," Sonny Vaccaro says. "Go to the skill positions"—the stars. "Ninety percent African Americans." The NCAA made its money off those kids, and so did he. They were not all bad people, the NCAA officials, but they were blind, Vaccaro believes. "Their organization is a fraud."

Vaccaro retired from Reebok in 2007 to make a clean break for a crusade. "The kids and their parents gave me a good life," he says in his peppery staccato. "I want to give something back." Call it redemption, he told me. Call it education or a good cause. "Here's what I preach," said Vaccaro. "This goes beyond race, to human rights. The least educated are the most exploited. I'm probably closer to the kids than anyone else, and I'm 71 years old." . . .

In 2010, the third Knight Commission, complementing a previous commission's recommendation for published reports on academic progress, called for the finances of college sports to be made transparent and public—television contracts, conference budgets, shoe deals, coaches' salaries, stadium bonds, everything. The recommendation was based on the worthy truism that sunlight is a proven disinfectant. But in practice, it has not been applied at all. Conferences, coaches, and other stakeholders resisted disclosure; college players still have no way of determining their value to the university.

"Money surrounds college sports," says Domonique Foxworth, who is a cornerback for the NFL's Baltimore Ravens and an executive-committee member for the NFL Players Association, and played for the University of Maryland. "And every player knows those millions are floating around only because of the 18-to-22-year-olds." Yes, he told me, even the second-string punter believes a miracle might lift him into the NFL, and why not? In all the many pages of the three voluminous Knight Commission reports, there is but one paragraph that addresses the real-life choices for college athletes. "Approximately 1 percent of NCAA men's basketball players and 2 percent of NCAA football players are drafted by NBA or NFL teams," stated the 2001 report, basing its figures on a review of the previous 10 years, "and just being drafted is no assurance of a successful professional career." Warning that the odds against professional athletic success are "astronomically high," the Knight Commission counsels college athletes to avoid a "rude surprise" and to stick to regular studies. This is sound advice as far as it goes, but it's a bromide that pinches off discussion. Nothing in the typical college curriculum teaches a sweat-stained guard at Clemson or Purdue what his monetary value to the university is. Nothing prods students to think independently about amateurism—because the universities themselves have too much invested in its preservation. Stifling thought, the universities, in league with the NCAA, have failed their own primary mission by providing an empty, cynical education on college sports. . . .

Without logic or practicality or fairness to support amateurism, the NCAA's final retreat is to sentiment. The Knight Commission endorsed its heartfelt cry that to pay college athletes would be "an unacceptable surrender to despair." Many of the people I spoke with while reporting this article felt the same way. "I don't want to pay college players," said Wade Smith, a tough criminal lawyer and former star running back at North Carolina. "I just don't want to do it. We'd lose something precious."

"Scholarship athletes are already paid," declared the Knight Commission members, "in the most meaningful way possible: with a free education." This evasion by prominent educators severed my last reluctant, emotional tie with imposed amateurism. I found it worse than self-serving. It echoes masters who once claimed that heavenly salvation would outweigh earthly injustice to slaves. In the era when our college sports first arose, colonial powers were turning the whole world upside down to define their own interests as all-inclusive and benevolent. Just so, the NCAA calls it heinous exploitation to pay college athletes a fair portion of what they earn.

Seth Davis  **NO**

Should College Athletes Be Paid? Why, They Already Are

Hoop Thoughts

A lengthy article in an esteemed national publication criticizes the hypocrisies of college athletics. The author details a multitude of scandals involving seedy recruiting, nefarious boosters and academic fraud. The narrative winds to a damning conclusion: "[T]hanks to the influence of the colleges, there is growing up a class of students tainted with commercialism."

You might think I'm referring to the essay by Taylor Branch that was published last week in *The Atlantic* under the headline "The Shame of College Sports." But I'm not. I'm actually referring to an article that appeared in the June 1905 edition of *McClure's*, a prestigious monthly academic journal. The two-part series, authored by a former Harvard football player named Henry Beach Needham, makes a compelling case that the enterprise of amateur athletics is doomed. In *The Atlantic*, Branch also writes that "scandal after scandal has rocked college sports," but while that phrase implies this is a recent trend, Needham shows us that it actually extends back more than a century.

I mention this as a counterweight to the prevailing conventional wisdom—namely, that the publication of Branch's article is a landmark event that has skewered the NCAA's bogus amateurism model for good. The piece has certainly spurred much discussion. A post on *The New Yorker's* website deemed it a "watershed." Jeff MacGregor of ESPN.com suggested "a kind of cultural critical mass has finally been reached." Frank Deford called it "the most important article ever written about college sports." From NPR to MSNBC to *Business Insider* to every sport outlet in between, the story has been hailed as a slam-dunk, once-and-for-all indictment of the NCAA.

To be sure, Branch's article represents a brilliant piece of reporting, which is not surprising considering he won a Pulitzer Prize for his three-volume series on the American civil rights movement. Branch lays out in fascinating detail the structural and legal history of the NCAA that has led us to this point. However, when it comes to analysis, fairness and context, Branch's work leaves much to be desired. If there is a reasonable counter-argument to be made, Branch ignores it. If there is a fact that contradicts his conclusions, he omits it.

Indeed, the entire article is based on a faulty premise, which is introduced right away in the sub-headline: "[S]tudent-athletes generate billions of dollars for universities and private companies while earning nothing for themselves." This is indisputably untrue. Student-athletes earn free tuition, which over the course of four years can exceed $200,000. They are also provided with housing, textbooks, food and academic tutoring. When they travel to road games, they are given per diems for meals. They also get coaching, training, game experience and media exposure they "earn" in their respective crafts. Despite all that, Branch asserts that "[t]he tragedy at the heart of college sports is not that some college athletes are getting paid, but that more of them are not."

If Branch or anyone else wants to argue that college athletes should be paid *more*, let them have at it. But to claim that college athletes earn "nothing"? Pure fiction.

So then: Should college athletes be paid more? As the subject of Branch's most recent bestseller, Bill Clinton, might say, it depends on what the definition of "paid" is. There is a significant and growing gap between the value of a scholarship and what a student-athlete genuinely needs. This is what is referred to as the "cost of attendance" issue. Many people in college sports, from NCAA president Mark Emmert on down, have argued that the scholarship model needs to be updated so this gap can be closed. Part of the challenge is that the gap exists for every athlete in every sport, so the fix must be applied broadly—and expensively. Yes, I'll believe it when I see it, but at least the discourse on this front is moving in the right direction.

However, when Branch and so many others talk about college athletes getting "paid," they are not talking about merely the cost of attendance. They're talking about giving athletes what they're "worth." It's a convincing argument when cast alongside the mind-boggling dollars that are pouring in. Branch points out the SEC recently surpassed the $1 billion mark for football receipts. The Big Ten is close behind at $905 million. He reminds us that the football programs at Texas, Florida, Georgia, Michigan and Penn State earn between $40 million and $80 million each year in profits. The NCAA received $771 million from CBS and Turner to broadcast last year's basketball tournament, a sum that Branch asserts was "built on the backs of amateurs—unpaid labor. The whole edifice depends on the players' willingness to perform what is effectively volunteer work."

So we learn a lot in this article about how much the schools are making. We learn almost nothing, however, about what they're spending. Branch virtually ignores the basic profit-and-loss structure of college sports. For example, did you know that out of 332 schools currently competing in the NCAA's Division I, fewer than a dozen have athletic departments that are operating in the black? And that of the 120 programs that comprise the Football Bowl Subdivision, just 14 are profitable? That means some 88 percent of the top football programs *lose* money for their universities—and that doesn't even include the reams of cash the schools are spending on the so-called nonrevenue sports. Those are some basic, salient facts, but you won't find them anywhere in Branch's 15,000-word opus.

We might want to believe that the reason schools lose so much money is because of the runaway spending on coaches' salaries, new facilities and frivolous items like private jets. Those are indeed reckless expenditures; Myles Brand, the late NCAA president, frequently railed against them. They don't, however, begin to account for just how expensive it is to operate an athletic program. Branch derides college athletics as "Very Big Business," but the truth is, it's actually a "Very Lousy Business."

People who say that college athletes should be paid as professionals like to invoke the principles of the free market. That's the framework advanced by an entity called the National College Players Association, which recently issued a study that put some dollar figures on this question. The NCPA says those numbers demonstrate what the players would be worth "if allowed access to the fair market like the pros."

Left unsaid is the fact that the players *do* have access to the fair market. If they want to be compensated for their abilities, they can simply turn professional. Yes, the NFL and NBA have draft age minimums, but those rules were put in place by the leagues, not the NCAA. Does that not fall under the rubric of the "fair market"? Since the NFL won't accept a player who is not yet three years removed from his senior year in high school, the "fair market value" for a freshman or sophomore in college is actually zero. Yet, the NCAA is still "compensating" those players with a free education and other expenses, even if they are among the 98 percent who will never make a dime playing football. If anything, most of these guys are overpaid.

The NCPA found that, at the highest end, the fair market value for a football player at the University of Texas is $513,922. Setting aside that this number does not account for the money the university is spending on the athlete (for starters, out-of-state tuition at the school runs north of $45,000 per year), I can't help but wonder what's "fair" about the market the NCPA describes. Clearly the starting quarterback generates much more revenue for Texas than does the third-string safety. Would the NCPA argue those two players should be paid the same? There's nothing fair about that.

If we're going to say that players be paid according to their value, then we should pay them less if their team doesn't make a bowl game. That's only fair. Or maybe the school should enter into individual contracts mandating that in return for access to its training program, practice facilities, game experiences and television exposure, the players should pay the school a percentage of their future earnings. If the players don't like the deal, they can sign somewhere else. Hey, it's just business, right?

These are just the first small steps down a long and slippery slope. That's why Ben Cohen's assertion last week in *The Wall Street Journal* that the case for paying salaries to college athletes was "gaining momentum" is so wrong. The only place this idea is gaining momentum is in the media. There is no movement—none—within the actual governing structure of the NCAA to professionalize college athletes. It's not just that it would ruin the amateurism ideal. It's that from a business standpoint, it makes no sense.

The other arguments in favor of paying athletes also do not hold up. Some people claim it would serve as a deterrent against the temptation to accept largesse from agents. This insults our intelligence. Does anyone really think that if the schools give athletes another three thousand bucks a year that those kids are going to turn away a fist full of Benjamins proffered by an agent? On what planet?

Then there's the idea, promulgated by Jay Bilas among others, that athletes should have limitless opportunity to pursue ancillary marketing deals. This works much better in theory than it would in practice. Do we really want a bidding war between Under Armour and Nike to determine whether a recruit attends Maryland or Oregon? Do we want Nick Saban going into a kid's living room and saying, "I know Bob Stoops has a car dealership who will pay you $50,000, but I can line you up with a furniture store that will give you $75,000?"

To be sure, there are a lot of legitimate questions about whether many of the NCAA's policies are in line with laws governing trade and copyrights. This terrain is in Taylor Branch's wheelhouse, and his article is at its best when he dissects the various cases that are currently making their way through the courts. The most interesting one is the class action suit being spearheaded by former UCLA basketball player Ed O'Bannon, who claims the NCAA is violating licensing law by continuing to make money off his likeness without compensating him. I'm not a lawyer, but it seems to me O'Bannon has a reasonable argument, and I certainly have no problem with anyone suing the NCAA to address such grievances. But when someone like Branch characterizes these issues as part of a larger civil rights struggle, he loses me. And I suspect he loses a lot of other open-minded people who agree with him that the system needs fixing.

We need look no further than the current conference expansion madness to understand that many of the presidents who are running college sports are feckless, greedy hypocrites. It's also apparent that the NCAA's enforcement process has gone off the rails. Still, in the final analysis, it's not the NCAA's responsibility to stop schools and athletes from cheating. It's the responsibility of those schools and athletes not to cheat. Any system is only as good as the people who are in it. You can make all the reforms you want, but at the end of the day, where there's money, there's corruption. It's a problem as old as time.

We spend way too much energy worrying about how the system affects a very small number of elite athletes, young men who are going to be multimillionaires as soon as they leave campus. Thus, it was disappointing to see Branch fall back on the argument that these select young men are being exploited. As the father of three children under the age of eight, I can only pray that someone "exploits" my sons someday by giving them tuition, room and board at one of America's finest universities. Branch also relies on some surprisingly lazy reporting. He reveals without a dollop of skepticism that a basketball team (he doesn't say which one) decided it would not play in the NCAA championship game (he doesn't say which year) out of protest. Thankfully, Armageddon was averted when said team lost in the semifinal (Branch doesn't say to whom, or explain why the players couldn't have boycotted the semifinal). Given that this fantastic scenario has been peddled for decades without ever materializing, it is remarkable that a reporter of Branch's stature would accept the account at whole cloth.

In the end, the greatest flaw of Branch's article is his failure to address the question of why schools operate athletics programs despite having to incur such financial losses. Could it be that maybe—just maybe—they really do believe there is educational value in competing? That they think sports is a worthy investment because it gives tens of thousands of young people the opportunity to learn discipline, teamwork and time management alongside calculus and English lit? Could it be that the schools really do want to enrich the lives of their "student-athletes" regardless of whether they are turning a profit?

As I read through Branch's essay, I kept waiting for him to acknowledge that the student-athlete gets something of value from all of this. I finally found it in the last paragraph, when Branch quotes a member of the Knight Commission as referring to the "free education" a student-athlete receives. For Branch, this is the final straw. It is, he writes, "worse than self-serving. It echoes masters who once claimed that heavenly salvation would outweigh earthly injustice to slaves."

Giving someone a free college education is akin to enslavement? If that's the great watershed idea of our time, then we are living in a very dry world indeed.

POSTSCRIPT

Should College Athletes Be Paid?

Again, I'll consider the case of football, since it is probably the central sport in this controversy. Since only a very small percentage of college players ever go on to the NFL, playing professional football is mostly an unrealistic dream for college football players.

So one way of keeping the amateurism at the college level, but realizing that for most players there will be no big NFL payoff, could be to take a percentage of the money earned through selling broadcast rights (and perhaps through other sources, such as the sale of images of the team's leading player), put the money into an escrow account, and pay the departing players—as long as they graduate from college (but are not entering the NFL). That way some payment could be made to the college athletes without putting their college amateurism in jeopardy. The payments would come after they graduate. And those fortunate few athletes who do progress to the NFL will have their own pot of gold anyway. In addition, if the payment is withheld until the college athletes actually graduate, they will have some incentive to do the academic work that is required for graduation.

There has long been a tension between the special amateur status of college player and the money that sports bring into play. The preceding suggestion is just that: a suggestion about how to handle the situation. Unless one side or the other (i.e., amateurism or pay) comes to prevail, some compromise position or some as yet untried position will have to be found workable.

Further reading on this controversy can be found in "How to Pay College Athletes," *Sports Illustrated* (November 7, 2011); Allen L. Sack and Ellen J. Saurowsky, *College Athletes for Hire: The Evolution and Legacy of the NCAA's Amateur Myth* (Praeger Publishers, 1998); Andrew S. Zimbalist, *Unpaid Professionals: Commercialism and Conflict in Big-Time College Sports* (Princeton University Press, 1999); Walter Byers, *Unsportsmanlike Conduct: Exploiting College Athletes* (University of Michigan Press, 1997); Geoff Griffin, ed., *Should College Athletes Be Paid?* (Greenhaven, 2007); Ronald A. Smith, *Pay for Play: A History of Big-Time College Athletic Reform* (University of Illinois Press, 2010); and Michael Oriard, *Bowled Over: Big-Time College Football from the Sixties to the BCS Era* (The University of North Carolina Press, 2009).

ISSUE 17

Is It Right to Produce Genetically Modified Food?

YES: Ronald Bailey, from "Dr. Strangelunch—Or: Why We Should Learn to Stop Worrying and Love Genetically Modified Food," *Reason* (January 2001)

NO: Michael W. Fox, from *Killer Foods: When Scientists Manipulate Genes, Better Is Not Always Best* (Lyons Press, 2004)

ISSUE SUMMARY

YES: Ronald Bailey is a strong supporter of genetically modified food (GMF). He argues that it is feared by many activists, but there is no strong proof that there are any problems with it. In fact, he suggests that there are great benefits that can be provided by GMFs, especially to the world's poor and to those suffering from natural calamities.

NO: Michael Fox is cautious about the spread of *scientism* and the morally blind push for technological development. This scientism, when combined with an aggressive spirit of enterprise, threatens to upset the balance of nature. We may try to rearrange natural things (including plants and animals) to serve our own purposes, but Fox believes that in this way we end up alienating ourselves from the natural world.

Is it right to produce genetically modified foods (GMFs)? The technology that produces GMFs is a powerful technology that can have effects that are very good and also effects that are very bad. There are two mail sorts of problems here. First, there are the problems that we know about or can reasonably anticipate. Second, there are unanticipated problems that may arise. By way of illustration, consider the idea of environmental impact. We can anticipate certain concerns and make efforts to control them. For example, we may be worried about the cross-pollination of some GMFs with cultivated crops or wild plants. This sort of thing is easily anticipated and maybe controlled or taken into account. On the other hand, the second kind of problem is one that we cannot anticipate. Suppose, for example, that some genetic modification will make an important crop resistant to certain pests. So far, so good. But if the pests don't destroy the genetically modified plants, they may end up as pests of other plants, plants that were until then relatively safe. In this case, we may have a serious problem on our hands; and it may be too late to do much about it.

Consider an analogous case. There have been problems in the past when a non-native animal was induced into a new environment in order to deal with some problem there. But this non-native species may cause widespread and unanticipated damage. This is exactly what happened with the introduction of European rabbits into Australia. A small group of 12 rabbits were released by an Englishman living in Australia, who thought that he could use them to hunt (as he was used to doing in England) and that in any case 12 rabbits would have no great impact on the land. But these rabbits proliferated at an enormous rate and became pests, eating the very crops that the European settlers were trying to grow in Australia. In addition, the rabbits consumed much of the ground cover and ate the bark around the bases of trees that the settlers tried to plant. The erosion and environmental damage that resulted was huge. Throughout the 1800s, the rabbits continued to spread across Australia. In the early 1900s, a rabbit-proof fence was built, and further fencing was added until the whole fence extended over 2,000 miles. Today, there are hundreds of millions of rabbits in Australia. Estimates of annual damage caused by them in recent times range from $200,000,000 to $600,000,000.

So, a wise choice would be to proceed with caution—perhaps with utmost caution—when it comes to GMF. Supporters of GMF tend to be optimistic, as if the only problems are the kind that we can anticipate. But even if the optimists are correct that these concerns can be addressed, there are still the unanticipated problems. There are really two reasons for proceeding slowly and carefully. One has to do with the unanticipated problems that I have mentioned, but another has to do with people and their having to get used to new ideas—especially when the new ideas have to do with what sort of food they will consume. The problems are connected in this way: if there should arise one of these unanticipated problems, people will be *very* resistant to GMF. Hence, it is in the interest of the optimists themselves to be cautious.

Some critics of GMFs are worried about the powerful connection of capitalism and biological technology. Genetically modified organisms are developed for profit; they are patented. Individuals tend to do what is best for themselves and not necessarily what is best for other people, animals, or the environment. We have already seen how the "family farm" has given way to the "factory farm," in which huge numbers of animals are kept in close quarters, given hormones, and raised and slaughtered as quickly as possible. Some critics worry that the changes made possible by genetic modification would only exacerbate this sort of problem.

In the following readings, we can regard Ronald Bailey as an optimist. He foresees only good result from GMFs. And he is surely correct that there are many good results. But in the next piece, Michael Fox warns us of the dangers of GMFs. These, he would say, are not only of a physical kind, but also spiritual.

YES

Ronald Bailey

Dr. Strangelunch—Or: Why We Should Learn to Stop Worrying and Love Genetically Modified Food

Ten thousand people were killed and 10 to 15 million left homeless when a cyclone slammed into India's eastern coastal state of Orissa in October 1999. In the aftermath, CARE and the Catholic Relief Society distributed a high-nutrition mixture of corn and soy meal provided by the U.S. Agency for International Development to thousands of hungry storm victims. Oddly, this humanitarian act elicited cries of outrage.

"We call on the government of India and the state government of Orissa to immediately withdraw the corn-soya blend from distribution," said Vandana Shiva, director of the New Delhi–based Research Foundation for Science, Technology, and Ecology. "The U.S. has been using the Orissa victims as guinea pigs for GM [genetically modified] products which have been rejected by consumers in the North, especially Europe." Shiva's organization had sent a sample of the food to a lab in the U.S. for testing to see if it contained any of the genetically improved corn and soybean varieties grown by tens of thousands of farmers in the United States. Not surprisingly, it did.

"Vandana Shiva would rather have her people in India starve than eat bio-engineered food," says C.S. Prakash, a professor of plant molecular genetics at Tuskegee University in Alabama. Per Pinstrup-Andersen, director general of the International Food Policy Research Institute, observes: "To accuse the U.S. of sending genetically modified food to Orissa in order to use the people there as guinea pigs is not only wrong; it is stupid. Worse than rhetoric, it's false. After all, the U.S. doesn't need to use Indians as guinea pigs, since millions of Americans have been eating genetically modified food for years now with no ill effects."

Shiva not only opposes the food aid but is also against "golden rice," a crop that could prevent blindness in half a million to 3 million poor children a year and alleviate vitamin A deficiency in some 250 million people in the developing world. By inserting three genes, two from daffodils and one from a bacterium, scientists at the Swiss Federal Institute of Technology created a variety of rice that produces the nutrient beta-carotene, the precursor to vitamin A. Agronomists at the International Rice Research Institute in the Philippines plan to crossbreed the variety, called "golden rice" because of the color produced by the beta-carotene, with well-adapted local varieties and distribute the resulting plants to farmers all over the developing world.

Last June, at a Capitol Hill seminar on biotechnology sponsored by the Congressional Hunger Center, Shiva airily dismissed golden rice by claiming that "just in the state of Bengal 150 greens which are rich in vitamin A are eaten and grown by the women." A visibly angry Martina McGloughlin, director of the biotechnology program at the University of California at Davis, said "Dr. Shiva's response reminds me of . . . Marie Antoinette, [who] suggested the peasants eat cake if they didn't have access to bread." Alexander Avery of the Hudson Institute's Center for Global Food Issues noted that nutritionists at UNICEF doubted it was physically possible to get enough vitamin A from the greens Shiva was recommending. Furthermore, it seems unlikely that poor women living in shanties in the heart of Calcutta could grow greens to feed their children.

The apparent willingness of biotechnology's opponents to sacrifice people for their cause disturbs scientists who are trying to help the world's poor. At the annual meeting of the American Association for the Advancement of Science last February, Ismail Serageldin, the director of the Consultative Group on International Agricultural Research, posed a challenge: "I ask opponents of biotechnology, do you want 2 to 3 million children a year to go blind and 1 million to die of vitamin A deficiency, just because you object to the way golden rice was created?"

Vandana Shiva is not alone in her disdain for biotechnology's potential to help the poor. Mae-Wan Ho, a reader in biology at London's Open University who advises another activist group, the Third World Network, also opposes golden rice. And according to a *New York Times* report on a biotechnology meeting held last March by the Organization for Economic Cooperation and Development, Benedikt Haerlin, head of Greenpeace's European anti-biotech campaign, "dismissed the importance of saving African and Asian lives at the risk of spreading a new science that he considered untested."

Shiva, Ho, and Haerlin are leaders in a growing global war against crop biotechnology, sometimes called "green biotech" (to distinguish it from medical biotechnology, known as "red biotech"). Gangs of anti-biotech vandals with cute monikers such as Cropatistas and Seeds of Resistance have ripped up scores of research plots in Europe and the U.S. The so-called Earth Liberation Front burned down a crop biotech lab at Michigan State University on New Year's Eve in 1999, destroying years of work and causing $400,000 in property damage. . . . Anti-biotech lobbying groups have proliferated faster than bacteria in an agar-filled petri dish: In addition to Shiva's organization, the Third World Network, and Greenpeace, they include the Union of Concerned Scientists, the Institute for Agriculture and Trade Policy, the Institute of Science in Society, the Rural Advancement Foundation International, the Ralph Nader–founded Public Citizen, the Council for Responsible Genetics, the Institute for Food and Development Policy, and that venerable fount of biotech misinformation, Jeremy Rifkin's Foundation on Economic Trends. The left hasn't been this energized since the Vietnam

War. But if the anti-biotech movement is successful, its victims will include the downtrodden people on whose behalf it claims to speak.

"We're in a war," said an activist at a protesters' gathering during the November 1999 World Trade Organization meeting in Seattle. "We're going to bury this first wave of biotech." He summed up the basic strategy pretty clearly: "The first battle is labeling. The second battle is banning it."

Later that week, during a standing-room-only "biosafety seminar" in the basement of a Seattle Methodist church, the ubiquitous Mae-Wan Ho declared, "This warfare against nature must end once and for all." Michael Fox, a vegetarian "bioethicist" from the Humane Society of the United States, sneered: "We are very clever little simians, aren't we? Manipulating the bases of life and thinking we're little gods." He added, "The only acceptable application of genetic engineering is to develop a genetically engineered form of birth control for our own species." This creepy declaration garnered rapturous applause from the assembled activists.

Despite its unattractive side, the global campaign against green biotech has had notable successes in recent years. Several leading food companies, including Gerber and Frito-Lay, have been cowed into declaring that they will not use genetically improved crops to make their products. Since 1997, the European Union has all but outlawed the growing and importing of biotech crops and food. Last May some 60 countries signed the Biosafety Protocol, which mandates special labels for biotech foods and requires strict notification, documentation, and risk assessment procedures for biotech crops. Activists have launched a "Five-Year Freeze" campaign that calls for a worldwide moratorium on planting genetically enhanced crops. . . .

To decide whether the uproar over green biotech is justified, you need to know a bit about how it works. Biologists and crop breeders can now select a specific useful gene from one species and splice it into an unrelated species. Previously plant breeders were limited to introducing new genes through the time-consuming and inexact art of crossbreeding species that were fairly close relatives. For each cross, thousands of unwanted genes would be introduced into a crop species. Years of "backcrossing"—breeding each new generation of hybrids with the original commercial variety over several generations—were needed to eliminate these unwanted genes so that only the useful genes and characteristics remained. The new methods are far more precise and efficient. The plants they produce are variously described as "transgenic," "genetically modified," or "genetically engineered."

Plant breeders using biotechnology have accomplished a great deal in only a few years. For example, they have created a class of highly successful insect-resistant crops by incorporating toxin genes from the soil bacterium *Bacillus thuringiensis*. Farmers have sprayed *B.t.* spores on crops as an effective insecticide for decades. Now, thanks to some clever biotechnology, breeders have produced varieties of corn, cotton, and potatoes that make their own insecticide. *B.t.* is toxic largely to destructive caterpillars such as the European corn borer and the cotton bollworm; it is not harmful to birds, fish, mammals, or people.

Another popular class of biotech crops incorporates an herbicide resistance gene, a technology that has been especially useful in soybeans. Farmers can spray herbicide on their fields to kill weeds without harming the crop plants. The most widely used herbicide is Monsanto's Roundup (glyphosate), which toxicologists regard as an environmentally benign chemical that degrades rapidly, days after being applied. Farmers who use "Roundup Ready" crops don't have to plow for weed control, which means there is far less soil erosion.

Biotech is the most rapidly adopted new farming technology in history. The first generation of biotech crops was approved by the EPA, the FDA, and the U.S. Department of Agriculture in 1995, and by 1999 transgenic varieties accounted for 33 percent of corn acreage, 50 percent of soybean acreage, and 55 percent of cotton acreage in the U.S. Worldwide, nearly 90 million acres of biotech crops were planted in 1999. With biotech corn, U.S. farmers have saved an estimated $200 million by avoiding extra cultivation and reducing insecticide spraying. U.S. cotton farmers have saved a similar amount and avoided spraying 2 million pounds of insecticides by switching to biotech varieties. Potato farmers, by one estimate, could avoid spraying nearly 3 million pounds of insecticides by adopting *B.t.* potatoes. Researchers estimate that *B.t.* corn has spared 33 million to 300 million bushels from voracious insects.

One scientific panel after another has concluded that biotech foods are safe to eat, and so has the FDA. Since 1995, tens of millions of Americans have been eating biotech crops. Today it is estimated that 60 percent of the foods on U.S. grocery shelves are produced using ingredients from transgenic crops. In April a National Research Council panel issued a report that emphasized it could not find "any evidence suggesting that foods on the market today are unsafe to eat as a result of genetic modification." *Transgenic Plants and World Agriculture,* a report issued in July that was prepared under the auspices of seven scientific academies in the U.S. and other countries, strongly endorsed crop biotechnology, especially for poor farmers in the developing world. "To date," the report concluded, "over 30 million hectares of transgenic crops have been grown and no human health problems associated specifically with the ingestion of transgenic crops or their products have been identified." Both reports concurred that genetic engineering poses no more risks to human health or to the natural environment than does conventional plant breeding.

As U.C.-Davis biologist Martina McGloughlin remarked at last June's Congressional Hunger Center seminar, the biotech foods "on our plates have been put through more thorough testing than conventional food ever has been subjected to." According to a report issued in April by the House Subcommittee on Basic Research, "No product of conventional plant breeding . . . could meet the data requirements imposed on biotechnology products by U.S. regulatory agencies. . . . Yet, these foods are widely and properly regarded as safe and beneficial by plant developers, regulators, and consumers." The report concluded that biotech crops are "at least as safe [as] and probably safer" than conventionally bred crops. . . .

Activists are also fond of noting that the seed company Pioneer Hi-Bred produced a soybean variety that incorporated a gene—for a protein from Brazil nuts—that causes reactions in people who are allergic to nuts. The activists fail to mention that the soybean never got close to commercial release because

Pioneer Hi-Bred checked it for allergenicity as part of its regular safety testing and immediately dropped the variety. The other side of the allergy coin is that biotech can remove allergens that naturally occur in foods such as nuts, potatoes, and tomatoes, making these foods safer.

Even if no hazards from genetically improved crops have been demonstrated, don't consumers have a right to know what they're eating? This seductive appeal to consumer rights has been a very effective public relations gambit for anti-biotech activists. If there's nothing wrong with biotech products, they ask, why don't seed companies, farmers, and food manufacturers agree to label them?

The activists are being more than a bit disingenuous here. Their scare tactics, including the use of ominous words such as *frankenfoods,* have created a climate in which many consumers would interpret labels on biotech products to mean that they were somehow more dangerous or less healthy than old-style foods. Biotech opponents hope labels would drive frightened consumers away from genetically modified foods and thus doom them. Then the activists could sit back and smugly declare that biotech products had failed the market test. . . .

It is interesting to note that several crop varieties popular with organic growers were created through mutations deliberately induced by breeders using radiation or chemicals. This method of modifying plant genomes is obviously a far cruder and more imprecise way of creating new varieties. Radiation and chemical mutagenesis is like using a sledgehammer instead of the scalpel of biotechnology. Incidentally, the FDA doesn't review these crop varieties produced by radiation or chemicals for safety, yet no one has dropped dead from eating them.

Labeling nonbiotech foods as such will not satisfy the activists whose goal is to force farmers, grain companies, and food manufacturers to segregate biotech crops from conventional crops. Such segregation would require a great deal of duplication in infrastructure, including separate grain silos, rail cars, ships, and production lines at factories and mills. The StarLink corn problem is just a small taste of how costly and troublesome segregating conventional from biotech crops would be. Some analysts estimate that segregation would add 10 percent to 30 percent to the prices of food without any increase in safety. Activists are fervently hoping that mandatory crop segregation will also lead to novel legal nightmares: If a soybean shipment is inadvertently "contaminated" with biotech soybeans, who is liable? If biotech corn pollen falls on an organic cornfield, can the organic farmer sue the biotech farmer? Trial lawyers must be salivating over the possibilities.

The activists' "pro-consumer" arguments can be turned back on them. Why should the majority of consumers pay for expensive crop segregation that they don't want? It seems reasonable that if some consumers want to avoid biotech crops, they should pay a premium, including the costs of segregation. . . .

Under the "precautionary principle," regulators do not need to show scientifically that a biotech crop is unsafe before banning it; they need only assert that it has not been proved harmless. Enshrining the precautionary principle into international law is a major victory for biotech opponents. "They want to err on the side of caution not only when the evidence is not conclusive but when no evidence exists that would indicate harm is possible," observes Frances Smith, executive director of Consumer Alert.

Model biosafety legislation proposed by the Third World Network goes even further than the Biosafety Protocol, covering all biotech organisms and requiring authorization "for all activities and for all GMOs [genetically modified organisms] and derived products." Under the model legislation, "the absence of scientific evidence or certainty does not preclude the decision makers from denying approval of the introduction of the GMO or derived products." Worse, under the model regulations "any adverse socioeconomic effects must also be considered." If this provision is adopted, it would give traditional producers a veto over innovative competitors, the moral equivalent of letting candlemakers prevent the introduction of electric lighting.

Concerns about competition are one reason European governments have been so quick to oppose crop biotechnology. "EU countries, with their heavily subsidized farming, view foreign agribusinesses as a competitive threat," Frances Smith writes. "With heavy subsidies and price supports, EU farmers see no need to improve productivity." In fact, biotech-boosted European agricultural productivity would be a fiscal disaster for the E.U., since it would increase already astronomical subsidy payments to European farmers.

The global campaign against green biotech received a public relations windfall on May 20, 1999, when *Nature* published a study by Cornell University researcher John Losey that found that Monarch butterfly caterpillars died when force-fed milkweed dusted with pollen from *B.t.* corn. Since then, at every anti-biotech demonstration, the public has been treated to flocks of activist women dressed fetchingly as Monarch butterflies. But when more-realistic field studies were conducted, researchers found that the alleged danger to Monarch caterpillars had been greatly exaggerated. Corn pollen is heavy and doesn't spread very far, and milkweed grows in many places aside from the margins of cornfields. In the wild, Monarch caterpillars apparently know better than to eat corn pollen on milkweed leaves.

Furthermore, *B.t.* crops mean that farmers don't have to indiscriminately spray their fields with insecticides, which kill beneficial as well as harmful insects. In fact, studies show that *B.t.* cornfields harbor higher numbers of beneficial insects such as lacewings and ladybugs than do conventional cornfields. James Cook, a biologist at Washington State University, points out that the population of Monarch butterflies has been increasing in recent years, precisely the time period in which *B.t.* corn has been widely planted. The fact is that pest-resistant crops are harmful mainly to target species—that is, exactly those insects that insist on eating them.

Never mind; we will see Monarchs on parade for a long time to come. Meanwhile, a spooked EPA has changed its rules governing the planting of *B.t.* corn, requiring farmers to plant non-*B.t.* corn near the borders of their fields so that *B.t.* pollen doesn't fall on any milkweed growing there. But even the EPA firmly rejects activist claims about the alleged harms caused by *B.t.*

crops. "Prior to registration of the first *B.t.* plant pesticides in 1995," it said in response to a Greenpeace lawsuit, "EPA evaluated studies of potential effects on a wide variety of non-target organisms that might be exposed to the *B.t.* toxin, e.g., birds, fish, honeybees, ladybugs, lacewings, and earthworms. EPA concluded that these species were not harmed."

Another danger highlighted by anti-biotech activists is the possibility that transgenic crops will crossbreed with other plants. At the Congressional Hunger Center seminar, Mae-Wan Ho claimed that "GM-constructs are designed to invade genomes and to overcome natural species barriers." And that's not all. "Because of their highly mixed origins," she added, "GM-constructs tend to be unstable as well as invasive, and may be more likely to spread by horizontal gene transfer."

"Nonsense," says Tuskegee University biologist C.S. Prakash. "There is no scientific evidence at all for Ho's claims." Prakash points out that plant breeders specifically choose transgenic varieties that are highly stable since they want the genes that they've gone to the trouble and expense of introducing into a crop to stay there and do their work.

Ho also suggests that "GM genetic material" when eaten is far more likely to be taken up by human cells and bacteria than is "natural genetic material." Again, there is no scientific evidence for this claim. All genes from whatever source are made up of the same four DNA bases, and all undergo digestive degradation when eaten. . . .

The environmentalist case against biotech crops includes a lot of innuendo. "After GM sugar beet was harvested," Ho claimed at the Congressional Hunger Center seminar, "the GM genetic material persisted in the soil for at least two years and was taken up by soil bacteria." Recall that the *Bacillus thuringiensis* is a *soil bacterium*—its habitat is the soil. Organic farmers broadcast *B.t.* spores freely over their fields, hitting both target and nontarget species. If organic farms were tested, it's likely that *B.t.* residues would be found there as well; they apparently have not had any ill effects. Even the EPA has conceded, in its response to Greenpeace's lawsuit, that "there are no reports of any detrimental effects on the soil ecosystems from the use of *B.t.* crops."

Given their concerns about the spread of transgenes, you might think biotech opponents would welcome innovations designed to keep them confined. Yet they became apoplectic when Delta Pine Land Co. and the U.S. Department of Agriculture announced the development of the Technology Protection System, a complex of three genes that makes seeds sterile by interfering with the development of plant embryos. TPS also gives biotech developers a way to protect their intellectual property: Since farmers couldn't save seeds for replanting, they would have to buy new seeds each year.

Because high-yielding hybrid seeds don't breed true, corn growers in the U.S. and Western Europe have been buying seed annually for decades. Thus TPS seeds wouldn't represent a big change in the way many American and European farmers do business. If farmers didn't want the advantages offered in the enhanced crops protected by TPS, they would be free to buy seeds without TPS. Similarly, seed companies could offer crops with transgenic traits that would be expressed only in the presence of chemical activators that farmers could choose to buy if they thought they were worth the extra money. Ultimately, the market would decide whether these innovations were valuable.

If anti-biotech activists really are concerned about gene flow, they should welcome such technologies. The pollen from crop plants incorporating TPS would create sterile seeds in any weed that it happened to crossbreed with, so that genes for traits such as herbicide resistance or drought tolerance couldn't be passed on.

This point escapes some biotech opponents. "The possibility that [TPS] may spread to surrounding food crops or to the natural environment is a serious one," writes Vandana Shiva in her recent book *Stolen Harvest.* "The gradual spread of sterility in seeding plants would result in a global catastrophe that could eventually wipe out higher life forms, including humans, from the planet." This dire scenario is not just implausible but biologically impossible: *TPS is a gene technology that causes sterility; that means, by definition, that it can't spread. . . .*

As one tracks the war against green biotech, it becomes ever clearer that its leaders are not primarily concerned about safety. What they really hate is capitalism and globalization. "It is not inevitable that corporations will control our lives and rule the world," writes Shiva in *Stolen Harvest.* In *Genetic Engineering: Dream or Nightmare?* (1999), Ho warns, "Genetic engineering biotechnology is an unprecedented intimate alliance between bad science and big business which will spell the end of humanity as we know it, and the world at large." The first nefarious step, according to Ho, will occur when the "food giants of the North" gain "control of the food supply of the South through exclusive rights to genetically engineered seeds."

Accordingly, anti-biotech activists oppose genetic patents. Greenpeace is running a "No Patents on Life" campaign that appeals to inchoate notions about the sacredness of life. Knowing that no patents means no investment, biotech opponents declare that corporations should not be able to "own" genes, since they are created by nature.

The exact rules for patenting biotechnology are still being worked out by international negotiators and the U.S. Patent and Trademark Office. But without getting into the arcane details, the fact is that discoverers and inventors don't "own" genes. A patent is a license granted for a limited time to encourage inventors and discoverers to disclose publicly their methods and findings. In exchange for disclosure, they get the right to exploit their discoveries for 20 years, after which anyone may use the knowledge and techniques they have produced. Patents aim to encourage an open system of technical knowledge.

"Biopiracy" is another charge that activists level at biotech seed companies. After prospecting for useful genes in indigenous crop varieties from developing countries, says Shiva, companies want to sell seeds incorporating those genes back to poor farmers. Never mind that the useful genes are stuck in inferior crop varieties, which means that poor farmers have no way of optimizing their benefits. Seed companies liberate the useful genes and put them into high-yielding varieties that can boost poor farmers' productivity.

Amusingly, the same woman who inveighs against "biopiracy" proudly claimed at the Congressional Hunger Center seminar that 160 varieties of kidney beans are grown in India. Shiva is obviously unaware that farmers in India are themselves "biopirates." Kidney beans were domesticated by the Aztecs and Incas in the Americas and brought to the Old World via the Spanish explorers. In response to Shiva, C.S. Prakash pointed out that very few of the crops grown in India today are indigenous. "Wheat, peanuts, and apples and everything else—the chiles that the Indians are so proud of," he noted, "came from outside. I say, thank God for the biopirates." Prakash condemned Shiva's efforts to create "a xenophobic type of mentality within our culture" based on the fear that "everybody is stealing all of our genetic material."

If the activists are successful in their war against green biotech, it's the world's poor who will suffer most. The International Food Policy Research Institute estimates that global food production must increase by 40 percent in the next 20 years to meet the goal of a better and more varied diet for a world population of some 8 billion people. As biologist Richard Flavell concluded in a 1999 report to the IFPRI, "It would be unethical to condemn future generations to hunger by refusing to develop and apply a technology that can build on what our forefathers provided and can help produce adequate food for a world with almost 2 billion more people by 2020."

One way biotech crops can help poor farmers grow more food is by controlling parasitic weeds, an enormous problem in tropical countries. Cultivation cannot get rid of them, and farmers must abandon fields infested with them after a few growing seasons. Herbicide-resistant crops, which would make it possible to kill the weeds without damaging the cultivated plants, would be a great boon to such farmers.

By incorporating genes for proteins from viruses and bacteria, crops can be immunized against infectious diseases. The papaya mosaic virus had wiped out papaya farmers in Hawaii, but a new biotech variety of papaya incorporating a protein from the virus is immune to the disease. As a result, Hawaiian papaya orchards are producing again, and the virus-resistant variety is being made available to developing countries. Similarly, scientists at the Donald Danforth Plant Science Center in St. Louis are at work on a cassava variety that is immune to cassava mosaic virus, which killed half of Africa's cassava crop two years ago. . . .

Biotech crops can provide medicine as well as food. Biologists at the Boyce Thompson Institute for Plant Research at Cornell University recently reported success in preliminary tests with biotech potatoes that would immunize people against diseases. One protects against Norwalk virus, which causes diarrhea, and another might protect against the hepatitis B virus which afflicts 2 billion people. Plant-based vaccines would be especially useful for poor countries, which could manufacture and distribute medicines simply by having local farmers grow them. . . .

[O]pponents of crop biotechnology can't stand the fact that it will help developed countries first. New technologies, whether reaping machines in the 19th century or computers today, are always adopted by the rich before they become available to the poor. The fastest way to get a new technology to poor people is to speed up the product cycle so the technology can spread quickly. Slowing it down only means the poor will have to wait longer. If biotech crops catch on in the developed countries, the techniques to make them will become available throughout the world, and more researchers and companies will offer crops that appeal to farmers in developing countries.

Activists like Shiva subscribe to the candlemaker fallacy: If people begin to use electric lights, the candlemakers will go out of business, and they and their families will starve. This is a supremely condescending view of poor people. In order not to exacerbate inequality, Shiva and her allies want to stop technological progress. They romanticize the backbreaking lives that hundreds of millions of people are forced to live as they eke out a meager living off the land.

Per Pinstrup-Andersen of the International Food Policy Research Institute asked participants in the Congressional Hunger Center seminar to think about biotechnology from the perspective of people in developing countries: "We need to talk about the low-income farmer in West Africa who, on half an acre, maybe an acre of land, is trying to feed her five children in the face of recurrent droughts, recurrent insect attacks, recurrent plant diseases. For her, losing a crop may mean losing a child. Now, how can we sit here debating whether she should have access to a drought-tolerant crop variety? None of us at this table or in this room [has] the ethical right to force a particular technology upon anybody, but neither do we have the ethical right to block access to it. The poor farmer in West Africa doesn't have any time for philosophical arguments as to whether it should be organic farming or fertilizers or GM food. She is trying to feed her children. Let's help her by giving her access to all of the options. Let's make the choices available to the people who have to take the consequences."

Michael W. Fox

Killer Foods: When Scientists Manipulate Genes, Better Is Not Always Best

Scientific and Bioethical Issues in Genetic-Engineering Biotechnology

> Every creature has its own reason to be. All its parts have a direct effect on one another, a relationship to one another, thereby constantly renewing the circle of life.
>
> —Johann Wolfgang von Goethe

Through genetic-engineering technology, we now have the power to profoundly alter all life forms and the very nature of nature—the natural world, or earth's creation. What are the short- and long-term consequences for humanity, animals, and nature, and what are the ethical principles and boundaries? What risks are justified by what benefits?

This new technology is complex, with many risks, costs, and benefits that need careful consideration because it could permanently and irreversibly alter the biology of life forms, the ecology, and natural evolution.

Through various techniques, the genetic composition of animals, plants, and microorganisms can be altered in ways radically different from those achieved by traditional selective breeding. Genes can be deleted, duplicated, and switched among species. Animal and human genes have been incorporated or "spliced" into the genetic structure or germ plasm of other animals, plants, bacteria, and other microorganisms. Human genes are now present in the genetic makeup of some mice, sheep, pigs, cattle, fish, and other animals.

The creation of transgenic plants, animals, and microorganisms, along with a host of other developments in genetice-ngineering biotechnology, are touted as progressive, if not necessary, and as promising great benefits to society (and investors). Although I have found no coherent argument based on reason, science, or ethics to support any of these claims unconditionally, the biotechnology life-science industry and its supporters, just like the supporters of factory farming and vivisection, give enthusiastic and unconditional endorsement to new developments in biogenetic manipulation and to the industrialization and patent protection of its processes and products. The hyperbole employed on behalf of such new developments, coupled with a highly competitive and volatile world market, is driven by risk-taking venture capitalists whose cavalier attitude toward such significant risks as socioeconomic inequity, ecological damage, and animal suffering is neither progressive nor visionary. Unfortunately, this attitude is understandably often shared and rarely challenged by bioengineering scientists and academics in their employ, and by politicians and policy makers, who are generally scientifically illiterate.

This is not a good foundation for any new technology, least of all for such a profound and complex one as bioengineering. It is incumbent upon all who do not feel so sanguine about the directions this new technology is taking to challenge its assumptions and presumptions.[1] The doublethink and newspeak logic* of the biotechnocracy evidences some disturbing warning signs, notably of historical amnesia, ecological and biological illiteracy, ethical and moral dyslexia, blind faith, and ideological rigidity.

An international bioethics council within the United Nations would be a beginning to help ensure that this technology is applied with the minimum of harm to further the good of society and the integrity and future of the planetary biosphere. Insofar as its applicability to organic agriculture, biogenetic engineering is, from a philosophical perspective, anathema. It is mechanistic, deterministic, and reductionistic, while organic agriculture is seen as emulating nature—i.e., ecologistic, dynamically indeterminate, holistic, and regenerative. There is also an inimical difference in attitude that separates these two worldviews and in the kinds of medicine, industry, and market economy they aspire to. It has to do with reverential respect for the sanctity and intrinsic value of life, which is more evident on a well-operated (and well-loved) organic farm than in a biotech laboratory or on an industrial farm.

The ideal of value-free objectivity in the method of scientific investigation provides no ethical basis for determining the risks, costs, and benefits in the technology transfer of biotechnical discoveries from the laboratory setting to the real world. A technocratic society runs the risk of serious error in believing that the "truth" of the scientific method is an ethically objective yardstick. This belief system of *scientism*, which is like a religion in the late twentieth century, accounts for the rigid "science-based" criteria and policies that corporations and governments—the entwined limbs of the technocracy—so adamantly adhere to. Yet this yardstick is as linear as it is simplistic. A broader bioethical framework is urgently needed in order for society to transcend technological enchantment, so that the fruits of scientific research may be realized for the benefit of the entire life community of the planet. . . .

Two contexts of particular interest to me are agriculture and the use of animals for biomedical research and biopharmaceutical industrial purposes. I am especially concerned about applications of genetic-engineering biotechnology in agriculture, because it is being applied primarily to maintain a

---

*E.g.: *Knowledge is Power and Science is Truth.* From *1984* by George Orwell.

dysfunctional system. We have an animal- rather than a plant-based agriculture in the industrial world, which causes much animal suffering and isn't good for the environment, for consumers, or for the social economy of rural communities. And it is now well documented that conventional agricultural practices are ecologically unsound, inhumane, and in the long term unsustainable, even with ever more costly corrective inputs. Some of these are being developed and misapplied by agricultural biotechnologists, who endeavor to maintain and expand globally a bioindustrialized food and drug industry that must be opposed by all because it fails to meet any of the following bioethical criteria of acceptability: that it be humane, ecologically sound, socially just, equitable, and sustainable. Rather, it is a major threat to biodiversity and to the social economies of many more sustainable farming communities.

Now, via GATT, the World Trade Organization, and Codex Alimentarius, the life-science industry, with its new varieties of patented seeds and other bioengineered products and processes, is moving rapidly to a global agricultural and market monopoly.

With regard to the patenting of animals, plants, and other life forms, I believe that it is demeaning to refer to them as "intellectual property" and that there are unresolved questions of ethics and equity over the patenting of life.

The spirit of enterprise and state of mind behind genetic engineering evidences an ethical blindness to the natural integrity, purity, and sanctity of being. Otherwise, how would we ever consider inserting our own and other alien genes into other species, drastically altering their nature and future to make them more useful to us rather than fulfilling their biologically ordained ecological, evolutionary, and spiritual purposes?

The domestication of plants and animals and the transformation of their habitats and ecosystems to serve human ends have had profound consequences on their nature and on the entire natural world. But do thousands of years of domestication and ecosystem alteration provide a historically valid and ethically acceptable precedent for even more profoundly altering the intrinsic nature of other living beings through genetic engineering?

We must ask: Is it necessary? Who are the primary beneficiaries? What are the direct and indirect costs and risks? Are there safer, less invasive and enduring alternatives? Does a cultural history of exploiting life justify its continuation and intensification through genetic-engineering biotechnology?

"Hard" and "Soft" Paths

There are two basic paths that this new technology can take, and I have designated them as "hard" and "soft." The hard path results in permanent physical changes that may be transmissible to subsequent generations. These changes in animals' physiology or anatomy may result in their suffering. For purely ethical, humanitarian reasons, I am opposed to all hard-path applications of genetic-engineering biotechnology of which there is no demonstrable benefit to the animals themselves.

Where such benefits can be demonstrated, as in efforts to conserve endangered species and to prevent or treat various animal diseases of genetic origin, and there are no alternative strategies to achieve the same ends, then I would accept on a case-by-case basis some hard-path applications. But those applications that design animals for purely utilitarian ends should be questioned and opposed in the absence of demonstrable animal benefit.*

Likewise, any nontherapeutic product of genetic-engineering biotechnology, such as recombinant (synthetic) bovine growth hormone (rBGH), that is used to increase animals' utility and can result in animal sickness and suffering, or increase the risk thereof, is not ethically acceptable.

The creation of transgenic plants that are resistant to herbicides and virus infections, or that produce their own insecticides, belong in the hard-path category. They do not accord with accepted standards and principles of organic and sustainable agriculture and are a potential threat to wildlife and nonharmful insects, microorganisms, and biodiversity.

Soft-path developments with this technology include the creation of new-generation vaccines, veterinary pharmaceuticals and diagnostic tests, and genetic screening to identify defective genes and those that convey disease resistance and other beneficial traits. The most promising of these soft-path developments that I would endorse are immunocontraceptives, new-generation contraceptive implants for humans and other mammals.

Soft-path genetically engineered products are acceptable, provided they are safe and effective without side-effects that could cause animal suffering; provided they cannot be transmitted to or harm nontarget species (as with modified live virus vaccines); and provided they are not used to help prevent diseases in animals kept under stressful, inhumane conditions (as on factory farms), rather than changing the conditions that contribute to increased susceptibility to disease. A full socioeconomic and environmental impact assessment is needed prior to approving these soft-path products for animal use. For example, a new vaccine for cattle to combat trypanosomiasis (to which wild ruminants are immune) could result in an unacceptable loss of biodiversity and an ecologically harmful expansion of livestock numbers. . . .

Genetic Determinism

The broad range of potentially beneficial applications of genetic-engineering biotechnology in agriculture and in veterinary and human medicine are being overshadowed and undermined by an overarching narrowmindedness. This is the reductionist view that since there is a genetic basis to disease, then genetic engineering is the answer to preventing and treating various human, crop, and farm-animal health problems. And that along the way we may even discover ways to genetically engineer (and patent) life forms to enhance their usefulness and "improve" their nature, be it the stature and intelligence of our own species, the growth rates of chickens and pigs, or the herbicide and pest resistance

---

*Utilitarian ends such as to increase appetite, growth, muscle mass, leanness, fertility, or milk or egg production or to deliberately create developmental abnormalities and genetic disorders.

of corn and beans. This simplistic view of genetic determinism is a potentially harmful one because even though it claims to be scientific and objective, i.e., value free, it is extremely subjective and biased since it puts so much value (and faith) in the genetic approach to improving the human condition and the disease resistance and productivity of crops and farm animals.[2]

A more interdisciplinary and holistic approach to human, animal, and crop health and disease prevention is urgently needed. Seeking purely genetic solutions is too narrow and reductionistic, and because of the uncertainty principle inherent in the genotype-environment interface, genetic determinism is unlikely to bring the benefits that its proponents and investors hope and believe are possible.

In its unsubstantiated promises to feed the hungry world, and its promises of great profits for investors, genetic-engineering technology drains human resources from funding more sustainable, eco-friendly, and socially just ways of producing food. It likewise impedes the medical sciences from breaking free of a reductionistic and mechanistic paradigm of human health that blames either nature or our genes for most of our ills. Once people blamed the gods, but as Hippocrates advised, "Physician, do no harm." Conventional medicine has yet to realize this wisdom and put it into practice.

Had the dominant Western culture based its foundation on the worldview of Pythagoras or Plato, rather than that of Aristotle, with his hierarchical, linear thinking, and not on interpreting the book of Genesis as giving man unconditional dominion over God's creation, then our powers over the atoms of matter and the genes of life would probably be applied to very different ends: wholeness and healing, rather than commodification, monopoly, and selfish exploitation.

The original meaning of *dominion* in the book of Genesis does not rest in the Latin *domino*, to rule over, but in the root Hebrew verb *yorade*. *Yorade* means to come down to, to have humility, compassion, and communion with all of God's creation. It is an injunction of reverential care, of humane stewardship. Hence, genetic engineering is antithetical to Judeo-Christian tradition and ethics. It also violates the precept of Islam, where it is regarded as a sin to willfully interfere with God's creation, and would be considered a blasphemy of hubris to engage in creating transgenic life forms and then to go and patent them.

Genetic engineering is anathema to Buddhists, Hindus, and Jains, since it is a direct violation of the doctrine of *ahimsa*, of noninterference and non-harming. It is also a fundamental biological interference with the earth's creative process of natural unfoldment and thus a disruption in the spiritual process of incarnation.

One would think that an enlightened biotechnology industry would make every effort to protect the remaining integrity and biodiversity of genetic resources of the first creation—the last of the wild. Future generations, with a more sophisticated understanding of genetic engineering, will need wild places as a source of uncontaminated genetic resources. This "biobank" must be protected now and not ransacked by the industries of timber, mining, real estate, and other business enterprises, and by the millions of poor people who are malnourished and either landless or without sustainable agriculture or way of life. I have seen them in India and Africa leaving an imprint similar to that left by the clear-cutting of old-growth forests and totally obliterated prairies that the U.S. government still permits. To this destruction by the rural poor—especially from grazing too many livestock, plowing marginal land that erodes easily, and killing trees for firewood—we must add industrial and agrochemical pollution in both the "first" and "third" worlds.

An important step to protect the biobank is to eliminate all possibilities of genetic pollution from transgenic crops, bacteria, insects, oysters and other mollusks, shrimp, and other genetically engineered seafoods, which will be the first foods of animal origin on the market.[3] The second step must be to label all foods to indicate whether any product or ingredient has been genetically engineered. To have this information is a consumer's right, on religious and ethical grounds, since many, regardless of assurances as to food quality and safety, would prefer not to unknowingly purchase genetically modified foods. The public has a right to be informed and a right to be able to choose natural foods if they prefer, especially since genetically altered foods violate many people's religious principles.

The third step entails international cooperation on the scale of a United Nations environmental paramilitary police force to help countries protect their wildlife preserves and biodiversity, both aquatic and terrestrial, from further human encroachment, wholesale exploitation, and genetic piracy.

There is no way to collect all potentially useful life forms and store them in culture media, or in seed, sperm, embryo, and cell banks. Many seeds lose their vitality when stored and need to be frequently germinated and harvested, genetic changes due to local environmental influences notwithstanding. They must be protected *in situ* and *in toto*.

The late Professor René Dubos, a renowned biologist from Rockefeller University, said, "An ethical attitude to the scientific study of nature readily leads to a theology of the earth." His concerns, expressed in 1972 in his book *A God Within,* are extremely relevant today with the advent of genetic engineering.[4] He cautioned, "A relationship to the earth based only on its use for economic enrichment is bound to result not only in its degradation but also in the devaluation of human life. This is a perversion which, if not corrected, will become a fatal disease of technological societies." Without an "ethical attitude," beginning with a reverential respect for all life and based on internationally accepted bioethical principles and values, . . . this disease is very likely to be fatal to the dominant culture.

The ethics of preserving the earth's bio-integrity must serve to direct and constrain the emerging biotechnocracy. The biotechnology industry must adopt these ethics; otherwise, the costs and risks to future generations will far outweigh the short-term profits of the present.

Obedience to natural law, which is based on the bioethics of sound science and moral philosophy, must be absolute, like compassion, or else it is not at all. Through science, reason, and reverence, we learn the wisdom of obedience. Industry and commerce must conform to natural law and, like human society, do nothing to jeopardize natural biodiversity, bio-integrity, or the future of earth's creation. The first task of science and of biotechnology is to begin the healing of humanity, which is biologically, economically, and spiritually dependent on the protection and restoration of what is left of the natural world: first creation first!

The application of bioethics, which is the foundation of natural law, to establishing the necessary limits and boundaries of new technologies like genetic engineering is long overdue. Every nation-state needs to have a bioethics council that would function to maximize the benefits and minimize the risks and costs of all new technologies and related commercial activities, and to ensure international harmonization of their policies and guidelines with all countries via the United Nations Council on Sustainable Development.

Beyond Genetic Determinism and Reductionism

Genes "intelligently" organize structural proteins into myriad environmentally co-evolved, living forms. These life forms are variously self-healing, self-replicating, even marginally self-conscious to varying degrees; and they form mutually enhancing or symbiotic communities. Collectively, for example, they help create and maintain the soil and the atmosphere that sustains the body-earth and life community; much like our digestive, circulatory, and respiratory systems are cellular communities that sustain the body-human. We find phenomenological parallels between the ecological roles of a living forest or a watershed of streams and swamps, and the functions of our own lungs, circulatory system, and kidneys.

In order to know, therefore, *how* genes, organs, and forests function, we must understand their purpose within the larger functional systems in which they participate. Therefore, we must seek to understand the *contexts* in which genes operate, their history (or evolution and development), and their consequences. Such knowledge of temporal and spatial relationships within the intersecting biofields of organisms and their environments is lacking in the reductionistic paradigm of conventional scientific inquiry, and in conventional medical practice, which has been so reticent to recognize the myriad connections between healthy forests and a healthy people. Hence, most of our agricultural, medical, and technological inventions and interventions have caused more harm than good.[5]

The direction being taken by the life-science industrial biotechnocracy today, especially its investment in creating and patenting transgenic life forms that have been engineered to serve narrow human ends, is cause for concern, as the science base is unsound and there is no ethical or ecological framework. . . .

It is unlikely that genetically engineered crops will ever help compensate for nutrient-deficient soils, polluted water, or a contaminated food chain. Using biotechnology to make farm animals more productive and efficient in the context of intensive industrial agriculture will only extend the animals' suffering and prolong the adverse environmental, economic, and consumer health consequences of this kind of agriculture.

Genetic-engineering reductionists might find it advantageous to further reduce life conceptually to its next level—primordial energy, vital force, or chi—and then reflect upon the possibility that the final frontier of materialistic and mechanistic science, molecular genetics, is a grand illusion, a mirage created by a defective worldview and a misconception of human purpose and significance. The antidote is a paradigm shift that broadens our understanding of life by fostering a sense of reverence and awe and a feeling for the spirit or essence of life that is omnipresent in all matter and manifest in all sentient beings.

Ecological and Social Concerns

In relation to ecological concerns, I would concur with Mario Giampietro that:

> Current research on agricultural applications of genetic engineering seems to be heading exactly in the same direction as the green revolution. The main goal is to provide yet another short-term remedy to sustain, if not increase, the scale of human activity. . . . Genetic engineering aimed only at increasing economic return and technological efficiency is likely to further lower the compatibility of human activity and natural ecosystem processes. . . . Before introducing a massive flow of new transgenic organisms into the biosphere, a better understanding of the endangered equilibrium of the biosphere should be achieved.[6]

Philosopher, scientist, and activist Vandana Shiva eloquently expresses my concerns over the harmful consequences of this new technology and the need for public input to minimize potential harm:

> My major concern these days is with the protection of cultural and biological diversity. I am preoccupied with the ecological and social impacts of globalization of the economy through free trade on the one hand and the colonization of life through genetic engineering and patents on life forms on the other hand. My sense is that unless we can put limits and boundaries on commercial activity and on new technologies, the violence against nature and against people will become uncontrollable. The question I constantly ask myself is, What are the creative catalytic linkages that strengthen community and enable communities of people to exercise social and ecological control of economic and technological processes?[7]

One of the major risks of genetic-engineering biotechnology has a conceptual basis that Craig Holdrege thoroughly dissects in his book *Genetics and the Manipulation of Life*.[8] It stems from scientific reductionism, objectivism, and the mechanomorphizing and reification of genetic and developmental processes and shows no concern and responsibility for effects on the organism and the environment. The belief in genetic determinism is as dangerous ethically as it is flawed scientifically because it is based on the central dogma that genes alone determine how an organism develops and functions.[9] The antidote that Holdrege offers is in seeking an understanding of relationships via contextual thinking, based in part on regarding heredity as potential or plasticity complemented by heredity as limitation or specificity. *Genetics and the Manipulation of Life* is an important book for all students of the biological sciences and for those proponents and critics of biotechnology in particular.

We must be mindful of the fact that nothing that exists originated independently. Therefore, all existences are ultimately interconnected, co-evolved, and interdependent. Genes are not the sole or even the primary controllers and regulators of life processes. It is a product of hubris and reductionism that in isolating and manipulating DNA, we believe we can gain control over life. If we do not act quickly to address all the factors that are leading to the death of nature, then the virtual reality that the global life-science industrial biotechnocracy is fabricating will collapse. We have neither the wisdom nor the resources to develop a viable analog of the earth's atmosphere, or of an old-growth forest, a mountain stream, or a coral reef. . . .

How then can we expect unnatural, genetically engineered life forms to do any better in the virtual world of global industrialization, even when we too are engineered to withstand the harmful, somatic effects of chemicals, pathogens, and radiation?

Some Bioethical Concerns and Solutions

I am deeply concerned by what I see as a lack of vision in the agricultural biotechnology. industry, which is limiting its benefits to humanity and its potential for profitability and sustainability. The cavalier attitude of corporations, governments, and much of academia toward the release and commercialization of transgenic crops is especially troubling. A related concern is over the fact that agricultural biotechnology is focused primarily on major commodity crops and not linked in any significant way with ecologically sound and sustainable crop and livestock husbandry. It therefore cannot play any significant role in helping relieve world hunger or, especially, in implementing appropriate practices and inputs to restore agricultural and rangelands now sorely degraded worldwide.

Lester Brown writes in *State of the World 1994* that University of Minnesota agricultural economist Vernon Ruttan summarized the feeling of a forum of the world's leading agricultural scientists when he said, "Advances in conventional technology will remain the primary source of growth in crop and animal production over the next quarter century." Biotechnology should not be seen as a panacea, or as a substitute for conventional technologies, the most basic of which are good farming practices in accordance with the land ethic and the principles of humane sustainable agriculture. My opposition to conventional agricultural biotechnology is based on its evident band-aid and high-input roles in conventional, nonsustainable agriculture. As such, it represents a major obstacle to the research, development, and adoption of more sustainable, ecologically sound, and in the long-term more profitable farming practices. . . .

The conservative Hastings Center has published a report that details the complexity of bioethics, especially the creation of genetically engineered animals.[10] This report emphasizes the difficulties of developing a "grand monistic scheme" that "establishes a hierarchy of values and obligations under the hegemony of one ultimate value." Such an approach to dealing with contemporary ethical concerns is dismissed by the authors because, while it "may serve the peace of the soul by reducing internal moral conflict," it would, they believe, work only in relatively small and homogeneous communities. It "invariably is bought at the price of the variety and richness of human experience and significant cultural activity. In this sense it impoverishes the human soul."

I would argue to the contrary. There are moral absolutes such as reverence for life, compassion, and *ahimsa* (nonharmfulness) that can provide both a goal and a common ground for a reasoned and scientific approach to resolving ethical issues. These absolutes are the cornerstones of a monistic hierarchy of human values that could effectively incorporate the plurality of interests of various segments of society and of different cultures. . . .

References

1. *Cancer Weekly Plus,* via News Edge Corp., April 8, 1998.
2. C. McKee et al., "Production of biologically active salmon calcitonin in the milk of transgenic rabbits," *Nature Biotechnology* 16 (1998): 647–49.
3. P. B. Thompson, *Food Biotechnology in Ethical Perspective,* London, England: Chapman Hall, 1997.
4. R. Goldburg, "Something Fishy," *Gene Exchange* (Union of Concerned Scientists), Summer 1998, p. 6.
5. Genetic engineering news email: rwoifson@concentric.net (November 14, 1998).
6. *Eurobarometer Survey,* London, 46.1.
7. See: M. W. Fox, *Eating with Conscience: The Bioethics of Food,* Troutdale, OR: NewSage Press, 1997.
8. V. Shiva, *Biopiracy: The Plunder of Nature and Knowledge,* Boston, MA: South End Press, 1997.
9. *New Scientist,* February 14, 1998, pp. 14–15.
10. S. Nec and R. May, "Extinction and the loss of evolutionary history," *Science* 278 (1997): 692–94.

POSTSCRIPT

Is It Right to Produce Genetically Modified Food?

At first sight this dispute might seem hopeless. Ronald Bailey can hardly find a problem with GMF and Michael Fox can hardly find anything good about it. But this is to draw too strong a conclusion. Bailey is right that GMFs are widely used and there haven't been the kinds of dire problems that some critics have predicted. (In fact, some of the objections of the critics have been shown by Bailey to be based on groundless misunderstandings.) And the greatest problem that Fox sees with GMF is really a problem about the relationship between people and the rest of the natural world. It's not something that could have a technological fix; his very complaint might be said to be that we modern Western human beings tend to look for a technological fix when what we really need is to be one with nature.

Fox, for all his criticism of GMF, is dismayed that what he calls a "lack of vision" limits the benefits that are possible through genetic modification. He also laments the "cavalier attitude of corporations, governments and much of academia." We could benefit from genetic modification of living things if, for example, this modification were focused on restoring damaged ecologies, bringing back degraded rangelands, etc. But instead, biotechnology is focused on major commodity crops. We human beings end up consuming more and more. If the genetic modification of plants leads only to more crowded factory farming conditions, then we are going in the wrong direction. What we really need, in his view, is not a technological fix at all, but a change in attitude.

One may be quite sympathetic with Fox's concerns, but still the problem he identifies is not one that is limited to GMF; it is a much wider problem. Farmers and animal breeders have changed the genetic structures of plants and animals over generations. One way of looking at GMF is to think of it as a speeded up kind of breeding. Where cows, for example, were bred from some original wild animals over generations and generations, we can now make more immediate changes in living things in a single generation at the gene level.

Fox may be right that more thoughtful oversight is needed.

More research and readings about GMF may be found in: Michael Ruse and David Castle, eds., *Genetically Modified Foods* (Prometheus, 2002); Lisa H. Weasel, *Food Fray: Inside the Controversy over Genetically Modified Food* (AMACOM, 2009); Nina Fedoroff and Nancy Marie Brown, *Mendel in the Kitchen: A Scientist's View of Genetically Modified Food* (Joseph Henry Press, 2006); Gary E. Marchant, Guy A. Cardineau, and Thomas P. Redick, eds., *Thwarting Consumer Choice: The Case Against Mandatory Labeling for Genetically Modified Foods* (Aei Press, R&L, 2010); and Paul Lurquin, *High Tech Harvest: Understanding Genetically Modified Food Plants* (Basic Books, 2004).

Contributors to This Volume

EDITOR

STEPHEN SATRIS was born in New York City. He received a BA in philosophy from the University of California, Los Angeles, an MA in philosophy from the University of Hawaii at Manoa, and a PhD in philosophy from Cambridge University, England. He has written on moral and philosophical issues for professional journals, and he is the author of *Ethical Emotivism* (Martinus Nijhoff, 1987). He has taught at several American universities, and he currently teaches philosophy at Clemson University in Clemson, South Carolina. Professor Satris is a former president of the South Carolina Society for Philosophy and is currently C. Calhoun Lemon Fellow in Clemson University's Rutland Institute for Ethics.

AUTHORS

JOHN ARTHUR is a philosopher at the State University of New York at Binghamton. He has published works on social, political, and legal philosophy.

MIRKO BAGARIC is a professor of law at Deakin University's School of Law in Australia. He has published on a wide variety of social issues. His latest book is *How to Live: Being Happy and Dealing with Moral Dilemmas* (University Press of America, 2006).

RONALD BAILEY is science editor of *Reason* magazine. He has published articles in *The Washington Post, The Wall Street Journal, Commentary,* and *Forbes.* He has given lectures at many institutions, including Harvard University, Rutgers University, the Cato Institute, and the American Enterprise Institute.

WALTER BLOCK earned his PhD in economics at Columbia University. He is an author, editor, and coeditor of many books, including *Defending the Undefendable; Lexicon of Economic Thought, Economic Freedom of the World 1975–1995; Rent Control: Myths and Realities; Discrimination, Affirmative Action, and Equal Opportunity; Theology, Third World Development and Economic Justice; Man, Economy, and Liberty: Essays in Honor of Murray N. Rothbard; Religion, Economics, and Social Thought;* and *Economic Freedom: Toward a Theory of Measurement.* Dr. Block has written more than 500 articles for various non-refereed journals, magazines, and newspapers, and is a contributor to such journals as *The Review of Austrian Economics, Journal of Libertarian Studies, The Journal of Labor Economics, Cultural Dynamics,* and the *Quarterly Journal of Austrian Economics.* He is currently a professor and chair of economics, College of Business Administration, at Loyola University.

HILARY BOK teaches philosophy at the Johns Hopkins University in Baltimore, where she is Luce Professor in Bioethics and Moral and Political Theory. Her publications and research interests are in ethics, bioethics, free will, and the philosophy of Kant.

DAVID BOONIN is an associate professor and chair of the Department of Philosophy at the University of Colorado. He is the coeditor of the book *What's Wrong?: Applied Ethicists and Their Critics.*

TAYLOR BRANCH is an American writer and editor, best known as the author of *America in the King Years, 1954–63,* part of his three-volume biography of Dr. Martin Luther King, Jr., and a book for which Branch was awarded the Pulitzer Prize. Branch has written on a wide range of subjects, including politics, history, and sports.

LEWIS BURROWS, MD, is Professor Emeritus, Surgery, at Mount Sinai School of Medicine, City University of New York.

JAMES F. CHILDRESS is the John Allen Hollingsworth Professor of Ethics and Professor of Medical Education at the University of Virginia. Professor Childress is the recipient of several prestigious academic awards, is the author (or coauthor) of scores of books and articles, and has served on numerous advisory bodies, including the presidentially appointed National Bioethics Advisory Commission. With Tom L. Beauchamp, he is the coauthor of *Principles of Biomedical Ethics,* 5th ed. (Oxford University Press, 2001), a classic work in its field.

JULIE CLARKE teaches law at Deakin University's School of Law in Australia.

MEAGHAN CUSSEN is a graduate of the College of the Holy Cross in Worcester, Massachusetts. She is currently the director of Business Development at Navigate Health International.

ANTHONY DANIELS (THEODORE DALRYMPLE) is a retired prison psychiatrist and writer. He is the author of numerous books including *Life at the Bottom: The Worldview That Makes the Underclass.*

SETH DAVIS is a writer for *Sports Illustrated* and a regular contributor to CBS Sports. He primarily covers basketball and golf.

PHILIP E. DEVINE is a professor of philosophy at Providence College.

RICHARD DOERFLINGER is deputy director of the secretariat for Pro-Life Activities at the U.S. Conference of Catholic Bishops in Washington, DC. He is also adjunct fellow in bioethics and public policy at the National Catholic Bioethics Center in Boston. Speaking on behalf of the Catholic Bishops, he has prepared policy statements and given congressional testimony on abortion, euthanasia, human embryo research, and other bioethical issues.

AUTUMN FIESTER is a senior fellow at the Center for Bioethics at the University of Pennsylvania. She teaches and conducts research in moral philosophy, animals and bioethical issues, and clinical professionalism.

MICHAEL ALLEN FOX is professor of philosophy at Queen's University in Canada and adjunct professor of social science, University of New England in Australia. He is the author of *Deep Vegetarianism* and *The Accessible Hegel.*

MICHAEL W. FOX is a well-known veterinarian, the author of over 40 adult and children's books about animal care, animal behavior and issues in bioethics.

ALAN H. GOLDMAN is now Kenan Professor of Philosophy at the College of William and Mary. (Previously, he taught for 25 years at the University of Miami in Florida.) He is the author of numerous books and articles on aesthetics, moral knowledge, and the philosophy of law. His most recent book is *Practical Rules: When We Need Them and When We Don't* (Cambridge, 2002).

GILBERT HARMAN is Stuart Professor of Philosophy at Princeton University. He has published extensively in ethics, epistemology, metaphysics, cognitive science, and the philosophy of language. His most recent book is *Explaining Value and Other Essays in Moral Philosophy* (Clarendon Press, 2000).

TIMOTHY HOWELL is associate professor of psychiatry and director of the geropsychiatry program at UW Health—a health and medical network affiliated with the University of Wisconsin. He is active in both teaching and clinical care.

JEEF JORDAN is professor of philosophy at the University of Delaware. He works in metaphysics and the philosophy of religion.

C. STEPHEN LAYMAN is professor of philosophy at Seattle Pacific University. He has published in logic, metaphysics, and the philosophy of religion. His books include *The Shape of the Good* (University of Notre Dame Press, 1991), *The Power of Logic*, 2nd ed. (McGraw-Hill, 2002), and *Letters to a Doubting Thomas: A Case for the Existence of God* (Oxford University Press, 2007).

MARGARET OLIVIA LITTLE is an associate professor in the Philosophy Department at Georgetown University. She is also a senior research scholar at Georgetown's Kennedy Institute of Ethics.

DON MARQUIS is professor of philosophy at the University of Kansas in Lawrence, Kansas. He has written on issues in medical ethics.

ALBERT G. MOSLEY, philosopher and musician, is currently at Smith College in Massachusetts. He is the editor of *African Philosophy: Selected Readings* (Pearson Education, 1995) and coauthor, with Nicholas Capaldi, of *Affirmative Action* (Rowman & Littlefield, 1996).

LOUIS P. POJMAN (1935–2005) was a prolific American philosopher who published (as editor or author) over 30 books and wrote more than 100 articles. His writing extends widely and embraces many areas of philosophy, but Pojman is best remembered as a writer on ethical, social, and political issues. He was particularly concerned to make ideas clear to nonphilosophers.

VINCENT C. PUNZO is Professor Emeritus at Saint Louis University in St. Louis, Missouri. His specialties are ethics and political philosophy.

JOHN A. ROBERTSON holds the Vinson and Elkins Chair at the University of Texas School of Law at Austin. He has written and lectured widely on law and bioethical issues. He is the author of *The Rights of the Critically Ill* (Ballinger, 1983) and *Children of Choice: Freedom and the New Reproductive Technologies* (Princeton University Press, 1994). He is also the author of numerous articles on reproductive rights, genetics, organ transplantation, and human experimentation. Robertson has served on or has been a consultant to many national bioethics advisory bodies and is currently chair of the Ethics Committee of the American Society for Reproductive Medicine.

HOLMES ROLSTON III is an internationally known philosopher of the environment. He is University Distinguished Professor at Colorado State University in Fort Collins, Colorado. He has written extensively and lectured widely on the environment, science, and religion. His works have been translated into many languages.

MICHAEL J. SANDEL is the Anne T. and Robert M. Bass Professor of Government at Harvard University, where he has taught political philosophy since 1980. He is the author of *Liberalism and the Limits of Justice* (Cambridge University Press, 1982, 2nd ed., 1997; translated into eight foreign languages), *Democracy's Discontent: America in Search of a Public Philosophy* (Harvard University Press, 1996), *Public Philosophy: Essays on Morality in Politics* (Harvard University Press, 2005), *The Case Against Perfection: Ethics in the Age of Genetic Engineering* (Harvard University Press, 2007), and the bestseller *Justice: What's the Right Thing to Do?* (Farrar, Strauss and Giroux, 2009). He has also written for publications such as *The Atlantic Monthly, The New Republic,* and *The New York Times.*

JEREMY SNYDER is an assistant professor in the Faculty of Health Sciences at Simon Fraser University.

ERNEST VAN DEN HAAG (1914–2002) was a distinguished lecturer at Columbia University, Yale University, and Harvard University. For many years, he was John M. Olin Professor of Jurisprudence at Fordham University and also a scholar at the Heritage Foundation. Van den Haag was both a psychoanalyst and a criminologist. He is coauthor, with John P. Conrad, of *The Death Penalty: A Debate* (Plenum, 1983).

DAVID T. WATTS is a practicing physician, a poet, a radio commentator, and an author. His most recent book is *Bedside Manners: One Doctor's Reflections on the Oddly Intimate Encounters Between Patient and Healer* (Three Rivers Press, 2006).

MICHAEL WELCH is a sociologist and professor of criminal justice at Rutgers University. His work focuses on the ideas of punishment and social control. He is the author of *Detained: Immigration Laws and the Expanding I.N.S. Jail Complex* (Temple University Press, 2002). Welch is the author of several books, including, most recently, *Scapegoats of September 11th: Hate Crimes and State Crimes in the War on Terror* (Rutgers University Press, 2006).

MATT ZWOLINSKI is an associate professor of philosophy at the University of San Diego. He is also the codirector of the University of San Diego's Institute for Law and Philosophy and a member of the editorial board of *Business Ethics Quarterly.*